THE VIOLENCE INSIDE US

THE VIOLENCE INSIDE US

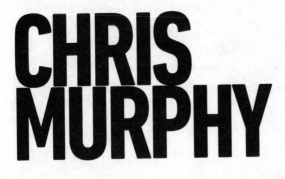

A BRIEF HISTORY OF AN ONGOING AMERICAN TRAGEDY

CHRIS MURPHY

RANDOM HOUSE
NEW YORK

Published in the United States by Random House, an imprint and division of Penguin Random House LLC, New York.

RANDOM HOUSE and the HOUSE colophon are registered trademarks of Penguin Random House LLC.

LIBRARY OF CONGRESS CATALOGING-IN-PUBLICATION DATA

Names: Murphy, Chris (Christopher Scott), author.

Title: The violence inside us : a brief history of an ongoing American tragedy / by Chris Murphy.

Description: New York : Random House, [2020] | Includes bibliographical references and index.

Identifiers: LCCN 2019030481 (print) | LCCN 2019030482 (ebook) | ISBN 9781984854575 (hardcover) | ISBN 9781984854582 (ebook)

Subjects: LCSH: Violence—United States—History. | Gun control—United States. | United States—Social conditions. | United States—Politics and government.

Classification: LCC HN90.V5 M87 2020 (print) | LCC HN90.V5 (ebook) | DDC 303.60973—dc23

LC record available at https://lccn.loc.gov/2019030481

LC ebook record available at https://lccn.loc.gov/2019030482

Printed in the United States of America on acid-free paper

randomhousebooks.com

9 8 7 6 5 4 3 2 1

First Edition

Book design by Jo Anne Metsch

FOR SHANE, DYLAN, AND THE
COUNTLESS OTHER BRILLIANT YOUNG
LIVES CUT FAR, FAR TOO SHORT

"It was always the becoming he dreamed of, never the being."

F. Scott Fitzgerald, *This Side of Paradise*

PREFACE

For the life of me, I can't remember what my first-grade classmate Paul did to prompt me to challenge him to a fight after school. I vaguely recall that an exchange of mean words in the classroom immediately brought to mind an instruction from my mother to stand up for myself if bullied. So I told Paul to meet me after school at the bottom of the hill, next to the woods behind Emerson-Williams Elementary School. I probably overreacted to whatever slight I perceived, but it soon became the buzz of our classroom, and a hive of kids followed us down the short incline to watch us square off. The bout lasted all of ten seconds. Before I could get in a swing, Paul leveled me with an open hand, right across my mouth, knocking out one of my loose front teeth.

Though the details of my first fistfight are fuzzy, I do have a strong recollection of the adrenaline surge that raced through my body as I readied for the fight, and my desire to seek revenge once I had been embarrassed. I was rail thin, the skinniest kid in my class, but at that moment I felt like I was hardwired to fight. Of course, I was wrong about my pugilistic skills, but what I felt that day was real. What I connected to was an instinct for violence, created by a complicated intersection of genetics, biology, and neurology, that is buried deep inside all of us.

Our bodies are fighting machines, and our minds are wired to use violence as needed to protect ourselves from danger and advance our own interests. Human beings have a trigger for violence that is virtually unmatched in the animal kingdom, prompting both pint-sized tantrums and adolescent brawls, all the way to world wars. Maybe once or twice in your life you've sensed an uncomfortable desire to put your hands on someone who has harmed someone you loved or done something to send you into a momentary rage. Maybe you've even acted on this instinct. If you have, you're not alone. Violence is unquestionably inside us, whether we want it or not.

This American land, dating all the way back to before Europeans ever set foot on this soil, has always been particularly fertile ground for violence. Pre-Columbian America, according to some estimates, was one of the most violent places on earth, as many Native Americans used violence and the threat of it to settle disputes over living, hunting, and fishing space. European settlement did nothing to help. A relatively new technology, firearms, allowed the settlers to brutally take from the Native Americans the same living, hunting, and fishing space that had been the subject of intertribal conflict for centuries.

Then the original settlers were joined by waves of new migrants from Ireland, Scotland, Italy, Germany, Poland, and Russia. The same friction that had sparked conflict between colonists and Native Americans now brought these new Americans, vying for economic and political space, to blows at abnormally high rates. Weapons innovators Samuel Colt and Oliver Winchester were there to exploit these tensions and provide both sides with increasingly efficient guns to turn ordinary arguments deadly in an instant.

But the defining violence of early America—the violence that propped up our nation's economy; that inspired a nation-altering civil war; that led to the creation of a caste system that exits to this day—was the quotidian violence necessary to compel enslaved people from Africa to work the New World's land for free. America became a nation anesthetized to physical harm because the entire country's economic, political, and social structure was predicated on the brutal subjugation of black Americans. Guns, of course, were an obvious mechanism for white oppressors to maintain the social and economic order.

A predilection to violence exists inside every human, but America's practice of violence is unique. It is definitional. And it is persistent. How else can one explain why a white police officer, after questioning an African American man about a report of a simple counterfeit twenty-dollar bill, would feel justified pressing a knee to the man's neck for eight and a half minutes, unconcerned that the man might be unable to breathe, unmoved by his dying cries for his mother? How else can we understand why a young African American man could choose to go out for a jog in his neighborhood and within minutes find his path obstructed by shotgun-wielding vigilantes intent on administering private justice?

Right now, following the killings of George Floyd, Ahmaud Arbery, and others, America is convulsed by a moral reckoning over our nation's systematic use of violence by white Americans against African Americans and other people of color. This is a long overdue and vitally necessary exercise, and I endeavor in this book to tell the story of America's long history of white majorities using violence for repression and control. If you come to this book freshly heartbroken over the murder of Floyd or Arbery or Breonna Taylor or Trayvon Martin, you will find here a map of how America arrived at this moment of reckoning.

But American violence also takes many other forms, and its roots stretch far beyond the realm of racial division. At this critical moment in our nation's history, our duty as citizens—and the mission of this book—is to examine the long, tangled roots of American violence. We must ask why humans of all races and creeds, in America and all over the world, are drawn to violence, instinctively, as a way to protect ourselves or settle grudges or advance our interests. We must figure out why young men in this country, robed in military-style clothing and carrying wildly lethal weapons, walk into schools and churches with the goal of killing as many people in as short a time as possible. We must reckon with the systemic oppression that still denies so many

African American men legitimate pathways to success, forcing them to resort to violence as a means of survival in blighted neighborhoods. It's time to figure out why more Americans than ever are killing themselves quickly with guns, and more slowly with illegal drugs and alcohol. And no discussion of violence can conclude without questions about our nation's insistence on exporting American violence to the rest of the world, through the sale of arms and the dispatch of our armies.

What we will find are some hard truths: Some of America's violent tendencies *are* inevitable. The nature of our country—a melting pot of different racial and ethnic and national identities—likely means that we will remain a more violent place than others. From my perch in the United States Senate, I plan to be a forceful ally in a new civil rights movement arising in the wake of the protests of summer 2020. We should not give up on breaking down the unreasonable, nonsensical prejudices that exist between people who look or sound different from one another. But tribalism is deeply ingrained in biology and sociology, and we're not going to completely overcome the instinct to view other groups as a threat to our own anytime soon. America's commitment to heterogeneity is our core strength, but it also exposes us to rivalry and conflict and, for the time being, to rates of human-on-human harm that separate us from other nations.

But this reality should awaken in us a special responsibility to ameliorate it. And if we choose this calling, there is good news to greet us, because the evidence proves that human beings in general, and Americans specifically, have inside us the power to reduce the frequency of human-on-human violence. History shows us methods through which we can set up rules and social norms to reduce the likelihood that bloodshed will be used to advance economic or social interests. Time and again, as responsive governments and large, integrated economies provide individuals with less risky ways to prosper, violence rates plummet. We also know that the growth of empathy—the ability to walk in the shoes of others (and thus to understand the consequence of doing violence to them)—depresses rates of violence. We have discovered that the proper enforcement of laws plays a role, too—communities where the police are received as honest brokers are the places where fewer citizens feel the need for their own private systems of justice. And, of course, controlling the means of violence is perhaps the most impactful lever we have to pull. Today, the safest places in America are those that make it just a little harder for people who want to hurt others to get their hands on a gun that will do the job.

The second piece of good news is that, while the rules don't change themselves, today there are more Americans bent on reform than ever before. The Black Lives Matter movement is seeking to tear down the systems of violence used for centuries to subjugate people of color. In the last eight years, American citizens have risen up to make the case to their neighbors that private gun ownership and gun safety can co-exist. The gun industry, nearly omnipotent for decades, is reeling as movements to keep guns away from criminals, and to keep military-style weapons in the hands of professionals, gather momentum. A new generation of progressive agitators has begun to advance an agenda of top-down economic reforms that would restore the American dream of true economic mobility to families across these United States, reducing the need for citizens to turn to violence as a mechanism of survival. And peace organizations have convinced Congress to pass legislation to stop American wars overseas. This book will also tell these hopeful stories and explain why they matter.

Lastly, it's important to note that this book is also a personal account of my own journey over the past eight years. Prior to the morning of December 14, 2012, I knew virtually nothing of what you will read on these pages. I am embarrassed to admit that now. It was a bone-chilling phone call on a train platform in Bridgeport, Connecticut, and a crowded community room in the north end of Hartford weeks later, that started me on a life-changing journey and helped me discover what truly lies inside me. My narrative of self-examination, I hope, might inspire you to undertake a similar review.

What follows on these pages, then, is a deeply personal exploration of the biology, history, and politics of American violence, and the story of how, by coming to grips with the violence that lies inside all of us, we may learn to overcome it.

—Chris Murphy, June 2020

CONTENTS

THE VIOLENCE INSIDE US

1

SOS

Pastor Sam Saylor looks like he could protect you—from all sorts of things. Tall, muscular, as thick as an oak tree, Sam has presence. Lots of it. His powerful oratory and baritone voice can overtake a room, and his burly frame can alter the dynamics of a conversation. He wears a thin, carefully groomed beard and mustache, and often sports petite reading glasses, as if intentionally trying to soften his effect on you. His temper is quick, and he admits it has worsened over the years as the pain he has witnessed and experienced continues to well up inside him. But the anger abates faster than it builds, and grudges never hold. Still, his face at rest cannot conceal the hurt inside; Sam's eyes are always heavy.

On a sunny, crisp afternoon, the twentieth day of October 2012, Sam was having a great day. Maybe *the best day* he'd ever had during his time as a pastor. Back in 2012, he was the pastor at Blackwell Memorial Church on the corner of Blue Hills Avenue and Euclid Street in the north end of Hartford, Connecticut, the poorest and most violence-prone section of the state's capital city. This was the job Sam felt he was created to do—mentoring dozens of kids at risk of falling into a cycle of unemployment, incarceration, and poverty. No one understood the north end better than Sam. He grew up there, raised his six children there. He built a small business with customers all over the neighborhood. So he knew that the young African Americans who came through his church had a greater chance of spending their twenties in jail than in college, and that parents would leave his services on Sunday ravaged with anxiety over their inability to afford food for their children, many of whom would often go to bed aching with hunger.

To make matters worse, the streets of the north end had become a killing field over the previous two decades. Already nineteen people had been murdered that year. Sam was a drum major in what he called Hartford's "parade of pain," the nonstop cascade of gun crimes that rippled through the neighborhood. He was often among the first community leaders to arrive at a crime scene or a victim's house, offering consolation and understanding. In the aftermath of the most horrific shootings, he organized street patrols and vigils and marches.

After the violence-filled summer of 2012, Sam knew that the neighborhood surrounding Blackwell needed a way to release the stress that had built up, shooting after shooting. So he put all his energy into making that year's annual fall festival the biggest party the neighborhood had ever seen. Sam spent weeks putting it together with a group of volunteers from the church. There was a baking contest, games for the kids, a tag sale teeming with affordable housewares for the parents, free food galore. And in the middle of it, Reverend Saylor, spinning hits at the DJ booth. It was an *epic party*.

"The best day of my life as a pastor," he told me.

When the festivities were finished, Sam sped home, hoping to get a few hours of rest before starting the third shift at his overnight job.

· · ·

Shane Oliver had a busy afternoon planned, too. Shane was the only child of Sam Saylor and Janet Rice, the product of their brief relationship. At twenty years old, he was starting a life as a businessman, using a little insurance money he got from an automobile accident earlier in the year to start a small car-flipping operation. Shane bought near-junked cars, repaired and refurbished them, and then sold them for a small profit. He managed to scrape out a little spending money, but he and his girlfriend, Maria, were still living with his mother, Janet, in her crowded Hartford apartment. Shane had been hustling for money since he was in elementary school, and he imagined a day when he would be able to pay his mom rent, or maybe even afford a place of his own for Maria and him.

"He was an industrious kid," said Sam, beaming.

That Saturday, Shane and Maria planned to head to a vigil for his close friend, Angel "Ito" Garcia. One year ago to the day, Ito had been riding dirt bikes with friends in Colt Park, just south of downtown, when a truck began driving recklessly near him. The swerving truck forced Ito to steer his bike off the street and into an adjacent open field. When his friends circled back to check on Ito, he was gone. No Ito. No dirt bike. Nothing. And no one had seen Ito since.

It was the type of case, Sam thought, that would have warranted wall-to-wall cable television coverage if Ito had been named Rebecca or Sarah, and had long blond hair and pierced ears instead of cornrows and knuckle scars. A nineteen-year-old boy is riding his dirt bike and vanishes, and no one cares because it happened in Hartford. If it happened a few miles away, in middle-class Wethersfield, for instance, it would have been different. Sam knew this, and it hurt.

Ito was just in the *wrong place at the wrong time,* went the argument. Sam hated that phrase. These kids get shot next to their school, at the playground, on their own front porch, Sam howled. Ito was out riding his bike with friends, minding his own business. How is that the wrong place? So, a full year after Ito's disappearance, a small group of family and friends were keeping his story alive, and they planned to gather that night to mark the anniversary of his vanishing.

But before going to the vigil, Shane and Maria had to swing by the Sheldon Oaks Apartments to pick up the final payment for a Nissan Maxima that Shane had just fixed up for a new customer. The meeting was to take place at the small housing development near downtown

Hartford where Shane had once lived—the exact spot, in fact, where he had taken his first steps.

Walking had not come easily to Shane. When Janet was pregnant with him, he'd had a stroke in utero and was born with a form of cerebral palsy that dramatically affected the right side of his body. He walked with a noticeable limp, and he regularly hid his curled-up right hand inside a pants or jacket pocket. Sam and Janet were worried, at first, that the disability would hold Shane back. Right from the start, though, Shane was relentless, so stubborn. He compensated for his weak right side by building up remarkable strength in his left. "He rode a bike, climbed trees, played basketball, played football. He did everything," remembered Janet.

In a different neighborhood, maybe that would have been enough. Not in the north end, a place where the decades upon decades of discrimination, and economic desperation coupled with the daily threats of violence, fold layer after layer of trauma into the lives of children. There are few success stories in the north end—kids who did well in school, got a good-paying job, and reinvested that money in the neighborhood. Success really meant getting out, but first you had to survive. And survival meant learning how to punch your way out of trouble.

When I asked Janet and Sam to describe Shane to me, the first thing they wanted me to know, after explaining his cerebral palsy, was his greatest asset as a young man growing up in Hartford: "Shane was an *excellent* fighter," said Janet, proudly. "Some kids gave him a nickname. Sugar Shane."

Sam recalled hearing a story one day about a young man who assaulted two members of a high school football team as they disembarked from a city bus. The assailant apparently had been waiting for the football players at the bus stop, and attacked them so mercilessly that the two victims both ended up in the hospital. Sam was so distressed by this report that he called Janet to suggest that they approach Shane and his friends to track down the culprit and report him to the police.

"Sam, that was our son. That was *Shane!*" howled Janet over the phone.

Shane never told Janet the complete story, but from what she could gather, the two players had been harassing Shane—picking on him because of his disability—and one day, he decided he'd had enough of the bullying, and took the two kids down.

"He wanted to let you know, right there, he was no punk," Sam explained to me. "He had to hold his. Boys in the hood, you need to establish your position, and let people know you're not a punk, because once people assume you're one, they're always going to come and challenge you."

.   .   .

Shane's customer arrived at Sheldon Oaks with several friends in tow. It's unclear what caused the meeting to go off the rails so quickly, but the crowd of young men had taken note of Maria and began to make suggestive comments about what they might do with her if they had the chance. Among the group of taunting young men was twenty-year-old Luis Rodriguez, who was a casual acquaintance of Shane's. It was Rodriguez's taunts that were the loudest. Maria got out of the car to try to settle down the escalating verbal exchange, but her protests had little effect. Sam guesses that the boys pressed so hard because they had noticed Shane's disability—took note of his weakness—and needled him, thinking Shane couldn't fight back.

But Sugar Shane did fight back. *He wasn't a punk.* He looked back for a second at Maria and charged up to meet Rodriguez chest to chest. A scuffle broke out, and Shane cocked his famous left arm. At least one punch landed, and Maria watched, worried, as Rodriguez and his friends, shocked at the ferocity of this crippled young man and embarrassed to have been on the receiving end of his blows, retreated to their car.

The next few seconds were a blur. Rodriguez emerged from his vehicle with a pistol—an illegal gun without a permit, as it turned out—and pointed it at Shane.

Shane knew what was coming. He turned and began to run back to the car. But it was too late. Rodriguez had made the decision to pull the trigger, and emptied the chamber of its bullets. One chased Shane down, entered his body through his back, and split open the bottom of his heart, his liver, and his abdominal artery. Shane's body crumpled and fell to the pavement. "It was just something that escalated too fast," Rodriguez said later.

Janet was home that afternoon with a bad migraine headache. A nephew called to tell her to get down to Sheldon Oaks—fast. Janet focused on the fact that Shane was *hurt*, blocking out the detail that he was *shot*. The difference mattered; it helped her keep her composure while she drove to see Shane, to get to him while he was still alive. She drove fast, getting there before the paramedics. He was still on the ground and conscious. Janet remembers looking into his eyes, holding him tightly as his lip quivered uncontrollably. He didn't say anything. But the look in his eyes told her that he loved her.

Maria rode in the ambulance to the hospital with Shane, and Janet followed. She was optimistic. "I really didn't think he wasn't going to make it," she recalled. But in the emergency room, events moved fast, and Shane could feel himself drowning as his blood flooded out of the severed artery. As Maria stood over him, Shane knew he was losing consciousness, and he began to panic.

"He felt himself dying," remembered Janet. As doctors began to prepare him for emergency surgery, Shane alternated between making Maria promise to tell his mother how much he loved her and protesting his imminent death. *"It's too soon . . . it's too soon . . . it's too soon,"* Shane repeated, over and over and over. The doctors rushed him up to surgery, and Janet took her phone out of her pocket to call Sam.

.   .   .

Sam was at home, basking in the afterglow of his afternoon at church, getting some rest before heading out to his job on the night shift. When he got the call, he ran out the door and into his car—he had made this trip so many times, as a pastor rushing to a crime scene or a hospital waiting room to counsel grieving parents. Now, this was different, and he drove too fast. He was pulled over by Hartford police officers for speeding, but managed to spit out enough of his story that the officers got back in their patrol car and escorted Sam the rest of the way to the hospital, sirens blaring.

As he burst into the waiting room, the pastor immediately began negotiating with God. "I tried to do all the biblical Lazarus-raising promises to God that I could," Sam explained. "I tried to give reasons why he needs to bring this boy back."

But that's not what happened. Shane bled to death on the operating table. He was twenty years old, dead from gunshot wounds inflicted by another twenty-year-old. The twentieth shooting victim in Hartford of 2012, on the twentieth day of October.

OCTOBER 20, 2012

Two quick left turns out of the Sheldon Oaks Apartments, where Shane was born and where his body fell to the pavement that bright Saturday afternoon, you find yourself on Main Street, the road connecting Hartford and Wethersfield. Along the next five miles of that road, you will pass almost every landmark of my childhood: The restaurant where my grandparents took me to breakfast every Saturday morning. The middle school where I spent seventh grade awkwardly following around pretty Sue Sassano, my first mad teenage crush. The town hall where my classmates and I protested the slow pace of our high school's renovations my senior year. Eventually, on the southern border of the town, you reach the shopping plaza on Town Line Road where I chose to locate my headquarters after I launched my campaign for the U.S. Senate in 2011 at the age of thirty-seven.

Shane Oliver was born the year I left Wethersfield to head to college, but the geographies of our childhoods are within earshot of each other. Hartford and Wethersfield border each other—thousands of people, including my father, travel back and forth each day from home in one town to work in the other. The high schools play each other in every sport each year. The area's popular public golf course overlaps the line dividing them. The two towns even have the same historical roots—Wethersfield was the primary port city along the Connecticut River during colonial times until the river shifted, forcing traffic five miles north to Hartford.

Yet Shane Oliver and I might as well have grown up in different universes.

I remember the look on Sam's face after he explained to me his son's impressive pugilistic skills. He could tell the prideful way he was telling the tale of Sean's fighting exploits wasn't landing with me. He paused.

"Sam, it's funny," I started to explain. "I'm just realizing—I have no idea if I was a good fighter as a kid. I have no idea whether any of my friends were good fighters. We just didn't need to think about that." I have that memory of Paul slapping me on the playground after school in first grade and knocking out a loose tooth, but that's the closest I ever got to an actual fight as a child. Later, as a candidate and elected official, I'd succumb to the tired practice of describing nearly every political conflict as a "fight" or a "battle," even though the days of politicians trading blows were long past. I thought now about how disconnected and insensitive that language must sound to someone like Sam.

I put my Senate campaign office right along the southern border of my hometown because, in my mind, there was no safer place than Wethersfield, Connecticut. I took over an old piano showroom wedged in between three businesses owned by campaign supporters, Town Fair Tire, Edible Arrangements, and Wood-n-Tap Bar and Grill. The icing on the cake was the proximity to my childhood home, where my parents still lived and which allowed my retired, type A mother to adopt the office as her own, maintaining a fully stocked snack and soda table just inside the front door, and reliably vacuuming and cleaning the full space a few times a week.

Despite this fortuitous location, in the fall of 2012, as my campaign for Senate was drawing to a close, I was a mess. I had come to find out the hard way that running a political campaign against a billionaire is kind of like having an enema. You understand there is a purpose to it.

You know it will end. You submitted to it voluntarily. But while it's happening, it's excruciating. Every minute of it.

But on the morning of October 20, as Shane was preparing to pick up his final payment for that Maxima only a few miles up the road, it looked like we might have weathered the storm. Polls suggested that my opponent's withering negative ad campaign was backfiring. Our risky move to spend our scant campaign cash on positive ads was paying off. Only two weeks left in the campaign, I could see the light at the end of the tunnel.

That Saturday, I started my day in my small, windowless office where I was expected to spend 90 percent of my time dialing for dollars. My fund-raising staff had plastered the walls of my office with pictures of my two sons, Owen and Rider. I smiled, faintly, as I entered the room, reminded that there were at least two people in the world who weren't paying much attention to the billionaire's negative attack ads.

Then, the Bearer of Crappy News appeared in the frame of my open office door. With his tightly cropped hair, glasses, and slight build, Eli Zupnick looked completely harmless. He had been brought into the campaign late in the game to head up our communications team. He was a pro, and he made our campaign better. But because he was an outsider who had no plans to stay after the election, Eli was frequently given the unenviable task of breaking bad news to me.

I smiled at Eli nervously as he poked his head into the office.

"The *Connecticut Post* profile dropped this morning," he said sheepishly.

"Not good?"

"Could be better. Could be worse. The reporter definitely had a point he wanted to get across. I don't think you're gonna like it."

I took the small stack of papers out of Eli's hands and leaned back on my metal office-supply-store desk to read the story.

Chris Murphy defines "middle of the pack." He's a quiet member of the minority party in the House of Representatives, a moderate-to-

liberal with a voting record very similar to that of his four Connecticut colleagues. As his three-term tenure comes to a close, he's seen
as a solid and unspectacular swimmer in the seat of 435 members of
the House. And that's the problem: Murphy's biggest enemy, other
than his well-heeled Republican opponent, is obscurity.

Oomph.

Politicians, for the most part, run for office for the right reasons. At
the core of every elected official is a foundational set of convictions or
beliefs that drove that individual to public life. There's no other reason
to put yourself through the unique grinder of intense public scrutiny
that comes with political service unless you have an internal drive that
comports with your value system.

But simply caring about a cause isn't enough to change the world
for the better. There are a lot of ineffectual members of Congress who
care deeply about the issues upon which they labor. If you want to do
something about your cause—if you want to make a difference—then
you need to find a way to move people to action. That's why the worst
thing a politician can be called is *obscure,* because in the era of C-SPAN
and social media and cable news, obscure congresspeople rarely get
anything done. Making waves, becoming known—*wearing your passions on your sleeve*—is generally a precondition for success in elected
office.

I had been called a ton of terrible names over the past year by my
opponent's campaign. *Corrupt. Incompetent. Irresponsible.* But *obscure*—
that one maybe hurt the most.

"Middle-of-the-pack is a little over the top, I think," mused Eli, trying
to soothe the wound.

I shoved the article back in front of Eli, walked around my desk,
and pulled out the rickety folding chair tucked underneath. I slouched
down in the seat and began to recount all the races I had run: Planning
and Zoning Commission, state representative, state senator, U.S. Congress. All the issues I had championed: ending the war in Iraq, land
preservation, universal healthcare. All the bills I had passed: Connecticut's workplace smoking ban, the country's first state-financed stem

cell research initiative, cleanup funds for abandoned factories in my congressional district. I wasn't a milquetoast moderate who refused to take controversial stands. I wasn't a calculating opportunist who just picked issues based on polling and public opinion. I was prodigious, on a range of serious issues.

But being thoughtful and productive isn't the same as being impactful. And deep down, I knew that the essence of the *Connecticut Post* story wasn't wrong. Maybe I wasn't obscure, but I knew that the driving, personal connection to a cause or an issue that drove many of my colleagues had eluded me. Maybe it was because of my relatively comfortable, trauma-free upbringing. Maybe it was because my brain tended to hew toward the intellectual, rather than the emotional component of policy debates. But whatever the reason, the story that Eli handed me that morning hurt because I knew there was a substantial grain of truth to it. And that afternoon, as Shane was pulling up to the Sheldon Oaks housing complex to collect on his debt, I was sitting in a folding chair, just a few miles away, trying to figure out what I was missing from my political makeup.

DECEMBER 14, 2012

For all the drama of the most expensive Senate race in the state's history, election night was a snooze. Ten minutes after the polls closed, the Associated Press called the race for me. A few days later, my mother presented me with a gift—a crumpled-up piece of paper that she had found buried in a desk drawer of my childhood bedroom, which she had meticulously smoothed out and placed in a small frame. It was a timeline that I had written as a freshman in high school, predicting the course of my life and career, year by year, up to and including my death (which, interestingly, I guessed would occur in 2037). She thought it was worth preserving because of how inaccurate my teenage predictions were. Back in 1988, I had guessed I would be a U.S. senator by age thirty-seven. I was a whole two years past due.

My climb had been swift and steady, but that anxiety—that I would be just as mediocre in the Senate as I was in the House—still haunted me. But as November turned to December, I did my best to calm my restless innards and mostly succeeded. I had won the election, and I was excited about the possibilities that lay ahead for our growing family. During my time in the House, my personal life had been a whirlwind. I got married, and Cathy and I had our first child, Owen, and our second son, Rider, all during my first five years in Congress. Cathy was named the head of the juvenile law division at Connecticut's statewide legal aid organization; our life was full of long days, sleepless nights, and constant scheduling conflicts. Over the course of the two-year Senate campaign, Cathy and the kids had borne the brunt of the vitriolic personal attacks and daily life with an absentee husband and father. So to make up for lost time, we took an early December trip to Disney World with my extended family, and then, midway through the month, planned a day trip to New York City that would be a dream come true for our four-year-old Owen.

We used to worry why Owen so seldom smiled when he was a newborn. He had a permanent furrow etched into his brow, and as a toddler, earnestness became his trademark. He smiled more often now, as a four-year-old, but you had to work for it. The small, silly things that delighted other little kids seemed to Owen to just be small and silly. But Owen did have his passions—he was just very particular about them—and that late fall, two things that excited him more than anything else were trains and Christmas, in that order.

So, on a crisp, breezy Friday morning in December, Owen stood with me on a platform about to board a train to New York City, where he was going to spend the afternoon with his parents and one-year-old brother basking in the holiday splendor of the city, skating at Rockefeller Center, viewing the storefront displays at Macy's, maybe even finding a department store Santa with whom to plant some last-minute ideas.

I had arrived at the train station ten minutes after Cathy and the boys, after having joined Bridgeport's mayor to announce a clean energy project coming to the city. The nondescript station, which lies between a lightly trafficked business district and the hulking oil-fired power plant that represents most people's impression of Bridgeport, was quiet that morning; the rush-hour commuters had already disappeared. My longtime chief political aide and Senate campaign manager Kenny Curran was with me. During the race, the stress literally caused Kenny's heart to fail, and he'd had a pacemaker installed mid-campaign. He'd stubbornly (and dangerously) insisted on missing only a few days of work.

An hour earlier, Kenny had received word of a shooting at a school in the Sandy Hook neighborhood of Newtown, a small, sleepy suburban town on the western edge of both the state and my current congressional district. We assumed it was a workplace dispute that had gone horribly wrong, and I convinced myself there was little I could do and decided to go to New York and monitor the situation remotely. As I began walking to the platform to meet up with Cathy and the boys, Kenny called out to get my attention. His face was ashen. Later that day, I remember trying to put myself in Owen's shoes at that moment. I imagined the raw four-year-old excitement that must have been pulsing through every muscle in his body as the train huffed into the station. That spine-tingling mixture of joy and wonder, anticipation and exhilaration. The entire circuitry of his brain fixated on the journey ahead of him, staring down the locomotive as it screeched into the station.

I thought about the disruption that must have occurred in his little heart when I greeted him at the station with a big hug, leaned over to him—his body tensed and ready—and whispered, "Buddy, I have some bad news. We can't go to New York City today."

Catastrophe.

The tears started welling up immediately. The chest convulsions quickly followed.

"Why . . . why . . . why?" Owen stammered through his sobs. "Why not, Daddy?"

"Something happened. I have to go."

The convulsions turned into a full-blown breakdown, and as my lip began to quiver, too, I feared it would become contagious.

"Let's just take the train one stop, and then you can get off and go," suggested my wife, struggling to hold our twelve-month-old, Rider, with one arm, while soothing Owen with the other. "It's basically on the way. It won't cost you any time, and we can try to explain to him what's happening."

Her alternative certainly made sense. Owen would get a ten-minute train ride, which would soothe his tears and potentially salvage the morning. Knowing where I was going, anticipating what I was about to see, I couldn't stand to leave my little boy in the lurch. His peace of mind, in that moment, seemed like the most important thing in the world.

But the other part of Cathy's plan—telling him what happened—was the harder part.

"Chris, there's kids involved," Kenny had said to me moments earlier, after calling me back to the car. "There . . . are . . . kids . . . shot."

An ice-cold shiver ran straight down my spine when I heard the words. My mind started racing—the horror of what might lay before the world and the people I had come to know in Sandy Hook. I had read about school shootings. I had watched coverage of them on television. I had spoken with colleagues who represented districts where shootings had occurred, who had tried in vain to offer consolation to grieving family members who brooked no consolation.

Kenny's words echoed over and over in my head. *There are kids involved. There are kids shot.*

I couldn't move. I was frozen.

"Jesus" was all I could muster.

I gathered myself. "How many?"

"I . . . I don't know," he stuttered, clearly having trouble keeping himself composed. "All I know is that this might be really, really bad."

DECEMBER 14, 2012

Janet went into a cold, dark place after Shane died. Her life—ordered around Shane's moods, his schedule, his friends—came to a functional end, as she saw it. Her purpose, her meaning, was gone. Her grief manifested itself in many ways. On the day of Rodriguez's arraignment, one of the shooter's cousins made a snide remark to Janet outside the courtroom. She snapped, charged at the young man, and set off a dizzying melee that ended with her in jail for assaulting a courthouse sheriff. This is actually how I first heard of Janet. In 2013, I sent a letter to the judge asking for a lenient sentence given the life-altering trauma she had experienced.

At home, Janet refused to talk to anyone, other than close family members, about Shane's death. She couldn't bear to be outside the house for longer than a few minutes at a time. Janet remembers driving everywhere, even to the bodega two blocks away, for fear that she would run into someone she knew around the neighborhood and be forced into small talk.

Sam fared only slightly better. He rededicated himself to parenting his five living children, only now with the daily, crippling fear that Shane's fate awaited them, too. After Shane's death, Sam never again answered his home phone, frozen by the memory of that Saturday afternoon call from Janet. He battled increasing anger, and eventually lost his pastorship at Blackwell because his sermons got too dark and disturbing. His supervising deacon moved Sam to a church in Springfield, Massachusetts, hoping his mood would lighten if he preached farther away from his son's murder scene.

Janet doesn't remember having many complex thoughts when she saw the news, that Friday morning, of the massacre at Sandy Hook. It had been almost two months since Shane's death, and her emotional temperature didn't really rise for anything not related to her own grieving process. The one thing she does recall is focusing on the number: *twenty. Twenty* kids killed. Just like Shane's age. Just like the age of Shane's killer. Just like the date he died. Just like the number of homicides in Hartford that year. She remembers feeling that day like there must be some reason for it—a cosmic connection between the horror of what was playing out fifty miles away in Newtown, and what had happened to her little boy.

Sam had two distinct reactions that day: grief and fury. He doesn't recall exactly where he was when he heard the news reports, but waves of sadness passed over him as he thought about twenty more kids extinguished from the earth. He knew the immeasurable pain their parents were experiencing right then.

But then quickly came the anger. Shane's death, and the nineteen lives lost in Hartford that year prior to Shane's murder, felt to Sam like trees dropping in the woods, unheard and unseen. And now, all of a sudden, the entire world—*the entire world*—was transfixed on a different twenty lives lost, in a place far different from Hartford.

"We couldn't get the drums to beat for our son," says Sam. "We couldn't get the drums to beat for our pain. And then—*BOOM*."

It's not that Sam didn't understand then, or now, the difference between the cataclysm of twenty first graders all losing their lives at the same time, and the slow but steady pace of pain in urban America. Since Sandy Hook, he often gets most worked up when talking about what those bullets, fired out of a military-grade semiautomatic weapon, did to those little bodies in Newtown. He understands why the reaction to Newtown was different—he knows Newtown *was* different. But that day Sam couldn't help obsessing over why America couldn't get that worked up about what was happening every day in places like the north end of Hartford.

OWEN AND SHANE

As we got off the train a few minutes after boarding in Bridgeport, Owen still hadn't pulled himself together. He remained inconsolable. We walked a few minutes to a coffee shop where Kenny was meeting me to drive to Sandy Hook. We found a four-top table so Cathy could compose herself and figure out what to do with the rest of the day.

As we unwrapped the kids' winter layers, it felt like the walls on the restaurant were closing in on me. The lunch crowd had begun to arrive, and the place was filling up. News of what had happened in Newtown had not broken widely yet, and so dozens of patrons were settling in for a long Friday lunch with friends or coworkers, oblivious to the news. I needed to leave—right now—but Owen had a question first.

"What happened, Daddy? Where are you going?"

I peeked across the table to Cathy. She shook her head. I read her loud and clear. *He's too young—he's not ready to hear this.*

"Some people got hurt, Owen. And part of my job is to help people who get hurt. I really, really wanted to go see the big Christmas tree with you today, buddy. But my job is to be a helper, and there are some folks who need some help today."

He sniffled, and wiped his reddened nose. He paused for a moment, adjusted his infamous furrow, and stared out into the restaurant, as if trying to access a thought that was proving hard to articulate. And then, miraculously, a switch flipped somewhere deep inside that kid. In an instant, his tears stopped. His spine straightened. And he looked me straight in the eye.

"I know. I know, Daddy." That was it. He reached over and pulled the saltshaker out of his little brother's hand and changed the topic. His protest was over. I slipped out the door and into a waiting car.

In the seven years since, *I've never told Owen about Sandy Hook.* He's now eleven—a mature, thoughtful, deeply insightful fifth grader. As Orlando and Las Vegas and Parkland unfolded, I walked him through those tragedies in real time. As he has gotten older, I haven't hesitated to educate him about the shootings that motivate my work. I talk through the reality of other kids his age who live in violent neighborhoods, and the safety and security that he shouldn't take for granted. By now, he can make the argument for universal background checks better than many congresspeople. His least favorite activity at summer camp was air riflery, he told me, because "it just didn't feel right, having a gun in my hands." He's proud of what I do, and passionate about changing the laws, just like I am. I'm not sure he knows what happened in Sandy Hook that day. But if he does, he doesn't know the story from me.

Maybe it's because the truth of what happened inside that school is too gruesome, the tale is full of too much evil, to sit inside an eleven-year-old's brain. Maybe it's because I just don't want to say it out loud—because I know I won't be able to hold it together if I have to look him in the eye and tell him what happened. But really, I think the reason I don't tell Owen the story of what happened inside that elementary school is because the story doesn't have an end yet.

Not a day goes by that I don't experience the broad, sinking pall of grief caused by this country's continued inaction in the face of mass slaughter. Having seen the horror so personally—in the hollow eyes of Sam Saylor, the emptiness of the Sandy Hook parents'—it is unfathomable to me that human beings would intentionally let this pain continue. It stuns me that my country does not see this horror—ninety people dying every day from gunfire, a rate ten times higher than other industrialized nations—and choose to act in a way that saves lives.

I was a firsthand witness to the immediate aftermath of Sandy Hook. Those parents are all my age—many are now close friends. My younger son recently finished first grade—and it was inconceivable to me that he might not survive the year, just as it was inconceivable to those parents who sent their children off to Sandy Hook Elementary seven years ago. The arc of thousands of people's lives changed that day in December 2012. Parents lost their sons. Brothers lost their sisters. Far away from Sandy Hook, a woman started a Facebook page entitled "Moms Demand Action" and created a movement. My friend Gabby Giffords, still recovering from her own wounds, decided to go public and start advocating for a better, safer world. And, of course, my life took a hard about-face. I now had my calling . . . my mission in life.

I've never told Owen and his brother, Rider, the story of Sandy Hook because the story is not finished. Those children did not die in vain. *I know this.* This *has to be.*

.   .   .

"I assume they noticed his limp," Sam guessed, talking about the kids who picked a fight with his son, Shane, the day he died. "I assume they thought he couldn't fight three kids . . . probably thought he couldn't fight even one, without full use of his right hand."

Shane's mom, Janet, had been toying with her phone, sitting across the room from Sam as I spoke to them. She raised her head back up and let escape a short, single laugh. "That's what they *thought*."

Sam smirked. "They just didn't know about that *other hand*."

Shane's grit—that hidden strength in his left side that Luis Rodriguez didn't see coming that Saturday afternoon—it's what Janet and Sam want you to know about their son. That he didn't let a disability hold him back. That he was an entrepreneur, a self-starter. That he wasn't a punk.

One summer when he was ten years old, Shane went to his father and asked what to do to keep away from a group of local drug-dealing boys who were pressuring him to work for them. Sam had an idea. It was a hot summer, and Sam had noticed that a group of neighborhood kids had started a small operation selling bottles of water, at prices marked up just enough to make a little money for themselves. Shane could do the same, in another spot, and tell the drug dealers that he already had a job for the summer.

"I'll invest in the business," Sam told his son. "I'll pay for the ice and the chest and the water, and you can pay me back. You stand right in front of the shop, while I'm working, so I can keep an eye on you."

Shane jumped at the opportunity, and quickly made the idea his own. After a few slow days in front of his father's lightly trafficked trophy store, Shane moved his table up to Central Baptist Church, where a day care center ensured lots of movement in and out of the building all day. Soon, Shane began selling juice to the kids and water to the parents, and business was taking off.

"He was paying for his own phone. He was buying food for his mother. He got new sneakers that year. He was making more cash than I was making!" exclaimed Sam.

The business, keeping him away from the drug trade and the dangerous idleness that comes with summers in the north end, was Shane's sanctuary. He worked the table during the day and spent his nights wrapped in the embrace of his mother. He didn't have to use that left hand very much that summer, his mother remembered.

After buying Shane the big white coolers and the ice and the bottles of water, Sam realized that one thing was missing for an effective business: a name.

Shane Oliver had found his way out that summer. And he was a natural salesman. Ten years later, as he drove to collect payment on a restored car, Shane believed his ability to sell would be his permanent way out—for him, his girlfriend, and his mother.

Sam asked Shane what he wanted to call his water stand.

"I'll make you a sign," he told his son.

Shane thought for a moment. Then it came to him.

"Shane Oliver Sells."

"Shane Oliver Sells?" asked Sam. "You sure?"

"Yup," replied Shane confidently. "Write on the sign, SOS. Shane Oliver Sells."

"SOS?" repeated back Sam.

"SOS," said his son.

.   .   .

Unlike the town in Connecticut, Sandy Hook, New Jersey is, in real life, a sandy hook—a spit of land jumping out from the Atlantic Highlands and protecting the southern end of New York Harbor from the ocean's open waters. On February 5, 1910, a steamship by the name of *Kentucky* sailed past Sandy Hook on her maiden voyage. The ship's log notes Sandy Hook prominently, because just 150 miles past the barrier spit, the vessel began taking on water and slowly started to sink. The hobbled cargo ship limped into port in Virginia and was patched up well enough that the captain decided to set off again on a long 14,000-mile trip to Seattle and then Alaska.

But it was not to be. Off Cape Hatteras, the *Kentucky* again began to sink, and the crew began to panic. Luckily, the ship was equipped with a technological wonder brand-new to seafaring: the wireless telegraph. A young operator, W. D. McGinnis, typed out a new code that he had learned just for this occasion.

Dot dot dot. Dash dash dash. Dot dot dot. The world's first-ever recorded SOS distress call from a sinking ship.

The SOS distress call has persisted over the hundred-plus years since W. D. McGinnis first punched it out that February evening in the Atlantic. Heaven knows how many lives have been saved by that simple signal. And what is important about the SOS call is that the signaler has to believe two essential things before sending it out: First, an SOS call is a method of last resort. All must be lost—the peril must have become so desperate, and all other options must have been exhausted, such that the only option is to abandon your ship and hope that help arrives. An SOS call is the ultimate act of desperation. Second, you don't make an SOS call unless you reasonably believe that help *will* arrive. If time is ticking down, and you know that anyone who could potentially rescue you is out of range, then an SOS call is pointless. You need to *believe* that help can and will arrive.

· · ·

Today, Americans are ten times more likely to be murdered by a gun than citizens in any one of the other twenty most prosperous nations in the world. American schoolchildren now practice active shooter drills once a year, crowding into bathrooms and classroom corners, told to hold their hands over their mouths to prepare for the eventuality of a "bad man" entering their building. Shane's cousins still fear for their lives while walking to the corner grocery in Hartford, ordering their lives around physical survival, not social or economic advancement. The American gun violence epidemic has put our nation in danger of sinking, and it's time to issue a distress call.

I've spent the seven years since that bone-chilling day in December 2012 learning everything I can about why Sandy Hook happened. I have sought to discover why Shane Oliver died over a boys' dispute that would have never become fatal in any other country. I have sought answers to every question: Are we born with a predilection to harm others, or is violence a learned behavior? Why is America such a disturbing outlier of violence in the industrialized world? What is it about America's history, culture, and politics that draws us toward guns and the unique violence perpetuated by those weapons? What are the similarities and differences between the different kinds of gun deaths—the

mass shootings, the grudge crimes, the domestic assaults, and the suicides? And, finally, what do we know about how to stop all of this?
What are the right policy interventions, and how do we reshape our
politics to make sure public leaders pursue these policies?

This book seeks to answer these questions by weaving together
three interconnecting narratives. One story is my personal journey
into, and through, the gun violence epidemic—a political coming-of-
age story that overlaps with the birth and maturation of the modern
anti–gun violence movement. The second story is the story of violence itself—why humans hurt one another, and why America's long,
unique relationship with firearms makes our nation number one in
global first world violence. The final story, told in the last several chapters of the book, charts the way out—how to demand commonsense
changes in our laws that will reduce episodes of life-altering violence,
while turning down the temperature on the white-hot politics that
currently surround the debate over guns in America. This book's ambi-
tion and scope are both large, and so I will do my best to carefully put
down all the pieces, one by one, that need to be on the table in order
for us to understand why America became this violent, and how we
can change.

My hope is that this book stands as an important guide for those
who want to understand why America has arrived at this place today,
where a twenty-year-old African American living in urban America is
more likely to be shot than a young American soldier patrolling the
streets of Syria. But this book is also a template for action. Because
none of what we experience in the United States—the mass shootings,
the suicides, the urban violence—is inevitable. It is our choice whether
we accept it, or rise together to demand a new deal.

Through all the searing pain and bottomless loss that I have witnessed, I remain confident America *will* rise up. From my earliest days
in politics, I have been a believer in positive visualization, and almost
every day during the past seven years, I run through in my head the
events of the day—maybe still years away—when I will walk out of the
U.S. Senate chamber having just helped pass the first meaningful legislation to crack down on gun violence in a generation. I will embrace

the victims and family members left behind that will be waiting outside the doors to the Senate floor. And then I will go home, sit Owen and Rider down on the living room couch, and tell them the *whole* story. What happened that day when we couldn't go to see the Christmas decorations in New York City. And how their country—*with their dad's help*—went and *did something about it.*

This book is the journey through the story of how we make that day a reality.

2

THE VIOLENCE INSIDE US

NATURAL VIOLENCE

At a rally for Montana Republicans in October 2018, President Donald Trump knew he needed to provide a major boost to beleaguered incumbent congressman Greg Gianforte. Polls showed ticket-leading Democratic senator Jon Tester comfortably ahead in his race, and worries were growing that Tester's popularity might drag Gianforte's opponent across the line for an unexpected Democratic victory. So Trump turned to what he believed to be Gianforte's primary selling point to the Montana electorate: his history of unprovoked assault.

"I heard that he body-slammed a reporter," Trump boomed. "This was the day of the election or just before, and I thought, 'Oh, this is terrible! He's going to lose the election.'" Trump continued: "And then I said, 'Wait a minute. I know Montana pretty well, I think it might help him.' And it did!" The line electrified the arena, and the crowd roared in approval. The clip, complete with the thunderous response, was played that night over and over again on every news outlet in the country.

The body slam to which Trump was referring had taken place a year and a half earlier, when in the final days of Gianforte's special election campaign for the U.S. House of Representatives, he had bristled at questions being asked of him by Ben Jacobs, a well-regarded reporter for the British newspaper *The Guardian*. With Jacobs's phone recording the entire incident, Gianforte refused to answer the questions, lurched into a fury of anger, and picked Jacobs up off the ground and slammed him to the floor. Within minutes, Jacobs and others had posted the audio proof of the assault on social media, leading to the filing of charges against the candidate by the local police.

I remember assuming Gianforte's campaign was a cooked goose. How could someone with such a hair-trigger temper, willing to assault a reporter simply for asking a question he didn't like, be elected to Congress? But, of course, I was wrong. Gianforte didn't suspend his campaign. He didn't step aside. He stayed in the race, and, incredibly, he won. He didn't suffer any drop in support after the assault. Some polling suggested he actually picked up new support.

And that explains why Trump chose the story of the body slam as his closing argument for the congressman's reelection. What else could make the case better for a candidate for Congress than his penchant to take out his frustrations on others through physical violence? What Trump knew, and what many Americans try to deny, is that deep inside all of us is an uncomfortable but natural predilection toward violence. Harming others—as a method of personal protection, or as a means of social or economic advancement—is part of our nature. It's been that way for humans for thousands of years. Gianforte's assault connected with the primal instinct for violence still lodged inside the human body and brain. That's what Trump knew, and that's likely why the Montana crowd cheered so loudly.

. . .

My journey into this question of the roots of human violence began the day I first heard the name *Adam Lanza*. Kenny and I sped northward through western Connecticut on the way to the Sandy Hook volunteer firehouse. I was trembling as I got out of the car and approached Chris

Lyddy, the dynamic young state representative from Newtown, in the parking lot. The small station sits at one end of Dickenson Drive. At the other, less than a quarter mile away, is Sandy Hook Elementary. As the school was evacuated, children were brought to the firehouse, and parents were directed to pick up their children there. Save for the six children who miraculously escaped Victoria Soto's classroom while Adam Lanza fumbled with an exchange of cartridges, most of the children ended up there that morning.

Except for twenty.

Gradually, as the firehouse grounds cleared out of kids and parents, there were forty parents who had not been reunited with their first graders. This was the moment I arrived there, and Lyddy explained to me, as I walked into the building, the terrible decision that lay before our hands-on governor, Dan Malloy, who was on-site managing the minute-by-minute emergency response. As rumors began to circulate about what had happened inside those two classrooms, Dan had a terrifying decision to make: follow protocol and wait until the bodies were identified before informing the parents of their children's fate, or explain to those who remained in the firehouse the likelihood that their children were still in the school, dead.

When Dan made the decision to enter the room where the parents were congregated to tell them about the scene inside the school, I accompanied him, and stood outside the door as he broke the life-altering news. The heartbreaking aftermath of that meeting is a story that is not mine to tell. It's personal to the parents who streamed out of that room, their lives changed forever. Frankly, much of it is a blur to me today. But I do remember thinking two things. First, I remember wanting to get back to Owen and Rider, as fast as I possibly could. Second, I began to wonder how any human being could be capable of that kind of horror—the premeditated murder of twenty first graders.

Three days later, I went to the first funeral—for Noah Pozner, the youngest of the twenty. The room was drowning in sorrow, and I fidgeted endlessly in my seat, trying to digest what was happening to this family in front of my eyes. It was the first funeral or wake for a child I had ever attended. I would go to a dozen more before Christmas.

I boarded a plane for Washington that afternoon, on my way to give a short speech to my colleagues in Congress before a moment of silence on the House floor. I sat down in my seat, pulled down the tray from the seatback in front of me, and began to draft my remarks. After fifteen minutes of writing and crossing out, I settled on four words to explain to the world what had driven Adam Lanza to slaughter children: *sickness masquerading as evil.*

That's what I said that evening, as my voice quivered through four minutes of remarks. But really, I didn't believe it. I had looked into the eyes of those parents, as they left that room, and there was no way what happened inside those two classrooms the morning of December 14 was *disguised* as evil. It *was* evil, the purest form I could imagine.

And this evil didn't come from a dangerous outside place, breaching the suburban defenses of Sandy Hook. No, the people in that firehouse, *they knew the Lanzas.* Their kids were in classes with Adam. They occasionally ran into his mother, Nancy, getting takeout from her favorite tavern, My Place. That December day, the veil that had existed between the violent places we saw on the news, like the north end of Hartford, and the safe places we knew, like Newtown, collapsed to the ground. And now people started to wonder: If that kind of evil lay somewhere inside a skinny kid with no prior history of violence, what lurks inside each of us that we don't yet know or comprehend? Are we all, potentially, unknowingly, just a few moments away from criminal violence? What shook me, and many Americans, to the core that weekend, was not simply the thought of what had happened in that school, but the idea that human beings have inside them the capacity to conceive of, and carry out, that kind of mind-bending horror.

As so, in the weeks after the shooting, I began to ask the most basic question: Where does violence *come from*? Is it a learned behavior that we choose to exercise, or is violence in our nature, an uncontrollable part of our biology?

Our first stop in our journey to understand American violence is to explore the nature of human violence itself. As we will see, humans have always been violent. Our biology has guaranteed that in our lifetimes we will not shake our violent predispositions. Violence is, indeed, in our nature. But in recent times, the human race has gone through a remarkable "civilizing process"—that is, the quelling and controlling of this predisposition toward physical aggression. While shootings still dominate the news, we have become a remarkably less violent species, thanks to centuries of willful decisions made by human beings. Yes, violence is in our nature, but we have proved, over and over, that we have the means to control it. I need to tell you both of these stories—the story of natural violence, and the story of our success in tamping it down—so that you will have hope for the future. And so that you will know that no matter how much violence continues to dominate American headlines, we are not helpless. It is within our power to do something about it.

A BRIEF EXPLANATION OF THE BIOLOGY OF HUMAN VIOLENCE

The story of violence, and where it comes from, is a complex one. All humans share a rage instinct, but not every human defaults to rage in even the most stressful situations. The explanation for violence has always involved a mix of natural and external influences—biology and free will. Even today, with reams of research on the derivation of human aggression, we struggle to understand where to set the blame for violent acts.

Consider, for instance, the case of Davis Bradley Waldroup, Jr. One fall night in 2006, Waldroup had been drinking heavily in his trailer in the mountains of Polk County, Tennessee, occasionally leafing through a King James Bible he kept close, as he waited impatiently for his estranged wife, Penny, to arrive for a visit with their four children. As the car pulled up, Waldroup, drunk and pestilent, stumbled outside carrying his .22 caliber hunting rifle. He began arguing immediately with Penny and her friend Leslie Bradshaw, who'd come along for the ride.

In an instant, Waldroup flew into a rage, emptied eight rounds into Bradshaw, and then, to finish the job, sliced her head open with a knife. His wife ran as fast as she could, but Waldroup caught her. He beat her with a shovel, butchered her with the knife and a machete, and then dragged her back into the trailer, demanding sex. She lay on the floor of the trailer, unresponsive and clinging to life, while their four children watched the entire massacre unfold. The crime scene was difficult for even career law enforcement officers to stomach. Blood everywhere—on the floors, the walls, the children's clothes, even on the Bible that Waldroup was reading before the rampage started. "There are murders, and then there are . . . hacking to death, trails of blood," said the local prosecutor. "I have not seen one like this. And I have seen a lot."

At the trial in a rural east Tennessee courtroom, there wasn't a question as to what happened. "I just snapped," said Waldroup. "I'm not proud of none of it." So his lawyers shifted the focus away from the facts of the assault and instead turned to the motivation. "It wasn't a whodunit," said Waldroup's defense attorney. "It was a why done it." Of course, the easiest answer was that Waldroup chose to do it. He had a time-tested motive—anger over his smashed marriage. As the victim of horrific abuse and beatings as a child, Waldroup had learned the devastating power of violence. And during the murder, he displayed a consciousness about his actions that made clear he was exercising free will. (At one point during the attack on Penny, Waldroup yelled to his children, "Come tell your mama goodbye!") The prosecution argued that though Waldroup may have snapped, as he claimed, it was his decision, and his decision alone, to kill Bradshaw and maim his wife who, amazingly, survived the attack. He did it, and he chose to do it.

The defense had another theory. They argued that free will played no meaningful part in the attacks because Waldroup was biologically predisposed to be violent. They offered studies of his DNA and scientific research showing that Waldroup was a victim himself. Powerful, biogenetic forces operating inside his body made him powerless to stop this heinous act of violence, they said. Waldroup didn't *choose* to be violent. He was *designed* for violence.

After eleven hours of deliberation, the jury returned with a split decision that suggested it had accepted *both* explanations of Waldroup's acts. The jury found him guilty, but structured their decision in a way that deliberately saved him from the death penalty. The justice system may rest on the assumption of behavior as a manifestation of free will, but as one juror said at the end of the trial, "A bad gene is a bad gene."

· · ·

Seventeenth-century philosopher Thomas Hobbes famously mused that humans, in their pre-civilization "natural state," lived lives that were "nasty, brutish, and short." Four hundred years later, President Barack Obama seemed to agree, when in his Nobel Prize speech, he noted that "war, in one form or another, appeared with the first man." Both were right—humans, more so than most other animals, have been a particularly violent species, beginning at our earliest moments.

In 2012, Marta Mirazón Lahr and a team of researchers from Cambridge University were hunting for prehistoric human remains when a hunch led them to a place called Nataruk, located in the high lakes region of Kenya. They hit the jackpot near now-dry Lake Turkana, when they stumbled across a trove of intact skeletons, preserved in a long-ago dried-up shallow lagoon where the bodies had come to rest. As Lahr began to remove the earth around the first complete skeleton, her team was puzzled why the body was fully prone, the face pressed into the sediment of the lagoon, an unusual position for a person in death, even ten thousand years ago. Lahr soon discovered the reason for the strange positioning. The perfectly preserved skull showed two clear major blunt-force traumas, one to the forehead and another to the left cheek. This young man had been clubbed to death, his skull shattered, and his spine snapped. Murdered in an instant, he fell to the ground, face-first, and stayed in that exact spot for ten thousand years.

What followed was even more startling: Twenty-six more skeletons were uncovered, including at least eight women and six children, all dating from the same moment in time, all displaying evidence of brutal, violent death. One victim was pregnant and likely bound before being killed. Two other bodies had projectiles lodged in their throats and heads. One victim survived an arrow wound to the brain, only to be later killed by a vicious blow to his forehead.

Here was clear evidence of large-scale premeditated murder from the time when giant mastodons walked the earth. According to Lahr, before humans even began to live close to one another, creating more friction points and contests for resources, premeditated violence was part of the human repertoire. After having spent a year unearthing the grisly scene, one of Lahr's co-researchers, Robert Foley, noted, "I've no doubt it is in our biology to be aggressive and lethal, just as it is to be deeply caring and loving. A lot of what we understand about human evolutionary biology suggests these are two sides of the same coin."

.   .   .

Spanish zoologist José Maria Gómez Reyes would likely agree with Foley. In 2006, he and a team of researchers published a remarkable work of breathtaking scope. The zoologists surveyed the behavior of 1,024 species of animals to determine which animals showed aggression toward other animals of their same species—a phenomenon called *conspecific violence*—and how frequently these animals engaged in this specific type of violence. The first finding was perhaps the most surprising: 60 percent of all the animals that Gomez and his colleagues observed showed no propensity to such violence. Bats and whales, for instance, though social animals who travel in large groups, demonstrate no propensity toward violence against other members of their community. On the other hand, many animals one might think of as peaceful, like horses and squirrels, showed high levels of violence against one another. The most violent of all the mammals Reyes studied were, in fact, the stars of a hit show on Animal Planet, *Meerkat Manor*. Meerkats kill one another at a stunning clip—one in five of these cute, cuddly little tunnel dwellers will die at the hands (or paws) of another meerkat, a conspecific violence rate of 20 percent.

Overall, the general rate of conspecific violence among mammals was very low: .3 percent. But among humans and our primate cousins, the number jumped to 2 percent, nearly the highest level of intraspecies violence of all the animals studied. And other research confirms that primates are indeed much more violent than other animals. In the

1980s, the renowned primatologist Jane Goodall described shocking examples of behavior among chimpanzees, often thought of as the closest primate cousins to humans. Groups of chimps, traveling together, would come upon a solitary chimpanzee from another group and launch an attack on the lone chimp with lethal savagery. In one instance, Goodall watched as two chimps held down a solitary male while the others bit off his appendages, ripped his trachea out of his body, and drank his blood. Goodall also witnessed a group of chimpanzees from one community methodically hunt down each member of another community until all the males had been executed.

Of course, humans are not chimpanzees, but six million years ago we shared an evolutionary ancestor, and today 99 percent of the DNA of humans and chimps is identical. Thus, it cannot be a coincidence that, in general, primates, from chimpanzees to humans, display a level of aggression far greater than more than half of all mammals. Primates are animals with built-in triggers for aggression, and we have passed down those triggers from generation to generation. Imagine the evolutionary pressures favoring human violence in the Stone Age, when those twenty-seven people in Nataruk were killed. Early humans were more likely to survive if they could win physical battles with other humans, and thus natural selection passed down the traits associated with more efficient aggression. Women chose to mate with males who were more likely to be able to protect them and their offspring.

When those twenty-seven people were killed in Nataruk ten thousand years ago, they were victims of an attack by a rival group of foragers. They are the first known victims of tribal conflict. And fear is one of the key drivers of our tribal nature. Belonging to a tribe or group is indispensable to survival. We're social creatures who are richly rewarded—materially and emotionally—by belonging to groups. So it's no surprise that our neurological systems have abundant pathways for deciding who's in our group and who is not. We have an in-group bias. We're faster and more accurate at recognizing the faces of people in our group than outside our group. We're quicker to habituate to and trust the face of a member of our tribe than an outsider's. We're more likely to feel empathy and concern when a member of our group feels pain. We might even have a little surge of positive hormones when we meet a new member that we perceive to be part of our group.

In contrast, research shows that outsiders or intruders trigger a cascade of processes in our brains and bodies, many of them associated with the way we become afraid and express it. Untrustworthy outsider faces spark "automatic, prepotent and conscious intentions" related to fear, according to a 2012 study published in *Nature*. All of this happens in our brains faster than the blink of an eye, often faster than we can assert conscious control. If you've ever felt a surge of fear connected to an unknown threat coursing through your body, you know how powerful it is. But even low-level, constant fear is an integral part of our lives. There is no stopping that constant bass line of fear about outsiders in our brains. For some people, the neurocircuitry of fear is turned to eleven, and for others the volume is set very low. But no matter what, us versus them is just wired into our brain.

This natural fear of others, and the instinct to revert to violence against outsiders, has been passed down from generation to generation. "Violence can be seen as an adaptive strategy, favoring the perpetrator's reproductive success in terms of mates, status or resources," wrote José Maria Gómez Reyes and his colleagues. The physical and psychological traits related to effective aggression became more likely to be passed down, as more aggressive males prevailed in contests for primacy and increased their reproductive opportunities. All of this is proof that our bodies and minds have been shaped by and adapted for violence.

.   .   .

Let's look at one single feature of human anatomy that sparks an interesting debate over how our bodies have been designed for physical conflict. Our species' evolutionary break from the pack can be explained by two codependent adaptations. First is the development of a fifth finger, independently maneuverable from, and opposite to, the hand's other four digits. Anthropologists believe that the opposable thumb began to develop almost as soon as early humans gained the ability to walk upright (making the hands available for tasks other than walking). The transformation of the hand that followed allowed humans to manipulate objects with a level of precision and dexterity previously unseen in the animal kingdom.

Thus began the world's greatest virtuous circle of anatomical development. These newly nimble hands allowed humans to diversify their diet. A variety of proteins and fats from fish and animals that could now be caught, and the vitamins and fibers from the fruits of vegetables that could now be collected, vaulted the human brain into developmental overdrive. Fed a steady and reliable diet of these new nutrients, our brains began to grow and mature, allowing for the discovery and mastery of new tasks for these miraculously dexterous opposable thumbs.

Thumbs, according to the conventional wisdom of human biology, were our ancestors' primary agent of separation from the rest of our primal competitors. We became the dominant species—the masters of our domain—in part because of our opposable fifth finger.

And then in 2013, along came biologist David Carrier. Carrier had a more brutish theory of the evolution of the human hand. One of the most important functionalities of the opposable thumb is the ability to tuck it into a fist, a feature unavailable to primates with non-opposable fifth digits. And that, it turns out, makes humans more powerful fighters. Carrier used human cadavers to show how the ability to tuck the thumb into a fist made throwing a punch more effective since the thumb was less likely to break or be damaged inside the fist. Carrier's basic theory was that the evolutionary advantage of the opposable thumb wasn't really about helping us advance mentally as a species; it was all about making *Homo sapiens* better fighters.

Carrier's research was immediately controversial. One skeptic exhaustively studied the strike impact of fists with tucked thumbs versus open palms and came to the conclusion that open palms did just as much damage, so early humans wouldn't have been so reliant on the effectiveness of a fist punch.

But Carrier's series of studies don't exist in a vacuum. Plenty of other science exists to show that the human form has been optimized for battle. Humans don't have one dominant physical feature designed for conflict (like a deer's antlers or a shark's teeth), but the long list of differences in the biology of men and women have led researchers to the conclusion that men's bodies in particular have likely evolved into more effective fighting machines over the years as a mechanism to win breeding partners and protect themselves and their offspring. From higher bone density to greater muscle-to-fat ratios, males have twenty-six biological differences from women that suggest male bodies are honed for efficient physical aggression. The human body may not present as ferociously as a hulking primate or a sharp-fanged jungle cat, but it is designed for violence nonetheless. The history of our biology tells us that.

. . .

Our bodies are built for violence, but so are our brains. In the weeks after Sandy Hook, I retreated to my home, and I tried to spend as much time as I could there, playing trains and trucks on the floor of our living room with Owen and Rider. My greatest optimism about human nature came from these moments. Kids in these early years harbor no prejudices; they draw no lines of arbitrary discrimination. They exude joy and wonder, and after you've come in contact with the sharpest edges of human behavior, soaking in the uncorrupted, unfiltered spirit of a child is the most wonderful tonic. A child's mind, in these first few years, exists in near pure form, and I took solace in the belief that if that purity of heart could exist inside us during our early years, then surely it must be part of our nature, accessible to us as adults.

But if young children are a window into our true nature, then we need to take a second look. Because, as it turns out, young children—toddlers, in particular—have a nasty side. Every parent remembers the seemingly unprovoked temper tantrums, where anything not tied or glued down was a potential weapon. At the beginning stages of writing this book, a friend texted me about a planned dinner between our two families: "I'm leaving [the two-year-old] with a babysitter. We're better off that way—she'll light your house on fire." His daughter isn't alone. Eighty percent of children engage in violent behaviors by seventeen months. Put another way, the average toddler is more frequently violent than members of the most ferocious organized street gangs. In 1972, Donald Hebb, one of great psychologists of the past fifty years, noted that toddlers don't have to learn how to throw a temper tantrum. They know it from birth, because lodged in tiny knots of neurons inside an almond-sized piece of our brain called the hypothalamus are the instructions for rage and aggression. It works differently in different brains, but in the hypothalamus lies the anatomical circuitry of instinctual violence.

In 2014, researchers at the University of Montreal placed an advertisement asking for parents of twins, both fraternal and identical, to take part in a study of violence in toddlers. What the researchers found lent more credence to the idea that violence is preset into some individuals' genetic makeup. First, among the identical twins, violence was an all-or-nothing proposition—in most cases, either both twins were abnormally violent, or neither was. In the fraternal twin sets, violence often showed up in only one child, even though both children were being raised in the same environment, under the same parental rules of behavior. Second, the children generally were able to unlearn violence, suggesting that while violence may be part of our nature, nurture plays an increasingly influential role as children gain more exposure to alternative methods of conflict and rage resolution. Rates of violence were highest among children ages two to four.

"As children grow," said Stéphane Paquin of the research team, "they learn how to manage their emotions, communicate with others, and deal with conflict. They are able to channel their aggressive impulses, whether proactive or reactive." Violence is biology, but it is not destiny.

According to researchers, during childhood we learn to manage the seven basic emotional networks lodged deep in our ancient brain structure: fear, grief, rage, seeking, lust, care, and play. You recognize each one of them as powerful motivators for your daily behavior: the desire to seek and accomplish a professional or personal goal; the lust for sexual relations with a person you find attractive; the instinct to care about the daily happiness of those close to you, like children and parents; the joy you get from playing a sport you love or having dinner with friends.

Rage and aggression are important emotional systems, too—instincts that have allowed humans to survive and advance over the centuries in often hostile environments. We need rage and fear. But children learn to suppress the negative emotions when they get in the way of fulfilling needs associated with the positive emotional systems. When he was younger and his little brother was doing something particularly annoying, Owen would often push or shove Rider to send a message. But Rider figured out how to make him pay for this. Owen is a storyteller, and when he was eight, he loved weaving complicated narratives of imaginary worlds for Rider. When Owen acted aggressively toward his brother, Rider would withdraw and become uninterested in Owen's stories. Owen quickly figured out that his physicality had consequences and adjusted his actions. For Owen and millions of other children with growing brains, the positive systems start to create feedback loops that quash the actions driven by the negative systems. This transformation in children is no different from the transformation that the human species has undergone over the course of millennia as the instinct to fear non–family members and strangers was, over time, counterbalanced by a desire to seek out the benefits of more integrated, cohesive communities.

But despite all this progress, there are still plenty of moments when the positive systems fail to override the negative impulses, and rage turns into a violent attack. And it's important for us to spend some time understanding how the brain still tricks some humans into believing physical aggression is the wisest course of action to settle conflict or protect oneself. Legions of scientists across the world have spent the past decades trying to explore this phenomenon, and they have focused on two key questions about the anatomy of violent acts. One, what is the neurological chain reaction in the brain that causes a human being to act out aggressively, often when logic would dictate a different path? And two, how are the keys to this violence-producing sequence in the brain passed down from generation to generation?

• • •

Kent Kiehl's childhood home in Tacoma, Washington, was just down the street from notorious serial killer Ted Bundy's house, and as Kiehl grew up he was perplexed by how someone that viciously deviant could have lived inconspicuously among his family, friends, and classmates for so long. Today, he's a neuroscience professor at the University of New Mexico, where he is developing a stunning database of four thousand brains of hardened criminals—murderers, arsonists, rapists. *They have different brains,* he's found. There's less gray matter; the amygdala, a key part of the brain where emotions are experienced, is smaller; and there are often defects in the limbic and paralimbic cortex, the parts of the brain used for focus and impulse control. Kiehl believes that as much as 50 percent of the time, these abnormalities have a genetic component. The defects, which are found in 1 percent of American adults, but 16 percent of American adults in prison, have dramatic impacts, sharply limiting the ability to feel empathy or remorse. Kiehl's work is backed up by other studies that show the same thing—brain scans of those prone to violence look different from those who are not.

Far more drives violence than brain structures. A veritable alphabet soup of brain chemicals regulates our rage system. Scientists are hard at work trying to figure out the role they play in our violent biology. One theory holds that when dopamine levels are off-kilter, the brain may offer higher reward signals to violence and aggression than in most humans. Dopamine is the critical hormone in the brain's reward system—creating the neurochemical loop that links a stimulus with pleasure and satisfaction.

Norepinephrine, on the other hand, is the neurotransmitter that is integral to the fight-or-flight instinct triggered when a human faces an immediate, unexpected threat. Some studies show that highly aggressive individuals have particularly high levels of norepinephrine and therefore are more likely to choose *fight* over *flight,* responding more violently to stressors and outside threats than other persons. And there's a similar story with testosterone, another popular theoretical cause of violence. Studies have shown higher levels of testosterone in prisoners versus the general population, but the consensus is that high testosterone alone, without environmental triggers, is not an automatic precursor to violence.

But perhaps the most interesting brain chemical related to violence is serotonin, the most intensely studied neurotransmitter and one that allegedly played a role in Bradley Davis Waldroup's murderous rampage. Five years after Waldroup committed his heinous crime, Dr. Phil, the talk show doctor, devoted an entire episode, entitled "Born to Rage," to what has been described as the "warrior gene." He invited a group of self-described "rageaholics" to sit on a panel and testify to their lives of violence. At the end of the show, Dr. Phil revealed that each of his violence-prone panelists carried the same genetic mutation, causing a deficit of the enzyme MAOA, which impacts serotonin.

The existence of this gene was first hypothesized in the 1990s, a result of a Dutch woman who walked into a local hospital seeking counseling for dealing with the abnormally violent men in her family. Clinicians—and then researchers—became fascinated by this unique family with a long, multigenerational history of exceptional male violence, ranging from attempted sibling rape to running a work supervisor down with a car. It seemed that virtually every man in this particular family acted out in extraordinarily violent ways.

German geneticist Han Brunner began a study of the family's genetic makeup, and came to a groundbreaking conclusion. Virtually all of the violent males in the family possessed a defective version of a gene, only found on the X chromosome, that regulates serotonin levels in the body. Brunner further noted that because the mutation was found to occur on the X chromosome, it might help explain why males, over history, have tended to be much more violent than females. Since men have only one X chromosome, a mutation on it can have profound effects, while women, who have two X chromosomes, can compensate with the other nonmutated X chromosome.

Serotonin is not a neurotransmitter you want to mess with. It relays the signals between nerve cells, regulating the intensity of those transmissions. Screwed-up serotonin levels negatively affect your mood, appetite, sex drive, sleep, memory, bowel function, and blood clotting—pretty much everything important to being a functioning human. Most important for our study of violence is the impact that high and low serotonin levels can have on aggression. The "warrior gene" causes the body to produce insufficient levels of the enzyme MAOA, which is partially responsible for controlling levels of serotonin produced by the brain. Without enough MAOA, serotonin floods the brain, causing a malfunction in the way the brain regulates aggression.

. . .

There is, of course, danger in going too far down this road trying to trace the biological roots of violence. At the end of Dr. Phil's show on the warrior gene, when the panelists were told that they all carried the genetic mutation, no one took it as an alarming discovery. These rageaholics seemed comforted to know that they weren't to blame for their aggressive behavior—it was just in the genes. One subject revealed to Dr. Phil, "It's a relief there's something linked to this anger, and it's not brought on because I want to do it."

As we are beginning to learn, biology—that fist you can form with your opposable thumb, that rage center in your hypothalamus, that smaller amygdala, those hormones and neurotransmitters coursing through your body, that genetic mutation—is clearly an important part of the story. But the risk of telling too much of the story of aggression through the prism of genetics is to give excuses to those who want to take agency away from human beings, or those who want to give up on trying to use rules and interventions as a means of quelling violence. As we will learn, there is plenty of evidence to suggest that free will plays a much bigger role in the perpetuation of violence than biology.

And there's an even greater risk to placing too much emphasis on genetics and biology. Only a century ago, the field of research making the connection between genetics and violence belonged almost exclusively to racists and eugenicists. In the early twentieth century, the American eugenics movement held sway over large portions of the nation's legal and medical establishment. This school of thought argued that certain types of individuals were "born criminal."

Criminality, one prominent researcher claimed, could be predicted by inspection of certain physical characteristics, most notably hawk-like noses, bloodshot eyes, and jug ears. Twenty-nine states enacted forced sterilization laws on the theory that crime could be controlled by purging the gene pool of these natural aggressors. And in 1927, the U.S. Supreme Court handed the eugenics movement its breakthrough victory, upholding the forced sterilization of Carrie Buck, a seventeen-year-old girl from Virginia whose offense, according to the state, was feeble-mindedness and sexual promiscuity. The great justice Oliver Wendell Holmes, Jr., wrote for the majority: "It is better for all the world, if instead of waiting to execute degenerate offspring for crime, or let them starve for their imbecility, society can prevent those who are manifestly unfit from continuing their kind. . . . Three generations of imbeciles are enough."

This regrettable piece of American scientific history causes current researchers in the biosociology space to tread lightly when arguing for the connection between biology and aggression. Modern scientists working in this field fill their work with caveat after caveat.

In 1989, UNESCO, the scientific arm of the United Nations, adopted a remarkable resolution, drafted by twenty of the world's preeminent biologists and scientists, entitled the Seville Statement on Violence. The key line: "It is scientifically incorrect to say that war or any other violent behavior is genetically programmed into our human nature." The resolution was designed as a response to a growing modern branch of research that built on the eugenics movement's attempts to link genetics to violence and theorized that evolution wasn't able to pass down only physical traits, but behaviors as well.

Just as John Calvin argued during the sixteenth century that a human's free will was celestially bound by inevitable, predestined sin, so did these new sociobiologists theorize that evolution had saddled humans with predestined, hardwired behaviors. For the United Nations, this idea, unchecked, threatened to unwind the entire postwar order, which was designed to use treaties and conventions and conflict-resolution mechanisms to convince humans that violence was unnecessary in modern existence.

You've got to be careful when mixing talk of genetics and violence—not everyone with elevated levels of MAOA or high testosterone or bloodshot eyes is a murderer in waiting. But what the growing evidence of the evolutionary roots of human violence reminds us is that under the right circumstances and in the right context, eons-old aggressive tendencies, baked into the human genetic code, can flash to the surface and push humans to violent eruption that may feel to them, and to us, impossible to understand. The fact that this potential sits inside each of us is not, as the United Nations feared, a reason to give up, to accept human violence as destiny. In fact, I would argue the opposite is true: The biology of violence is a reminder that without coordinated strategies to reduce violence, humans, left to their complicated evolutionary composition, will do bad things to one another.

A SHORT HISTORY OF TWO THOUSAND YEARS OF VIOLENCE

I was raised in a Protestant church, became an active member of the youth ministry as a high school student, and formed an early appreciation for the ways in which the Christian church teaches the importance of selflessness and community amid a world that often rewards selfishness and individual achievement. But the stories upon which the church is founded often perplexed me, given how difficult it was to square the biblical text I read at youth group with the history and science books I read in school. Cathy's church experience wasn't much different, so we decided to raise our kids in a home that enthusiastically considered religion and religious belief, but largely outside the confines of organized church. We go to our neighborhood Protestant church sometimes, but largely we find other ways to engage our kids in religious exploration. That's how I came to the practice, early in 2017, of reading excerpts from a children's Bible to my younger son, Rider, each night. It was a jumping-off point for discussions about the lessons inside the narratives, and I looked forward to every evening, tucked away in a cozy corner of my son's loft bed, discussing theology with a wide-eyed five-year-old.

One night, when I was away from home, Cathy took my spot and picked up where I had left off in the Old Testament. When I got home the next day, she pulled me aside. "I'll be honest," she admitted, "I haven't read the Old Testament in thirty years. And Chris, it is *way too violent* for a five-year-old. I mean, every story I read had siblings murdering each other, mass killings. Last night, I think I read a part where God orders a genocide. I know Rider really loves this, but we might need to stop reading the Bible to our son."

It was a thought that hadn't escaped me. For obvious reasons, Christians tend to focus more attention on the New Testament than the Old Testament portions of the Bible. Christianity's origin story really begins in the Gospels. And so, like Cathy, I don't remember my church spending a lot of time on the detailed narratives of the Old Testament. But as Rider spent time working through Genesis and Exodus, Leviticus and Deuteronomy, it dawned on me that there might be another reason my church didn't spend too much time on the first section of the Bible: It's full of mind-blowing, civilization-altering violence.

As Steven Pinker coyly notes in his groundbreaking, magisterial book on global violence, *The Better Angels of Our Nature*, the Bible begins with a family of four—Adam, Eve, Cain, and Abel. One day, out in the field, Cain smites Abel. "With a world population of exactly four," Pinker writes, "that works out to a homicide rate of 25 percent, which is about a thousand times higher than the equivalent rates in Western countries today."

The text doesn't get more peaceful from there. The basic rhythm of the Old Testament is God punishing society for its wickedness with horrific disease or pestilence or violence, followed by a biblical actor saving the society from God's wrath, followed by the society slipping back into wickedness, prompting more terrible vengeance from God. Along the way, God kills every single firstborn child of the Egyptians; the entire Egyptian army is wiped out by the sudden parting and closing of the Red Sea; Moses and his brother, Aaron, murder thousands of their followers under orders from God; and Joshua terrorizes the city of Jericho (again, with God's blessing), "destroy[ing] all that was in the city, both man and woman, young and old, and ox, and sheep, and ass, with the edge of the sword."

Let's put off a fully loaded discussion of whether the stories of the Old Testament are actually rooted in historical truth. What matters is the authors of the text, who were writing a persuasive text, either were telling a true story or were making up stories that were rooted in enough truth to be believable to readers who were still hearing histories passed down from generations that lived in these pre-Christ times. Maybe the violence in the late pre-Christ era wasn't as dramatic as the Bible describes, but it wouldn't have been an effective persuasive document if it had no grounding in reality.

. . .

The historical record from the time of Christ backs up the epidemic levels of violence portrayed in the King James Bible. Let's visit the Roman Empire in one single year—A.D. 69—as an example. The year before, Emperor Nero's reign came to an end by his own hand, as the ruler committed suicide rather than face execution for alleged treason against the empire, but not before he had presided over epidemic levels of slaughter during fourteen years in power. As the empire was growing, violent revolts and rebellions sprang up in all corners of Europe and the Middle East, and the Romans spared no one. Nero put down a Jewish rebellion in Palestine that may have taken the lives of nearly one-quarter of the region's total population. The historian Tacitus reports that Nero's efforts to quash another rebellion, this one launched against the Roman occupation of Britain, resulted in the deaths of eighty thousand Roman soldiers and seventy thousand Britons.

After Nero took his own life, Galba, the governor of the empire's largest Spanish province, marched on Rome to take the throne. Along the way he destroyed any village that did not accept his claim to power, and once in Rome, he executed scores of political opponents—including members of the Senate—whom he considered rivals for power. Rome quickly tired of Galba's terror, and an ambitious nobleman, Otho, convinced Galba's guards to kill both the emperor and his handpicked successor. Otho took power, but was forced to march

north to meet his rival for the throne, Vitellius, the governor of a powerful Germanic province.

At the Battle of Bedriacum, another forty thousand fell as Vitellius
prevailed. Otho immediately committed suicide, and Vitellius returned
to Rome and took power over a city in political and financial crisis.
Vitellius's fiscal strategy was simple: Kill anyone with a claimed debt
against the empire. His killing spree expanded when debt-ridden citizens began to name the emperor as an heir and Vitellius responded
by murdering each of them. Sensing an opportunity, the commander
of Roman forces in Judea, Vespasian (who had led the brutal massacre of the Jews under Nero), marched to Rome, burned down the
Temple of Jupiter, killed Vitellius, and, on December 21, named himself the fourth Roman emperor of the year 69.

It is hard to wrap your head around the scope of this carnage—all
occurring in one single year—today. Imagine, for a moment, in 1964,
as the country was still mourning the assassination of John Kennedy, if
Lyndon Johnson, the two following American presidents, and dozens
of congressmen were also murdered or committed suicide amid a civil
war that left hundreds of thousands more Americans dead. Modern
American political life is rough-and-tumble, but not that rough-and-
tumble.

·   ·   ·

For as wildly violent as biblical times were, in the middle of the fifth
century, the Roman Empire fell, and things got—unbelievably—much
worse. Europe in the Dark and Middle Ages was a deeply violent place.
I remember arriving at Oxford University in 1994 to study for a year at
one of the university's oldest colleges, Exeter, founded in medieval
times, and learning about the dining hall's curious table manners. The
dining room at Exeter dates later, to the 1600s, but looks positively
Arthurian. Several long wooden tables and accompanying benches run
the length of a dimly lit rectangular room with vaulted ceilings. Meals
when I was there were organized in two seatings, and all students ate
the same, family-style meal.

On my first day, I picked up my knife to cut the meat on my plate and then placed it down on the edge of my plate, cutting end facing in, as I was taught by my mother. A second-year student across from me leapt at the opportunity to instruct me on proper Exeter etiquette. "Don't put the knife down, hold it under the table, in your right hand, when you're not using it," he explained. My face conveyed confusion, and he continued. In the Middle Ages, he explained, when the college was young, fights would break out in the dining hall every night over the smallest offenses. It became dangerous to put down your knife. It left you defenseless and made a weapon available to those sitting close to you. So for hundreds of years, Oxford students had adopted the habit of eating with a knife in a hidden hand.

And that kid was right: Threats were everywhere in Europe during the Middle Ages. Nature was the deadliest player—plagues, other lethal diseases, and famines caused by bad harvest years wiped out millions of Europeans as life expectancy hovered around thirty years for the average male. But natural selection had built into the European a short temper and a preference for settling disputes with violence. Homicide rates were ten times higher in medieval Europe than today, and murder was often the result of humble disagreements. A study of coroners' inquests in medieval England concluded that the most frequent violent confrontations were between simple farmers arguing during planting and harvests, possibly over land disputes. The most common weapons were the knife and quarterstaff, the long wooden rod that most peasants carried to herd animals and walk on muddy roads.

Violence was not the exclusive province of the peasantry. The ruling class set the tone, using violence as a regular means to consolidate power and exercise dominance. Take the case of John of Arundel, an influential knight of the English court, when he set off in 1379 to lead a naval attack against the French fleet in support of Britain's ally, the Duke of Brittany.

Popular historical fiction casts medieval knights in a chivalrous hue, but they were more often brutish marauders. As Arundel and his soldiers waited out a storm at their launching port of Hampton, they took refuge in a convent. A night of heavy drinking ended in the squad of knights assaulting and raping the nuns before looting the convent of all its valuables. Arundel and his band then crashed a nearby wedding ceremony, took turns raping the bride, and then kidnapped her and dozens of the nuns to be concubines on their ships during the naval campaign. But the horror was not over. When the seas became rough, and the weight of the boats threatened to capsize the fleet, Arundel ordered the captives overboard. As the monk historian Thomas Walsingham recounts, "With the same arms with which they had lustfully fondled them, they now snatched them up and threw them into the sea; as many as sixty of the women, they say, were thrown overboard to be eaten by the fish and sea monsters."

Two centuries later, the Wars of Religion descended on western Europe, pitting Catholics against Protestants in an orgy of blood that is impossible to comprehend today. This forgettable stretch of the historical record is littered with episodes of apocalyptic mass violence, and to pick one as illustration threatens to miss the enormity of the hundred-year cascade of atrocities. But let's try. In Paris on St. Bartholomew's Day eve, August 24, 1572, the relatively new king, Charles IX, was twenty-two years old, and his mother, the infamous anti-Protestant Catherine de' Medici, dominated the court. With the Protestant population surging in France, she ordered the murder of hundreds of its leaders in an effort to stymie the growing political strength of the Protestant minority. Counter-assassinations of Catholic leaders came quickly in turn, and by August 24, the capital city was awash with sectarian fear and suspicion. Likely at the urging of Catherine, the king ordered a mass purging of Protestants, giving his troops the chilling order "Kill them all, so that not one will be left to reproach me for it." It is probable that the intent was only to eliminate the Protestant ringleaders who were in the city that night for a royal wedding, but the massacre went off the rails, and by the end of the night, fifteen thousand Protestants lay butchered on the bloodred streets. Paris "looked like a conquered city" according to one witness.

.   .   .

The year 69, Arundel's killing spree, and the St. Bartholomew's Day Massacre were not isolated instances. José Maria Gómez Reyes, the

Spanish zoologist who studied mammal violence rates, did more than just compare primate violence with that of other mammals like meerkats, squirrels, and whales. He and his team gathered evidence of conspecific human violence as far back as they could over the full history of our species, and found that from the emergence of the modern *Homo sapiens* approximately two hundred thousand years ago up until today, the rate of human-on-human violence has been similar to the high rates among other primates—2 percent.

There is enough of a historical record of human existence, however, for Reyes and his team to know that our rates have varied over the centuries. We were a relatively average lot during the Paleolithic period, when our violence rate was right at our species average of 2 percent. Then the number of human-on-human deaths start to spike right around the Nataruk massacre ten thousand years ago, and by the time the Bronze Age arrived five thousand years ago, some civilizations experienced catastrophic rates of 30 percent conspecific violence, likely because humans were beginning to live in closer proximity to one another. As denser human communities formed, the competition for scarce resources—food, shelter, and mating partners—made every other human look like a potential threat. Tribal rivalries, fueled by the biological "us versus them" instinct, also exacerbated violence as groups of humans began to bump up against one another more often. Faced with these threats and daily opportunities for friction in close quarters, the human brain turned to violence, a tried-and-true means of survival. Lethal aggression rates went up and down from there.

The Middle Ages were another time of high violence. In Oxford, England, where I was schooled about medieval table manners, the murder rate in the 1340s was about 110 per 100,000 people. Keeping a knife by your side was a good idea then. In nearby London, in the first half of the fourteenth century, the homicide rate was about 36 to 52 per 100,000 people per year. To put that in context, in 1990, when murders hit an all-time high in New York City, the homicide rate was about 14 per 100,000. But today, the conspecific violence rate among humans is at its lowest point in our history—around 6 murders per 100,000. It has been a wild ride from the Bronze Age, when a quarter of humans were dying at the hands of other humans in some places, to modern times, when one in a hundred deaths are caused at the hands of another human.

. . .

The morning after sixty-four-year-old Stephen Paddock mowed down fifty-nine concertgoers from his thirty-second-floor corner suite at a Las Vegas casino hotel, Kentucky governor Matt Bevin turned to social media to tell "all those political opportunists who are seizing on the tragedy in Las Vegas to call for more gun regs . . . you can't regulate evil." Sensing he might be referring to me, I responded on Twitter, "I await your proposal to rescind Kentucky's laws banning assault, murder, and arson. One of government's core functions is to regulate evil." Both tweets went viral. It was a silly social media back-and-forth—both of us probably typing before thinking amid the emotional aftermath of the country's worst-ever mass shooting.

But Bevin's comments got a lot of attention, and many others leapt forward to amplify his theory. To Bevin and his defenders, certain people have a predisposition to wickedness and cannot be controlled by outside forces. Humanity, in this vision, is largely helpless in the face of the natural inclination toward malevolence that sits inside some individuals.

Setting aside the spiritual aspects of evil as a concept, Bevin's argument is not without some merit. Thousands of years of evolutionary change favored *Homo sapiens* who could physically best others in a contest for limited land and food and shelter and mating partners. The design of the body allowed humans to efficiently land blows against one another. The brain developed a specific rage circuitry to translate the fear of outside threats or the need for social dominance into physical action. And genetics hardwired a certain subset of humans with a fast track to aggressive behavior that has been handed down one generation to the next.

Even today, during an era of unprecedented peace and prosperity, the kind of evil that Bevin warned against trying to address is still found in spades. The last century has witnessed some of the worst incidents of mass casualties in human history. Historian Matthew White, a self-described "atrocitologist" and author of *The Great Big Book of Horrible Things*, notes that the two top acts of barbarism in historical memory—the Second World War (55 million deaths) and Mao's Cultural Revolution and government-caused famines (40 million deaths)—occurred just in the last century. People like Bevin who are looking for evidence of pure, unchecked evil can find it all over in modern times. The Holocaust alone, with its six million Jewish and five million non-Jewish victims, is a reminder of how truly diabolical and bloodthirsty modern humans can be.

But my response to Bevin was supported by the balance of evidence over the past one thousand years that suggests that violence is, in fact, many more parts nurture than nature. How else to explain the results of work done by the historian J. S. Cockburn, who scoured local records from the English county of Kent to divine just how far the murder rate—probably the best indicator of a society's predilection toward violence—had fallen from the Middle Ages to today. In 1600, Elizabethan Kent endured a homicide rate of 7 per 100,000. By 1900, in three hundred short years, that number had plummeted to less than 1 per 100,000. Surveys of murder rates in Italy, the Netherlands, Germany, and Scandinavia show a similar trend, with rates of violence beginning to bend down significantly at the turn of the seventeenth century and not flattening until the twentieth. In the next chapter, we will survey the history of American violence, but it's worth noting here that while American violence is almost always at a higher level than Europe's, America saw a similar dramatic drop in murder rates from 1600 to the twentieth century.

Human interventions (most notably, interventions by government) have gradually weaned humans off a reliance on violence as the primary method people use to gain advantage over one another. Over time, humans developed codes of behavior, increased empathy for others, and built commercial economies and legal structures, that, together, convinced humans that they were better off finding nonviolent ways to carry out grudges, increase one's wealth, or express displeasure. The trajectory of human violence can be explained by both biology and sociology, but the remarkable success of the civilizing process suggests that as humans continue our work to stamp out conspecific violence, self-determination, not genetic destiny, will rule the day.

. . .

So what happened? How, in the time between the Middle Ages and today, did the world get so much less violent? So *civilized*? The search for an answer to that question begins during one of the most uncivilized times in European history: 1933 Germany.

That year, German sociologist Norbert Elias saw his demise coming. As Hitler began his campaign to exterminate German Jews, Elias knew he had no choice but to leave his native land. He packed up and fled to England, where he toiled in obscurity on a massive two-volume work that seemed tin-eared for the times. In 1939, *The Civilizing Process*, a narrative of the rise of self-control mechanisms in humans, was published, to crickets. Not too long thereafter, Elias's parents, left behind in Germany, became two of those six million Jewish victims of the Holocaust, and Elias's work began to collect dust on academic shelves all across the continent. And then, thirty years later, in 1969, it miraculously vaulted out of hiding. In the wake of the political and social upheavals of the late 1960s, influential thinkers turned their focus to understanding why controls on violence put in place after the Second World War seemed to be breaking down. In that last year of the decade, President Johnson convened not one but two expert panels to study the causes of violence (more on this later), and sociologists began to scan the historical record for the drivers of prior flare-ups of individual and collective violence.

The Civilizing Process, which became the inspiration for Steven Pinker's later opus on the history of violence, was rediscovered, translated into English, and made required reading for smart thinkers and policy makers. To this day, it remains the most elegant explanation for the broad downward slope of human-on-human violence in the second half of the second millennium. Data not available to Elias in 1939 would later confirm that in the seventeenth century the world started to become a more diplomatic place, where physical aggression became less and less common as a means to display emotion, settle disputes, or project dominance over others. The pacification came slowly, but something clearly shocked the human race into a series of actions that tamped down the instinct of violence. Elias didn't need modern data analysis to notice the trend in favor of more humane and methodical dispute settlement, and he offered a three-part explanation for the phenomenon.

First, Elias simply noted that the invention of manners had a profound effect on rates of violence. We take for granted now the etiquette associated with every human activity, from dining to conversation to defecation. But six hundred years ago, few, if any, of these rules existed. People may have learned to group themselves into cities and nations, but their personal behavior was still often more reminiscent of their pre-civilization ancestors. Public nakedness and urination were regular sights, table manners were nonexistent, and sexual taboos were few (parents, for instance, often spoke openly with their children about their exploits). Scant value was placed on self-restraint, and thus, the Darwinian predilection for violence suffered little inhibition, either. Elias paints a picture of emotional control that sounds familiar to the parent of that temper-tantrum-prone toddler we discussed earlier:

> Not that people were always going around with fierce looks, drawn brows and martial countenances. . . . On the contrary, a moment ago they were joking, now they mock each other, one word leads to another, and suddenly from the midst of laughter they find themselves in the fiercest feud.

Elias's book is full of references to manuals of manners that grew wildly popular throughout Renaissance Europe. The most famous of these manuals was probably humanist scholar Desiderius Erasmus's *A Handbook on Good Manners for Children,* an etiquette guide he wrote in 1530. The book was widely read throughout Europe for the next two hundred years. In Louis XIV's France, diners were desperately trying to emulate the new etiquette used at Versailles, but old habits were hard to break. Says historian Georges Mongrédien, at dinner during this time, "the most delicate nuances of courtesy mingled with the most slovenly behavior." Pinker notes, interestingly, that many of the etiquette rules propagated in these early days had to do with knives. One list of dining rules included an instruction that directly contravened the advice I was given at Oxford. It read, "Don't hold your knife the entire time you are eating, but only when you are using it." As the Middle Ages turned to the Age of Enlightenment, it seemed as if dining hall fights were becoming less common, and table manners more in vogue.

The second pillar of the civilizing process was the change in human thinking that followed advances in education and commerce, as individuals' interdependence fostered an understanding and empathy for others and the realization that everyone's economic existence was made better by harmonious, rather than adversarial, relations with others.

The year 1536 was an unusually turbulent one for the uxoricidal English king Henry VIII, even by his standards. Two years before, Henry had formally broken from the Catholic Church over its refusal to grant an annulment of his marriage to his first wife, Catherine of Aragon, and had set himself up as the unitary head of the church in England. Now, isolated from the church and its allies on the Continent, Henry needed money to fund his lavish court and his growing European military ambitions, so he ordered the dissolution of monasteries all across the countryside, transferring their significant assets to the Crown.

The Dissolution of the Monasteries set off a peasant rebellion against Henry that almost toppled his regime—the most significant threat ever mounted to Tudor rule. The rebellion, which Henry eventually brutally put down, demonstrated, once again, what a tinderbox of violence Europe was in the late Middle Ages. But what stands out to me about the dissolution is the obsession—of both Henry and the monks—over one of the monasteries' most valuable treasures: their books. Henry sent one of his key advisers, John Leland, to catalog the monastic libraries and bring them to his court. Meanwhile, monks all over England quietly removed as many volumes as they could and created small, secret libraries all over the island.

The battle over the libraries of England's monasteries was emblematic of the scarce and valuable resource that books were in the time of Henry VIII. Johannes Gutenberg's printing press had not spread into widespread usage by Henry's reign, and in 1530 it is likely that nine of every ten of Henry's subjects were illiterate. Henry, Leland, and the monks cared so passionately about books in the 1530s because they were a scarce resource, and many important works existed only in dozens of hand-reproduced copies. That began to change quickly; the number of published works dramatically increased in the seventeenth century, and then skyrocketed after 1700. This brought to Europe what historian Rolf Engelsing calls the reading revolution. Beginning in the late eighteenth century, books and pamphlets and periodicals became available to millions of citizens, and literacy rates spiked.

It is not a coincidence that England would not see another violent peasant rebellion like that of 1536, as literacy spread across England. The reading revolution helped quell the violent instincts of individuals by increasing their capacity for empathy. Books gave readers a window into worlds other than their own, allowing them to better understand the experiences and perspectives of people different from them. The primary psychological system of caring triggers naturally when thinking of family and friends, but without empathy for strangers, this emotional system can be easily overcome by one of the negative emotional systems, like rage or aggression. And empathy comes from the ability to put yourself in the shoes of others, even those that seem very different from you.

The rise of reading during the Age of Reason (by 1800, the illiteracy rate in England was down to 50 percent) allowed millions of Europeans to internalize the perspectives of others. Explaining why medieval torture techniques began to fade from common usage during the period commensurate with the reading revolution, Steven Pinker writes:

Stepping into someone else's vantage point reminds you that the other fellow has a first-person, present-tense, ongoing stream of consciousness that is very much like your own but not the same. It's not a big leap to suppose that the habit of reading other people's words could put one in the habit of entering other people's minds, including their pleasures and pains. Slipping even for a moment into the perspective of someone who is turning black in a pillory or desperately pushing burning faggots away from her body or convulsing under the two hundredth stroke of the lash may give a person second thoughts as to whether these cruelties should ever be visited upon anyone.

Another development pushing through Europe in the late Middle Ages helped to increase the rate of perspective taking by individuals: the spread of nonfarm commerce. From peasant rebellions caused by bad harvests to farmers regularly beating others to death with quarterstaffs, the agrarian economy was a stimulant for individual and mass violence. Farming is, at its foundation, a zero-sum game—your wealth is directly proportional to the amount of land you own or farm. This creates an incentive for conquest and conflict. But the means of wealth began to diversify as the Tudors gave way to the Stuarts in England, and it was our own John Leland who provided one of the first catalogs of this transition.

After his partial victory in the battle over the monastic manuscripts, Henry, perhaps appreciating John Leland's gifts as an antiquarian, sent him off to survey the state of local governments and economies throughout England. For five years, from 1538 to 1543, Leland compiled what became known as his Itineraries, and they provide a fascinating portrait of a commercial economy that was beginning to mature beyond the field. He describes in detail new ports, markets, and infrastructure projects. He explains how the manufacture of cloth was quickly industrializing small towns, aided by private capital provided by a growing class of industrial investors.

During the reign of Henry's daughter Queen Elizabeth I, the English economy went into diversification overdrive. Farming still dominated the economy, but there were now more bankers, bakers, basket makers, blacksmiths, goldsmiths, bowyers, carpenters, fletchers, glaziers, and wheelwrights than ever before, and Elizabeth's economic reforms, including the establishment of indentured apprenticeships, brought stability to England's expanding commercial life.

No longer was the English economy a simple zero-sum game, where one player's loss was another's gain. Now, a positive-sum game flourished, wherein two individuals could trade their surpluses and both come out of the transaction having benefited. Markets, like the bustling Cheapside in London, created networks of supply and demand, and all of a sudden, a *customer culture* began to develop. Now, strangers were not simply Darwinian competitors; they were potential buyers of your goods or services. Treating people well and controlling your impulses became good business; raiding, ransacking, and pillaging were not smart commercial behaviors. As social and business networks became more important to one's economic survival, reflexive violence retreated further from the mainstream, and natural selection began to favor the planners and persuaders over the marauders and roughnecks.

The final pillar of the civilizing process is one worth paying the most attention to. In his seminal work *Leviathan,* published in 1651, Thomas Hobbes had a prescription to counteract the natural violence of man. He advised a simple social contract with individuals and a sovereign in which individuals make the following oath:

> I authorise and give up my right of governing myself to this man, or to this assembly of men, on this condition; that thou give up, thy right to him, and authorise all his actions in like manner.

Hobbes guessed that a unitary, controlling power was the only means by which to properly arrange human existence. And that is exactly what began to happen in the middle of the second millennium. The Spanish monarchs Ferdinand and Isabella expelled the Moors and unified their nation under one rule. Ivan the Great defeated the Mongols, expanded Russian territory, and consolidated power in a Moscow-based tsar. The number of small, autonomous baronies and principalities dwindled as more and more territory and people came under the control of centralized governments. With larger and fewer sovereign territories came fewer lines of friction and less reason for constant conflict.

Inside these large states, rulers during the middle of the second millennium began to accumulate a monopoly on the two primary powers of modern government, taxation and physical force. Louis XIV, "the Sun King," inherited a stable, consolidated France, and he went about the business of modernizing revenue collection throughout his kingdom. He used his riches to build a grand palace outside of Paris at Versailles, and invited all the leading noblemen and church leaders to join him at his new court. There he could keep a watchful eye on all of the most influential Frenchmen, and use his financial largesse to reward and punish.

"The art of governing is not at all difficult or unpleasant," Louis remarked to his heir. "It consists of knowing everything that people try to conceal from us, their secrets, and keeping close watch over them." The Sun King used his riches to keep contestants to his power under his thumb, and those individuals similarly used that wealth to keep their principalities under control. All of a sudden, currying and maintaining favor with powerful people was a much more reliable way to enrich yourself or protect your interests, than resorting to violence. Habits and behavior began to mold to this new order.

The monopoly on physical force was also transformative in Renaissance Europe. Once weapons became instruments of technology, rather than clubs and long staffs, governments could control the means of production and distribution of these new, more powerful weapons. When Rome put down rebellions in the first century, the empire's capacity for lethal force was easily matched by the rebels. A few decades prior to the bloody year 69, Emperor Augustus tried banning Roman subjects from carrying weapons—mostly swords and knives. But since these weapons were really just hard, sharp objects, easily made or manufactured by emperor or peasant alike, those with grievances against the state had little trouble arming themselves just as well as the emperor's guard.

But as the late Middle Ages arrived, insurrection became a harder proposition as the Crown's military advantage over a rebellious citizenry became significantly more favorable. In Spain, gun possession during the late medieval period was limited to members of the nobility, and in Britain, the first law banning gun ownership among the general population was decreed in 1523.

The first police forces also made a big dent in rates of violence. As Louis consolidated power and influence, he used it to create the first modern law enforcement organization. By royal edict in 1667, Louis established an agency in Paris with the goal of "ensuring the peace and quiet of the public and of private individuals, purging the city of what may cause disturbances, procuring abundance, and having each and every one live according to their station and their duties." In the eighteenth and nineteenth centuries, governments discovered that crime and violence could be preempted by instilling in citizens the belief that law enforcement was lurking just around the corner to catch you in the act and hold you accountable.

Like Hobbes predicted, as governments got bigger, violence declined. Why rely on violence to protect yourself if a king or a police force could do it for you? Why take a chance on political rebellion if you know the monarch's army will outgun you from the start? Why bully your way to prosperity when a well-ordered, rules-based economy allows ambitious individuals to become wealthy without having to throw a punch? Powerful modern governments, with big incentives to reduce violence, were beginning to prove that humans' biological penchant for violence was not inevitable. All you needed were rules that handed people options other than physical aggression to protect themselves and advance their interests.

I DO NOT UNDERSTAND MYSELF THESE DAYS

I remember the first time someone I knew committed suicide. I was fifteen years old; it was the summer between my freshman and sophomore years in high school. One day, my parents received a call with horrifying news—the older brother of my closest female friend had committed suicide. It shook me to my core.

He was a model student—fun loving, studious, handsome. It was inconceivable to me that his mind was contorted in a way that would make him think that taking his own life was his only option. Clearly, something had gone wrong inside this young man's head that none of us—even his family—could see. That summer, my family took a month-long driving trip to the national parks of the western United States, and I wrote my friend postcards from nearly every stop—just trying to stay connected to her in any way I could (in those pre-Internet days).

Lethal violence—the kind that ends up taking lives—is an alien species to most of us. There is just no way for most of us to relate to the way a brain rationalizes a premeditated murder or suicide. And so, we try to rationalize and understand violence by putting it into boxes that allow us to argue to one another that *we* could never do that. *That would never happen here. Our son's brain isn't broken like that. My town isn't like Hartford.* But that's not how violence works. It lies inside each of us, and the brain is a cruel master that reveals its flaws often without warning.

On the first day of August 1966, Charles Whitman climbed to the top of a clock tower on the campus of the University of Texas in Austin. By that time, he had already killed his wife and his mother, and from the top of the tower, he gunned down seventeen more and left thirty-one others injured. Whitman had not led a perfect life—he had apparently beaten his wife twice and as a marine was disciplined for gambling. But he had a near genius level IQ, he was an Eagle Scout, and was generally well thought of as an engineering student on the University of Texas campus. The cause of Whitman's break with reality is still a mystery—he was killed by two Austin police officers that afternoon—but he did begin to draft a suicide note, recommending a scientific study of his brain, that provides a hint as to how he had begun to lose control of his thoughts:

> I do not quite understand what it is that compels me to type this letter. Perhaps it is to leave some vague reason for the actions I have

recently performed. I do not really understand myself these days. I am supposed to be an average reasonable and intelligent young man. However, lately (I cannot recall when it started) I have been a victim of many unusual and irrational thoughts.

No one saw Whitman's rampage coming. On the outside, he looked no different from any other student crossing the quad that summer afternoon. Only Whitman knew that there was something sinister and abnormal occurring in his brain.

In this chapter, I've tried to make three overlapping arguments to help you understand what Whitman could not: First, that all of us share a violence-prone biology, and thus none of us can escape it. Find me an adult who didn't throw a single temper tantrum as a toddler. Second, that there are certain brains, as Kent Kiehl says, that just *work differently*. Usually, these brains need outside agitation to spring into violent action, but the triggers likely operate differently in some minds. And third, that the human race has demonstrated that it has the power to quell and control these predilections to aggression. Violence is prewired, but not predestined. It's our decision to allow it to spread, or to control it.

.   .   .

One final story, from the days following the Sandy Hook shooting. H. Wayne Carver had been suffering from health problems that had kept him out of the office for the better part of the fall of 2012. He decided to put in for retirement. After twenty-four years as Connecticut's chief medical examiner, it was time. He came back to the office in early December, planning to spend a few months tying up loose ends, and then his life changed.

"My sensibilities may not be the average man's, but [Sandy Hook] is probably the worst I have seen or the worst that I know of any my colleagues have seen," he said. Carver remembers those awful, long days, trying to perform autopsies on twenty small bodies carefully enough to be able to tell the story of the gruesome crime, but quickly

enough so that the bodies could be turned over to the parents for funeral after funeral after funeral.

And then there was the question of what to do with Adam Lanza's
body. Carver performed a standard autopsy, but paid special attention
to Lanza's brain. He found no obvious abnormalities, no tumors or
visible deformities. But Carver felt that in this case, he had to do more.
Lanza left few clues as to why he did what he did—there was no easily
identifiable motive—and so the question of what was happening inside Lanza's brain in the hours and days leading up to his decision to
kill his mother and twenty-six others was a mystery. More reason,
Carver thought, to learn as much as possible from the evidence available. And so he snipped off a piece of Lanza's brain before turning the
cadaver over to Lanza's remaining family members, and sent it off to
the genetics lab at the University of Connecticut.

And that's where the story ends, because the team at UConn has
never chosen to make public the results of their inquiry, which likely
included an assessment of whether Lanza possessed the warrior gene,
the size of his amygdala, and the levels of testosterone and dopamine
in his brain. I briefly considered asking for the results as I began the
process of writing this book, but thought better of it for two reasons.
First, the information is not mine to possess—it belongs to the Lanza
family, and, arguably, to the victims' families as well. Second, I'm not
sure I need the information, because I already know the answer.

It's complicated.

3

AMERICAN VIOLENCE

THE OUTLIER

A few months into his posting as U.S. ambassador to England, Matthew Barzun called me from London. It was late 2013, and he wanted to share a story with me. I had met Barzun during his confirmation hearing before the Senate Foreign Relations Committee, which I had chaired, but our relationship was cursory, so I was somewhat surprised to get the call.

Barzun explained to me that he had begun a practice of visiting schools all over Britain to explain to them the importance of the "special" U.S.-Britain relationship and hear their impressions of America. During these visits, Barzun would hand out two note cards to each student and ask them to write on one card a word that represented something they admired about the United States and on the other a word representing a negative association they had with America. Barzun wanted to talk to me about the latter set of note cards.

"What would you say if I told you that on two-thirds of the negative association note cards, the exact same word showed up? Not similar words . . . not the same phrase. The same single word."

I started noodling around words in my head. The middle part of 2013 had been consumed by news of a complicated international U.S. surveillance program that had tapped the phones of several world leaders. Britain was also still going through a painful inquiry of their nation's participation in the Iraq War.

"Kind of surprising, I guess. Is it *spying*, or *Iraq*?" I asked.

"Nope," replied Barzun. "It's *guns*. On, like, two of every three cards, it says the same thing. Just *guns*."

.　　.　　.

America is, and always has been, an abnormally violent place. Compared to other high-income nations, the chance you will die a violent death at the hands of another person is ten times higher if you live in the United States than any other place. This is driven by a gun homicide rate that is a mind-blowing twenty-five times higher than that in other advanced countries, but rates of rape and assault are also much higher in the United States. And America's outlier status as a wildly violent nation isn't new. Since the middle of the nineteenth century, America's homicide rates—the primary historic means to compare violence across societies—has been in a class by itself.

To those students in Britain, America's inability to quell its gun violence must appear curiously inconsistent with so much else they have learned about America. You can argue that on almost every great social, political, and economic question of the modern era, America has delivered the answer. The global economy and financial system are largely governed by standards created by America—the dollar is the world's currency and Wall Street still dominates global finance. Though we certainly borrowed all our civic ideals from our European parents, modern participatory democracy is an American invention, and billions of people around the world live under governments that look a whole lot like the one our founders created 240 years ago. Even the way we communicate with one another was created in America—

first the telephone and now the Internet were and are American inventions.

These are all important human concerns—how economic activity is ordered, how people are governed, and how we communicate. But these are all secondary matters to the most fundamental worry of human existence: How do I keep myself and the people I love safe from physical harm? And on this question, it isn't just that the United States is failing to lead; it's that we are the constant, stubborn laggard. And it's no secret. Breaking news of school shootings and movie theater rampages mingles with the drumbeat of grim coverage from Chicago and New Orleans and Baltimore, causing kids in England and all around the world to view America as a heavily armed, wildly violent place with no apparent interest in making itself less armed or less violent.

In this chapter, we will survey this story of American violence and focus on the two factors that explain our outlier status. First, the core of America's genius lies in her ability to mold together people of different national origins, religious practices, skin colors, and natural languages, into a nation with an overlaid common identity and system of beliefs. I am white, Irish/Polish, and Protestant. But first, I consider myself American. This is the United States as the great, precedent-breaking "melting pot." But this constant inflow of new peoples comes with a friction and a never-ending, constant, and open battle for supremacy among these different groups. It has resulted in a well-worn practice of dominant groups (what I will call "in-groups") using violence to control and repress subordinate groups (I will label these "out-groups").

As we will find out, America's violence problem is rooted, first and foremost, in violence erupting as in-groups and out-groups fight for finite social and economic territory in tight spaces. First it was the early Americans massacring the Native American tribes. As waves of immigrants landed on America's shores, contests erupted between ethnic groups, and also second- and third-generation immigrants resorting to force to maintain their social and economic priority over first-generation entrants to the country. And then, of course, throughout our nation's long history, the most violent of all in-group/out-group conflicts has been that between white Americans and African Americans. At the beginning, it was southern whites using chains, whips, and brutal executions to terrorize and enslave the burgeoning slave population. Then it was massacres and lynchings and a coordinated system of private justice that whites perpetuated on blacks in the post–Civil War era. And today it is police beatings and mass incarceration that extend this history of white violence against African American communities.

This constantly renewed tempest of social-group conflict, whether it be between settlers and tribes, immigrant groups, or white and black Americans, acted as the tinder for the conflagration of violence that engulfed America soon after its founding. But the catalyst, from the very start, has been firearms. This is the second part of our story in this chapter. Those early battles with Native Americans were bloodier because almost every male settler was required to own a musket. The subjugation of slaves was much easier when plantation owners stockpiled veritable arsenals of firearms. Crime in the growing American cities of the nineteenth and twentieth centuries was more serious because scores of men carrying pistols caused verbal arguments to turn deadly with regularity.

Guns, and their liberal usage, have been built into the fabric of America from the beginning, and there is no way to tell the story of American violence without placing much of the blame on the widespread marketing and ownership of these highly lethal weapons. One of the most comprehensive studies of historic American violence rates came to the conclusion that if not for America's unique relationship with guns and the gun industry, the American homicide rate, over the long course of our nation's history, would be cut in half. The grand heterogeneous experiment of America was going to be a tinderbox of violence no matter what; guns just set it on fire.

BEARING ARMS

In 2002, I was running for an open seat in the Connecticut State Senate, in a historically Republican district that included the hardscrabble working-class neighborhoods of the east end of Waterbury, Connecticut's fifth largest city. This was the hometown of the state's popular Republican governor, John Rowland, who was a strong favorite for reelection that year. I knew that with Rowland at the top of the ticket, I would be hard-pressed to find votes in Waterbury, especially since the east end had a reputation for social conservatism that didn't match well with my progressive voting record.

That August, I paid a visit to the most popular fall festival in the city, the Italian Festival at the historic Pontelandolfo Community Club in the northeastern corner of the city. This wasn't particularly friendly territory for me, and I was on edge as I parked my car and walked up the hill into the festival. A middle-aged man in worn jeans, dark sunglasses, and a VIETNAM VETERAN baseball cap was walking back to his car, and I breathed deep to ready myself for my first pitch of the afternoon.

"Hi, can I just introduce myself for a second?" I asked. "I'm Chris Murphy, and I'm running for State Senate in Waterbury. I just wanted to say hello."

"Guns," he said, flatly.

I swallowed. "Excuse me?"

"Guns. What's your position on the Second Amendment?"

Life changes fast. If a voter asked me that question today in Connecticut, chances are better than not their views on guns are similar to my own. After Sandy Hook, the people in Connecticut that are most interested in a candidate's position on gun policy tend to be supporters of stricter guns laws. But in 2002, anyone who asked you about the Second Amendment on the campaign trail—and in a right-leaning district like this, the topic arose frequently—didn't want to hear about your plans to tighten up America's loose gun laws.

Back then, the issue of guns did not animate me in the slightest. I supported all the right things—universal background checks, an assault weapons ban—but when I ran into someone like this, I knew two things for certain. First, he likely knew a lot more about the issue than I did. I had a basic knowledge base about firearms and firearms laws, but voters who proactively asked about guns normally spent a lot more time thinking about guns and gun laws than I did. Just like when you try to argue with your mouthy uncle over the Second Amendment at Thanksgiving dinner, I was likely to lose the argument. Second, I knew that given how little I cared about the issue, the satisfaction of having a heated argument frankly was not worth losing a vote.

"You know, I really think that we need to focus more on why people are pulling the trigger, instead of spending so much time focusing on the gun," I said, like I was reciting scripted National Rifle Association talking points. "You know what I'm talking about? If you don't address the reasons why the crime is happening, what good is trying to control the gun?"

Today, knowing what I know—having experienced what I've experienced—I'm embarrassed, deeply, by how I answered this question and questions like it twenty years ago. But I wasn't unlike most passive supporters of stronger gun laws. The people on the other side—the gun rights champions—always seemed to know more about, and care more about, guns than we did. And so we stayed silent, or in my case, fudged.

In the weeks following Sandy Hook, the first task I undertook was to cure my naïveté about the history of guns in America, and in particular, the history of the provision in the U.S. Constitution that provides individuals with a right to own a firearm. I decided that if I was going to wade into the waters traditionally populated only by those who subscribed to the NRA monthly newsletter, I had better have a more informed position on the role of violence and firearms in America than the one I sputtered out in the parking lot of the Pontelandolfo Community Club. So here's what I learned.

·   ·   ·

The first thing to know about violence in America is that our continent was a violent place long before Europeans set foot on it. In fact, in the centuries leading up to the European settlement of the New World, Europe was becoming less and less dependent on human aggression as an organizing principle, while in America, intertribal violence was as regular as rain. Oral histories of pre-Columbian America suggest that raiding parties were constantly in transit between tribes, and violence was used regularly to settle disputes. Clearly, not all Native American communities were abnormally violent, but some estimates suggest that one in four Native Americans died at the hands of other humans in the time before European settlement—a remarkable rate of homicide. To wit, in 1978, researchers discovered the site of the Crow Creek massacre, a mass grave in southern South Dakota where nearly five hundred individuals were murdered in one single event a century before Columbus set foot in the Americas. The Native Americans that the first Europeans confronted carried with them a legacy of violence, which does not explain or justify the campaign of extermination waged by early settlers, but might explain why the colonists so quickly armed themselves to the hilt.

Understandably, Native Americans did not take kindly to the invading British, Dutch, French, and Spanish who commandeered the most protected harbors, the most fertile farming land, and the best forests for hunting. Conflict was immediate, and the colonists made sure that the fight was not a fair one by importing to America the means to massacre the Native Americans: the rifle. The first recorded gun murder in colonial times was recounted in William Bradford's *History of Plymouth Colony*. John Billington, an original settler who, Bradford noted, belonged to one of Plymouth's "most profanest families," shot a more recent arrival to the colony, John Newcomin, in 1630, ten years after the *Mayflower* arrived in the New World. Billington was himself taken to the woods and hanged, also the first recorded execution in European America. This was an example of colonist-on-colonist gun violence, but the true brutality of these times was mostly reserved for the campaign against the Native American peoples.

The legend of the Thanksgiving holiday is designed to intentionally gloss over the regular massacre of Native Americans by the settlers (and, to be fair, the regular preemptive and retributive violence against settlers by Native Americans). But some historians wonder whether Thanksgiving was actually a celebration of violence against, rather than fellowship with, the Native Americans. On May 26, 1637, a group of settlers descended upon the Pequot tribe camp in present-day Mystic, Connecticut, and proceeded to murder all but a handful of the four hundred inhabitants of the settlement. William Bradford described the "streams of blood" and the sickening "stink and scent" of the piled dead bodies.

The next day, though, Bradford shook off memories of the bloody mess and declared "a day of Thanksgiving kept in all the churches for our victories against the Pequots." It's certainly not clear whether this day of Thanksgiving is the precursor of the national holiday created more than two hundred years later by a proclamation signed by President Lincoln. What *is* clear is the massive level of violence that occurred regularly between early Europeans in America and Native American tribes in the colonies' early years. From the establishment of the first colony to the end of the Indian Wars of the late nineteenth century, various American governments authorized 1,500 wars and raids on Native Americans, and the pre-Columbian Native American population of somewhere between five to fifteen million cratered to less than 250,000.

Guns were the facilitator of this campaign of murder. The new Americans could never have achieved their lightning-quick dominance over Native Americans if not for the advantage of the firearm. Among the 104 original Jamestown settlers in 1607, initially only the top men were allowed the "privilege" of firearms ownership. This reflected the tradition of gun control in England, where only high-status individuals were allowed to own them. Colonial leaders quickly found this policy unwise in the New World and chose instead to press their technological advantage over local tribes. Thus, the first American gun control statutes did not restrict ownership of firearms; instead, these first laws mandated gun ownership.

By 1630, half of Virginia's five thousand European inhabitants owned a gun. In Plymouth Colony, a 1623 law required every male to own a gun, and in 1630 this requirement, along with mandatory militia service, was extended to all inhabitants of the Massachusetts Bay Colony. And in my home state of Connecticut, the laws were even more adamant. While today Connecticut has on the books laws forbidding guns from being carried into most public places, in 1643 the legislature passed a law *requiring* every male to carry a gun when at church or a public meeting.

Throughout the 1600s, American violence rates were six times higher than those of the countries from which the colonists had emigrated. And gun ownership rates were sky-high—by the dawn of the eighteenth century it is likely that 60 percent of American households owned a firearm (in those days, most likely it was a bulky and finicky five-foot-long musket). While the most horrific large-scale violence was directed against Native Americans, this reliance on brutality as an organizing tool meant that disputes between colonists also tended to be settled by bloodshed. Rates of European-on-European clashes are also very high during the period. In early America, violence as means to control out-groups begot violence among members of the in-groups. This would become a repeating theme of the next four hundred years of American history.

In a way, the story of American violence was set in stone during the first century of European colonization. Violence became a means for domination and subjugation in a wildly unstable and changing social ecosystem, and guns made the murderous campaigns of the dominant classes all the more efficient. Famed American historian Bernard Bailyn penned an epic survey of the 1600s titled, appropriately, *The Barbarous Years*, in which he chronicled the waves of violence that defined life in prerevolutionary America. Bailyn agrees that this founding century foreshadowed the future of American social norms. In the 1600s, one civilization (white Europeans) relied on violence as a means to control another (Native Americans), setting a precedent that America would never reverse. "A legacy of brutality in intercultural relations developed through this period," Bailyn explains, "of which, of course, the overwhelming legacy was slavery."

.   .   .

We're getting closer to a deep dive into the history of the Second Amendment, but we need to make one more pit stop. We've seen that from a practical standpoint, America was super violent right from its genesis, and this likely had implications that have lasted until modern times. But what did colonists *think* about guns and violence? To understand whether or not the Second Amendment includes a right for everybody to own and carry guns—the primary means of American violence—we need to know what the Revolutionary generation actually thought about guns and the damage they did.

Let's start by going all the way back to Renaissance Britain, the place and time from which many of America's founding ideas and legal principles derive. Gun ownership during this time—in Britain and Europe—was sparse. Guns were expensive, cumbersome, and often unreliable. Records from the 1500s show that only one in ten homicides were committed with a firearm (in colonial America, a century later, this number would be four times higher), and few estates listed guns as being in the possession of wealthy families.

The advent of the English Civil War, in which elements loyal to the monarchy battled those who favored parliamentary government during a ten-year period in the middle of the seventeenth century, dramatically increased gun ownership rates. Guns were all over England in the years that followed, and in the 1680s, the newly installed King James II began the process of confiscating weapons, especially those in the possession of his political opponents, through the Militia Act of 1662, which called for guns to be taken from anyone deemed "dangerous to the Peace of the Kingdom." When James's regime began to collapse (largely due to his increasingly Catholic sympathies), prominent Protestant noblemen arranged for James's daughter and son-in-law, Mary and William of Orange, to cross into England and lead a largely peaceful takeover of power, dubbed the Glorious Revolution. As a condition of this handoff of power, the English aristocracy required William and Mary to concede to certain limits on the authority of the Crown, conceived as a Bill of Rights for English citizens.

Among those rights was a highly conditional right to bear arms:

"Subjects which are Protestants may have Arms for their Defense suitable to their Conditions and as allowed by Law." The new rule was important, but so were the exceptions. As clearly stated, the right only applied to Protestants; Catholics were still prohibited from owning guns. And other pre–Bill of Rights restrictions remained, like the requirement that an individual must maintain a minimum income level to purchase a gun (thus ensuring that the peasantry could not effectively arm itself against the landed class).

Amid the tinderbox of Revolutionary-era America, the British conceded this conception of a private right of firearms ownership in their reluctance to press for gun confiscation in the days leading up to the breakout of rebellion. The present-day gun lobby's argument that the American Revolution was, at its heart, a reaction to the attempts at gun confiscation by the British is laughable. The underlying reasons for the colonists' rebellion, mostly economic and philosophical, had little to do with the individual right of firearms ownership. But there is no doubt that General Thomas Gage's increasingly aggressive seizures of the colonists' weaponry grated on Americans terribly.

After the British broke up a town meeting in Salem in 1774, the popular *Boston Gazette* noted that the imprisonment of several of the leaders of the meeting "irritated people next to the seizing their Arms and Ammunition." In other words, the right to bear arms was equally, if not more, important to Bostonians than the right to assemble. Two years later, faced with an increasingly hostile citizenry, Gage made the fateful decision to follow through on the long-threatened disarming of the militias. The men of Lexington and Concord got to their armory of muskets first, and the Revolution was off and running.

Though Revolutionary-era Americans took their guns seriously and believed that their liberty was closely related to their ability to be armed, they also saw no conflict between the importance of private firearms ownership and a host of local laws that severely regulated the purchase and possession of these weapons. For instance, during the Revolution, many states passed "loyalty oath laws," requiring citizens to pledge their allegiance to the American government before being allowed to carry a firearm. Gun registration laws were popular, mainly to take inventory of the guns available to local militias, and penalties were stiff for those that failed to report their weapons. The storage of gunpowder was highly regulated and restricted. And, of course, many large segments of the population—including slaves, free African Americans, and Catholics—were prohibited from owning guns altogether. Guns were built into the fabric of early America, but so was the heavy regulation of these weapons.

.   .   .

Now let's dig into the centerpiece of all the modern talk around gun rights: the Constitution's Second Amendment. To understand what was at stake when the document and its first ten amendments were conceived and approved, let's start with an important but mostly forgotten event that took place during George Washington's second term in office.

In the early years of the American republic, no one was certain how long this trial nation would last. The Constitution had transferred massive powers to a faraway federal government, and it was unclear whether Americans would accept this new national seat of government as legitimate. In 1794, the fledgling national authority was put to its first real domestic test. Americans were outraged about a major tax imposed throughout the country on the sale of their beloved elixir, whiskey. In western Pennsylvania, distillers outright refused to pay the tax, which had been conceived and championed by Treasury secretary Alexander Hamilton, and began to threaten anyone who tried to collect it with violence. In July, the gathering revolt reached a tempest as an angry mob burned down the house of a tax collector in Allegheny County and mustered seven thousand men with a plan to march on Pittsburgh to seize a government garrison full of weapons.

For a moment, it looked as if the Whiskey Rebellion would spread, and the experiment of a federal government would collapse. Washington worried, "If the laws are to be trampled upon with impunity, and a minority is to dictate to the majority, there is an end put at one stroke to republican government." But Washington was close to powerless to meet the threat. Why? Because Washington and Hamilton had no actual mechanism to repel the growing rebellion.

America in 1794 had no standing army, and for good reason. With memories of British troops quartered in Boston homes fresh in the founders' minds, the first generation of Americans was dead set against re-creating a permanent military apparatus like the British version that had come to terrorize colonial America. Here was James Madison, normally among the staunchest defenders of sturdy federal authority, at the Constitutional Convention in Philadelphia:

> A standing military force, with an overgrown Executive will not long be safe companions to liberty. The means of defense against foreign danger, have been always the instruments of tyranny at home. Among the Romans it was a standing maxim to excite a war, whenever a revolt was apprehended. Throughout all Europe, the armies kept up under the pretext of defending, have enslaved the people.

So that summer, Washington had no actual army to draw upon as the Pennsylvania rebels gathered strength and threatened to take down his government. Washington instructed Hamilton to quickly assemble as many state militiamen as possible and build a kind of eighteenth-century pop-up army. Hamilton went to work ordering horses, tents, shoes, blankets, and uniforms and did his best to quickly professionalize the purely amateur soldiers, but to little effect. Luckily, the sheer quantity of militia troops—twelve thousand at the campaign's peak—along with the imposing command of the imperial Washington, was enough to scare off the tax scofflaws, who relented without a fight.

Why should we care about this infrequently studied episode in American history? Because the Whiskey Rebellion is a useful prism through which to understand the founding generation of Americans' obsession with militias and paranoia about standing armies. In the Revolutionary era, with the legend of Lexington and Concord already baked into American mythology, few topics aroused greater passion than that of preserving young America's amateur military and viewing a national army contrary to the still-in-formation idea of American liberty. Standing armies were to be avoided. And the only way to preserve the peace without a standing army was to protect the ability of citizens to organize militias. No discussion of the Second Amendment is worthwhile without understanding this early American mindset.

. . .

The Second Amendment, adopted with little fanfare as part of the Bill of Rights, is a mess of a run-on sentence, with commas seemingly randomly dropped in between words to make its plain meaning impossible to derive. It reads in whole:

> A well regulated Militia, being necessary to the security of a free State, the right of the people to keep and bear Arms, shall not be infringed.

Read it again, and ask yourself, what is the thing that is not to be infringed? The militia or the right of the people to bear arms? Or maybe both? What makes these questions even harder to answer is the almost complete lack of historical backup to the drafting or writing of the amendment. Madison, its primary author, leaves us no clues as to whether the purpose is to protect militias or to protect an independent right of Americans to own and carry weapons. Maybe most notably, there is not a single reference to an individual's right to own weapons in Madison's copious notes from the Constitutional Convention. Also, the way we hear the words in the Second Amendment have changed drastically over time. Today, we use the term "bear arms" to talk of an individual's right to carry weapons, but in 1776 the term was used almost exclusively in the context of organized military activities.

This textual uncertainty of the Second Amendment is why the historical context of the Whiskey Rebellion matters. Washington had no standing army because the drafters of the Constitution and its first ten amendments believed that one of the greatest threats to personal liberty was the creation of a new American standing army, to be used and deployed at the whim of the newly created chief executive. The men who created America believed that the country could keep order and

defend itself with militias, but only if the federal government protected the ability of the states to keep their militias in good order.
Hamilton called the state militias "the most natural defense of a free
country," and even critics of the Constitution believed that "a well regulated militia, composed of the Yeomanry of the country, have ever
been considered as the bulwark of a free people." Thus, the need for
specific language in the Constitution that protected the right of militias to exist and for citizens to own weapons that could be used in militia service.

Consider Madison's original version of the amendment, which was
passed by the House of Representatives:

> A well regulated militia, composed of the body of the people, being
> the best security of a free state, the right of the people to keep and
> bear arms shall not be infringed, but no one religiously scrupulous of
> bearing arms, shall be compelled to render military service in person.

One step forward and one step back in understand the meaning of
the amendment, right? In this version there isn't a comma between the
right to bear arms and the prohibition on infringement, giving credence to the argument that the text protects the individual right of gun
ownership. But more important, this original text, with additional
flowery language about the importance of militias, makes it even
clearer that the whole focus of the amendment is to protect and advance state militias. In fact, this version has a conscientious objector
provision, suggesting the point of the amendment was to allow states
to compel militia service rather than advance some notion of firearms
ownership divorced from military service.

For the first 220 years of American jurisprudence, courts agreed
that the Second Amendment did not include an individual right to gun
ownership, reflecting a consensus among legal analysts that the amendment was primarily about enabling militias and thereby protecting
America from a standing army. From 1888, when law reviews first
began to be indexed, through 1959, not one article on the Second
Amendment came to the conclusion that the Constitution guaranteed

a right to private gun ownership. But beginning in the 1970s, powered by an increasingly reactionary gun lobby (we will get to this later), a new reading of the Second Amendment began to take shape, in which the founders had actually been out to make sure every American could own any type of weapon he or she wanted without hassle from the government.

The 1984 movie *Red Dawn* hit theaters just as this new spin on the Second Amendment was becoming en vogue among gun advocacy groups and a handful of conservative legal scholars. It was a revelation for an eleven-year-old kid like me growing up during the final throes of the Cold War. The film, in which Patrick Swayze, Charlie Sheen, and a few of their friends retreat to the Colorado woods with a small store of arms to fight a guerrilla war against the invading Russian army, prompted legions of kids to grab their plastic rifles and play endless hours of "Red Dawn" in the woods. For the gun rights movement, *Red Dawn* is a cult classic—a perfect encapsulation of their belief that the framers' true intent was to protect citizens' right to arm themselves against tyrannical government or even invasion. Any abridgment of the ability of Americans to own firearms, these Second Amendment "absolutists" claim, cannot be squared with the founders' belief that private gun ownership is an essential individual right, instrumental in keeping state authority in check.

Ultimately, this interpretation of the amendment prevailed, when in 2008, five conservative Supreme Court justices decided to overturn two centuries of precedent to hold that the Second Amendment included a right to individual gun ownership. The decision, *District of Columbia v. Heller*, was not a complete win for the absolutists, however. Justice Antonin Scalia's decision noted that this newly discovered right was subject to restriction and regulation, giving as examples ways that government could properly and constitutionally control the right to private gun ownership: bans on certain dangerous weapons and mandatory background checks.

And here's my bombshell: *I think* Heller *is basically correct.* This may come as a surprise to some readers who watch me regularly trade blows on television and online with the Second Amendment absolutists. But if I'm honest with myself, I need to admit that whether or not the Second Amendment is primarily concerned with militia management, our founders likely believed in a common-law right for citizens to own guns. That doesn't mean I agree with all of Justice Scalia's ruling, but I think it's important to concede that our founders didn't so much love the militias as they hated the idea of the government possessing an exclusive monopoly on the power of violence. But *Heller* also conceded that while the government cannot comprehensively disarm Americans, it *can* regulate the ability to buy and possess weapons. The constitutionality of firearms restrictions is also deeply rooted in constitutional-era history, given how much gun regulation existed at the time of the adoption of the Second Amendment. America may have been well armed during our formative years, but our founders clearly recognized the legitimacy of the government's broad authority to regulate firearms.

Historian Pieter Spierenburg wrote a controversial journal article in 2006 entitled "Democracy Came Too Early: A Tentative Explanation of American Homicide." In it he argues, quite persuasively, that since firearms came into widespread use in Europe during the period of monarchial control, kings and queens, recognizing the threat these weapons posed to order, were able to dispossess their populations of weapons before democracy took root. They established a principle of government monopoly on violence and the most lethal means to violence. Thus, by the time the English Bill of Rights was recognized by William III and Mary II, and long before the popular vote was granted to all British people in the early twentieth century, strict gun control was an accepted norm.

In America, says Spierenburg, the British monarchy was too weak and too far away to disarm Americans. And when the British finally did attempt to press forward on gun confiscation, it was too late—the colonists were too well organized, the grievances against the state were too large, the guns in their possession were too many. The founders did not want to create a relationship between the government and governed where the state could wield its military might as a way to control the people. Militias, in the 1700s, were the mechanism by which the citizenry shared responsibility with the government for the physical protection of the nation. But the value that is encapsulated in the Second Amendment is the belief that the government's sole control of the means of violence is a threat to the freedom of the public. That is a hard thing for many liberals to admit, because it suggests that the *Red Dawn* view of the Second Amendment is closer to right than that of pre-*Heller* courts, but I think that it's time for my side of the argument to admit the Second Amendment does protect an individual's basic right to firearm ownership.

Of course, I also believe the gun-rights crowd conveniently ignores the way in which colonial and early state governments assiduously regulated firearms ownership, suggesting that those who wrote and ratified our Constitution were comfortable with a heavy regulatory hand on the bearing of arms. Responsible citizens should be able to buy and own guns, and society, through its elected government, should be able to control the kind of people who can own guns, and the types of guns that can be owned. If my side were to concede the constitutional right to private firearm ownership, and gun-rights advocates were to concede the constitutional ability of government to regulate aspects of this right, maybe we could land on a much more rational debate free from the tyranny of fear created by each side believing the other is seeking to either completely eliminate the ability of Americans to possess guns or completely eliminate the ability of government to decide how to regulate gun ownership.

THE FIRST WAVE OF AMERICAN VIOLENCE (1840–60)

The first instruction I gave my skeletal Connecticut staff after getting sworn in to the U.S. Senate was "Get our office out of downtown Hartford."

It had nothing to do with a lack of affection for downtown Hartford. Good things were happening there in 2013. Residential apartments were popping up all over the business district, bringing after-hours life back to the city. The Front Street District, a new riverside dining and entertainment development, was under construction.

And the new Connecticut Science Center was attracting thousands of families back into the capital city. But best of all, the downtown office space inherited from my predecessor, Senator Joe Lieberman, was in the same building as Shipman and Goodwin, my father's law firm. I would be working just a few floors down from my dad.

But with the exception of Shane Oliver's murder, the killings in Hartford weren't happening downtown. They were happening in the neighborhoods north and south of the business district, and after New-town . . . after meeting Sam Saylor . . . I knew that if I wanted to be part of the solution to the epidemic of gun violence, I couldn't wall myself, and my staff, off from it, like most people did who worked downtown during the day and then went back to their tree-lined suburban en-claves at night. I needed to be in the north end or the south end if I wanted to understand the problem and live the solution. And I felt like the unique prestige that comes with a U.S. Senate office was kind of wasted on a downtown that already had plenty of respected law firms, insurance companies, and banks in residence. In a different part of the city, our office could serve as a signal that some politicians were willing to walk the walk, not just talk the talk, about making these places safer.

Unfortunately, we quickly found out why almost every in-state Sen-ate office is in a fancy high-rise or office park. Because of the myriad security threats that congressional offices face, Senate security man-dates make it almost impossible to locate an office in any structure other than a large, fortified commercial building. So Kenny Curran, who became the director of my Connecticut operations after my swearing-in, went off to search for a large building outside of down-town Hartford, but inside an emerging neighborhood that could be buoyed by a U.S. Senate office anchoring a redevelopment effort.

As he was nearing the end of his search, Kenny called me one after-noon.

"I have good news, and I have bad news."

"Good news first," I replied.

"I found an office building that basically fits your requirements. Out of downtown. Up-and-coming neighborhood. Plenty of room for security upgrades."

"But?"

"It's the Colt firearms factory."

. . .

After a blood-soaked start to postsettlement American history, violence in the United States quieted in the late 1700s and early 1800s, settling back down to levels on par with European nations. In the first decades after the drafting and enactment of the Constitution, the U.S. economy grew vigorously, but with Europe bogged down in unending internecine warfare, most adult European males were unable to leave their families and migrate to the New World. Thus, American labor demand outstripped American labor supply, and the population remained relatively homogeneous. The growth of out-groups that the in-groups needed to suppress slowed. And America was only beginning to push westward—eastern tribes had largely been brutally subjugated by the late eighteenth century, and the days of the Wild West were not yet upon us.

That all changed in the two decades leading up to the Civil War—the greatest of all American bloodlettings. Sometimes called the "riot era," violence dramatically spiked upward during the time that Samuel Colt began to build his firearms empire, anchored in the south section of Hartford, Connecticut, and U.S. violence rates have not come back to earth since. In his excellent book, *American Homicide*, historian Randolph Roth summarizes:

> It was at this time that homicide rates in the United States truly diverged from rates elsewhere in the Western world. In the late 1840s and 1850s they exploded across the nation, not only in the plantation South and the Southwest, where higher rates already prevailed, but also in the mountain South and the North, which had previously had extremely low rates. The least homicidal places in the Western world suddenly became the most homicidal.

What happened to so permanently change the course of human-on-human aggression in America? One part of the explanation lies in the explosion of two out-group populations during this time—immigrants and enslaved African Americans—and the retreat to physical force as a means to control and subordinate them by the founding generations of white Americans.

First, let's talk about the effect of the seismic wave of postrevolutionary European immigrants that began to pour into the country in the middle portion of the nineteenth century. The Napoleonic Wars had come to an end, and young men, unburdened by conscription and facing economic hardship at home, could freely relocate to the opportunity-rich American continent. Irish, Scots, and Germans began to pour into America's growing cities, where the Industrial Revolution was spinning out urban-based job opportunities faster than companies could fill them.

Take Hartford, for example: In twenty short years, from 1840 to 1860, the time during which the Colt firearms factory was being built, Hartford's population nearly tripled. Other American cities experienced the same explosive growth, which rapidly expanded the nation's gross domestic product, but also created friction points between young males. These new groups of citizens were a threat to more established classes in every way: a threat to take away jobs, a threat to overcrowd housing resources, a threat to usurp mating opportunities. If there is one constant in the history of violence, it is that aggressive acts are most often undertaken by anxious men, ages eighteen to twenty-five. American cities were teeming with this demographic in the middle 1800s.

Unapologetic xenophobia ran wild as America's urban centers crowded with immigrants. During this time, an entire political movement—the ironically titled Native American Party—congealed around the economic and social fear of immigrants. Better known as the Know Nothings, this movement made the argument that migrants from places like Ireland and Scotland and Germany were inherently prone to violence and thus presented a natural danger to native-born Americans (more evidence that the debate between genetic and learned violence has been around for a long, long time). Of course, the truth of the matter is that those who came to America during this second wave of American immigration were not, in fact, naturally more violent. Indeed, rates of violence in the origin countries were lower than the rates of violence in America. Again, Randolph Roth:

> The Irish were four or five times more homicidal in the United States than they were in Ireland in the 1850s and 1860s. Had they continued to kill at the same rate they did in Ireland, they would have been the least murderous of all Americans.

The xenophobic American environment explains much of the spike in violence that occurred when these immigrants came to America. The claims of immigrant violence by Know Nothings were circular and self-fulfilling, given that much of the violence in American cities was occurring in conflicts between native-born Americans and the Irish and Scottish newcomers. The cause of the violence was not the immigrants themselves, but the irrational hysteria caused by the increasing number of ingredients in the melting pot.

• • •

It was also during this period in American history when violence rates in the South and West began to greatly outpace the rates in the more established areas of the American Northeast. There is no way to account for this diversion other than the second great demographic phenomenon of the middle 1800s—the explosion of the slave population in cotton-producing states. In 1793, the year that Alexander Hamilton was trying in vain to collect his whiskey tax, Connecticut inventor Eli Whitney patented the cotton gin, and by the 1840s, it had reached full penetration into the southern cotton economy. The highly efficient and extremely productive gins revolutionized the manufacture of cotton into commercial products, and created a need for more and more enslaved people to pick enough cotton to feed them. In 1800 there were 850,000 slaves in the South. By 1840, just four decades later, that number had tripled to 2.4 million.

The involuntary enslavement of a human being, enforced by never-ending, constant, dehumanizing actual and threatened physical harm, is perhaps the most purely distilled example of violence in human his-

tory. As the southern slave population grew, the use and accompanying desensitization to violence spiraled exponentially. These decades
prior to the Civil War were the peak of the slave economy in the South,
and the levels of violence everywhere must have been truly epidemic
in order to keep control of the more than two million enslaved humans. Published crime data shows that reported violent crime spiked
higher in the South during this time compared to the North, but of
course almost none of the *actual* violence taking place in the South
was reported to anyone because most of it was fully sanctioned.

It's interesting to note that when African Americans began to travel
north during this time, violence greeted them upon arrival in their
new homes. One of Randolph Roth's most fascinating data sets re-
gards homicide rates from 1800 to 1950 in both New York City and
Philadelphia. Murder rates for white citizens and African American
citizens of both cities remained almost identical through the early
1800s. But then around 1850, the lines began to diverge, drastically, and
by 1900, African Americans in New York were being killed at a rate five
times higher than their white neighbors. In Philadelphia, at a rate ten
times higher. Harvard's Steven Pinker concedes that the increasing fear
of an expanding African American population likely accounts for the
high violence rates these out-groups faced when they left the slave
states. But Pinker also has another idea, and it's central to his entire
theory of why some parts of the United States, including the South,
began to experience higher rates of violence.

Pinker's theory is that in some parts of the country, "self-help" enforcement systems, in which private vengeance and retribution replaced legal systems organized by the state, became the norm. Pinker
notes that often this was not by choice. In northern cities, communities of free African Americans found the official state apparatus of justice and dispute resolution was simply not available to them like it was
to their white neighbors. "Communities of lower-income African
Americans were effectively stateless, relying on a culture of honor
(sometimes called 'the code of the streets') to defend their interests
rather than calling in the law," says Pinker. Recall, now, how proud
Sam Saylor was of Shane's ability to self-police his disputes in the heav-

ily African American north end of Hartford. We'll return to this idea in a later chapter as one way to explain the epidemic levels of violence in modern American cities.

Pinker, though, argues that self-help justice was also a preferred, even idealized, built-in feature of some communities in early America. The duel remains the most famous of these private means of dispute resolution. Though originally a creature of Renaissance-era Europe, it found favor in early America as a way for "men of honor" to uphold their integrity in the wake of an insult or a slander. The most famous of American duels is, of course, that between Alexander Hamilton and Aaron Burr, but many other early American luminaries, like Henry Clay and Andrew Jackson, found themselves taking paces, turning, and firing on colleagues who had maligned their reputation. This growing practice of vigilantism caught the eye of a young lawyer who had just set up his practice in Springfield, Illinois. In 1838, Abraham Lincoln wrote:

> When men take it in their heads to day, to hang gamblers, or burn murderers, they should recollect, that, in the confusion usually attending such transactions, they will be as likely to hang or burn some one who is neither a gambler nor a murderer as one who is. . . . Thus it goes on, step by step, till all the walls erected for the defense of the persons and property of individuals, are trodden down, and disregarded.

The duel persisted in the South and West of the United States long after it had faded away in the Northeast. Those were regions where weak governments led individuals to rely on informal violence to enforce codes of conduct. Andrew Jackson's mother gave him this piece of maternal advice, growing up on the border of North and South Carolina: "Never . . . sue anyone for slander or assault or battery; always settle those cases yourself." Homicides in the early American South, for instance, often went unpunished so long as the killings were considered "reasonable" and resulted from a personal dispute.

Some of this preference for "self-help" has survived to modern day. When I arrived in the Senate, I became interested in ending the practice of using physical restraints on disabled students as a way to control their aggressive behavior when it careened out of control. It was a practice used rarely in Connecticut, but I felt there was no justification for schools ever using force as a way to mete out discipline. What I quickly realized was that the rest of the country didn't think like my state. I was shocked to find out that nine states still allowed teachers to paddle students for bad behavior. All nine—Alabama, Arkansas, Georgia, Louisiana, Texas, Tennessee, Mississippi, North Carolina, and Oklahoma—were in the South. Violence without due process as a means of maintaining order is still alive and well in parts of America.

A concern with Pinker's argument is that governments weren't weak in the southern and western states by accident. They were kept impotent in part so that slaveholders, and later postbellum white landholders, could whip, beat, and lynch African Americans to maintain their economic and social dominance while suffering no legal consequences for their brutality. Today, lynchings may be largely confined to the history books, but in those states that allow for corporal punishment in school, guess who actually gets beaten in class? In reviewing the reported physical punishment in schools in seven of those nine states, the Brookings Institution found that African American students suffer in-school beatings at twice the rate of white students in the southern states that still allow for it.

The foundation of America's violence explosion in the pre–Civil War years was certainly the need for in-groups to assert their authority over the growing numbers of out-group members who threatened them economically and socially. But the massive spike in violent injury and death during this period of American history, cementing the country's status as a violent outlier in the civilized world, could not have occurred without one more historical development. To finish our survey of the turning point of American violence, we need to return to Hartford, Connecticut, and to the genius of Samuel Colt.

.   .   .

Samuel Colt was born in Hartford and endured a difficult childhood. His mother died when he was six, and his despondent father sent him to work as a kind of indentured servant on a farm across the river in the agrarian town of Glastonbury. One of Samuel's most treasured possessions during those years was the flintlock pistol handed down to him by his grandfather, an officer in General Washington's Continental Army.

During his time on the farm, Colt preferred to study scientific encyclopedias rather than cavort with the other children. At age fifteen, he finally rejoined his father, who had by then moved to Massachusetts, but the reunion would not last long. Even then, Colt had a fascination with gunpowder, and a pyrotechnic experiment gone wrong ended with a section of his boarding school burning to the ground. Now sixteen, young Colt was sent by his father to be a laborer on a brig bound for India to mature and learn a useful trade. But Colt's passion for firearms was undeterred. Inspired by watching the endless motion of the ship's rotating capstan, Colt came up with a new idea for a revolver that relied on the cocking mechanism to rotate a cylinder. When he arrived in India, he whittled a wood version of the gun.

Once back in the United States, Colt continued to perfect his design and pursued a commercial application for his innovative new firearm. In 1836, at age twenty-two, he filed a patent on the Patterson repeating revolver, which eventually became the first commercially available handgun capable of firing multiple rounds without manual reloading. Colt's profits were small, with only occasional sales to the U.S. Army and other military and law enforcement agencies, and he was forced to earn his living selling a variety of other inventions, including underwater mines and waterproof telegraph cables.

Then came the Battle of Walker's Creek in June 1844. Texans—not yet Americans—were busy trying to exterminate the Comanche tribe, which that summer had taken to the offensive, raiding settlements north of San Antonio. A band of fifteen Texas Rangers, armed with Colt Pattersons, rode out to the Guadalupe River and engaged an eighty-strong Comanche war party. The fearsome Comanches were no match for the repeating revolver, and half of the war party were felled by bullets in a short skirmish. A Comanche complained that the Rangers "had a shot for every finger on the hand."

One of the Rangers injured in the battle, Sam Walker, met Colt shortly afterward and eagerly told him the story. Colt recognized the marketing power of the Comanche massacre immediately, and hired Walker to help him develop a new version of the repeating revolver, appropriately named the Walker. The legend of Walker's Creek spread, helped by Colt's mass-marketing campaign. When Walker, still a Texas Ranger, became a hero of the Mexican–American War, the good press wrote itself, and President Zachary Taylor ordered one thousand of the Walker revolvers to supply his wartime army. The sales over the course of that war launched Colt's enterprise, and he moved back to Connecticut to build a manufacturing facility that could meet the burgeoning demand for his breakthrough firearms.

The war had provided Colt with a small taste of commercial success, and the ambitious entrepreneur certainly wasn't going to let peace get in the way of growing his business. As we will find later in this chapter, guns were plentiful in early America. Perhaps as many as half of all households counted a gun as one of their possessions. But gun ownership before Colt was seen as a responsibility of citizenship, still connected to the duty of militia membership. Guns were not romantic objects in early America. They were instruments of utility—frustrating, bulky machines that malfunctioned with regularity.

Colt changed all that. He saw how America's imagination was captured by the Rangers' daring raid on the Comanches and Walker's heroic exploits against the Mexican army. He launched a massive advertising campaign associating his new revolver with the exploits of those seeking to protect America from its enemies and tame the wilds of the West. Colt was among the first marketers to regularly use celebrity endorsers. Walker helped bring Sam Houston into the Colt fold, and Colt invented the practice of sending free merchandise to cultural and political leaders in the hopes that they would vouch for his products in public. He hired famed American painter George Catlin to paint scenes in which Colt guns had saved the lives of settlers in the American West, and he produced endless pamphlets depicting the heroic efforts of Colt firearms owners throughout the country.

Colt wasn't alone in marketing the handgun to a mass audience.

While the outbreak of the Civil War was the principal stimulating event for the domestic gun industry, companies like Smith and Wesson, Winchester (then the New Haven Arms Company), and Remington were, like Colt, finding an ample private sector market for handguns as the romanticizing of gun ownership spread through popular culture. American companies saw the handgun market as their opportunity to outflank the long-dominant European gunmakers, who were still focused on selling larger, traditional long guns. Plus, the relative lack of gun regulation compared to Europe created few barriers to market for the growing domestic firearms industry. Led by Colt, the American companies drastically decreased the manufacturing costs of these smaller weapons, and prices plummeted, making the guns affordable to more and more Americans who bought into the growing allure of firearm ownership.

The revolution of small arms, combined with the rising fear of violence in America's teeming cities, created a perfect storm of incentives for gun purchases. The gun marketers played upon people's fears of Native Americans and immigrants, and soon it was social custom to carry a gun while walking the street. The great New York diarist George Templeton Strong wrote worryingly of the growing fear of violence coupled with increasing rates of gun ownership among his peers:

> An epidemic of crime this winter [1856–57] . . . Most of my friends are investing in revolvers and carry them about at night, and if I expect to have to do a great deal of late night street-walking of Broadway, I think I should make the like provision; though it's a very bad practice carrying concealed weapons.

If the repeating revolver could protect Walker against marauding Comanche Indians, then certainly it could ward off drunk Irish hooligans in the mean streets of Manhattan, went the argument. Colt's endless storytelling of gun-wielding Western heroes who righteously gunned down wicked Native Americans drilled into consumers' minds the potential for guns to protect oneself against the threats—real or imagined—that seemed around every corner to pre–Civil War Americans. What better way to protect against the genetically violent Irish and Scottish than a small handheld killing machine? How better to keep newly freed southern African Americans in line than to make sure every white man in town has a firearm in his holster? Gunmakers marketed to the in-groups, feeding off a growing sense of threat coming from the expanding out-groups, while enthusiastically selling guns to the out-groups, too.

The physical properties of Colt's handgun also deeply impacted the potential for interpersonal violence. Guns weren't hulking, unreliable long rifles any longer—they were compact, efficient instruments that could fit inside a coat pocket. Guns could now be carried easily in public. In his majestic history of homicide in the United States, *Murder in America,* historian Roger Lane notes that Colt's guns were "small, cheap, easily hidden on the person, with the potential to turn any drunken shoving match into an instant fatality."

Handguns also further depersonalized firearms violence. Prior to the invention of projectile weaponry, the effort necessary to kill with a knife or a club or one's fist was significant and messy. Deciding to kill someone in a way that put you in close physical contact with that individual naturally put you at risk as well. Common sense tells us that physical and moral costs associated with hand-to-hand assault would have had a chilling effect on human violence. Guns, which can execute your target from a distance without your ever having to lay a hand on the subject, changed this equation. But rifles required the shooter to go fetch the weapon, individually load each round, and hoist to one's shoulder a device weighing as much as ten pounds. That's still a lot of effort. The handheld Colt revolver, which could shoot multiple rounds and had a weight one-quarter that of a rifle, essentially eliminated any physical effort connected to murder, further depersonalizing the act.

The Colt revolver flew off the shelves, and the firearms industry got a taste of the limitless success that could come from creating consumer demand based on the promise of an affordable weapon to ward off perceived dangers and threats. Fear became a commercial tool, as did the manufactured belief that gun ownership could conquer those fears.

Records of gun ownership dry up between the Revolutionary period and the twentieth century, but there is plenty of evidence to suggest that handgun ownership took off as soon as Colt started marketing his history-changing invention. Consider this: No businessman in America had sold a million of anything until Colt sold his millionth handgun. Given that others besides Colt were selling large numbers of handguns, and the population of the United States in 1850 was only twenty-three million, it is likely that a large number of Americans quickly became proud owners of these exceptionally lethal instruments. And unlike in Europe, where centuries-old restrictions limited the size of the private marketplace, American gun laws in the early days of the nation posed few barriers to ownership. One of the few data sets for the period comes from the late historian Eric Monkkonen, who found that one of every ten Americans likely owned a handgun in 1850, only fourteen years after Colt got his patent for the repeating revolver, a rate of "short gun" ownership ten times higher than gun ownership fifty years earlier.

In addition, newspapers and journals are full of reports in the middle and late 1800s of citizens armed to the hilt, and guns spilling out of every crevice of American city life. Roger Lane reports on an 1856 election in Baltimore that makes today's political bickering seem like child's play:

> In October 1856 a local Baltimore election was entirely dominated by . . . youth gangs: the police either stood by or actively cooperated as Blood Tubs, Stingers, Plug Uglies, and Tigers took over the polls to drive out German and Irish immigrant voters. Pistols, rifles, then cannons were again brought in by the private gangs, and a contemporary historian claims that "more men were killed than were lost on the American side in the battle of Palo Alto, in the war with Mexico," just ten years earlier.

Violence was back, at a pace far above the European norm, and it has been that way ever since.

.   .   .

By the 1850s, Colt's early handgun sales had made him a raging business success. He returned to his hometown in Connecticut and acquired land alongside the Connecticut River in Hartford to build his new armory. The Connecticut River valley, now nicknamed "Gun Alley," had become the epicenter of the nascent but growing American gun industry.

Samuel Colt had grand ambitions for his new factory: He set out to build a utopian industrial community, where employees and executives lived, worked, and worshipped on the same plot of land. He built the largest factory floor in the United States, creating the modern assembly line that would become the template for Henry Ford's early plant designs. Next door to his factory he built worker housing, a grand chapel, and his own opulent home. For nearly 150 years, Coltsville, as it became known, dominated the landscape in southern Hartford, employing tens of thousands of immigrants who poured into the city for the good-paying employment Colt offered.

After losing several major military contracts at the beginning of the 2000s, the company filed for Chapter 11 bankruptcy and ended its operations in Hartford. But the factory building, the worker housing, the church, and the Colt home still remain as a living memorial to the American Industrial Revolution. In 2014, I partnered with my friend Hartford-area Congressman John Larson to win congressional approval to designate Coltsville a National Historical Park.

A new owner began the work of rehabilitating the hulking factory, capped with its famous onion dome (apocryphally thought to have been built in an effort to disguise it as an Orthodox church to fool potential enemy bombers during World War II), for new commercial tenants. And in 2015, the most vocal antagonist of the American gun industry in the U.S. Senate opened his brand-new office on the fourth floor of the most famous gun factory in the world.

THE SECOND WAVE OF AMERICAN VIOLENCE (1865–1935)

After Appomattox and through the beginning of the twentieth century, homicide rates settled back down, holding steady in some places and decreasing in others. After more than six hundred thousand American soldiers perished during the Civil War, the nation was tired of fighting. But during the second half of the 1800s, two new but familiar waves of violence began to develop: the epidemic levels of violence during the settlement of the western frontier and the new kinds of violence directed toward newly free American blacks in the former Confederacy.

From 1935 to 1960, Hollywood made a staggering 1,400 Westerns, movies set in the days of westward expansion during the second half of the nineteenth century. *Winchester '73* from 1950 is a prototype of the midcentury Western. Starring Jimmy Stewart, Tony Curtis, Shelley Winters, and a young Rock Hudson (regrettably playing a Native American), the movie is subtitled *The Gun That Won the West* and follows Stewart's character as he pursues a vigilante who steals his prized Winchester rifle. Oliver Winchester, the founder of the Winchester Repeating Arms Company in New Haven, Connecticut (and Connecticut's lieutenant governor from 1866 to 1867), would have been pleased that his relentless marketing campaign to associate his firearms with the settlement of the American West had borne fruit. By the middle of the twentieth century, his advertising phrase for the Winchester rifle had been so routinely accepted as fact that it had found its way into the title of a major motion picture.

The maturation of the American firearms manufacturing industry coincided perfectly with the timing of America's population migration west of the Mississippi River, and the industry quickly discovered that the young men leading the exodus were prime targets for the new romantic association of firearm ownership. It's hard to know whether the legitimate and imagined dangers of western expansion produced a natural demand for gun ownership, or whether brilliant marketers like Colt and Winchester created that demand with their ribald stories of gun battles with Indians, but there is no doubt the West was indeed wild, with "annual homicide rates . . . fifty to several hundred times higher than those of eastern cities and Midwestern farming regions," as Pinker notes in *The Better Angels of Our Nature*.

And the West was awash in guns. William Swain was a twenty-seven-year-old farmer's son from Youngstown, New York, when he left his wife and daughter to become a forty-niner—a seeker of personal fortune in the California gold rush of 1849. He lasted only two years, returning home empty-handed and shaken by the high rates of violence in the western territories. He wrote in his journal that "all emigrants are armed to the teeth. It is like one continual glorious 4th of July." Swain described his fellow gold rushers as "walking arsenals" and detailed frequent injuries from accidental shootings.

It was during this era that gunmakers and gun marketers began to capitalize on the growing value Americans were placing on individualism and self-reliance, the very ideals that were driving so many young men to leave their families behind to seek success, alone, in the new frontier. Winchester's marketing campaign was driven by his vision of "single individuals, traveling through a wild country." The incessant use of Wild West imagery in gun advertisements burned in the image of the firearm as the symbol of heroic westward expansion, hinting to those who stayed behind in the East that the purchase of a Smith and Wesson, Remington, Colt, or Winchester could give them an association with the gallant cowboys and gunslingers without ever leaving home. As the self-made man became more tightly tied to American mythology, the gunmakers succeeded in making ownership of a firearm a symbol of rugged individualism.

The final development during the late 1800s that facilitated this rapid commercialization of handguns and rifles was the plummeting cost of the mass-market revolver. Hartford's Mark Twain, upon visiting the Colt armory, described it as "a tangled forest of rods, bars, pulleys, wheels, and all the imaginable and unimaginable forms of mechanism. . . . It must have required more brains to invent all those things than would serve to stock 50 Senates like ours."

By the 1870s, at least fifty companies were producing small revolvers with catchy names like "Banker's Pal," "Tramp's Terror," and "Protector." In 1850, a Colt revolver cost twelve dollars. By the end of the century, multiple sellers were marketing two-dollar "suicide specials," and Sears was retailing Colt's .22 caliber "Defender" in its mail order catalog for sixty-eight cents plus ten cents shipping. Cost was no longer a barrier to getting your piece of the growing American mythology of gun ownership.

. . .

The end of legalized slavery did not stem the tide of violence in the South and the West. With the conclusion of the Civil War, the passage of the Thirteenth and Fourteenth amendments granted African Americans constitutionally protected equal status with the white Americans who had used systemic, legalized violence to keep them subjugated for more than two hundred years. In 1877, as Reconstruction governments run by "carpetbaggers" and "freedmen" ended, Southern whites took back control of state and local governments and began to enact laws establishing the legalized separation of African Americans and whites, and enthusiastically took up the practice of using a variety of extralegal means to reimpose their temporarily lost dominance over African Americans. The most effective of these informal mechanisms of dominance was white–on–African American violence.

Lynchings were the most infamous of these methods—mobs of anywhere from dozens to thousands would round up African American citizens suspected of wrongdoing and execute them without trial, most often by various means of torture followed by being hanged from a tree and set on fire. The scenes described by eyewitnesses evoke the most gruesome executions in medieval Europe.

"Whole families came together, mothers and fathers, bringing even their youngest children. It was the show of the countryside—a very popular show," read a 1930 editorial in the Raleigh, North Carolina, *News and Observer*. "Men joked loudly at the sight of the bleeding body. . . . Girls giggled as the flies fed on the blood that dripped from the Negro's nose." Bodies were usually then dismembered with parts gifted to the executioners and onlookers as keepsakes. W.E.B. Du Bois, in his autobiography, wrote that after the 1899 lynching of Sam Hose in Georgia, the dead man's knuckles were kept on public display at a local store in Atlanta and his heart and liver were presented as a gift to the state's governor.

Of course, racial violence wasn't limited to lynchings. In certain areas of the South, white–on–African American homicide reached staggeringly high levels. In rural Louisiana, homicide rates were 35 per

100,000 (today, Louisiana has the highest homicide rate in the United States, at a comparably meager 12 per 100,000), and whites killed African Americans at a rate eighteen times higher than African Americans killed whites. The regular use of violence by whites to brutally dominate African Americans was a foundational truth of the post–Civil War South, but also of every other corner of the nation.

The worst incident of racial violence in Louisiana occurred in 1873, at a time when the Reconstruction governments still tried to protect African American participation in local and state governments. A mob of Ku Klux Klan members marched on the Grant Parish courthouse in Louisiana demanding that the Republican government in the parish, split between whites and African Americans, surrender power. An all-black militia took up arms in the courthouse but were forced to surrender to the more heavily armed white mob. As the African American militiamen filed out of the building, a massacre ensued, and up to 150 of the African American soldiers were shot and hanged by the KKK mob. The bloodbath set off a chain of events that expedited the end to the biracial Reconstruction governments of the South, and to this day, unbelievably, a plaque stands on the site of the massacre, proudly stating, "On this site occurred the Colfax Riot in which three white men and 150 negroes were slain. This event on April 13, 1873 marked the end of carpetbag misrule in the South."

Skeptics of explaining increasing violence rates in the South mainly through the prism of racial violence often cite data suggesting that white-on-white violence also dramatically increased in the postbellum South. Steven Pinker suggests that the overriding "honor culture" of the region, where private justice was socially preferred over justice rendered through law enforcement and court systems, explains why general violence in the South was so high during this period of U.S. history, and remains so today. There may be some truth to this, but I still believe that racism was the driving force behind the high rates of violence in this part of the nation, largely because there are easy ways to also explain the high rates of white-on-white violence through this lens of racial subjugation.

First, it stands to reason that a society whose very social foundation is predicated on violence would become anesthetized to the effects and consequences of physical aggression. Once violence had become rationalized as a mechanism for social control against African Americans, why wouldn't it become contagious, easily rationalized as a way to settle other conflicts unrelated to race? Second, whites likely owned many more firearms in the postbellum South than during the years prior to the war and used them rather indiscriminately, against both African Americans and whites. Explains Roth:

> Before the Civil War, blacks in plantation counties in Georgia and South Carolina used guns in 7 percent of the homicides they committed and whites in 38 percent: roughly the same percentages as pre– and post–Civil War Virginia. But after the war, blacks used guns in 57 percent of the homicides they committed and whites in 80 percent. . . . Carrying guns to perpetrate interracial violence or to defend themselves against it also increased the likelihood that whites would kill whites and blacks would kill blacks.

The Johnson and Grant administrations chose not to disarm Confederate soldiers after the war, so the glut of weapons that flooded into the South during the conflict remained. And white governments, understanding the power of gun ownership to reassert dominance over African Americans, passed laws forbidding or making it increasingly difficult for African American southerners to carry or own firearms, giving whites a near monopoly on gun violence in the South, and, consequently, an incentive to purchase more guns. And so it was no coincidence that homicides, especially against African Americans but also among whites, dramatically increased.

·　·　·

As the twentieth century dawned, a new societal menace began to emerge, mainly in the cities of the Midwest, but also in parts of the Eastern Seaboard: heavily armed groups of unrepentant criminals, often organized around the illegal sale of alcohol during the Prohibition years, who rejected the authority of local law enforcement units.

John Dillinger was among the most notorious of the Depression-era gangsters who captured the public's imagination with his daring prison escapes and bloody confrontations with police. From the fall of 1933 to the summer of 1934, Dillinger terrorized the Midwest, killing ten and wounding seven more, robbing banks, stealing police arsenals, and staging no fewer than three jailbreaks. He was eventually killed in the summer of 1934 in a shootout with FBI agents who had received a tip that he was taking in a movie at a Chicago theater.

Americans became obsessed with the exploits of dashing, unabashed bandits like Dillinger, Bonnie Parker and Clyde Barrow, George "Machine Gun" Kelly, and Charles "Pretty Boy" Floyd. Of particular interest was the gangsters' weapon of choice—the small machine gun dubbed the "Tommy gun."

The "Maxim gun," a recoil-operated fully automatic firearm, capable of firing multiple rounds with a single trigger pull, was invented by American-born British inventor Hiram Stevens Maxim (who also invented the spring-loaded mousetrap that is still in widespread use today) and was used frequently by British forces in their colonial campaigns. But it was heavy and awkward, requiring a team of four to six men to operate. The technology, though, was revolutionary, and in the middle of the First World War, the chief engineer at the Remington Arms Company, John T. Thompson, patented a firearm capable of firing an astonishing six hundred rounds per minute. Debuting on the commercial market in 1920, this highly destructive weapon immediately appealed to gangsters like Dillinger. The Tommy gun retailed for $175 (about $2,000 in current dollars) and could be bought by mail, making it "expensive but affordable to a thriving criminal syndicate."

Today, the Prohibition-era gangster is a romantic figure, the subject of Academy Award–winning films. But even during the time of their audacious rampages, there was widespread sympathy, and even some admiration, for these early century machine-gun-wielding bandits.

First, the unpopularity of Prohibition itself lent the rum-running gang credibility. Gangsters taking up arms against an unjust law were seen as sympathetic crusaders just as often as they were viewed as contemptuous killers. Second, the new American out-groups of the twentieth century, southern and eastern European Catholics along with another wave of Irish immigrants, saw these syndicates, often composed of members of their own ethnic groups, as noble champions against the dominant Protestant in-groups. In a way, the immigrant out-groups of the early 1900s were flipping the script on the dominant in-groups. They found a way to use violence to protect and advance their position, and like the swashbuckling outlaws of the Wild West, the gangsters of the early 1900s helped rationalize violence as a legitimate means of settling scores and gave the weapons industry even more material to use in their advertisements.

.　　.　　.

The increased violence during the Tommy gun era was not a fiction created by newsreels and movie scripts—it was real. And while the gangsters got all the ink, much of this increase in violence can be explained in the same way we explained the crime surge of the 1840s. The third and biggest of the immigration swells of America's first two hundred years arrived in the first decade of the twentieth century. Made up of Italians and Russians and more Irish, more than eight million immigrants landed in America between 1900 and 1910, a number nearly twice as high as any other previous decade in American history. And just like in the 1840s, violence began to rise. In 1900, the rate of homicide in the United States was just over 6 per 100,000. By the middle of Prohibition, it had increased by 50 percent, to around 9 per 100,000.

What made this particular spike in violence different was the speed with which news—especially bad news—could travel with the rapid growth of the media and entertainment business. Newsreels were full of harrowing depictions of gangster violence. One, from 1931, showed footage of a bullet-riddled New York City streetscape and children who were caught in the crossfire. "Here is Samuel Davino, only five years old, pointing to where he was shot in the leg by gangland's ruthless gunmen," the voiceover explains. "But poor little Samuel is more fortunate than Michael Vengali, also five. Michael met death. And this casket will hold his tiny body, broken by machine gun bullets." Even given the sympathies that the gangs drew from some parts of American society, it became increasingly unsustainable for political leaders to allow these crime gangs to openly flout the law and pitch open warfare against law enforcement.

When former New York governor Franklin Delano Roosevelt became president, he vowed to stand up to the machine-gun-toting gangs, and he had a growing movement to tighten the nation's firearms behind him. The first American laws regarding guns may have mandated gun ownership by colonists under threat of attack from Native Americans, but soon thereafter, state and local governments got into the business of trying to regulate the ownership of firearms, passing nearly one thousand gun laws from colonial times to Prohibition. For instance, during the pre–Civil War riot era, southern states rushed to adopt bans on carrying concealed weapons.

In Kentucky, when a state court struck down the state's concealed carry law, the state amended its constitution to make clear the general assembly had the power to stop people from carrying concealed weapons. The western frontier, which Winchester claimed was won by the gun, actually had some of the most onerous restrictions on guns.

In the infamous Tombstone, Arizona, there were much more restrictive gun laws than there are now. "Today, you're allowed to carry a gun without a license or permit on Tombstone streets," notes UCLA law professor Adam Winkler. "Back in the 1880s, you weren't." Historian Robert Dykstra compared the strength of gun laws and the gun violence rates in a set of frontier towns and came to the conclusion that the towns that restricted weapons inside their boundaries had few if any killings, compared to towns with looser laws. Policy makers quickly figured out that restricting gun ownership was a quick way to quell gun violence.

During the gangster era, a powerful conglomerate of gun owners stepped forward to help pass the nation's first comprehensive gun control law. In 1871, George Wingate, a New York lawyer, and William Church, a writer for *The New York Times*, founded a new organization called the National Rifle Association, with the stated intention of improving what Wingate and Church believed was the feeble marksmanship skills of soldiers in the U.S. Army. But as an organization dedicated to raising the standards associated with gun stewardship, the NRA soon got into the business of advocating for state laws that would assure that only serious people owned firearms. In the early 1920s, the group pushed states to pass comprehensive gun control legislation, including requiring a permit to carry a concealed weapon (more on this later). Eighteen states adopted some version of the laws the NRA was proposing.

When Roosevelt arrived in the White House, he inherited a mature national gun control movement, with the NRA at its center. In the early 1920s, the NRA had 3,500 members. By 1934, its membership had grown tenfold, and it was unquestionably the largest organization of gun owners in the nation. Senator Royal Copeland of New York pushed a federal ban on Tommy guns and other automatic weapons toward a floor vote, but Roosevelt balked, not because of the Second Amendment, but because of the Supreme Court's strict interpretation of the commerce clause.

Eventually, Congress passed and Roosevelt signed the nation's first two laws regulating the commercial gun market. The 1934 National Firearms Act and the 1938 Federal Firearms Act were significant pieces of legislation—together, the acts imposed registration requirements and high fees ($3,500 in today's dollars) on the most dangerous weapons (like Tommy guns), required gun dealers and manufacturers to register with the federal government, and prohibited felons from buying guns.

The NRA successfully objected to stronger versions of the legislation, most significantly convincing Congress to drop pistols from the licensing and taxation included in the 1934 bill. But the organization did endorse the legislation that eventually came to Congress for a vote. Said NRA president Karl Frederick in testimony before Congress on the 1934 act, "I do not believe in the general promiscuous toting of guns. I think it should be sharply restricted and only under licenses." He further mused that he had given no thought to whether the laws would violate the Second Amendment. "Protection for firearms does not come from the Second Amendment," wrote Frederick elsewhere. "It comes just from wise public policy."

Now comes the most fascinating part of the story. In the wake of the passage of the nation's first laws controlling the sale and possession of firearms, homicide rates began to plummet. Like, *really* plummet. In ten short years, from 1935 to 1945, homicide rates in the United States dropped an astonishing 50 percent, and then held relatively steady until the outbreak of violence in America in the mid-1960s. Violence rates were still much higher in America than in Europe—five times higher than in England, for instance—but America had never before witnessed such a rapid de-escalation of violence.

In *American Homicide,* Randolph Roth argues that the recovery of the American economy from the depths of the Depression and the resulting restored faith in centralized government explains the rapid drop in violence rates. No doubt the decreasing desperation of Americans likely calmed the tinderbox of potential conflict that existed between the immigrant out-groups and the legacy in-groups during the worst of the Depression, but there is no other corollary in American history where a robust economic recovery led to sharp declines in homicide rates like what occurred from 1935 to 1945. Almost all murders in the 1920s were committed with guns; the American Bar Association found that 90 percent of all homicides during the decade were committed with firearms. Thus, the contraction of dangerous weapons from the marketplace, and the restriction that only nonfelons possess guns, likely had a significant effect on gun ownership and violence rates.

THE THIRD WAVE OF AMERICAN VIOLENCE (1965-95)

There were a lot of puzzled faces on the floor of the 1968 Republican National Convention in Miami Beach when Richard Nixon announced that he had picked obscure Maryland governor Spiro Agnew as his running mate.

"I hardly know who Agnew is," said one Iowa delegate. "I hope he fits the bill."

But Richard Nixon knew Agnew and what his selection would telegraph to the nation. The assassination of Martin Luther King, Jr., had set off waves of violence in several American cities, including Baltimore. That city, in 1968, was a case study in the new segregation of the late 1900s. Starting in 1950, whites began flushing out of Baltimore and into the suburbs, replaced by African Americans, who could take advantage of the truly national economy of post–World War II America and move fluidly from the Jim Crow South to northern cities with a less overt racial caste system. Northern white governments, like that of Agnew in Maryland, funneled government spending to the places to which whites were moving, leaving behind blight and underinvestment in the cities. In some neighborhoods in Baltimore, unemployment was 30 percent.

In April 1968, when Agnew judged that Baltimore's Democratic mayor, Tommy D'Alesandro (brother of Speaker of the House Nancy Pelosi), couldn't quell the growing riots after the King assassination, he initiated a brutal put-down, calling up ten thousand National Guard and Army troops and arresting more than five thousand individuals. A week later, he met with African American leaders from the city to discuss their concerns with the ferocity of his response. Instead of taking part in a polite listening session, Agnew turned on the fifty attendees at the meeting, haranguing them for a "perverting sense of race loyalty" and blaming them for not controlling the organic frustrations of their community. Many of the African American leaders stormed out of the meeting in protest, and Agnew's defiant performance captured national attention. A young aide to candidate Richard Nixon, Patrick Buchanan, handed Nixon a newspaper clipping describing the heated meeting.

Nixon ran as the "law and order" candidate in 1968, recognizing that the rising violence of the 1960s had set off an anxiety in America about a changing society. Nixon wanted Agnew because he played to a fear consistent with the long history of American violence: the rise of African American civil, economic, and social rights. The civil rights

movement, bridging the 1950s and '60s, represents the political awakening of African Americans after the century of severe oppression that
followed the official abolition of slavery. The movement led by King
and others was nonviolent, but there were also incidents of open conflict between African Americans and whites as urban riots flared up in
dozens of cities during the 1960s. I will cover one particular riot in
Newark in a later chapter, but these conflicts were triggered by decades of incessant oppression by white in-groups of African American
out-groups, and pent-up frustration combined with the civil rights
movement led to outbreaks of violence.

As we saw with the massive immigration waves of the 1840s and
early 1900s, unexpected social dislocation is a trigger for violence
spikes, as anxiety and fear generally rises in both in-group and out-
group populations. Thus, the increase in violence in the 1960s came
both from out-group African Americans who were occasionally using
it as a means to protest or break the dominance of white in-groups,
and through the increased usage of force by in-group whites to project
dominance over rising African Americans. (And, as we saw in the post–
Civil War South, violence *within* out-group and in-group communities
also increases when the general level of economic or social anxiety
rises between the dominant and subordinate groups.)

Nixon and Agnew, playing to the "silent majority" who wanted a
firm response to the empowerment of African Americans, triumphed
in 1968. Having won by exploiting the fear of increasing racial violence, they did nothing but exacerbate the politically advantageous
trend. Nixon did not share Johnson's enthusiasm for government
spending, through the so-called Great Society programs, and so the
federal war on poverty stalled during his administration. This helped
lead to a growing concentration of poverty in small, defined neighborhoods, as wealthier white individuals continued their exodus from
urban America.

As we will learn later, the strongest correlation to violence is income (though poverty by no means inevitably leads to violence), and
as more and more Americans began to live in areas of highly concentrated poverty and the suffering and trauma the poverty begot, vio-

lence started to increase in those places. This then allowed Nixon to conveniently tailor his "war on drugs" to those cities that were increasingly populated by people of color. He began to militarize urban police departments, using funding programs started under the Johnson administration to send heavier weaponry into U.S. cities, further reinforcing violence as the primary method of social control in urban settings.

.   .   .

We can't end a discussion of the violence spikes in the middle of the twentieth century without talking about what was happening in the firearms industry during this time. The NRA, though ultimately supportive of the 1930s gun laws, had worked in a loophole to allow handguns to remain largely unregulated by the federal government. American men continued to purchase cheap handguns in large quantities in the early half of the twentieth century, and World War II and the buildup of militaries in its aftermath prompted international gun companies to begin competing vigorously to sell the new holstered weapon of choice to soldiers and law enforcement officers: the semiautomatic handgun. In 1963, Gaston Glock began designing a new semiautomatic handgun for the Austrian army, and today, the Glock 19 is one of the best-selling guns in the world, finding its way into the hands of more than 60 percent of all U.S. federal, state, and local law enforcement organizations.

Due in part to the popularity of these powerful but affordable handguns, by the 1960s, gun ownership rates were back to Revolutionary-era levels, with more than half of American households owning at least one gun. Between 1958 and 1968, gun homicides increased by 51 percent, and assaults using a firearm shot up by 84 percent. Colt and Winchester were still selling millions of handguns, but now foreign competitors like Glock were entering the American market at stunning levels. In 1955, sixty-seven thousand guns were imported to the United States. By 1968, that number was one million.

Shortly after the assassination of Robert Kennedy, Congress passed an update to the 1930s gun laws, but it broke little new ground, in part because of the growing power of the gun lobby. The main purpose of the Gun Control Act of 1968 was to reestablish much of the framework of the 1934 act, part of which had been struck down as a violation of the Fifth Amendment by the Warren court. There were a few new wrinkles, like a minimum age of twenty-one for handgun purchases, but by and large, the 1968 act did little novel to address the growing rates of personal violence in America. And coming on the heels of the King and Kennedy murders, the legislation was interpreted largely in the context of high-profile political violence. Predictably, the law did little to affect murder or assault rates.

But then, like magic, that all changed. Virtually overnight, in the middle of the Clinton administration, America got a whole lot safer. Homicides, assaults, arsons, and rape—indeed every kind of violence—began plummeting around the year 1995, so that by the time Barack Obama was elected president, America was as pacific as it had been during the 1950s. Just like that, the crime surge was over. So what the hell happened?

Pinker and Roth are both essentially stumped for an explanation for why violence rates suddenly nosedived in the late twentieth century. Historical models would suggest that the new waves of Latino immigrants coming into the United States, engendering the same kind of racial and economic fears as previous immigrant bursts, should have pushed violence rates up, not down. Pinker suggests a "recivilizing" took place during this time, but that theory would be questioned by the Christian conservatives of the era who regularly bemoaned the rise of violence-glamorizing rap music and the increasing prevalence of anti-authority figures in popular culture. Roth offers his tried-and-true explanation that faith in government rose with the election of centrist Democratic president Bill Clinton. Of course, that's an interesting way to remember an eight-year period marked by congressional investigations, a government shutdown, and an impeachment trial.

The best explanation for the fulcrum point of the mid-1990s is, in fact, not hard to find. During a twelve-month period from November 1993 to October 1994, Congress passed two sweeping pieces of legislation designed to attack the decades-long simmering epidemic of violence in America. In the fall of 1993, Congress passed the Brady Handgun Violence Prevention Act—or Brady bill—the first significant piece of legislation regulating ownership of the highly efficient and lethal handgun that Colt had popularized a century and a half earlier. The bill was named after President Reagan's press secretary, James Brady, who was shot during the 1981 assassination attempt, and mandated that every handgun purchaser in America pass a criminal background check and imposed a waiting period on sales for a period of five years as the instant background check system was built and implemented.

Then, in October 1994, right on the precipice of the midterm elections, Clinton pushed through Congress the Violent Crime and Law Enforcement Act, commonly called the crime bill, which included a ban on all semiautomatic "assault rifles," like the one used by Adam Lanza and most other modern mass shooters, and on ammunition clips of more than ten bullets. These bills also extended the "American imprisonment binge" that began in the 1970s and extended to the Clinton administration. In the two decades beginning in the mid-1970s, the prison population in the United States increased by a factor of five, reaching an incredible two million incarcerated citizens by the time Obama became president, the highest rate of any country on the planet.

The two anticrime bills of 1993 and 1994 were the most significant pieces of legislation regulating firearms—the primary means of American violence—in sixty years. From 1999, when the National Instant Criminal Background Check System (NICS) became operational, until the time of the Sandy Hook shooting, 1.5 million people were denied a firearm because of felony conviction or a serious mental illness. Of the twelve worst mass shootings in the history of the United States, none occurred during the ten years following 1994, when assault weapons were banned from sale or purchase. Eight of those twelve—67 percent—have occurred in the fourteen years since the ban lapsed, and in six of those shootings, rifles were used that were banned by the 1994 law.

·　　·　　·

One afternoon, shortly after the October 2017 Las Vegas shooting, a Republican senator grabbed my arm as we were passing each other in the hallway just outside the Senate floor.

"You know, my father thinks you're the devil," he quipped. I was confused by the deadpan look on his face, which suggested he wasn't kidding.

"What did I do to him?" I replied with a hopeful grin.

"He just can't believe the way you talk about us on Twitter. The way you say that we're murderers and that we're complicit in these shootings."

I froze up a bit, never having been confronted directly by a colleague over my habit of personalizing the consequences of Congress's inaction on guns in the wake of shooting after shooting. He was referring to my regular chastising of Republicans for knowingly allowing gun murders to persist due to their unwillingness to pass laws that evidence clearly demonstrates would lower violence rates. But after the Las Vegas shooting, the most deadly in American history, I went a little further, suggesting that Republican silence was actually an endorsement of these rampages. At a press conference two days after the Las Vegas tragedy, I said that "in the minds of these mad men, when they see Congress doing absolutely nothing, shooting after shooting, they read that as quiet acceptance of the carnage." I thought my language was purposeful but careful, but clearly I had touched a nerve, at least for one senator's family.

"I'm sorry he felt that way," I said. "My point is that there are real things that happen to people when we make bad decisions here. And when we don't use our positions to do anything to stop these shootings, I really think these people, whose minds are breaking, think that we're giving them the okay."

I remember the conversation trailing off after that—I'm not sure either of us wanted to get into an argument over which particular senators were to blame for kids and concertgoers being gunned down in cold blood. But he'd made his point.

I thought back to that conversation when I was doing research on the precipitous fall of gun violence rates in America after the passage of the two most significant gun control acts ever passed by Congress. In the next chapter we'll get into the modern phenomenon of mass shootings that started with the Columbine massacre and was seared into the public consciousness in December 2012. But since Sandy Hook, there has been a dramatic uptick in the times a man has chosen to deploy a semiautomatic rifle like the one used by Adam Lanza to indiscriminately kill scores of victims. This isn't a coincidence—these are copycat killings. In fact, among the evidence collected from Lanza's room was material suggesting he had meticulously researched earlier mass shootings to study methods and weapon choice.

My point about Congress's complicity is rooted in the theory that these young men, as their minds descend into a dark, shadowy place, unimaginable to you and me, where they rationalize the decision to exorcise their personal trauma through mass violence, take note of the silence at the highest levels of their nation regarding the choice they are contemplating. Yes, presidents and governors and senators send out statements condemning each mass shooting, and offer "thoughts and prayers" to the victims and their families. But these are empty words, and everybody knows it, especially after no actual policy changes are enacted as the mass shooting era continues to grip America. When Congress passes a major change in law, it is a legislative action *and* a moral action. Individuals look to leaders—yes, even leaders in government—for cues about the boundaries of acceptable behavior, and adjust their actions accordingly.

I remember sitting in a briefing in 2014 with Republican economist Douglas Holtz-Eakin as he tried to explain why healthcare inflation had stabilized in the years following the passage of the Affordable Care Act, even though, in his opinion, there were only a few real cost control measures in the bill. He explained a well-known social science experiment in which the productivity of factory workers was tracked in a factory where signals were given to workers that they were being observed by a supervisor, and in another where workers thought they were unobserved. The theory emanating from this study and others like it is called the Hawthorne Effect—the concept that people behave in different ways if they are being watched and judged. Holtz-Eakin surmised that costs had been contained because the relatively minor cost control provisions in the Affordable Care Act were a signal to the market that the federal government valued lower costs, and hospitals and health systems responded by going above and beyond the law's requirements to implement cost reduction measures. The values signal from a piece of legislation led to changes in behavior by private sector actors.

Could this same phenomenon have occurred in the aftermath of the 1930s gun control bills and the legislation of the early 1990s? The increase in gun homicides, especially those carried out by organized gangs and gangsters, were big news in the 1920s and early '30s, as was the violence of the 1980s and '90s. The Los Angeles riots had captured the nation's attention only six months before Clinton was elected president.

It would be a wild coincidence if the two biggest nosedives in violence in the last one hundred years began in the immediate aftermath of the passage of the two biggest gun control acts in the last one hundred years, and the former had nothing to do with the latter. Passing laws—taking automatic and semiautomatic weapons off the street and making it hard for violent criminals to buy guns—has had a dramatic effect on gun crimes. That's what study after study tells us, and we'll cover that in more detail in chapter 7. But likely so did the message that the government was sending about the *moral value* it, and the country, placed on decreasing violence in the years following the highly publicized escapades of the 1920s-era gangsters and the crime spree of the 1970s and '80s. Government took action to set a new expectation of society—that gun crimes were not to be glorified but eradicated—and individuals, in turn, responded by restraining their more violent instincts.

4

THE VIOLENCE WE SEE

THE NEW NORMAL

Shane Oliver's father, Pastor Sam Saylor, said something important to me the night we spoke in the north end of Hartford, almost under his breath. Complaining about how the local newscasters describe murders in Hartford, he noted that when talking about crime, "It's always 'the suspect is known to police.'"

Sam's point was simple but important—the local media, in covering urban crime, want to put their largely suburban viewership at ease by letting them know not to worry about the images they are seeing of police tape and flashing cruiser lights in Hartford. When the media say the shooting suspect is "known to police," they mean it's someone from Hartford. Probably someone with a criminal record. Probably African American. Probably poor. You have nothing to worry about in quiet suburbs like Wethersfield or Glastonbury or Simsbury, implies the anchor. It's just the same small circle of young African American men shooting one another, and you have little to fear so long as you never set foot in the north end of Hartford, which you don't need to do anyway because Connecticut has made sure few critical services or state offices or companies that you do business with are in the north end of Hartford.

Violence, if it doesn't threaten your family or your neighborhood, is relatively easy to ignore. You can turn on the television for the late evening news and remain a voyeur. It's always been that way. I grew up just blocks away from Hartford, and there was not a single day of my life when I worried that I would be shot walking to school. I had not a single close friend or relative who had ever been assaulted with a weapon of any kind. I read about what happened in places like Hartford and New Haven in the newspaper, but I just made sure that I didn't spend any more time in those places than I absolutely needed to. And when I applied to colleges, I just left the University of Hartford and Yale off my list. There were plenty of other safe small towns where I could go spend four years.

For Sam Saylor, the way that the news constantly marginalized and explained away gun homicides in Hartford was a dismissive construct to allow in-group leaders to make sure that no one outside of the north end really had to worry about what happened to Shane. Nobody in Wethersfield ever had to come to Hartford's rescue because Hartford's problems showed no signs of spilling across its southern boundary. That's what the newscasters told us every night. So Shane's death was Sam and Janet's private pain, and nothing was going to change that.

Until it all changed.

· · ·

There are many days that I wish I had not seen and heard the things I did that day, at the Sandy Hook firehouse. And to be honest, you won't get much of the details of that day in this book. I felt strongly, upon making the decision to write this, that the story of what happened inside that elementary school during those earth-shattering five minutes, and what happened in the firehouse as twenty sets of parents came to the crippling realization that their children were not coming out of the school alive, is, by and large, not my story to tell. Nor is the story of the indescribable grief and sorrow that the families of those children have lived with, from that day until this day. Though the parents of so many of the children killed in Sandy Hook are now close friends, I was merely a witness—an interloper—on that horrible day. I often say my life changed that afternoon, but that description feels cheap and over-blown given that so many other lives changed that day, too, in ways that make my transformation feel inconsequential.

So this isn't a book about what happened in Sandy Hook. But I do want you to know what happened to *me* that day, and what happened to *the country*. Because in many ways, America awoke that day, and the nation has not closed its eyes since. All of a sudden, nowhere felt safe. Adam Lanza wasn't "known to police." Sure, he was a loner and an outcast, but he had no history of violence, and every town has its share of loners and outcasts. Adam Lanza didn't live in a blighted neighbor-hood that you never had to visit. He lived in Sandy Hook—a town that looks like every other small suburban hamlet in America.

All of a sudden, gun violence was unavoidable. If the epidemic was contained to Hartford or Chicago, then it could happen only in places that looked like Hartford and Chicago. And most Americans don't live in places that look like Hartford and Chicago. But if twenty first grad-ers could vanish in the space of five minutes of gunfire in Sandy Hook, Connecticut, then this kind of mass violence could happen anywhere. Now, *everyone* was a potential target. The tectonics of the modern American conversation on violence policy shifted beneath our feet that day.

But the tectonics of the gun lobby had shifted, too, in the decades leading up to the Sandy Hook shooting. Unprepared and unready to stop the 1934 and 1994 laws, they had since the 1990s transformed themselves into a political juggernaut, able to channel the fears and insecurities of Americans into a ruthless political movement designed to protect the profits of the gun industry and ward off any attempts to make the sale of firearms any more difficult or onerous. The gun lobby was ready for the moment that was created by the Sandy Hook shooting. This chapter is the story of America's mass shooting epidemic, and the story of how the gun industry became so powerful as to block any changes in law to do something about it.

· · ·

I've never experienced a feeling of helplessness quite like that afternoon at the Sandy Hook firehouse. An hour after Governor Malloy delivered the grisly news to the parents there, I was glad to get a phone call from one of my close friends in the U.S. House of Representatives, Colorado Democrat Ed Perlmutter. Ed is a generation older than me but has the energy of a man in his twenties and the excitability of an adolescent. We formed a close bond during my six years in the House of Representatives, and I knew why Ed was so eager to call.

"You know I've been through two of the damned things, Murphy. Columbine and Aurora. And it's just horrifying. Horrifying," Ed said as his voice cracked slightly.

"What am I supposed to do right now, Ed?" I asked.

"Three things. First, just be there. Be there today. Be there tomorrow, the next day. I know it won't always feel right, to just be hanging around, but trust me, folks want you there. And you never know when you might be needed."

"Okay."

"Second, don't be afraid to talk to the press. I get it—it doesn't feel right to be on TV talking about other people's pain. But you were elected to be their voice—so do it. Take the pressure off the families and the first responders and talk to the press. You're good at it, and people will appreciate that they don't have to do it."

"Got it."

"And third, take care of yourself, Murph. Hug Cathy and your kids a lot these next few days. And talk to somebody if you can't get over the sadness."

I hung up the phone and stepped away to the back wall of the firehouse, hoping to collect my thoughts. The world was descending on Sandy Hook—thousands of journalists, television crews, and evening news anchors—and I knew that Ed was right. I needed to help translate to the country what had happened and how Sandy Hook was going to survive and recover. But I was consumed at that moment by a crippling realization: This wasn't just about this little town. Newtown was simply the confirmation moment for the nation that this new phenomenon of disgruntled, tortured young men turning powerful weapons on innocent civilians was not going away. Sandy Hook was not an outlier. It was the new normal. And the hairs on the back of my neck straightened as I tried to understand how on earth I would explain such a chilling idea to the nation.

. . .

Here's the undeniable, frightening reality: Over half of the twenty deadliest mass shootings in the 240-year history of the United States have occurred in the past twenty years. The massacre of 27 in Sandy Hook was followed by 12 gunned down at the Washington Navy Yard; 14 dead at a San Bernardino, California, holiday party; 49 murdered at the Pulse nightclub in Orlando, Florida; 58 killed at a concert in Las Vegas, Nevada; 26 fatally shot at a church in Sutherland Springs, Texas; and 17 murdered at a high school in Parkland, Florida. Another data set of mass shootings analyzed by *Mother Jones* found that since 2011, the pace of mass shootings has tripled. Up until 2011, there were an average of 172 days between mass murders. Now we average a mass shooting every two months.

Before we go any further, it's probably important to define what I mean by *mass shooting,* because depending on your definition, the data can tell us different things. I'm going to refer to a mass shooting, for the purposes of this book, as the murder of four or more people in public by someone who had no specific connection or relationship to the victims before the incident. But I acknowledge that this is a fairly arbitrary distinction, especially since the pain associated with a mass murder doesn't change whether the assailant and victim knew each other beforehand. Admittedly, in my public comments I often use a broader definition—for instance, on New Year's Eve 2015, I got worked up into such a lather reading an article on all the mass killings that year that received no national press attention that I stayed up all night personally sending 149 separate tweets detailing the 372 incidents where four or more people had been shot at one time in 2015.

But I think that it makes sense, in the context of this book's broader review of American violence, to think of the more random episodes of mass violence as worthy of separate attention, largely because whether I like it or not, the American public has simply decided to place a different premium on nonpersonal mass violence. As Sam Saylor poignantly noted, our brains process random, nonpersonal violence differently than other types of crime. When there is no clear, personalized motive, lethal violence is much harder to explain or rationalize and, as we covered in chapter 2, that causes us to struggle with what in our nature could cause such a seemingly unprovoked explosion of human violence. And for now, public policy conversations are driven by these kinds of shootings. Knowing the public's fascination with nonpersonal violence, journalists flood these crime scenes while leaving family violence or gang-related mass shootings on the back pages of local newspapers.

It's worth noting that the fear we feel when watching the news cover another public mass shooting is, actually, pretty irrational. While coverage of random, public mass shootings clog our airwaves, you are more likely to die by a weather event or by choking on your food than you are in a mass shooting. That stands in contrast to the other kinds of gun violence that do not seem to provoke such intense interest and fear. Interpersonal gun homicides, suicides, and accidental shootings are on the rise, too, so much so that today gunshot wounds kill more Americans than automobile accidents and house fires.

Whether or not the fear of a mass shooting is justified, it is real. The indiscriminate mass killings compel us to think about what has gone so wrong in this nation that someone would feel so aggrieved, so left out, as to take out their misery on so many innocent people. Many who obsess over mass shootings might not actually worry too much that they will be next. They just want to know what's wrong with us, what *has changed,* and why this cataclysm is happening over and over and over. Is the sickness that causes shooters to do such damage a reflection of a broader sickness that infects all of us, even if we don't all manifest the symptoms in violent rages and criminal acts? *Half of the twenty worst mass killings in the country's history have happened in the past twenty years.* This cannot be a coincidence, right?

"PSEUDO-COMMANDOS"

By early afternoon, the name *Adam Lanza* was whipping through the gathered masses at the firehouse. Rumors began to swirl about the murderer's background, his motive, and his movements in the hours leading up to the massacre. The more we learned, the more familiar Lanza became. Like almost every mass murderer in America, he was male. He had an affinity for powerful, military-style firearms and a fascination with prior mass shootings and other killers. He had many diagnoses, but, like other shooters, he had not been diagnosed with a mental illness. And, perhaps most important, like all of those other mass shooters, Adam Lanza felt he was an American outcast, with real and imagined grievances against his peers—and society in general—that caused him to believe that the only mechanism to exorcize his grudges was mass murder. While each shooting is unique, the similarities outweigh the differences, and so it makes sense to spend some time trying to figure out who these mass shooters are, and why these massacres happen over and over and over.

Eighty percent of all murderers are male. So the small sample of mass murderers likely simply reflects the broader trend of male violence. Over the course of millennia, males have been bred for violence. They may have started out more violent, in pre-civilization eras, because their bodies were adapted to combat, but now that the physical action required to commit murder is the simple pull of a trigger, anatomy cannot explain why men still carry out the overwhelming majority of lethal crimes. Men's brains, and the social pressures that interact with those brains, are just different from the neurological and psychological makeup of women.

In a 2012 paper, Michigan State University professor Melissa McDonald gathered up all the data in favor of the "warrior hypothesis" to explain male violence. Men are more likely than women to harbor prejudicial and dehumanizing feelings toward out-groups, which can spur the motivation and rationalization for violence. More men than women prefer group hierarchies dependent on the perpetuation of in-groups and out-groups, and thus end up acting out in order to reinforce these hierarchies. (For many mass shooters, envy resulting from being an involuntary member of an out-group is their primary motivation.) And research shows that men are more likely than women to use violence as a tool early in a dispute. McDonald refers to a number of studies in which during war game simulations men are much more willing to use "preemptive strikes" against an adversary without any real provocation.

. . . .

As it turns out, I was wrong when I told my colleagues that Sandy Hook was "sickness disguised as evil." Adam Lanza was never diagnosed with a mental illness, and neither are most mass shooters. Dr. Michael Stone, a forensic psychiatrist from Columbia University, produced an exhaustive study of these kinds of murders and found that only one in five mass killers had what could be diagnosed as a mental illness. Most of these, like Congresswoman Gabby Giffords's assailant, were paranoid schizophrenics. But a lack of diagnosis doesn't equate to a lack of illness, so Stone went further and examined the behaviors and medical records of the mass killers and found that half of them had no clear evidence of an undiagnosed mental health disorder. This squares with larger data sets of perpetrators of violent crime, of which people with severe mental illness make up only 5 percent.

Let's spend a minute unpacking what I mean by *mental illness*, because when you hear that few mass killers are actually mentally ill, that probably sounds absurd. *If you choose to shoot up a church or a movie theater or a school, you must, by definition, be mentally ill,* most Americans would argue. But making a terrible decision—even choosing to commit mass murder—does not automatically mean you have a mental illness. Most Americans would concede that someone who carries out a single homicide in a fit of rage—maybe killing an estranged girlfriend or a member of a rival gang—is not automatically mentally ill. But taking a life intentionally, whether it be one or a dozen, is a cataclysmic, sociopathic act no matter the number of victims. Why, then, do we assume that mass killers are mentally ill, but those who just take one life are not?

Mental illnesses are defined, diagnosable conditions. There are 297 of them listed in the fifth edition of the hulking 947-page *Diagnostic and Statistical Manual of Mental Disorders* (called the "DSM–5" by healthcare insiders), the mental health practitioner's bible of symptoms and diagnoses. In Congress today, I have become what passes for an "expert" on mental health (in politics, expert status is achieved by working on the topic a shade more than the rest of your colleagues), and as much as I rely on the DSM–5 to make policy, I am admittedly more and more wary of the ability of doctors and medical professionals to accurately label the different ways our brains function. There are absolutely clear ways to diagnose certain mental illnesses, but the more I learn about the human brain the more I believe that its malformations and misfirings resist convenient categorization. The disciplines of mental health and developmental disabilities rely on neatly organized diagnoses and billing codes, but in truth, I think there are probably not clear distinctions between "developmental disorders" and "mental illnesses."

But whether or not the DSM–5 accurately categorizes the disorders of the brain, there is simply no correlation between the conditions that we label today as mental illness and violence of any kind, certainly not mass violence. Yes, anyone who carries out a preplanned mass murder is likely working with a brain that is different from mine or yours, but that's not the same as saying the person is mentally ill. Charleston church shooter Dylann Roof was dangerously angry, virulently racist, socially marginalized, and full of conspiracy theories. The mix of these influences contributed to his decision to commit an abominable act. But he didn't have a mental illness.

Adam Lanza's youth and adolescence were consumed with a process of trying to discover what was "wrong" with him. He was antisocial and "wracked by anxiety," according to the mother he would later murder in her bed. He was eventually pulled out of formal schooling, and in his final two years of life he basically retreated from society and into his darkened room, communicating only with his mother and a ghoulish group of Internet acquaintances. His diagnoses over his twenty years were numerous (sensory integration disorder, obsessive-compulsive disorder, Asperger's syndrome), but these are developmental disabilities and disorders, not mental illnesses.

The danger of reflexively describing all murderers, or at least all mass murderers, as mentally ill is that this deepens the already debilitating stigma for those who suffer with mental illness. Society constantly falls into the trap of equating mental illness with violence, and it makes my blood boil every time.

In March 2015, Andreas Lubitz was piloting a Germanwings plane carrying 144 passengers from Barcelona to Düsseldorf, Germany, when he locked his copilot out of the cockpit and deliberately plunged the plane to its demise in the French Alps. No one survived, and the press immediately obsessed over Lubitz's history of depression and the "discovery" that as many as one in eight pilots may suffer from clinical depression. Lubitz's act of mass murder was unforgivable, but it doesn't mean that pilots with depression (or even those with previous suicide attempts) are more likely than anyone else to do something horrific like intentionally crash a plane. All that likely happened in the wake of the Germanwings crash was that fewer mentally ill pilots sought out diagnosis and treatment because of their worries that their careers would be affected by being lumped in with Lubitz. That's what happens when we assume that the mentally ill have a propensity toward violence.

Of course, the trope of using mental illness as a facile explanation for incidents of mass gun violence is a favorite of the gun lobby. Within hours of a mass shooting, your television will be filled with gun industry allies arguing that mass shootings are a "mental illness problem." One of my colleagues, Iowa Republican Joni Ernst, summed up this position beautifully days after Parkland. "The root cause is not that we have the Second Amendment," she said. "It is that we're not adequately addressing mental illness across the United States. We need to focus on that, and we need to focus on substance abuse."

But more than 60 percent of all mass murders in the world since 1983 have happened in America, a mass violence rate twelve times higher than one would expect for a nation that comprises less than 5 percent of the world's people. So if mental illness is to blame, shouldn't we have a much higher rate of mental illness than all these other countries that have virtually no mass killers?

Of course, America has no higher rate of mental illness than the rest of world. We just have all the mass killings. Further, if mental illness were to blame, and 97 percent of mass shooters are men, you would expect men to disproportionally suffer from mental illness. But in fact the opposite is true. Women in America suffer through the same life experiences and stresses as men, but they are 40 percent more likely to develop a mental health condition than men. Yes, it's true that shooters' brains work differently than others. But it's both wrongheaded and dangerous to explain away the phenomenon of mass shootings through the prism of mental health.

. . .

So if America doesn't have more men than other countries and doesn't have more mentally ill people than other nations, then what is different about us that causes this almost exclusively American epidemic? Well, here's the simplest and perhaps most important truth: It is just much easier to commit mass murder in America. Why look for a more complicated answer when the simple one is staring you in the face? It's easier in general to get a gun here than anywhere else. And it's much easier to get your hands on guns that will kill many people very quickly. And it's easy to transport those weapons to your chosen place of assassination.

There were likely people on Adam Lanza's mass shooting message boards from all over the world, but if you are chatting about mass murder in countries in Europe or Asia, the barriers to obtaining the machinery that would make it possible are often prohibitive. And if you don't think the gun matters, just ask the parents of twenty-two children in the village of Chengping, China, where on the exact same day Adam Lanza shot and killed twenty kids in Connecticut, a young man by the name of Min Yingjun walked into a local elementary school with similar homicidal notions. But Min had a knife instead of a gun, and while he managed to injure twenty children, not a single one of them died.

Access to guns matters.

An obsession with weapons, combined with the means to easily obtain them, is at the heart of the American mass shooting experience. In Adam Lanza's case, he didn't become a gun enthusiast on his own. Adam's mother first took him to a shooting range at the age of four, and over the course of their twenty years together, purchasing and using guns became a rare bonding activity for mother and son. By the time that Adam turned one of those weapons on his mother, their house's weapons cache rivaled many military arsenals. That morning at Sandy Hook Elementary School, Lanza brought with him a twelve-gauge semiautomatic shotgun, a Bushmaster .223 caliber semiautomatic rifle, and two semiautomatic handguns. He left at home three other guns and hundreds of rounds of more than thirty different varieties of ammunition. On his wall in his room was a seven-by-four-foot poster he had created detailing the five hundred most deadly mass shootings, ranked by the number of fatalities, and scattered around were the boxes to the first-person shooter video games he played, like Doom and Half-Life.

But Lanza's focus on deadly weapons mirrors that of other mass killers. Stephen Paddock, the Las Vegas killer, had twenty-three guns in his hotel room and another twenty-four back at his two homes. Nikolas Cruz, the Parkland teen who killed seventeen at his former school, filled his social media accounts with talk and pictures of weapons. "Everything he posts is about weapons," said a classmate. "It was sick."

An important question is whether the ability to carry weapons of mass destructive capability and don tactical gear designed for the military gives shooters a perverse false confidence that spurs them to do things they would not if they couldn't dress up like the characters they control in video games. Would Paddock have carried out his assault if he could shoot only pistols equipped with ten-round magazines out his hotel window? Would James Holmes have entered that Aurora movie theater if he wasn't able to suit up in a ballistic helmet, vest, leggings, throat protector, and tactical gloves? Elliot Rodger, the college student who killed six in Isla Vista, California, in 2014, posted a chilling YouTube video prior to his shooting, describing the feeling of buying his first semiautomatic handgun. "After I picked up the handgun, I brought it back to my room and felt a new sense of power. Who's the alpha male now, bitches?"

And for young American men contemplating mass violence, coming up with a rationalization is often just as easy as finding the weapon. It isn't coincidence that these shootings, including the type of weapons used and the attire worn, have followed a disturbingly similar script. Lanza's wall chart is the most chilling example, but research clearly shows that mass shootings are "contagious"—the more that occur and populate the news, the more that follow.

Why does this happen? One theory is that media coverage of mass shootings can "plant a seed" in the mind of someone who is on the verge of carrying out a similar crime, legitimizing their homicidal thoughts. Jesse Osborne, an eighth grader who opened fire on a playground in Townville, South Carolina, followed the news of previous mass shootings closely. "I HAVE TO BEAT ADAM LANZA . . . At least 40," he wrote on a message board nine days before the September 2016 shooting. He googled on his phone, "deadliest US mass shootings" and "youngest mass murderer." As the American public begins to accept mass shootings as the new normal and as the news media gives relentless coverage to these "pseudo-commandos," it serves to unintentionally rationalize and encourage the nascent plans of other potential mass murderers who are looking to justify their homicidal urges.

. . .

The final uniquely American aspect of mass shootings is perhaps the hardest to discuss—the insecurity that convinces these men to convert their intense sense of persecution and mistreatment into an excuse to commit horrible acts of awesome violence. James Knoll, a psychiatry professor at the Syracuse campus of the State University of New York who coined the term "pseudo-commando," neatly describes a common through line in the typical modern mass killer:

> [He] is an injustice collector who spends a great deal of time feeling resentful about real or imagined rejections and ruminating on past humiliations. He has a paranoid worldview with chronic feelings of social persecution, envy, and grudge-holding. He is tormented by beliefs that privileged others are enjoying life's all-you-can-eat buffet, while he must peer through the window, an outside loner always looking in.

Adam Lanza's grievance was against society in general, which he excoriated online for trying to control and deaden individuals, which is perhaps what he felt that his mother and the therapists she hired had tried to do to him. He equated civilization with mind control, and though he took his specific motive for targeting the elementary school to his grave, he became fascinated with mass killings and seemed to clearly justify murder as a proper response to society's efforts to impose social conformity on others.

Other killers share this intense feeling of exclusion and resentment that builds until it explodes: Dylann Roof in Charleston toward African Americans. Elliot Rodger in Isla Vista toward the people he believed looked down on him. Devin Patrick Kelley in Sutherland Springs had a more personal motive—revenge against family members—but his rationale was no doubt connected to grudges that he had collected over time.

In other countries, these resentments don't turn into mass shootings. And maybe the easy access to the means of mass slaughter in America, combined with the copycat phenomenon, explains much of our epidemic. But there's one final avenue to explore: a pair of developing American pathologies that may make these grievances more acute and thus more likely to trigger dangerous, outlandish reactions.

The first is the growth in the value of self-admiration and personal celebrity that has spread like a virus in the late stages of the twentieth century and early parts of the twenty-first. The election of Donald Trump, whose primary personal achievement was, in fact, celebrity, was the final confirmation that fame, realized by nearly any means, is a worthy end in and of itself. Decades ago, the most famous Americans achieved their status by accomplishment—through song or sport, valor or innovation.

Today, perhaps the most famous American—Kim Kardashian—is famous, well, just because she's famous (and maybe the sex tape). Teens measure their worth by how many people amplify their Instagram posts, and millions of Americans pay close attention to how many followers they gain and lose every day on Twitter. America is in the midst of an epidemic of vanity, and for those on the outside of the fame parade, the judgment, real or simply perceived, can feel heavy, embarrassing, and unjust. So, for unstable minds, the mass shooting can be viewed as the quickest mechanism to make an elusive imprint. Christopher Harper-Mercer, the killer of nine at an Oregon college in 2015, wrote prior to his rampage, "Seems the more you kill, the more you're in the limelight." Columbine shooter Dylan Klebold mused that "directors will be fighting over this story" in a video made shortly before the massacre.

The second developing pathology that intimately relates to this culture of conceit is the growing narcissism of younger generations of Americans. In 2009, psychologists Jean Twenge and Keith Campbell published a powerful and influential book entitled *The Narcissism Epidemic: Growing Up in the Era of Entitlement*. Narcissists, the authors explain, "believe they are better than others, lack emotional warmth and caring relationships, constantly seek attention, and treasure material wealth and physical appearance." Backed by extensive personality survey data, Twenge and Campbell make the case that millennials (roughly those born in the 1980s and 1990s) are much more likely to exhibit these egocentric personality traits than prior generations of Americans. This trend would, of course, logically dovetail with a society that has come to place an increased premium on personal notoriety, but narcissists are different from simple attention seekers in that they believe that they alone have a power and ability to control the reality around them.

The outcast narcissist, thus, presents a unique danger. Twenge and Campbell suggest that while overall crime rates have dropped over the past twenty years, crimes connected with damaged outsized egos—a category into which many mass shootings would fit—have actually increased. And this makes some sense. When narcissists fall behind their peers, or face painful exclusion from in-groups, they take it harder than others. For the tiny portion of outcast narcissists who end up committing mass violence, it may be that their belief in their own power allows them to rationalize taking drastic personal responsibility for remedying a wrong that may be personal, but is extrapolated to a wider set of victims. In an America where self-obsession is no longer a personality flaw but a virtue, damaged minds can find toxic ways to rationalize extreme action.

MY COLD DEAD HANDS

The community of Sandy Hook struggled to keep from drowning in the days following the shooting. The parade of wakes and funerals was incessant. Memorial processions and TV satellite trucks competed for space on the few roads that bisected the town. The surviving schoolchildren and teachers began to pass through the early stages of their own trauma, and schools remained closed day after day. The crush of media meant that no grieving survivor could go anywhere in town without having a camera and microphone thrust in their face. I was there every day that I could be, and the scene was nightmarish.

The counterweight to this chaotic aftermath was the overwhelming grace that showered down on Sandy Hook from outside the town. A campaign was launched to send teddy bears to the children of Sandy Hook. Within weeks, town leaders who had rented out a local warehouse to store the sixty-seven thousand stuffed animals that had flooded into the town had to launch a counter-campaign to beg caring, generous people to stop sending teddy bears to Sandy Hook. A charitable fund was launched to support the families of the victims and pay for the mental health and grief counseling needs of the community. It raised an astounding $28 million.

It felt like the conversation about gun violence was changing quickly, too. That weekend, I watched my future colleagues in the Senate go on television and do the unthinkable: reverse their position on guns. Bob Casey of Pennsylvania, who ran for the Senate in 2006 as a "pro-life, pro-gun" candidate, announced that after a long talk with his wife and daughters about the implications of Sandy Hook, he would now vote for a ban on both assault weapons and magazines holding more than ten bullets. Mark Warner, an NRA-supported senator from Virginia, announced that "enough is enough" and stated his willingness to support gun restrictions he had opposed in the past.

I followed Ed Perlmutter's advice and started accepting offers to speak for Sandy Hook on the national news shows. That Sunday, all the weekend news shows converged on Connecticut to broadcast live from Newtown, and I was scheduled to appear on two of them with my soon-to-be Senate partner Richard Blumenthal. But I was still hesitant—I knew I would be asked about gun control measures, and it felt wrong to introduce the issue into the ongoing tragedy so soon after the shooting. My staff warned me about the danger of "politicizing" the shooting, and I readied noncommittal, milquetoast answers to the expected queries about the legislative path ahead.

I arrived early for my appearance on *This Week with George Stephanopoulos,* and the show's producer took me to a waiting room where the show's guests were gathered. My jaw dropped two inches when I looked across the Newtown High School classroom that had been turned into a green room and recognized Utah congressman Jason Chaffetz, one of the chief opponents of new gun laws in the House of Representatives, sitting in a chair getting his makeup done. I was there because as the congressman for Sandy Hook, I had an obligation to speak for and represent my district. But what the hell was an NRA ally from across the country doing here, in Newtown, forty-eight hours after the shooting? I thought to myself, What cold-blooded gall it must take, to travel all the way from Utah to suburban Connecticut to stick your finger in the eye of parents who have yet to bury their children, and do the bidding of the gun industry. It was my first indication that a big fight lay ahead.

On Monday, I returned to Washington to lead the moment of silence in the House. All week, the buzz increased about the possibility of Congress taking up legislation to crack down on illegal and military-style weapons. More and more congresspeople were expressing an openness to re-imposing the ban on assault weapons or high-capacity magazines, and discussions started again of reforming the broken national background check system, which no longer applied to many gun sales that occurred online or in gun shows. As the week wore on, the complete silence from the NRA gave the impression that they knew the national conversation had shifted away from their hardline position. I imagined gun industry leaders holed up in the organization's Virginia headquarters, drafting a legislative proposal that would be their first gambit in the inevitable coming debate.

On Thursday, six days after the shooting, Richard Blumenthal and I flew back from Washington and returned to Newtown, this time for the wake of little Grace McDonnell. As we stood in the endless, slow-moving line, I started up a conversation with a young couple in front of us who had two rambunctious children scampering about at our collective feet.

"How do you know the McDonnells?" I asked.

"Our daughter was in first grade with Grace," the mother said, stone-faced.

I froze, stuttering out a few inaudible sounds as I tried to figure out what the right next thing to say was.

"She was out sick on Friday," the woman said, looking at the floor. "She was out sick."

I tell people, when they ask how Newtown is doing these days, that the town will never, ever be the same. When twenty children vanish from the face of the earth, in five minutes, in a town as small as that, there is no recovery. Four of the children lived on the *same street*. And then . . . gone. It is impossible to truly comprehend the scope of the cataclysm until a mother tells you that all of her daughter's friends are *dead*.

When Blumenthal and I finally got up to the McDonnells, I was glad that he was the first to greet the grieving mother and father. We had a brief conversation, and then, as we were readying to move on, Blumenthal said to the McDonnells, carefully, "You know, whenever you're ready to talk to us, about what you want us to be doing to make sure this doesn't happen again, just let us know."

I winced. I worried it was too soon to be engaging parents in the political fights of Congress. But Mrs. McDonnell didn't flinch. She looked Blumenthal in the eye, and said, purposefully and calmly, "We are ready. *Now.*"

I remember her words feeling like permission. Yes, it was the sentiments of only one of twenty sets of parents, but I needed a mother or a father to tell me that I wasn't "politicizing" the death of their child by forcefully advocating for the laws to change.

We left the wake and walked across the street to a church basement where several dozen Newtown parents and citizens had arranged an impromptu meeting to begin organizing for action on gun laws. It was a quick window into a national movement that was forming, at that very moment, all across America. The individuals in that church cellar would come to form the Newtown Action Alliance, today one of the most powerful voices for gun safety in the country. That night, it was simply an angry but committed group of parents who knew that, somehow or some way, everything must change.

.   .   .

The next day was Grace's funeral. One week had passed since the shooting, and the day began with a short memorial service on the steps of the town meeting hall. With Christmas fast approaching, I needed to get back home; Owen was having trouble understanding why his father had disappeared right in the middle of his favorite time of year. I was gone every night for memorials and wakes, community meetings and television appearances, and I would limp home late every night, after the kids were in bed, emotionally and physically exhausted. So my plan was to spend a full day in Newtown on Friday, attend the funerals for both Grace and Dylan Hockley, and hope that I had enough emotional energy left to spend the weekend with Cathy, Owen, and little Rider, cramming a month's worth of holiday traditions into two days.

Grace's funeral was a backbreaker, though. Both of her parents spoke, and the entire church's sobs rippled across the hall as her father stood at the pulpit, speaking directly to his deceased daughter, telling her how he was "so, so sorry" for having failed to be there, seven days earlier, to protect her. I sat there, slouched down in the pew, thinking to myself that there was no way I would be able to make it through a second service in the afternoon.

As the mourners filed out of the church, I pulled my phone out of my pocket and began scrolling through my Twitter feed. I noticed a social media fury growing around a speech recently delivered by NRA chief Wayne LaPierre, who had chosen Friday to break his organization's silence on Sandy Hook. I figured the uproar was over the insufficiency of the policy proposals he outlined in his remarks, and I pulled up the video of his speech as I stood next to my car, enjoying a few moments of fresh air before heading off to Dylan's memorial.

As the video played, my face went pale, and my body began to tingle with a combination of fury and fear. LaPierre wasn't offering *any* policy proposals to control the flow of illegal and dangerous weapons. He was brazenly advocating for the exact opposite response— increasing the number of guns in our schools. "The only thing that stops a bad guy with a gun is a good guy with a gun," LaPierre rumbled. He called for schools to arm themselves against potential future Adam Lanzas, asking "Would you rather your 911 call bring a good guy with a gun from a mile away, or a minute away?"

I was floored and deeply shaken. The NRA was *doubling down*.

· · ·

For most of the first three decades of the NRA, the long-term survival of the organization looked dubious. The state government of New York, the group's primary early patron, had ended its generous subsidy to assist in the mission of improving the marksmanship of soldiers in the wake of the Civil War. As funds dried up, the NRA sponsored shooting matches that were all the rage in the 1870s but began to fall out of favor. So the group's leaders decided to go after a bigger fish as their new sponsor—the U.S. government.

In 1907, the National Rifle Association made it official—their new headquarters would be in Washington, D.C. Their friend and card-carrying member Theodore Roosevelt was in the White House, and the NRA and other gun owners' groups decided to press their favor with the buccaneering chief executive by requesting the federal government sell surplus firearms to them at cost. Roosevelt agreed to the arrangement. Soon the NRA found other innovative ways for the government to keep them afloat. In 1912, Congress began providing funding for NRA-sponsored marksmanship events, and the army even detailed troops to assist in administering the competitions. After World War I, the NRA convinced Washington to limit the sales of surplus government guns to just their members, and membership began to increase as the allure of cheap weapons brought more people into the group's ranks. Between the two world wars, 200,000 army rifles flooded into the hands of recently signed-up NRA members. Hard-wiring the NRA to Washington's political class had saved the organization and made it the most powerful gun owners' advocacy group in the country.

Throughout the first seventy years of the twentieth century, the NRA remained primarily focused on helping its members obtain firearms and improve their marksmanship. It had a powerful political voice, but saw its role as trying to help, not hinder, Congress to adopt sensible laws restricting gun rights. The model firearms legislation that the NRA backed in the 1920s, and that many states adopted, would today probably be too radical even for some modern gun control enthusiasts. It required universal gun registration and a forty-eight-hour waiting period for all purchases, and conferred on local police departments the authority to refuse gun permits to anyone found to be a "drunkard, convicted criminal, drug addict, or minor."

In the halls of Congress, the NRA worked to soften gun laws passed in 1934 and 1938, but ultimately supported both on the House and Senate floor. In 1968, the NRA once again fought against a more aggressive version of the legislation but, in the end, supported a bill that reflected the group's view that the Second Amendment accorded only limited rights to gun owners. Shortly after the 1968 bill's passage, NRA president Harold Glassen explained to an audience of Duke University law students, "Does [the right to keep and bear arms] mean that every individual has a right to carry a gun at all times, concealed or openly? Obviously not." This position was widely shared by the leadership of the 1960s NRA.

But Glassen and the "old guard" NRA leadership had miscalculated by weighing in so definitively for the 1968 law, especially at a moment when the American conservative movement was entering a volatile era. Increasingly, new hardline conservatives believed that government regulation, in and of itself, constituted an evil to be resisted. Firebrand 1964 Republican nominee Barry Goldwater had set off a movement within the conservative ranks to brook less compromise, and had shifted the right toward more uncompromising, reactionary positions. In the 1970s, Jerry Falwell founded the Moral Majority, Howard Jarvis and Paul Gann launched the radical anti-tax Proposition 13 campaign in California, and the "sagebrush rebellion" against Department of Interior rules in the West gained steam. The NRA would not be immune to this revolution of conservative politics in America.

.　　.　　.

Harlan Bronson Carter was seventeen years old in 1931, when he walked into his family's home in the small Mexican border town of Laredo, Texas, to find his mother in tears. The border was the Carter family's livelihood—Harlan's father was a border agent, and Harlan was a few years away from joining the federal border patrol, an organization that he would eventually lead for the duration of the Eisenhower administration.

Harlan's mother told him she was worried about a group of Mexican Americans who had been loitering around the house all afternoon. She told her son she suspected they might have had something to do with the theft of their family's car a few weeks earlier. The teenager flew into a rage, grabbed his family's shotgun, and stormed off to confront the young men. He found them quickly, just as they were preparing to go for a swim, and demanded that they return to the Carter family home to be questioned about the stolen car.

They refused, and one of the men drew a knife for protection. Harlan pulled out his shotgun, and the young men scoffed at his bravado. *You'll never pull that trigger,* the young men yelled. But Harlan did, and shortly thereafter, seventeen-year-old Harlan Bronson Carter was convicted of murder. The conviction was eventually overturned due to improper jury instructions, but the damage to Harlan's reputation was already done. So he fixed it. He changed the second *a* in his first name to an *o,* and successfully covered up his gun murder for fifty years, until *The New York Times* discovered it in the course of reporting on the NRA in the wake of the attempted assassination of President Reagan.

In the 1970s, by then bald and nicknamed "Ol' Bullet Head," Harlon Carter had become the leader of the hardline wing of the National Rifle Association. He and his friends, plugged into the increasingly strident antigovernment wing of the conservative movement, were apoplectic that their organization had helped Congress pass the 1968 law that seemed to make arbitrary distinctions between legal and illegal firearms and that had set up a new bureaucracy—the Alcohol, Tobacco and Firearms (ATF) unit of Treasury—to be in charge of gun regulation. Carter wrote a letter to the entire NRA membership suggesting that in the future, the NRA take a different tack on any proposed legislation regulating firearms. "We can win it on a simple concept—No compromise. No gun legislation."

When, in 1976, the old guard fired seventy-four of Carter's allies from the organization and announced the group was moving its headquarters from politically charged Washington to Colorado Springs, Carter and his hardliners planned their takeover. At the 1977 NRA convention in Cincinnati, they packed the hall with more than one thousand of their supporters, voted down the move to Colorado, threw out the entire NRA leadership, and replaced them with Carter and his top lieutenants. Just before winning his new job, Carter took the convention dais and proclaimed, "Beginning in this place and at this hour, this period in NRA history is finished." He was right.

. . .

Gun sports scarcely mattered to the NRA any longer. Now it was about politics—all the time. Led by Carter, the group began building a case that the government's secret agenda was to disarm America, and any victory for the gun control movement was simply a move toward gun confiscation. Carter started hiring the best talent to lobby Congress and to fan out across the country to state capitals, including a young Democratic activist from Virginia by the name of Wayne LaPierre, who had turned down a job offer from Tip O'Neill.

Carter's team quickly scored a series of important victories, adding provisions to state constitutions in Nevada, New Hampshire, North Dakota, and Utah creating a state right to bear arms. In Congress, the NRA successfully flexed their new "no compromise" muscle, defeating any attempts to amend or improve the 1968 act. And then in 1980, it made its first-ever endorsement of a presidential candidate: Ronald Reagan. It sent field organizers all across the country to rally gun owners to his side, and mailed out more than eight hundred thousand postcards in battleground states.

Carter and his conservative allies also changed the vocabulary of the gun rights movement. Echoing Colt and Winchester, he rebranded the gun as the primary means by which Americans could secure and defend individual liberty amid a nation full of emerging threats to personal freedom. The primary enemy was the government, as the NRA relentlessly spun a narrative of a federal bureaucracy full of Second Amendment enemies (whom they later referred to as "jackbooted thugs") just waiting to enact their secret plan of gun confiscation.

But the NRA leadership also used the rising crime rates of the 1970s and '80s to inject a dose of racial and ethnic fear into their rallying cries. By the 1990s, the NRA had seamlessly melded together a broad patina of cultural gripes against ascendant out-groups into their agenda on gun rights. Said eventual NRA president Charlton Heston, in 1997, the year he joined the board:

Why is "Hispanic pride" or "black pride" a good thing, while "white pride" conjures up shaved heads and white hoods? . . . I'll tell you why: cultural warfare. . . . Mainstream America is depending on you—counting on you—to draw your sword and fight for them. These people have precious little time or resources to battle misguided Cinderella attitudes, the fringe propaganda of the homosexual coalition, the feminists who preach that it's a divine duty for women to hate men, blacks who raise a militant fist with one hand while they seek preference with the other.

Many white gun owners, fearing that if they remained unorganized they might lose their in-group status, responded to the new socially conservative, racially tinged direction of the NRA. When Carter took over in Cincinnati, the NRA had slightly over one million members. By the dawn of the 1990s, membership had more than tripled, to 3.7 million members. Clearly not all of the NRA's new members were drawn to the group by its new racially charged agenda, but the shift in tone and the surge in membership are certainly not coincidental.

And then, in 1981, John Hinckley, Jr., shot President Reagan. The attempted assassination gave birth to the first real organized political counterweight to the NRA, as Reagan press secretary Jim Brady, wounded badly in the attack, and his wife, Sarah, jump-started an organization dedicated to improving background checks and establishing a waiting period for handgun purchases. Sixty years before, this was the exact law that the NRA had suggested every state legislature enact. But now, the NRA set about destroying the case for stronger background checks and went on the offensive, pushing a bill that would repeal the 1968 protections and loosen restrictions on gun purchases.

It was a brazen strategy in the wake of an attempted gun murder of a U.S. president, and it worked. Though nominally supportive of the Bradys' goals, Reagan did little to push them forward. Instead, a Republican Senate and a Democratic House in 1986 sent to his desk the Firearm Owners' Protection Act. The bill was opposed by Democratic House leadership; demonstrating its new political power, the

NRA had organized a seldom-successful parliamentary maneuver called a discharge petition to force a vote in the House and had won.

Hailed by the NRA as "the law that saved gun rights," the legislation curtailed the ability of the ATF to oversee the private firearms market and greatly expanded unlicensed gun sales (including protecting gun shows from background check requirements). It was a stunning achievement for the gun rights movement.

But as crime rates spiraled throughout the 1980s and the Brady organization began to gain supporters, interest in gun control increased. The NRA was caught on its heels by this sudden surge in the power of the newly invigorated anti–gun violence movement, and some gun enthusiasts worried that Carter's crowd of revolutionaries (Carter himself retired from the organization in 1985) had by then become the "old guard," unable to meet the new challenges of an empowered change movement. In 1991, at the annual convention in San Antonio, just 150 miles due north on Interstate 35 from the town in which Harlon Carter had murdered that young Mexican American boy sixty years before, a new group of radicals took over the NRA leadership and installed Carter's protégé, Wayne LaPierre, as the group's new executive vice president.

The NRA, shortly after LaPierre took over, was caught resting on its laurels after the passage of the 1986 bill, and it couldn't stop a new Democratic president and emboldened Democratic Congress from finally passing the Brady bill in 1993. A year later, the ban on the sale of assault weapons and high-capacity magazines pushed by two new crusading members of the House and Senate, Brooklyn congressman Chuck Schumer and freshman California senator Dianne Feinstein, passed. But LaPierre smartly used these setbacks as a catalyst to once again grow the political muscle of the NRA. The group tied its fortunes to the brash, outspoken House minority leader Newt Gingrich and raised an unprecedented $70 million for the 1994 midterm election to target Democrats who had supported the Brady bill and the assault weapons ban.

Democrats were wiped out, and LaPierre went about the work of building a political mythology around the impact of the gun issue on swing races around the country. The truth is, the assault weapons ban was wildly popular in 1994. When none other than Ronald Reagan sent a letter to Congress pushing for the ban (along with former presidents Ford and Carter), he noted that a recent CNN/*USA Today*/Gallup poll had posted public support for the measure at an astounding 77 percent.

The ban and the Brady bill certainly may have helped energize some NRA members to vote Republican, but the actual defining issues of the 1994 elections were an unpopular President Clinton, an even more unpopular tax increase, and the failed healthcare reform effort. Clinton, unwilling to allow his personal unpopularity or his signature tax and healthcare bills to bear the blame for the defeat, and eager to memorialize his laudable courage on the gun bills, provided LaPierre with an unintended assist in exalting the NRA's influence. In his 2004 autobiography, Clinton wrote, "The NRA . . . could rightly claim to have made Gingrich the House Speaker." That was not true, but it became an article of political faith.

Testament to this new political reality, during the two decades that followed 1994, few prominent politicians dared take on the gun lobby and the NRA. In the House, when a high-profile shooting occurred, there was usually only one member willing to even talk about gun control to the press: New York representative Carolyn McCarthy, whose husband had been killed in a mass shooting on the Long Island Rail Road. Sensing the vacuum, the NRA and their allies rushed into the breach, racking up an overflowing bounty of legislative wins. They included:

- The 1996 Dickey amendment to the 1996 Omnibus Consolidated Appropriations Bill, barring the federal government from researching the causes of gun violence.
- A 1997 budget rider stopping the ATF from computerizing any of its gun sales records.
- A 2003 budget rider that required the ATF to wipe clean background check information within twenty-four hours, thus eliminating the ability to track gun trafficking.
- The 2004 expiration of the assault weapons ban.

- The 2005 Protection of Lawful Commerce in Arms Act, providing near-blanket immunity for gun manufacturers and dealers.

At the 2000 NRA convention, a buoyant and self-congratulatory Heston raised a flintlock rifle above his head and uttered the words that came to be synonymous with the NRA's no-compromise style and their justified political bravado. Warning the assembled gun enthusiasts that Democratic presidential candidate Al Gore would no doubt come for their weapons if elected, he raised a gun above his head and exhorted the vice president that the only way he would get his weapon was by prying it "from my cold dead hands!"

LOVE WINS

A week after the Sandy Hook shooting, *The Washington Post* published a long weekend piece entitled "History of Gun Control Is a Cautionary Tale to Those Who Want More Regulation." By and large, it was a fairly written article summarizing the previous twenty years of gun politics in America, but the headline summed up the conventional wisdom that had cemented in the decades following 1994: If you choose to take on the NRA, you're fucked.

Wayne LaPierre certainly believed *The Washington Post*'s analysis was correct. He was drawing another hard line in the sand in his speech the Friday after the shooting because he was making a wager—the same kind of bet that had paid off time and time again for the gun lobby. He believed, justifiably, that if he barked loud enough, the reputational power of his movement would stop any nascent gun control renaissance in its tracks. He believed he had taught smart, sensible politicians a lesson, over and over: Taking on the gun lobby wasn't worth it.

And that's exactly who and what I was, walking into St. Rose of Lima Roman Catholic Church that afternoon for one of the twenty-six memorial services that would occur in and around Newtown during the Christmas holiday. I was the dictionary definition of smart and sensible. And by being smart and sensible, I had become the youngest U.S. senator in America. And then, suddenly, as I slunk down in the passenger seat of my car to take the short drive from six-year-old Grace McDonnell's funeral to six-year-old Dylan Hockley's funeral, I had a revelation. A true-to-life epiphany—the first in my fifteen-year political career.

I did not care anymore what the smart, sensible thing to do was.

Sometimes, looking back, I wonder whether it was just a coincidence that it was during Dylan's funeral that I resolved to change myself politically, to live and act fearlessly in pursuit of the cause of anti–gun violence legislation. Of all the children who died that day, it would be Dylan that I would get to know best. It was his parents whom I would become closest to. It was his story that I would tell in the fifteenth hour of my filibuster in the summer of 2016 (following yet another massacre, this one in Orlando). Of course, that Friday afternoon, as I listened to the sobs from the audience as Dylan's favorite book, *Goodnight Moon,* was read aloud from the lectern, I had no idea this little boy with autism would become part of me. But there I was, struggling to pay attention as I began to plot how to build a movement that could finally *beat the gun lobby.*

Of course, I wouldn't be alone. The rest of Newtown's delegation— Senator Blumenthal and incoming congresswoman Elizabeth Esty— were just as committed to taking on the gun lobby. And there were signs that the scales were slowly tipping outside Washington. A CNN poll taken shortly after the shooting showed that national support for an assault weapons ban was up to 62 percent, with only 37 percent opposing the measure. As my swearing-in day approached in early January, there was reason to believe that Sandy Hook, by itself, had fundamentally changed the politics of gun violence.

On January 3, 2013, I became Connecticut's junior senator. At the ceremonial swearing-in with Vice President Biden, I was holding Rider in my left arm as Vice President Biden issued the instruction to raise my right hand for the oath of office. Without time to put Rider down, I hastily followed instructions, and mimicking his father, so did Rider. The result was a viral video, and a priceless, once-in-a-lifetime photo of Rider and me, raising our hands together, both getting sworn in to the U.S. Senate.

But I quickly came face-to-face with the impossibility of the task ahead of me. I was brand-new to the Senate—I had met only a handful of my colleagues, mostly those in the freshman class with whom I was going through orientation. I didn't even have an office yet. The small staff I had brought with me from the House and I were temporarily squirreled away in a tiny, cramped space in the basement of the Dirksen Senate Office Building, right across from the Senate office supply store. But now I had to perform an unmanageable multitask: introduce myself to senators and in the same breath lobby them on the most controversial bill upon which we would likely vote in 2013. *Ugh.*

I remember one particularly awkward phone call with Maine senator Susan Collins. She and I had spoken a few times over January, and I knew she was likely supportive of, at the very least, a universal background checks bill. But I needed her to go further, and so on a Saturday morning I called her from our house in Cheshire to convince her to join me on legislation to ban the kind of thirty-round high-capacity magazines that Adam Lanza had used in Sandy Hook.

I had no prior friendship with Susan. We didn't have a lot of life experiences in common, other than being senators. We hadn't worked on legislation together, of course, since I had been in the Senate for all of thirty days. So she knew I wasn't calling just to shoot the breeze, and it made for a pretty uncomfortable, perfunctory exchange of pleasantries. She was just waiting for me to get to the point, and when I did, she dropped the hammer.

"Chris, we don't know each other well, and I do really hope we'll get to work on things in the future. And you know I'm supportive of background checks, right?"

"I do, and I'm deeply appreciative of that. I wish there were more Republicans like you."

"But I think that's as far as I'm willing to go right now. I hope you understand."

I said I did, but I really didn't.

Twenty children had just been snuffed out by a skinny kid who weighed 115 pounds dripping wet. He probably didn't have enough strength to kill a single one of those children with his own hands, yet in less than five minutes he murdered twenty of them. That's largely because the bullets that emerge from the barrel of an AR-15-style rifle travel at four times the speed of bullets coming out of a Colt revolver.

One emergency room doctor told me once to fill up my sink with water and slowly run my fingers through the standing water, watching the ripples that extend from my moving fingers. Then, he instructed me, let the water settle and then run my fingers through at four times the speed, and watch how the ripples turn to waves and splashes, with water spilling over the edges of the sink. That, he said, is the difference in the damage done to your organs when a pistol bullet enters your body compared to a bullet from an AR-15. Little six-year-old bodies simply cannot survive the damage done by a projectile entering flesh at that speed, and none did that day.

The modern assault weapon was designed for the military, with the specific purpose of killing human beings as quickly and as efficiently as possible. Why would any thinking, compassionate human being believe that a weapon of that power—with no logical use other than to kill humans—should be in civilian hands?

Even harder to understand was Republicans' unwillingness to ban the thirty-round magazines Lanza and other mass shooters used. The less time mass shooters need to reload, the more they kill. It's that simple. Six children escaped one classroom in Sandy Hook, likely when Lanza fumbled with an exchange between cartridges. To fire 154 rounds, Lanza had only to change magazines a few times. What if he was able to bring only ten-round cartridges into the school, and he had to reload fifteen times instead of five or six? How many more kids would have had the chance to run out of the classroom and to safety? How many of those twenty would be alive today?

In Tucson, shortly after shooting Gabby Giffords in the head, Jared Lee Loughner fumbled with an exchange, and that's when bystanders were able to jump on him. There is no reason anyone using a gun to hunt, to target shoot, or to protect his or her home needs a thirty-round magazine or a hundred-round drum. They are the tools of mass murderers, and I was frustrated that I didn't have a preexisting relationship with people like Susan Collins so I could press more effectively as to why so many senators didn't see it the way I did.

But as the opening months of the legislative session wore on, I began to realize that Susan Collins was the least of my worries. In the weeks after Sandy Hook, I had assumed that a bill expanding criminal background checks to all gun purchases was the floor of what was possible to pass the Senate. Our case was simple—we weren't asking to change the intent of the original background checks law, which was to require a criminal check on commercial sales. But since commercial sales had migrated from brick-and-mortar stores to the Internet and gun shows, we needed to update the law and make sure the increasing numbers of gun buyers in these forums weren't criminals or the seriously mentally ill.

This change wouldn't have had an effect in Sandy Hook—the Lanza family bought their guns in licensed gun stores—but the families, many of whom were now regulars in the halls of Congress, were committed to making changes in laws that would cut down on gun murders wherever they happened, and they knew that universal background checks was a proven tool to reduce gun violence.

But only a few Republicans—including Susan Collins and John McCain—were willing to publicly endorse even this commonsense proposal. And several Democrats remained undecided, even after traditional NRA allies like Casey and Warner had shown the courage to break with the gun lobby. We weren't stuck because we were losing the argument on the merits; there wasn't a logical explanation for opposing making someone buying a gun at a gun show wait a few minutes while a background check is conducted. We were losing for a reason that was as simple as it was familiar: the power of the National Rifle Association. One afternoon in January 2013, after a particularly frustrating conversation with freshman Arizona senator Jeff Flake, who was spending the winter going back and forth on the background checks proposal, I was at my wits' end.

"We can't beat the NRA by working around them," I complained to

Joe Dunn, my top legislative staffer on guns. He was slated to focus exclusively on healthcare in my new Senate office, but given how shorthanded we were during the transition period, he was now working full-time on the still-in-formulation gun bill.

"Someone's got to just take them on directly," suggested Joe. "If we can't win on the merits, then let's show people that they aren't that scary."

And that's what we did. For the rest of the winter, as negotiations continued on the scope of the bill that would come before the Senate, Joe and I toiled in our little windowless basement space, doing a deep dive to understand the derivation of the power of the NRA. As we discovered vulnerabilities, we churned out report after report, trying to poke holes in the group's aura of political invincibility. We sent the reports around to other Senate and House offices. We pitched them to reporters. We held press conference after press conference. And along the way, I came to understand the influence of the gun lobby better than any other member of Congress.

. . .

The first thing we discovered was that the actual direct electoral power of the gun lobby was negligible. The NRA spent relatively modest sums of money compared to the growing array of super PACs that had come to dominate modern federal elections, and in many years the group lost substantially more races than it won. For instance, in 2012, the NRA-endorsed Senate candidate won only one out of seven races. From 2004 to 2010, the evidence suggests that there was no statistically significant advantage of an NRA endorsement, for either Republican or Democratic candidates. The NRA's reputation, it seemed, vastly exceeded the reality of their electoral muscle.

So where did the NRA's power come from if they didn't actually move the needle much in races? First, it's important to recognize that the most important principle in American politics is, perhaps, the squeaky wheel. Only 10 percent of Americans may oppose expanded background checks, but the NRA helps train that small coterie to amplify their voices to be louder than the 90 percent who support the measure. Second, the NRA's chief political success has been to transform their brand into a means for candidates to demonstrate their true conservative bona fides. As LaPierre and Heston used their bully pulpit to lead the fight on a broad array of conservative causes—opposition to affirmative action, gay rights, and abortion—the NRA endorsement became coveted as a conservative stamp of approval that communicated much more than simply a candidate's position on gun laws. While the data suggests the endorsement didn't matter as much in general elections, it became required to win in Republican primaries, and from 1994 to 2006, when Republicans controlled Congress, this was all that really mattered.

The second thing we discovered was that the gun industry had changed in the years since Harlon Carter revolutionized the firearms lobby. In 1993, when the Brady bill passed, you could find a gun in one-half of American households. Selling one or two guns to loads and loads of Americans was a sound business model thirty years ago. But after 1993, American attitudes about guns and gun violence began to change, and by the time Sandy Hook occurred, fewer than one in three households kept a gun inside. Along the way, the gun industry modified its business tactics, and the 2004 expiration of the assault weapons ban provided firearms companies with an important new profit center: expensive, powerful semiautomatic rifles and the countless accessories that can be attached to them. In 2006, gun dealers sold fewer than 400,000 of these "sporting rifles"; by 2016, just ten years later, the number had jumped to 2.3 million. And the profit margins were much bigger: AR-15-style guns sell for anywhere from $1,000 to $5,000, while the most popular handguns market for under $300. Just as the early gun marketers in the 1800s romanticized handgun ownership, so did the post-2004 gun advertisers link sporting rifle ownership with those same tried-and-true American ideals of liberty and individualism. It didn't hurt that these weapons were also being featured in increasingly popular first-person shooter video games, leading many gaming enthusiasts to see an AR-15 purchase as a way to pursue video game heroism in real life.

In addition to shifting their marketing strategy to these previously illegal weapons, the industry also figured out that they could make a lot more money by selling lots and lots of weapons to a small number of consumers, rather than fighting a losing battle by trying to sell one or two guns to a larger share of the potential market. This narrow focus has resulted in a mind-blowing concentration of weapons in the hands of a small number of Americans. Today, only 22 percent of Americans own any guns at all. But an even tinier percentage of Americans—3 percent—own a full 50 percent of all the weapons in private possession in the United States. That subset owns, on average, a personal arsenal of seventeen guns apiece.

One of the reports we released in early 2013 made the argument that the way that guns are sold has, of course, changed the way that the NRA lobbies and communicates. In fact, learning about this concentration of guns made LaPierre's post–Sandy Hook speech easier to understand. The NRA, which relies heavily on gun company funding, has little reason to speak to the full 22 percent of Americans who own guns when the industry's profits are driven by the 3 percent who buy most of the most profitable weapons. Many of these modern high-volume gun buyers are simply collectors and enthusiasts, caught up in the dizzying array of new models now available in a largely unrestricted marketplace. But many others are stocking up because they do, in fact, believe that private citizens need to be armed against a potentially confiscatory government, and an increasingly antigovernment, conspiratorial, uncompromising NRA platform is exactly the kind of talk that will convince these purchasers to keep bulking up their personal arsenals.

. . .

As winter turned to spring in 2013, it was clear that the NRA had successfully fought off the tougher measures, such as the reimposition of the assault weapons ban. I hadn't publicly given up, but the writing was on the wall that our best hope was to muster sixty votes (the threshold needed to pass legislation in the Senate) for a universal background checks bill. Unfortunately, there was one major problem with this idea—we didn't actually have a bill. Chuck Schumer, now a senator from New York and one of my early mentors in the Senate, had a version, but it had no Republican cosponsors, and it was generally agreed that a new, compromise bipartisan bill would have to be introduced if there was any chance of getting significant Republican votes. But still, with three months of the legislative session gone, and with momentum for change fleeting, there was still no bill.

Then an unlikely hero emerged from an unlikely place. Democratic senator Joe Manchin of West Virginia won his first race for Senate in 2010 by running a television ad in which he demonstrated how much he hated climate change legislation by picking up a shotgun and shooting a hole through the copy of the 2010 Democratic cap-and-trade bill. In thirty short seconds, he communicated to his conservative West Virginian voters how much he hated environmental legislation and how much he loved guns. But as he told me over and over again that winter, he was a politician second, and a father and granddad first. And like it did for so many others, Sandy Hook changed him.

Once I moved into my permanent office in the Hart Senate Office Building, we were located right next to Manchin's office, and I watched the Sandy Hook families move seamlessly from our office to his. Joe spent hours and hours with them, shedding tears and trying to figure out what he should do. He printed off pictures of all the children and put them up in his private office to serve as a daily prod to action. I watched him harangue and corral Republican senators all winter, trying to find a partner to work with on commonsense legislation. Finally, he got a tug at his line, and Pennsylvania Republican Pat Toomey, getting ready to run for reelection in a state that increasingly favored stronger gun laws, agreed to sit down with Joe to negotiate a bill. Joe told me that he thought they could get a background check reform bill that the NRA could support. I told him he was nuts but agreed to do all I could to help.

The Manchin-Toomey talks dragged on and on, and finally, Senate Majority Leader Harry Reid laid down the hammer—get a deal by the end of the day, Tuesday, April 9, or the Senate was going to move on to other business. That day, Manchin was scheduled to act as the presiding officer of the Senate. I saw him on the underground train that connects the Hart building to the Capitol, and I offered to preside in his place so that he could devote the entire day to finishing the bill. As I sat in the big chair on the dais of the Senate chamber, I was filled with conflicting emotions. Any time I got to sit in as the Senate president, occupying the seat reserved for the vice president of the United States, I was awed by the amazing privilege it was to serve in the Senate. But that day, I felt impotent as I sat helplessly inside the chamber while outside others were doing the real work of crafting legislation.

The next morning, Joe and Pat did indeed announce their compromise bill—expanding background checks to cover the gun shows that had been exempted in the 1986 NRA-backed law—and hope abounded that the Senate might break the historic logjam on gun policy and pass something meaningful. Back in Connecticut, we were preparing for President Obama's second visit to our state since the shooting. Sensing that the opportunity was upon us to get a bill passed, Obama gave a moving speech at the University of Hartford, with many of the Sandy Hook parents in attendance. "We have to believe that every once in a while we set politics aside," said Obama, "and just do what's right."

After the speech, Obama offered to let the Connecticut congressional delegation and the Sandy Hook parents hitch a ride with him on Air Force One back to Washington, so that the families could blanket Capitol Hill to lobby one last time for action. As I huddled on the plane with the families who were fast becoming my close friends, I came to a horrifying realization: No one had broken the news to them yet that the assault weapons and high-capacity magazine proposals—the changes that were most personal to the Newtown families—were effectively dead.

I perched on the edge of Nelba Márquez-Greene's seat. Her beautiful daughter, Ana, a musical prodigy just like her father, had been killed in Victoria Soto's classroom. "A background checks bill is the best we can do," I said. "I know it sucks. I know it's not enough. But we can't pass it if we don't have you all fighting for it."

The color drained out of the faces of the parents who had crowded around her chair. There was a moment of silence that felt like an eternity to me, as I awaited their judgment.

"I can't ever get Ana back," said Nelba. "But we can stop other kids from getting killed, and if this does that, then we have to push for it."

As we prepared to disembark at Andrews Air Force Base, Nelba pulled out a sheet of paper on which her niece had scribbled two words, and knowing that the cameras would be there to photograph the grieving parents arriving with the president to lobby Congress, she held it above her head as she descended the stairs. Her sign read LOVE WINS.

.   .   .

But love didn't win. The NRA pulled the rug out from under Joe and Pat and mounted a furious opposition to their bill. In the end, only four Republicans crossed the aisle to vote for the compromise bill, and it fell five votes short of sixty. My effort to expose the political fecklessness of the NRA hadn't put more than a dent in their political armor, and I walked out of the Senate chamber, fresh from defeat and full of mortal embarrassment. A group of Sandy Hook family members were waiting in a corridor just off the Senate floor.

"I'm so, so sorry," I whispered to Mark Barden, whose son Daniel was killed in the shooting. "I'm not giving up, Mark."

"We aren't either," he responded, wiping away tears. "This isn't about a four-month fight, Chris. This is the rest of my life."

We hugged and faced the cameras together to express our disappointment and heartache, but also our resolve for the future. It dawned on me that these relationships, forged in crisis over the four months following the shooting, would now become the most important personal bonds in my life, and that my self-worth as a legislator would be tied to my job approval among this small group of mothers and fathers and brothers and sisters. Nothing mattered more now than their belief in me, and their eventual satisfaction with the job I would do on their behalf.

Eventually, I snuck away from the scrum of reporters and walked the short distance to the rotunda of the Capitol, the second-floor space where above you is the majestic vaulted ceiling of the Capitol dome, and surrounding you are the vast, sprawling murals of American history. When I was sworn in to the House of Representatives in 2007, Nancy Pelosi, the incoming Speaker of the House, suggested that we use the rotunda as a refuge at the moments when the stresses of the job threatened to overwhelm us like a tidal wave. I took her advice, and from time to time, especially late at night, when the staff and tourists had cleared out, I would go quietly sit on one of the benches in the cavernous hall and marvel at the miraculous things that had happened in this building and reflect on how lucky I was, the son of a mother who grew up in public housing, to have a part in the grand theater of American politics.

As I sat looking up at the dome that afternoon, I realized that I wasn't the same person as the young, idealistic but analytic thirty-three-year-old congressman who'd showed up in Washington six years earlier. I didn't feel like just a politician anymore. I felt like an *activist*. The issue of gun violence—which had not occupied more than a handful of hours of my time prior to Sandy Hook—was now my political lodestone. And gone were the calculations of political pros and cons, and the assessments of what would be best for my own developing career ladder. Now, I was Sisyphus—waking each day to push the rock farther and farther up the hill, regardless of cost or risk or prospect of success, armed only with the blind faith that one day, we'd get that thing to the top.

5

THE VIOLENCE WE IGNORE

"Listen, we did three marches to the state capitol, talking about gun violence," the Reverend Henry Brown raged into the microphone, which his booming baritone voice had rendered totally unnecessary. "I didn't see none of you folks!"

I tried to find the right body language to convey the varying messages I thought appropriate while being yelled at in front of television cameras. *Sincere. Attentive. Remorseful. Unafraid.* How to do all that in one motion, I contemplated. After a few seconds of hesitation, I settled on leaning forward in my chair, resting my elbows on the table in front of me, and settling my chin down into my hands, shaped into a "v" and cupped over my mouth. Hopefully this will stop the yelling, I thought to myself.

Just seven days earlier, I had been sworn in to the U.S. Senate, and this was my first official visit to Hartford as their senator—a meeting with gun violence victims, their family members, and community activists to talk about the upcoming fight in Washington, D.C., over gun policy. I knew Reverend Brown from television but had never met him in person. The founder and leader of Hartford-based Mothers United

Against Violence, Brown himself was a survivor of gun violence. Years ago, while celebrating his discharge from the army with friends at a bar in rural Georgia, the then twenty-two-year-old went outside to the parking lot to help break up a fight. As he settled back into the club, one of the brawlers followed him in and shot him, point-blank, in the chest.

Brown spent the next week in a coma and, when he emerged, the bitterness and anger over what happened sent him into a personal descent that would last for years. His road to recovery was long but now, decades later in his adopted hometown of Hartford, Brown, burly, bald, and commanding in presence, had found his calling. He had emerged over the past decade as the most ferocious antiviolence voice in the city, and that afternoon, no halfhearted body language from me was going to settle him down.

In fact, whatever I was doing, sitting at a table in the front of the room, while Brown roared away from his seat in the audience, just seemed to make him more upset. "*Do* something! Stop *talking!*" he continued. "Because all you are doing is talking. Nothing is going to change with talk!"

Then Brown twisted the knife, deep and painful. "God knows, if Newtown didn't happen, why, none of you would be here today. *None. Of. You.*" My stomach turned, I unclasped my hands, and my gaze plunged to the floor.

For the next two hours, the mothers of fallen sons, the fathers of murdered children, the clergy who consoled those left behind, and the citizens just sick and tired of the nightly gunfire, laid bare their agony and frustration at the nation's latest sudden awakening to the terror of gun violence. They felt the pain of Sandy Hook more than anyone else, the mothers and fathers explained. "Because we understand the significant loss of life," said Brown. But the message was clear: Why does it take one murder of white children for politicians to show up here and talk about the yearly, monthly, and daily death of African American children? Why don't our kids matter just as much? Why have we been ignored for so long?

The meeting was, for me, one of those before-and-after moments.

I felt ashamed that having grown up just down the road from Hartford, and after having served in state and national government for a decade, I hadn't done anything meaningful about this epidemic in my state's cities. And having just watched the mothers and fathers in Sandy Hook stream out of a room in which they had been told their six- and seven-year-old children were never coming home, I felt a closeness that I could have never felt before to the pain of those Hartford parents. And I knew that my mission had expanded.

That day, one father who told the audience the story of his recent loss caught my attention, and at the end of the meeting, I pushed through the crowd to introduce myself to him. He seemed lost, not sure whether to flee the lingering, heavy sorrow of that room or to stay to commune with the other members of this club of which he was an unwilling new member. As I reached out my hand, he snapped back into consciousness and grabbed my forearm. "My name is Sam Saylor," he said.

. . .

Six years would pass between my introduction to Sam Saylor and the conversation with him about his son's death that I describe at the outset of this book. During that time, I spent countless hours with Sam, Reverend Brown, and the families affected by the violence that plagues certain discrete neighborhoods in our nation, and slowly, over time, my discomfort, so painfully apparent at that community meeting in early 2013, would dissipate.

I would also come to know the more private kinds of violence—the disconsolate individuals who take their own lives, and the manipulative men who assault their partners. Those left behind by these kinds of violence—which had been occurring at crisis levels long before Sandy Hook—became grieving partners in the growing anti–gun violence movement. They would become my friends, my constant allies. I grieved with inconsolable parents at funerals. I listened to teenagers describe the sirens they hear at night as their "lullaby." I sat across the table from hard kids, probably just like Shane, who were scared to death but for the gun tucked into their pants.

The violence that doesn't make the nightly cable news shows—the suicides, the domestic abuse, and the "normal" gun crime in certain American neighborhoods like the north end of Hartford—that's the violence we ignore. We ignore it because it accumulates like a slow snowfall. Each death doesn't make national news by itself, but on the day that twenty-seven were killed in Sandy Hook, ninety others were felled by gunfire in other parts of the country (and dozens more by other means). Individual homicidal acts or self-harm are never enough to capture the country's attention, even though the numbers of those lost in mass murders pale in comparison to those who die in smaller bursts of human rage or misery.

The other reason we largely ignore urban crime, suicides, and domestic violence is because the conversations about these tragic phenomena make us squeamish. A discussion of their causes requires us to confront our prejudices and the fundamental unfairness of American economic and social existence. I was uncomfortable as Reverend Brown harangued me because I, a privileged young white man who had represented a congressional district where people of color made up less than a quarter of my constituency, couldn't figure out how to relate to the experience of these African American fathers and mothers. I grew up in a town with almost no African American families, and violence is a lived experience—you can't understand how it feels to be assaulted, or to lose a loved one to an assault, if you haven't gone through it. So my discomfort was a result of my experience deficit, and as much as I knew I just needed to *get over it,* I couldn't. And to be honest, even having immersed myself in the experience of the north end and other places like it over the past six years, I still feel squeamish.

When I finished the first four chapters of this book, and I knew I had to write the story of urban violence and suicides and spousal abuse, I got cold feet. Not because I don't know the narrative, but because I worry that my telling of it will be inauthentic or unwanted. I skipped over this chapter and wrote chapter 6 first as a stalling tactic. You're reading this now, so you know I finally found the nerve to put into writing what I had learned over six years from Sam and Reverend Brown and so many others, but what you're about to read—the story of the violence we ignore—was the hardest to wrestle out of my head.

THE KERNER COMMISSION

The violence surges of the middle 1800s and early 1900s were arguably a result of new entrants to America demanding economic, social, and political space in which to live and the resulting hostility from more vested communities, all occurring at the same time as advances in the technologies of violence. The increase in American violence in the 1960s resulted from a slightly different set of circumstances. There were several contributing factors. The Vietnam War created a fundamental disruption in the covenant between the government and the governed, and the resulting free fall in respect for authority no doubt compromised the ability of the Leviathan to control violent impulses. With the maturation of the baby boom generation, historically large bands of young men were clustered in close proximity to one another, always a prescription for an uptick in aggression rates. And psychologist Steven Pinker's case for the collapse of civilized norms during this period is compelling, too.

But something else, much more familiar, was occurring during this time as well. As the national economy and its transportation links grew, so did the mobility of millions of African Americans in the South, still suffering under the hard, painful boot of Jim Crow. Often referred to as the Great Migration, from 1915 to 1970, about five million African Americans moved from southern states to northern (and to a lesser degree, western) states. The end of the Great Migration coincided with the civil rights movement, which finally opened an aperture for African Americans to envision the "Promised Land" Martin Luther King, Jr., described—where African Americans would have access to the civic, social, political, and economic rights that had been denied to them throughout American history. And now, especially in the northern cities crowded with newly empowered African Americans, increasingly unwilling to be held under by the white power structure, they began to assert themselves. As happened so many times before in American history, a claim for power from an out-group was met with a swift response from the threatened in-group desperate to reassert its dominance through violence. That was America when the simmering pot of U.S. race relations boiled to a tempest in the summer of 1967.

· · ·

The night of July 12 was a hot one in Newark, New Jersey. The residents of the run-down, crowded Rev. William P. Hayes Homes public housing complex were settling in for the evening when they heard a commotion on the street below. John William Smith, an African American cab driver in Newark, had been pulled over by two white police officers for an offense they described as "tailgating." An argument started, and the officers brutally beat Smith, tossed him into their squad car, and hauled him off to the Fourth Precinct headquarters, where they arrested him for assaulting and insulting the officers.

It was, for whatever reason, the proverbial straw that broke the camel's back in Newark, a community chafing badly from a white police force that regularly hounded the city's African American citizens. A rumor quickly spread throughout the massive high-rise buildings of the Hayes Homes development that once locked inside the police station, Smith had been murdered by the officers. (He was, in fact, badly beaten but alive.) A march was quickly organized, and at the Fourth Precinct a scuffle broke out between the largely African American protestors and the largely white officer corps.

The next day, another march was organized, and when a few of its participants became violent, the National Guard was mobilized, and local police were given the order to fire on protestors "if necessary." That night, the building that nurse's aide Rebecca Brown lived in shook under a barrage of gunfire from the National Guard. Brown, an African American, was killed in a volley of bullets as she tried to grab her two-year-old daughter from near her second-story window, and her death set off another round of protests. Over the next four days, chaos broke out; more than 12,000 bullets were fired, leaving 26 dead, 700 injured, and 1,500 arrested. A review of the violence concluded that most of the deaths were civilians killed by either National Guard troops or police officers.

Similar riots, met with comparable ferocity from authorities, broke out that summer in Cleveland, Detroit, and, by some accounts, around 150 other cities. President Lyndon Johnson responded by playing his favorite crisis response card: He formed a commission. Having served in government for two decades, I know a thing or two about commissions; you normally form them only to study problems you don't have the willpower to solve. And that's how Johnson, dubbed by his critics as "the Great Commissioner," looked at the National Advisory Commission on Civil Disorders, popularly known as the Kerner Commission for its stately and controversy-averse chairman, Illinois governor Otto Kerner.

The commission's membership was seemingly designed to make sure it made no waves. It was filled with conventional political figures, and, astonishingly, only two of the eleven members were African American (the NAACP's Roy Wilkins and Republican U.S. senator Edward Brooke of Massachusetts). The conventional wisdom was, as journalist Elizabeth Drew wrote, that the report would not "differ radically from the one that [Johnson] wants."

But implausibly, it did. Within weeks of its release, the Kerner Commission report was an American bestseller, flying off bookshelves as quickly as publishers could print it. It sold one million copies in a week and became such a sensation that Marlon Brando read portions of it aloud on a popular late-night network television show.

What the Kerner report said was, in fact, explosive, largely because it belied the vanilla expectations of the panel, but also because the frank language of the document put an official imprimatur on sentiments that were common currency among African Americans. The commission said, unflinchingly, that "white racism" was the primary culprit behind the rise in violence during the 1960s, and the riots of 1967.

"What white Americans have never fully understood—but what the Negro can never forget—is that white society is deeply implicated in the ghetto," the report stated. "White institutions created it, white institutions maintain it, and white society condones it." The punch line of the report was this passage: "Our Nation is moving toward two societies, one black, one white—separate and unequal." Speaking from the jail cell where he was detained for inciting a crowd to violence, African American militant H. Rap Brown said: "The members of the commission should be put in jail under $100,000 bail each because they're saying essentially what I've been saying."

In a nutshell, the Kerner Commission laid the blame for increased rates of violence in American cities on three factors. First, the commission argued that concentrated poverty created the preconditions for violence, as desperate, frustrated individuals no longer saw nonviolent means as effective ways to advance economically or to satisfactorily resolve disputes, and turned to violence as a way to protect their interests. Second, the commission laid the blame for increasing urban African American poverty squarely on the shoulders of a racist white power structure that systemically denied economic opportunities and jobs to African Americans and denied their neighborhoods access to basic human services like adequate housing. And third, the commission noted that it was the violence and illegal behavior of white communities—police brutality, the ruthless suppression of peaceful protests, and the defiance of court orders to end segregation policies—that triggered self-defense reactions from African American communities. "Discrimination and segregation have long permeated much of American life," argued the commission. "They now threaten the future of every American."

. . .

The residents of Newark recognized a lot of what was described in the Kerner report, which noted that from 1950 to 1969, almost all African American population growth—98 percent of it—had occurred in American cities, while 78 percent of white population growth had taken place in the suburbs. And none of this was accidental. The end of formal educational and social segregation led whites to simply set up *informal* systems of educational and social segregation by moving their families away from places where African American people lived to places with few African American people. Then whites established quiet, insidious rules to make sure the system of informal segregation persisted.

For instance, realtors, almost exclusively white, simply steered African American clients to African American neighborhoods, and white clients to white neighborhoods. I remember one of my first conversations with my friend Senator Cory Booker, during which he told me the story of the lengths to which his parents had to go to buy their first house in New Jersey. Over and over, they inquired about homes that were technically on the market until the sellers realized that an African American family was the potential purchaser. The only way his parents could eventually close on a home was to recruit a white family to express interest first, and then surprise the sellers by showing up at the closing instead. As if to perfectly underscore the tendency for in-groups to use violence as a method of controlling out-groups, the white realtor actually threw a punch at the Bookers when they unexpectedly arrived for the closing. And all too often, once families of color did make it into majority-white neighborhoods, they were (and still are) often met with more violence—houses broken into, possessions trashed, nooses and burning crosses placed in their front yards.

"Redlining" was another way the powers that be in New Jersey and other places kept a lid on economic opportunity in African American neighborhoods. Through this practice, a form of which still exists to this day, banks drew a line around the African American neighborhoods, deemed them unready for investment, and refused to make loans inside those areas, thus dooming these impoverished neighborhoods to a vicious downward cycle.

In 1994, the Hayes Homes were finally demolished, brought down by dynamite, but as *The New York Times* noted upon their destruction, the blighted development had for decades "long symbolized Newark's inability to provide decent shelter for its poor." In fact, as the summer of 1967 descended upon Newark, there was no city in America with a higher percentage of substandard housing. President Johnson's Great

Society programs, designed to target investments into places like New-ark, were falling apart as more and more federal funding was diverted to pay for the growing war in Vietnam. And the informal re-segregation of American schools with the flight of white families out of cities al-lowed state policy makers to comfortably construct a school funding system that relied on local resources to pay for education, ensuring that schools in poor, urban settings would never be able to match the funding or quality of schools in the white suburbs.

Finally, as the Kerner Commission wisely noted, the white power structure wasn't reluctant to use violence and illegality to quell any at-tempts by African American communities to assert their political rights. Though it panicked America that the nonlethal beating of one single cabdriver could spark a four-day citywide riot that left dozens dead, Smith's experience was simply the tip of the iceberg.

The residents of the Hayes Homes marched on the Fourth Precinct because they had experienced unprovoked police aggression every day, and they had been given the clear signal that nonviolent pathways to address their grievances were completely shuttered. All across Amer-ica during the 1950s and '60s, local white governments simply ignored court orders to desegregate schools and social spaces, and while occa-sionally the white intransigence was so spectacular as to draw the at-tention of the federal government, the flouting of desegregation orders mostly went unaddressed.

In Newark in 1967, African American leaders had vehemently op-posed the plans of the city and state to build a new state medical and dentistry school—largely for out-of-town white students—on a fifty-acre parcel right in the middle of the destitute Central Ward. Newark residents pleaded with the city to use the land for new affordable hous-ing, to no avail. Traditional political redress was just not available to the African American citizens of Newark and most American cities. During one field visit of the Kerner Commission to Cincinnati, a young Presbyterian minister calmly told the commission, "Look, man, we're hip to you white people. We know . . . it's no good trying to ap-peal to your morals; you've shown you don't have any morals. The only thing you believe in is your property—that's what this country is all about, baby. So we are going to burn it down." Said Martin Luther King, Jr., that same year:

> A riot is the language of the unheard. And what is it that America has failed to hear? It has failed to hear that the plight of the Negro poor has worsened over the last few years. It has failed to hear that the promises of freedom and justice have not been met. And it has failed to hear that large segments of white society are more concerned about tranquility and the status quo than about justice, equality, and humanity.

.   .   .

President Johnson was infuriated by the commission and its report, and *The New York Times'* decision to run articles on its findings for each of the seven days following its release must have boiled the president's blood. LBJ took its diagnosis of white racism as the primary cause of the riots as an attack on his administration and a rejection of the impact of the civil rights legislation that he had fought so hard to enact.

He instructed his staff to tell the commission that its provocative wording ("catchy but insidious slander" Johnson called it) would have the effect of making it less likely that the president would adopt its recommendations. He complained to anyone who would listen that the housing, education, and job training programs that the Kerner report recommended were too aggressive and too expensive. On the day the report was released, he fled to his Texas ranch and refused to comment publicly. Later, when Robert Kennedy announced his candidacy for president, he seized upon Johnson's coldness toward the commission's findings. "I would like to see the executive branch of government—the president, members of the cabinet—say this program is a valid plan of action. . . . We haven't had that at all," complained Kennedy, no doubt deepening Johnson's antipathy for the report.

American political leaders, searching in the late 1960s for explanations for the surge in urban conflict, had multiple theories. A 1965 California study following the Watts riots in Los Angeles posited the "riffraff theory," the idea that a group of nonconformist sociopaths (largely African American and originally from southern states) were primarily responsible for what appeared to be more general unrest. Sociologist and later U.S. senator Daniel Patrick Moynihan blamed the breakdown of African American family structure for the rise in violence in a widely read report he issued in 1965 for the Department of Labor.

The Kerner Commission felt these analyses were cowardly nibbling around the edges of the more nefarious problem. The toxic concoction of racism and poverty was the primary agent of the spike in violence that gripped all of America in the middle of the 1960s, it argued. And unless the federal government took bold steps to lift up communities of color and address the consequences of a separate and unequal American social structure, the violence would not abate.

Remove the historical references and read the Kerner report aloud today at a community meeting in the north end of Hartford, and residents would hear a convincing, real-time analysis of the roots of violence in their community. For as far as we like to believe we have progressed as a nation since 1967 (we elected an African American president, for heaven's sake!), the lens through which we should view the violence that occurs in America's cities should not be much different from the one used by Otto Kerner and his panel. Real estate discrimination still exists. Police brutality is still far too common. Bank redlining has not disappeared. Public housing is still falling apart. And economic mobility for urban African Americans isn't the same as it was in the 1960s—it's unbelievably much worse. The explanation of the causes for urban violence enumerated by the Kerner Commission are, tragically, just as true today as they were fifty years ago.

HUNGER, MAN, IT HARDENS YOUR HEART

On the morning of January 18, 2019, the public schools in Baltimore opened two hours late due to overnight snow. Corey Dodd volunteered to take his five-year-old twin girls to school and let his wife,

Marissa, have a quiet morning with their two other children, a three-year-old and a newborn. Life hadn't been easy of late for the Dodd family. Corey was working at his father's hauling company, but he wanted a career of his own. He had just finished a program to earn his commercial driver's license, and the family was planning to leave Baltimore as soon as he got a permanent job. That morning, I probably passed the Dodd twins, or maybe even rubbed elbows with Corey himself, in the foyer of Matthew A. Henson Elementary School in the Baltimore neighborhood of Sandtown. I was there because during the government shutdown of early 2019, I had found myself with some unexpected time on my hands. So, one Friday, with no votes planned in the Senate, I took a hastily arranged trip to Baltimore to visit the epicenter of the nation's plague of urban gun violence.

In 2017, the year that I decided to write this book, Baltimore was the deadliest city in America, with a homicide rate of 56 per 100,000 (for comparison, New York City's murder rate that year was just over 8 per 100,000). Baltimore families paid more than $3 million in burial expenses for gun murder victims that year. And, most troubling: 90 percent of the homicide victims were African American; 90 percent of the homicide victims were men; and 90 percent of the homicide weapons were guns.

I decided to visit Sandtown—a neighborhood about which I had read much, but seemed too heartbreaking to be real. Nestled in the northwestern quadrant of Baltimore, Sandtown is one of the poorest sections of one of the poorest cities in the nation. According to statistics, one out of every three Sandtown houses is vacant, but that number seemed far too rosy as I drove past block after block of endless, blighted, boarded-up row houses. Three percent of the residents are in jail at any given time, the highest percentage in Baltimore. One out of every three families make less than $20,000 a year. This is the neighborhood that produced Freddie Gray, the young African American man who died suspiciously after being transported in the back of a police van in April 2015, touching off three days of intense protests throughout the city.

I was visiting Matthew A. Henson Elementary School to check out an innovative program teaching young kids entrepreneurship skills. G. Travis Miller, the young principal brimming with empathy for his kids, described the challenges wrought by the crippling poverty facing his school's families. His focus today was on the kids who just disappear from school, into thin air. "I have twenty, thirty kids this year who just stop showing up, and never register for school anywhere else. We try to go get 'em, but these families move around so much, looking for housing or a job, just trying to survive."

I settled into a second-floor classroom with Joni Holifield, who founded the entrepreneurship program. Joni grew up in Baltimore and survived a trauma-filled childhood. Her brother had been in and out of trouble, but she built a successful career in the financial sector. After Freddie Gray's killing, her heart broken for her city, she decided to drop everything and devote her life to serving the children of Baltimore. Her experience as a child of Baltimore herself doesn't dim her optimism for the kids she serves. She explained to me, "I'm trying to change these kids' mindsets . . . show them what's possible other than what's in front of them."

And then, all of a sudden, fifteen minutes into our conversation, a booming voice on the school's loudspeaker system announced with a staccato urgency, "Code Green! Code Green! Faculty and staff, we are currently under a Code Green!"

"Do you know what that is?" I asked Joni.

"No, actually," she replied, trying hard to conceal her worry. "But Code Green is probably better than a Code Red, right?"

A teacher who moments before had been introduced to me, cheekily, as "the lady who runs this floor" burst into the room. "Shades down. Lights off. Door locked," she said with heart-attack seriousness, as if she had practiced this routine a dozen times before. "Code Green." And just like that, she disappeared back into the hallway.

A few minutes later, after we quickly complied with our instructions and darkened the room, the telephone rang. It was the front office on the line, explaining to Joni that a Code Green meant that there was an active shooting happening within blocks of the school, and the campus was on lockdown until given the all-clear from the police.

"It's ten-thirty in the morning and they're shooting?" I asked, my legs shaking a little bit under the table. And if *I* was worried, what were these first and second graders thinking? I put the question to Joni.

"Honestly, they're numb to it," she said in a deadpan voice. "Every single one of them has a cousin or uncle who has been shot. They listen to police sirens all day. It's just not news to them."

"That's how they may play it, but that trauma eats away, right?"

"Of course it does," replied Joni. "I had one of my third graders, who used to get into a little trouble here and there, say to me this fall, 'Ms. Holifield, I'm gonna have a great year this year!' I was so excited about his positive attitude, and so I asked him what had given him a new perspective. And then he says to me, totally matter-of-factly, with no drama at all, 'Well, Ms. Holifield, my brother got shot in the face this summer, and I don't want that to happen to me, so I'm going to have a great year.'"

"That's fucked up," I said.

"That's every day," Joni said back.

.   .   .

I was shaken by my first-ever school lockdown, and so that afternoon, I decided to take a walk. My escort around the streets of Sandtown was Walker Gladden III, whose life story, defined by the incarceration of his father and shooting death of his own son, was tragically representative of African American men's experience in Baltimore. Gladden's manner of speaking was meandering and often disconnected when in conversation with me, but he was a different person when he locked eyes with another Sandtown resident, all of whom he seemed to know personally. "Hey, fam!" he would bellow. "Hey, young blood!" "Hey, family!"

As we wandered around the four corners of Pennsylvania and North streets, on the edge of Sandtown, we snaked through dozens of small groupings of African American men and women, deep in conversation but seemingly in no hurry to get anywhere other than the corner of Penn and North. This was the economy of Sandtown, Gladden explained. Too many people, not enough jobs. Many of the people we talked with were working, but most had only part-time or temporary work upon which they couldn't rely.

Upon striking up each conversation and exchanging a few pleasantries, Gladden would ask a variation of the same question. "I got a senator here today. A real senator! And he wants to know what's going on here in Baltimore with all this killing. What do you think we need here to stop it?"

Like clockwork, almost every time, the answer was the same: "Jobs."

One high school junior was desperate for part-time work to help his family pay the bills. The topic was so familiar to the boy and Gladden that it seemed like they'd had this conversation several times before. "I apply for a different job every day. Every fucking day, man! And nothing. There's nobody who wants to hire me."

"I know this is going to sound like a dumb question, but how does that connect to the shootings?" I asked.

My disclaimer didn't stop him from giving me an exasperated look, confirming that it was, indeed, a dumb question. "We have to live, man. We have to live. And if I can't find a job, then I gotta do something else. I gotta steal, I gotta rob, or I gotta deal. Those are my only options."

The cycles of trauma—poverty, malnourishment, exposure to violence—rob these young people of the apparatus of opportunity that children like me simply took for granted during our upbringing. But the checks on violence that exist for children of means are also gone for young men like the one I spoke with on the corner of Penn and North. Political scientist Robert Putnam, who wrote of the chilling sociology of modern America in *Bowling Alone,* calls these checks "airbags"—the natural defenses against catastrophic life mistakes that exist for children who don't grow up in East Baltimore. *Los Angeles Times* columnist Doyle McManus explains, "Social airbags offer the same kind of protection as car airbags: In a collision, you walk away unharmed. When affluent kids stumble, a parent or someone else often jumps in to help—by hiring a lawyer, paying for therapy, making sure contraceptives are available, or merely finding a tutor." All young people are at risk of doing stupid things, but poor, repeatedly traumatized kids have fewer protections from the consequences of making a mistake, or ways to steer clear of the mistake in the first place.

That day in East Baltimore, I had a conversation with another, older man, who told us that he hadn't progressed further than fifth grade in school and had been shot nine times. He was eager to talk to us about how different Baltimore was today than twenty years ago.

"Nobody cares about nobody anymore. There's no *concern* for other people," he complained. "And you know why?" He waited for an answer.

I took the bait. "Why?"

"Well, I'll put it to you this way. You ever been hungry?"

"Sure."

"No, I mean you ever been *hun-gry?*" he asked again, drawing out the final word with delicate purpose, to make sure I knew he wasn't talking about a temporary state of feeling.

I got it. "No, I'm lucky that way, I guess."

"Well, me neither. I'm poor, but I never been hungry like that." He slowed down his words, wanting to drive home his message like a dagger. "But hunger, man . . . it hardens . . . your . . . heart. It makes you care about shit. Nothing other than . . . what's that word when all you think about is staying alive?"

"Self-preservation?" I guessed.

"Right. Self-preservation. That's all that matters, man, when you're hungry. You'll do anything—even shoot someone—just to *preserve* yourself."

. . .

The statistics surrounding the gun murders of African American men in America are simply mind-bending. In the five years following Shane Oliver's death in Hartford, another 35,689 African American men in America, ages fifteen to forty-nine, would be killed by a person firing a gun. An African American man in Maryland is fourteen times more likely to be killed in a gun homicide than a white man in Maryland. The rate of murder for African Americans in, for example, Missouri eclipses the gun murder rates of some of the most violent nations in the world, like Mexico, Honduras, or Afghanistan.

The slaughter of African American men in the United States is an epidemic, but it is largely ignored by the national media, which focuses on mass shootings or sensational murders of young white women. And I'm part of the problem, because my difficulty in writing this chapter clearly reflects my uneasiness in tackling this subset of American violence. But, really, the difficulty of journalists and researchers and politicians to square up to this crisis is understandable because of a confusing contradiction at the center of the explanation for the slaughter. As it turns out, when you search for the reason why African American men are killed at a rate ten times higher than white men, the answer has, at the same time, nothing to do with race and everything to do with race.

What do I mean by that? Well, let's start with the part of the explanation of the epidemic that has nothing to do with race. I want you to understand what life is really like in a place like Sandtown because one simple, knowable, preventable fact lies at the heart of the violence epidemic in the city: poverty. Being very poor and living in close proximity to other very poor people makes it much more likely that you will be the perpetrator or the victim of violence.

That finding may make you uncomfortable—why does having less money than someone else make you more likely to commit a violent act, or be unable to control your rage circuitry? But as we have seen throughout human history, when humans—especially young men, who are genetically designed for violence—are forced into a fierce competition for economic resources, whether it be in medieval Europe or mid-nineteenth-century America, violence tends to be a way to protect or advance one's interests. This doesn't mean that being poor makes you hardwired or predestined for violence—there is no straight line between income and the propensity to hurt someone else. But the historical record and modern data are clear that poverty is a condition that can increase the risk of violent behavior.

In fact, being poor, more than any other factor, including race, correlates with violence rates. In 2014, the U.S. Department of Justice released a groundbreaking comprehensive data set of violence rates, cross-referenced with income status and race. The basic finding of the report was, first, that violent crime is intra-racial, meaning that by and large, whites hurt whites and African Americans hurt African Americans. That makes sense, since a largely segregated country doesn't put many people of differing races in regular contact with one another. But the second and perhaps more revealing finding was that poor white Americans are actually more likely to be involved in violent crime (46.4 violent crimes per 100,000) than poor African Americans (43.4 violent crimes per 100,000). And maybe *most* interesting was the finding that when it came to the likelihood of violent attack, living in a city didn't increase your chances of being targeted. The DOJ data actually showed that poor urban blacks were less likely to be victims of violent crime than poor rural whites.

The Baltimore experience confirms this data. A recent Harvard University study concluded that Baltimore is the least economically mobile city in the nation, meaning that no city in America has a smaller percentage of poor people who climb out of poverty than Baltimore. Of the hundred most populous cities in America, the city with the highest number of children who never escape poverty during their childhood? You guessed it: Baltimore. This lack of economic mobility is by design, not by accident. In Baltimore's white neighborhoods, many of the buses are free, bike stations are plentiful, grocery stores with fresh produce dot the streetscape, banks offer prime rates, and small businesses are flush with loans. In the African American sections of Baltimore, though, the buses cost money, there aren't bike stations, supermarkets are almost nonexistent, predatory subprime lending is rampant, and small businesses can't find anyone to loan them money.

But poor concentrations of whites also witness higher levels of crimes, and as incomes have flattened for white Americans in rural America during the past several decades, it is no coincidence that violence rates have dramatically spiked. Guthrie County, Iowa, is 95 percent white but has a poverty rate that is close to double the national average. *The Des Moines Register,* in a 2018 article detailing the surge in violent crime in small-town, rural Iowa, noted that Guthrie's violent crime rates jumped 50 percent from 2006 to 2016. Since 1996, violent crime rates in the rural countries of New Hampshire and West Virginia have tripled. In sprawling, mostly white Ross County in Ohio, where violence rates have tripled in the last twenty years, the jail, built thirty years ago to house a maximum of ninety-two prisoners, now regularly has two hundred tenants. Poverty, and the desperation it often begets, is a trigger for violence everywhere.

·　·　·

So, if poverty, and not race, is the primary factor in violence rates, then why are so many more African American people than white people dying? The answer to this question comes in several parts, but let's start with the most obvious: There are simply more poor African American people living in high concentrations than poor white people. Here are the two most relevant sets of statistics: Twenty-one percent of African American families in America have incomes under the poverty line, while only 8 percent of white families are poor. And while poor whites are spread out all over the nation, poor African Americans tend to be clustered together in American cities. Consider this: While African Americans are only 12 percent of the nation's overall population, they are 79 percent of Detroit's population, 63 percent of Baltimore's population, and 50 percent of Newark's.

As the Kerner Commission found, this clustering of poor African American people in America's cities is systemic and intentional. As African Americans moved into the cities by the millions in the middle part of the twentieth century, white people moved out, and then the white political and economic elites fixed the rules to empty out the cities of economic promise and lock the remaining residents inside.

Bank redlining, property tax–dependent revenue systems, massive cuts in federal discretionary spending, and the creation of suburban corporate and industrial parks led to the cratering of the economies of American cities. As time went on, a handful of signature international cities like New York, Los Angeles, and Washington, D.C., were able to carve themselves out from the broader narrative of American cities in decline, but even those places made sure to keep their cities economically and racially segregated. Take the nation's capital, for instance: Head northwest from the White House and you will encounter some of the toniest, highest income neighborhoods in America with names you know, like Georgetown and Foxhall. Head the other direction, across the Anacostia River, and you're quickly in some of the poorest places in America, like Congress Heights and Barry Farm. And guess what? Whites live in the northwest; African Americans live in the southeast.

.　　.　　.

But it gets worse. Now, this isn't the book nor am I the person to catalog the series of economic and social injustices perpetrated on African Americans over the course of the last fifty years. But to understand the catastrophic rates of violence for African Americans in these poor neighborhoods, we need to quickly cover a few more of the contributing factors beyond modern, informal segregation.

Let's start with the violence against African Americans that replaced slavery and lynching: incarceration. You may not think of the act of imprisonment as an act of violence, but stuffing someone in a windowless steel box is no less of an act of physical domination than is a punch to the stomach or a knife to the side. As filmmaker Ava DuVernay points out in her groundbreaking documentary, *13TH*, the drafters of the constitutional amendment outlawing slavery thought of incarceration in the same terms as enslavement. They said so explicitly, writing an exception to the abolition of slavery for incarceration.

As DuVernay argues, with slavery and extrajudicial lynchings no longer available to whites as a way to exert physical domination over African Americans, white political leaders transformed the penal code into tools for targeting African Americans. They instituted black codes and pig laws to lock up large numbers of African Americans in prisons, and the threat of incarceration became the newest means for the in-group to control the out-group.

From 1970 to 2010, the total number of Americans in prison skyrocketed. In 1970, there were 200,000 incarcerated Americans; by 2010, that number had increased to over 1.6 million (the population of the country had increased by only 50 percent during those forty years). And throughout that entire period, African American men were disproportionately imprisoned. Today an African American man is six times more likely to be incarcerated than a white man. Hispanic men are twice as likely. An African American child is five times more likely to be tossed into the juvenile detention system than a white child. Meanwhile, one in ten African American children have a parent behind bars. Only one in sixty white children face those circumstances. Or what about this mind-blowing statistic: In 1980, one in ten African American men without a high school diploma was in prison (already a striking number); twenty years later, an incredible 27 percent of African American men without a high school education were incarcerated.

What happened to send one-quarter of poor, undereducated African American men to prison by the turn of the millennium? The short answer is the war on drugs happened. Under both President Nixon and President Reagan, and then under the Bush and Clinton administrations, a construct was created in which the illegal drug trade was presented as an existential threat to America that had to be met with increased law enforcement powers and longer prison sentences for drug sellers and users. This crackdown was carefully calibrated to put people of color in jail. Efforts were made to ratchet up penalties on the drugs primarily used in African American communities.

Prison sentences for possession of "crack" cocaine were one hundred times harsher than those for "powder" cocaine, the form preferable to white customers, even though the chemical effects of both were nearly identical. An African American man convicted of carrying five grams of crack, which is about the size of a dime, got five years in prison. But to get the same time for powder cocaine, you would have had to be caught with five hundred grams, enough to fill a medium-sized baggie. The media played along, happily telling stories and displaying images to create a narrative of "black criminality" driving the menacing drug trade. Today, more than half of all federal inmates are in jail for drug-related offenses, a result of these post–civil rights era policies.

While imprisonment itself is an act of violence, it turns out that locking up someone begets all sorts of other forms of violence, too. If being poor makes you more susceptible to using violence or being the victim of violence, then incarceration is the quickest way to become permanently poor and therefore forever at risk of victimization.

Author Michelle Alexander, in her bestselling book *The New Jim Crow*, argues persuasively that men of color who are targeted by our incarceration-obsessed society are trapped in a "closed circuit of marginality." The data backs up her claim: While the overall unemployment rate today is around 4 percent, for ex-offenders the rate is over 27 percent, higher than the unemployment rate during the Great Depression. And that number is especially striking because studies suggest that those with criminal histories actually try harder to find work than those who have never been imprisoned.

The closed circuit of marginality is insidious; it makes those with prison records economic pariahs once they emerge from prison, and makes it more likely that they will spiral back into the dangerous and violent drug trade, the only viable means of living for city dwellers with no other job prospects. The National Institute of Justice developed a list of "collateral consequences" of incarceration that is practically endless. It includes restrictions on obtaining a driver's license, qualifying for public housing, receiving public assistance, serving in the military, getting into college, applying for jobs, holding office, and serving on a jury. "If I can't find a job, then I gotta do something else," said the young man in Baltimore. That "something else" in Sandtown is selling drugs, a business white elites have been more than happy to allow to thrive in the cities.

Now, as Alexander points out, there isn't any evidence to suggest young African American men engage in any more drug selling than young white men (there were drug dealers at my mostly white high school, too), but with the entire infrastructure of the war on drugs focused on Hartford instead of the city's white suburbs like the one in which I grew up, the closed circuit makes sure that only the sellers with darker skin get cycled back into the criminal justice system. They don't have the airbags the young white drug dealers at my high school had. This lends a greater desperation and danger to the urban drug trade. The National Gang Center estimates that only about 13 percent of American homicides are gang related, but in cities like Baltimore that number is much higher.

.   .   .

During my conversation with Joni Holifield, I asked her how effective the police were in tracking down the perpetrators of violence in her childhood neighborhood, which she described as being plagued by crime.

"Would you call police when something happened?" I asked.

Joni raised her eyebrows and pursed her lips incredulously, like no one had ever asked her that question before. "The police aren't here for us. When I was young, I saw one of them pull a kid out of school and beat him senseless, for doing nothing. So we . . . don't . . . call . . . the police."

The relatives of gun violence victims in Baltimore simply didn't believe that the police or the prosecutors were there to protect their safety or their interests. They saw the police as their adversaries, much more interested in arresting their sons for nonviolent crimes than investigating the violent crimes committed against them. A sweeping 2017 federal consent decree, forcing the Baltimore Police Department to abandon its discriminatory policing tactics, was proof that this perception was not inaccurate. One Baltimore mother described to me the response she got from a white detective once she finally got up the courage to complain about the slow pace of the investigation into the murder of her son. "You're more likely to solve this case than me," the detective chastised her, clearly attempting to shift the responsibility for justice from law enforcement to the community he was supposed to serve.

It is this absence of justice that further contributes to the high rates of violence in African American communities. In *Los Angeles Times* crime reporter Jill Leovy's chilling book *Ghettoside*, she makes a compelling case that the violence in the poor African American neighborhoods of her city is driven in part by a perceived impunity for the murders of African American men, leaving the family and friends of murdered loved ones to seek out their own justice. In the thirteen years before the events described in her book, she notes an arrest was made in an embarrassingly paltry 38 percent of the 2,677 murders of African American men in the city of Los Angeles.

"The institutions of criminal justice, so remorseless in other ways in an era of get-tough sentencing and 'preventive' policing, remained feeble when it came to answering for the lives of black murder victims," she wrote. Her description of Los Angeles rang true with the mothers I met in Baltimore. When no arrest was made in one mother's son's death, even though all of his friends knew exactly who pulled the trigger, the offers came rolling in. "All his friends came and asked me, 'You want me to go handle it?'" she remembered. "But I couldn't do it. What I'm going through . . . it's not anything I would wish on my worst enemy."

This disbelief in the ability of law enforcement to uphold public safety has created an imperative to self-police in communities of color. This leads to some uncomfortable conversations in some community meetings. I remember one basement meeting with participants in a program called Street Safe in Bridgeport, Connecticut. The effort's organizers asked me to meet with several young men enrolled in the program to hear why they felt it so necessary to carry weapons.

"Nobody's gonna protect me except me," said one seventeen-year-old. "Everybody else is carrying. I can't be the only one who's not." He objected to any new gun laws because from his perspective, anything that made it harder for him to carry a gun put his life in jeopardy. Some social commentators try to psychoanalyze the decision of young African American men to carry guns, describing the weapons as a way to wield or project power that society has stolen from them through discriminatory policies and a dead-end economy. But I've found that most residents of violence-stricken poor neighborhoods who choose to carry guns find no joy or satisfaction in the exercise—it's just reflexive self-defense.

CHICAGOLAND

Though Baltimore stands as one of the most relentlessly violent cities in America, no American city has commanded more attention for its gun violence problem than Chicago, the crucible for the conversation about the role firearms play in the catastrophic rate of homicide in many American cities. Since the presidential election of Chicagoan Barack Obama, conservative activists and media personalities have been obsessed with assembling wall-to-wall coverage of gun violence in Chicago, painting the city as lawless, comparing Chicagoans' experience to the Holocaust, and equating the city to present-day Baghdad. Noting the regular attention on murder rates in Chicago during long holiday weekends, Wayne LaPierre said in a 2015 NRA video, "Nothing illustrates America's breakdown like the way the president's hometown celebrates its holidays," before describing the Chicago experience as a "kind of third-world carnage."

Chicago does not, in fact, even make the list of the twenty cities with the highest violent crime rates; in 2017, Chicago ranked 21st (Hartford was 23rd and Baltimore was 3rd). But the focus on Chicago was irresistible—high numbers of African American perpetrators and victims, and the connection of the city to the first African American president, allowed many conservatives to use the city's experience to lay the blame for America's urban violence epidemic at the feet of the African American community. It always seemed to me that "Chicago" had become code for "African American."

The ultraconservative website Breitbart sometimes looked like a local Chicago crime journal, posting endless stories of gun crimes carried out by African American Chicagoans. Matt Drudge did the same on his website, running an ongoing feature called "Chicagoland," detailing the constant flow of African American criminality in the city. When Chicago congressman Bobby Rush came to the defense of Trayvon Martin, the young Florida resident murdered simply because his hoodie made him look suspicious, Republican congressman Joe Walsh pounced. "I hope Congressman Rush will be as outraged with all of the black-on-black crime going on in the city of Chicago weekend after weekend." Added Fox News host Bill O'Reilly in defense of Martin's murderer, "The culture that we have in this country does lead to criminal profiling because young black American men are so often involved in crime."

The Chicago obsession, and the broader habit of anti-Obama conservatives to harp only on the African American perpetrators of crime, building upon decades of work by the NRA to construct a narrative of "black criminality," wore the American public into submission. Wrote Lisa Bloom in her book *Suspicious Nation:*

> The standard assumption that criminals are black and blacks are criminals is so prevalent that in one study, 60 percent of [television] viewers who viewed a crime story with no picture of the perpetrator falsely recalled seeing one, and of those, 70 percent believed he was African American. When we think about crime, we "see black," even when it's not present at all.

The media has been a consistent accomplice. Multiple studies confirm that local and national news focus on African American perpetrators and white victims disproportionately—remember Sam Saylor's amazement at the noncoverage of the disappearance of Shane's dirt bike–riding friend. One survey noted that while crimes with white victims and African American perpetrators comprise only 10 percent of arrests, they make up 42 percent of cases mentioned on television news.

· · ·

The second front of the Chicago obsession was to attempt to delegitimize gun regulation as a means to control violence. Throughout the 2016 Republican presidential primary, candidates repeated the claim that Chicago's tough gun laws were proof that firearms restrictions can't stop gun crimes.

Candidate Donald Trump said, "If you look at places like Chicago . . . it's got some of the single toughest gun laws in the United

States and it's a disaster." Once in the White House, his team kept returning to this argument as a defense mechanism against congressional proposals to tighten federal gun laws. Press secretary Sarah Sanders argued against passing any new laws in the wake of the Las Vegas massacre, saying, "If you look to Chicago, where you had over four thousand victims of gun-related crimes last year, they have the strictest gun laws in the country. That certainly hasn't helped there." Of course, as usual, Trump and Sanders were wrong. Chicago doesn't have the toughest gun laws in the nation. The state of Illinois actually prohibits Chicago from passing its own gun laws, and the state's gun laws, while certainly not the weakest in the United States, don't require gun registration or safe storage of firearms.

But the argument over the exact placement of Chicago on the national gun law spectrum was intended to obscure the more important conversation about how those laws and the practices of the gun industry affect urban violence. Illegal weapons (meaning weapons in the hands of individuals who should be barred from owning a gun due to their criminal record or mental health history) flood the streets of American cities. In 2018 alone, Chicago police seized nearly ten thousand illegal guns, likely representing just a fraction of the illegal weapons actually present in the city. In Baltimore, 86 percent of those arrested for gun murders had criminal records (nearly half had prior arrests for illegal gun possession), demonstrating the near complete futility of existing laws to keep guns away from individuals who have a history of violence and an intention to commit more violence. What has gone wrong, to let so many illegal guns flood our cities?

The most important thing to realize about an illegal gun is that it almost always starts off as a legal gun. Manufacturers sell guns to federally licensed gun dealers, who are required to conduct background checks on the people to whom they sell guns. Yes, there are some notable bad apples among licensed gun dealers, but the vast majority of gun stores are selling only to legal purchasers.

The secondary market—which includes private person-to-person transfers, Internet sales, and gun shows—is where the trouble happens, where criminals and gun traffickers can buy large numbers of weapons without having to go through any check. This is how the Mexican and Central American gangs get their guns, but it's also how many people in places like Chicago and Baltimore get their weapons, too.

A study of all traceable guns used in crimes in New York State found that 74 percent of those weapons came from states with looser guns laws. Sixty percent of the guns from out of state came from Florida, Georgia, North Carolina, South Carolina, Ohio, and Virginia—states that do not require background checks in the secondary market. More to the point, only 1 percent of guns used in New York State crimes originated in neighboring New Jersey, which has universal background checks. Chicago's numbers are not much different—60 percent of the guns recovered in crimes there came from out of state, and one out of every five crime guns came from Indiana, a state without universal background checks that directly abuts the city. Professional gun traffickers buy guns in unregulated markets in lightly regulated states and transport them to and sell them on the black market in places with tougher gun laws.

This "iron pipeline" of guns from states with loose gun laws into states with tougher laws is an intentional creation of the gun industry, which has for years opposed any and all laws that would make it harder for gun traffickers to flood cities with guns. As we covered in the previous chapter, the NRA fought to include provisions in federal law that effectively neuter federal enforcement authorities. Without the ability to repeatedly inspect those "bad apple" gun dealers or keep a register of guns sold by licensed gun dealers, the ATF simply cannot adequately track the movement of illegal guns around America. And by relentlessly opposing a national background check system, the gun industry ensures that the traffickers will have no problem getting their guns into markets where universal background checks prevent people with serious criminal records from purchasing guns.

●   ●   ●

In Baltimore, whenever Corey Dodd left his family's house, he knew what would be waiting for him when he came back. His three-year-old daughter, upon learning news of her dad's pending arrival, would take up her post right inside the front door of their row house in Sandtown and greet her father with a big hug as he walked through the door. On the morning of Friday, January 18, shortly after Dodd dropped his twins off at school, he turned around to make the short drive back to his house. He parked his car, as always, right outside, and stepped outside his vehicle.

The familiar sound of gunshots wouldn't have normally rattled Marissa, but these sounded too close for comfort. She rushed out the front door to find her beloved husband, the father of the couple's four children, lying on the sidewalk, struggling to breathe. She frantically waved down a passing police officer, and an ambulance rushed to the scene. It was too late. Corey Dodd became the latest victim in one of the most violent Januaries in any Baltimore resident's memory. He was the fourteenth homicide in eighteen January days, to go along with thirty-four nonfatal shootings in the barely begun new year of 2019. Over the course of the coming Martin Luther King, Jr., Day weekend, there would be thirteen more shootings in the city.

When I learned of Dodd's death, I couldn't stop thinking about those kids I left behind at Matthew A. Henson Elementary. I was there for only ninety minutes, and I experienced an active shooting within blocks of the school, and the victim was the father of two students. What must those kids go through, having to live in that neighborhood and go to that school every single day? My mind reeled knowing that there were two kids inside the school that day who were hours away from finding out that their father had been murdered. They would be the primary casualties inside Matthew A. Henson, but their father's killing, just around the corner from their playground, no doubt created layers of trauma for the rest of the student body.

It was a reminder that the measure we keep of the urban gun violence epidemic is virtually useless. We catalog deaths and shootings— the numbers of people killed or injured. But studies show that each gun murder results in diagnosable trauma affecting more than twenty other people connected to the victim. The ripples of grief extend, endlessly, to the deceased's mother, father, siblings, friends, and classmates.

Janet Rice and Sam Saylor are simply not the same people they were before Shane's death, nor will they ever be. And, of course, for that matter, neither are the families in Sandy Hook. If 299 people were killed by guns in Baltimore in 2017, then thousands more are dealing with the permanent health consequences of those deaths.

The most damage, though, is reserved for those kids in Sandtown, and millions of others who live in similarly violent neighborhoods all across America. Few Americans have heard of the hormone cortisol, but it's been called public enemy number one for children in places like Sandtown. Cortisol is your body's stress hormone, and it is released into your bloodstream and brain when you face traumatic events. Under normal circumstances, cortisol is your friend, because it temporarily elevates energy levels and brain functionality to allow you to step up your game during important, challenging moments. It's often associated with that "fight or flight" mechanism whereby humans are hardwired to make a quick choice when presented with a threat to their physical safety: fight back or run away.

For most of us, our "fight or flight" mechanism will be triggered only a few times in our lifetime. Think to yourself—how many times have you actually been so worried about your personal safety to be forced to make an instant lifesaving decision? Probably not many. But for children in Sandtown, who fear for their lives every day walking home from school (with good reason, given the events of that Friday morning), their brains are bathed in cortisol. The hormone pumps into their veins and brain circuitry on a near-daily basis. And too much cortisol is absolutely devastating to a child's growing brain. It crashes the brain's hard drive. Kids with high levels of cortisol can't sleep, their brains can't figure out how to work out conflict, they have trouble making strong emotional attachments, and they perform badly in school. The flood of cortisol, prompted by the stress of witnessing regular violence, effectively breaks a child's brain.

Those of us who work on the issue of gun violence every day refer to it as a public health epidemic, and the cortisol phenomenon is one of the reasons why. It's not a coincidence that the bulk of America's lower-performing schools are in the most violent neighborhoods—the brains of many kids in places like Sandtown have been damaged by trauma. The trauma of your friend's father being killed just blocks away from your school affects your ability to cope and learn. Just like our biology contributes to our aggressive, murderous instincts, so do those acts of violence loop back and alter our biology in turn. The circle of biology and violence is a vicious one if left unaltered.

Gun violence in America's cities, mostly targeting young African American men, *is* a public health epidemic. But we don't treat it as one. We continue to compartmentalize this phenomenon as something alien—a species of harm native to only a handful of places with no real potential contagion for the rest of America. And let's be brutally honest—we choose to ignore this plague because much of America still values the lives of young African American kids less than the lives of young white kids. That's what Reverend Brown knew, as he unleashed his fury on me that afternoon in Hartford. And that's what's communicated to those children at Matthew A. Henson Elementary when the father of two students is gunned down a few blocks away, and no one cares.

Television cameras don't descend upon *their* neighborhood. Deliveries of teddy bears don't start arriving. Grief counselors don't walk through the door. In research for this book, I found scant news coverage of Dodd's death. Imagine if a white suburban father was killed in front of his house after dropping off his twin white children at school? Do you think no one would cover that story? Those children at Matthew A. Henson Elementary aren't ignorant; they internalize the message that their lives—and the lives of their parents, siblings, and neighbors—don't matter to America as much as the lives of the more affluent white kids who live just miles away.

Inside that school, as I was trying to figure out what a Code Green was, were two five-year-old girls who likely giggled with their friends as the lights went off and schoolwork stopped for a few minutes. Maybe I walked by their classroom on my way out of the building a few moments later. What they did not know was that just two blocks away lay their father, breathing his last breaths. When they got home that day, their mother, Marissa, sat them down. "I told them Daddy's gone," Marissa said. "And he's never coming back."

Those twins, who will grow up with the memory of sitting through that Code Green and hearing those devastating words from their mother—they will know that their violence is the kind that America wants to ignore.

THE VIOLENCE OF DESPAIR

The shootings that occur in places like Sandtown and the north end of Hartford occasionally make news, if only for a moment. But what if there were a category of intentional death that occurred at three times the rate of homicides and almost never, ever made the headlines? What if people were dying every day of a completely preventable cause, at rates increasing each and every month, and barely anyone noticed? Welcome to America's growing suicide pandemic.

In the small town of Hooksett, New Hampshire, population fourteen thousand, Ralph Demicco hadn't thought too deeply about his state's suicide rates. He had friends who had taken their lives, but he was busy running a business and raising a family and just assumed that it wasn't his business to worry about the reasons why others chose to kill themselves. But something was happening in New Hampshire; though not many Granite Staters talked openly about it, the state was in the middle of a catastrophic spiral in suicide rates.

In 2005, 79 New Hampshire residents took their own lives with a gun. A decade later, that number would be 107, a roughly 35 percent increase. In 2009, in the middle of this tragic ramp-up in self-inflicted violence, Demicco received a phone call that would change his life. Elaine Frank, at the time the director of Dartmouth College's Injury Prevention Center, called Demicco to alert him to the fact that recently, in the course of six days, three area residents had committed suicide. And in all three cases, the victims had bought the guns they used from Riley's Sport Shop, the gun store that Demicco owned.

By all accounts, Riley's was a model gun shop. Demicco wasn't in business solely to turn a profit. He wanted to run an honest business that would provide "firearms to the responsible," as was his store's unofficial motto. He never let a customer leave his store without training on how to operate the complicated, lethal weapon they were purchasing, and he told his employees that if they didn't feel comfortable about any customer's motivation, to err on the side of caution—don't sell the gun. But the news that Frank delivered to him shook him to the core.

"Living with the idea that one of your customers has taken his or her life," said Demicco, "it's not a light burden. It's very uncomfortable."

When Frank approached Demicco about partnering on an anti-suicide campaign, he was, understandably, skeptical. "Not to stereotype, but generally people from the medical community and people from the firearms community don't share a lot of common ground," Demicco recalled recently, laughing. He knew that gun store owners would see a partnership with Frank as an attempt to lay the blame for homicides and suicides on gun sellers. But the more he considered the three individuals whose lives were ended by the guns he'd sold them, he knew he couldn't stand idly by.

In partnership with Dartmouth, Demicco launched a campaign that would eventually become known as the Gun Shop Project, an education program aimed at gun store owners and employees about the warning signs of suicidal behavior and the questions to ask if they suspect a buyer may be contemplating using the gun to take their own life. Posters went up in gun stores all over New Hampshire reminding both sellers and buyers that guns are the leading method of suicide and outlining the steps family members can take to remove guns from the hands of potentially suicidal individuals. And now, gun dealers in more than a dozen other states have adopted similar programs.

Mused Thomas Brown, a gun instructor who partners with Demicco in New Hampshire: "We as gun owners are constantly under attack, and one of the things that's constantly thrown in our face is the number of gun deaths. And when you realize that two-thirds, roughly, are suicides, that if we could reduce that number, wouldn't that be good for us?"

· · ·

The lion's share of American violence is inflicted by an individual on himself. That violence takes many, many forms. Suicide is its lethal incarnation, but every day millions of Americans cut themselves, starve themselves, drink themselves into unconsciousness, or knowingly inject potentially deadly foreign substances into their bodies. For all the—deserved—media attention on the times an individual ends the life of another, the vast majority of inward-directed violent acts go unreported. This is the scourge of American violence that gets the least attention, the fewest headlines, and we need to spend some time understanding why it happens.

First, what's the science? In 1897, Frenchman Émile Durkheim, one of the founders of the discipline of sociology, published a sort of treatise on suicides in which he upended modern thinking on the rationale behind the decision to take one's life. Prior to Durkheim's work, people believed that suicides were either the result of mental illness or a traumatic life event (like losing a job or the death of a loved one). Durkheim challenged that thinking, theorizing that it was, in fact, an individual's broken connection to his or her social environment that led to self-harm.

He sorted suicides into three categories: egoistic (individuals who had lost their sense of integration within their social group and no longer felt subject to social, family, or religious control); anomic (individuals who lived in a society that lacked collective order because it was in the midst of social change or political crisis); and altruistic (people who sacrificed their lives for the good of the community). And as it turned out, Durkheim had it largely right. More than one hundred years later, his work still stands as the foundation of the discipline. Depression and cataclysmic life events certainly contribute to or even trigger many suicide attempts, but the sensation that one's existence has become unmoored from social context lies at the heart of most decisions to hurt oneself. So, the stronger ties one has to the social environment, the less likely one is to come undone from it. Suicide is most often a consequence of personal demons mixed with weaker than normal connection to social structures.

Second, let's add some context. The American homicide rate in 2017 was about 5.3 per 100,000. That year, the suicide rate was nearly three times higher—14 deaths per 100,000. So why is the mainstream debate on violence in America so hyper-focused on murder when suicide takes so many more lives? Maybe part of the reason lies in the other context for this discussion: The American suicide rate is not as big a global outlier as the American homicide rate.

America's self-harm rate is on the global high end, but several other high-income nations, like France, Switzerland, and Japan, have suicide rates that are higher than ours. The more troubling trend is that American suicides have increased by 30 percent since 2000—a jump not matched by other nations. But measuring our overall rate against those of other countries still does not set off the alarms that the comparison of homicide rates does. Suicides in America are increasing, but overall they are just not as uniquely an American problem as gun homicides are.

There are, of course, explanations for why the suicide problem is largely hidden from public discussion. For the overwhelming majority of Americans who never experience suicidal thoughts, the threat of attack from another person is just much scarier, and more likely, than the threat of self-harm. We obsess over homicides because we feel we have much less control over what another person may do to us than what we may do to ourselves. Also, the unfortunate shame that many families feel surrounding the suicide of a loved one drives the discussion around causes and interventions underground. Murder is public spectacle. Suicide is private tragedy.

Another reason we spend so little energy studying the 129 people who choose to end their lives each day in America is that two of the most important discussions surrounding American suicides are the most uncomfortable to discuss. First, why do the racial disparities on homicide get flipped on their head when it comes to suicide? And second, what actually counts as suicide, and are we sure we have the definition right?

Here's the bottom line: America's high suicide rate is largely driven by a single demographic group: rural white men. If not for the suicidal propensity of Caucasian males living in low-population-density areas of America, our nation's suicide rate would be in the middle of the global pack. If you're an African American man in America, you are fourteen times more likely than a white man to be killed by a gun in a homicide. If you're a white man in America, you're three times more likely than an African American man to be killed by a gun in a suicide. So what gives?

Think about Durkheim's explanation for suicide: a seismic disruption in one's social context. *Disruption* is a funny word in modern America. For rich, largely coastal elites it has positive connotations (think of disruptive economic forces like the dot-com boom, globalization, and the sharing economy), but for those on the losing end of all this transformation, disruption comes with consequences. Nobel Prize–winning economist Angus Deaton put it this way:

> If you go back to the early '70s when you had the so-called blue-collar aristocrats, those jobs have slowly crumbled away and many more men are finding themselves in a much more hostile labor market with lower wages, lower quality and less permanent jobs. That's made it harder for them to get married. They don't get to know their own kids. There's a lot of social dysfunction building up over time. There's a sense that these people have lost this sense of status and belonging. And these are classic preconditions for suicide.

As journalist Jared Keller put it more bluntly, if less sympathetically: "Whites have taken their privileges for granted, and any relative deprivation is far more disconcerting and debilitating for them than marginalized groups that have spent their lives getting a raw deal in the U.S. political economy."

Indeed, studies show that both women and African Americans have developed better systems of resilience and of mutual support, each regrettably honed by years of subjugation and discrimination. Surveys show that poor African Americans are generally much more optimistic and show lower levels of stress than poor whites. Long the kings of American social and economic life, white males could afford the luxury of a more solitary existence, until the economic order came crashing down on top of them, too. Rural suicides are probably higher than urban suicides because the new economic order has hit rural America the hardest, as the jobs of the new high-tech global economy consolidate in mega metro areas, not America's small towns. Further exacerbating the crisis for rural men is the simple fact that in lower density population areas, social connections are harder to find to make up for the breach in one's economic existence.

Other factors likely contribute to the escalating levels of white male suicide: Depression rates for whites have consistently been higher than for African Americans or Hispanics. White men have much higher levels of alcohol abuse than African American men. And, perhaps most interestingly, the disparity between white and African American suicide rates may be self-reinforcing. In the early 1990s sociologists Kevin Early and Ronald Akers surveyed dozens of African American pastors and found that inside African American churches there was a widespread recognition of the divergence between African American and white suicide rates. In fact, that difference had become a built-in aspect of African American identity. They found that these church communities viewed suicide as an "unthinkable sin and define[d] it as a 'white thing' alien to the black culture."

. . .

Now, on to the even more difficult conversation: What do we define as a suicide? This might seem like an odd question to ask given that the definition, to most, would appear cut-and-dried. That's certainly true when the action is quick and deliberate—the pull of a trigger, for instance. But what about when the lethal behavior is spread out over a long period of time? What about actions that bring about death slowly, but only slightly less surely? What about activities where the risk of death is likely and knowable, though not definite? When death occurs under these circumstances, is it just the consequence of risky behavior, or is it suicide? Increasingly, these categories of preventable deaths are becoming a bigger and bigger percentage of deaths in the United States, and if we ignored them, we wouldn't be getting the full narrative of American violence.

Back to Nobel laureate Deaton for a moment. He lumps conventional suicides together with what he calls "deaths of despair": deaths caused by alcoholism, addiction, or overdose. Says his colleague Anne Case, "They are all suicide, either carried out quickly (for example, with a gun) or slowly, with drugs and alcohol." And while the conventional American suicide rate may not stand out globally, when combined with these other causes of death, America's chart line starts to veer far above the rest of the world's.

When you total up all deaths of despair (conventional suicides, overdoses, and addiction deaths), once again America is a global outlier, just as we are with homicides. In fact, our nation is one of only a handful in the world where life expectancy is actually dropping, and the reason is the rapid increase in these deaths of despair. Let's stipulate that not everyone who becomes addicted to a drug or alcohol is in "despair," and certainly most are not engaged in such activity as a means of purposefully ending their life. And, of course, addiction isn't a choice—it's a disease—so it may seem unfair to compare an overdose death with a firearm suicide, for instance, which sounds much more intentional.

But there are many reasons to think that Deaton and Case are right—that these deaths should be thought of as a unit. Many of the factors that drive conventional suicides seem to also correlate with these deaths of despair. While addiction does not discriminate—plenty of affluent individuals struggle with drugs or alcohol—it is also true that the burden of the addiction epidemic falls on the impoverished and economically marginal. If you're poor in America, you are just more likely to become addicted to opioids or heroin and a lot more likely to die from overdosing on your drug of choice. The same goes for conventional suicides. Again, lots of rich people kill themselves, but a person making less than $34,000 is 50 percent more likely to take their life than someone earning more. Like suicide, addiction takes its worst toll in rural areas, where there is less opportunity for connection between individuals and fewer services for those in the throes of crisis or illness. Overdoses are 50 percent more common in rural communities than urban ones.

In New Hampshire, where Ralph Demicco was building his anti-suicide program, locals know there is a clear intersection between the state's spiraling suicide and overdose rates (New Hampshire consistently has one of the nation's highest opioid overdose death rates). With a mostly white, rural population that has not benefited from the growth of the high-tech global economy and that does not have ready access to addiction and mental health services, the state is tailor-made to exist at the tip of both the suicide and addiction spear.

"In New Hampshire, Suicide Stressors Are Abundant," blared a headline in the *Concord Monitor.* A 2017 Trust for America's Health report that predicted New Hampshire would lead the nation in suicide rate over the next ten years received much attention in the state as well. New Hampshire knows what deaths of despair look like, and that's why good people like Demicco are so motivated to do something about it.

Now, here's where the discussion becomes even more fraught with peril. What about young men in places like Sandtown, who carry guns on the street, fully cognizant that gunplay could end their life at any moment? A devastating 2015 study from the American Sociological Association found that half of all African American children did not believe they would live to see age thirty-five, demonstrating a heartbreaking pessimism about the future. Do those that join the Baltimore drug gangs possess a subconscious death wish, or are they simply engaging in survival tactics that they feel give them their best chance to reach age thirty-five?

One study from 1993 reviewed urban murders and came to the conclusion that 30 percent were what criminologists call "victim-precipitated homicides," in which the victim of a homicide was the party that initiated the lethal conflict. Were these incidents just arguments gone horribly wrong, or did some of these victims have suicidal intent before initiating the conflict that led to their death? For years, law enforcement watchers have described a phenomenon called "suicide by cop," whereby an individual purposely provokes an officer to shoot them. The intent of risky behavior in violence-prone neighborhoods is impossible to divine, but we can't rule out that the measurement of American suicides should include some subset of the homicide deaths in urban settings.

.　　.　　.

Michael Scholtes still has dark moments, twenty-five long years after his last actual attempt to kill himself. "There are these moments when I am sure that suicide is the right choice," he explains. "But they're moments. It takes time to plan it. It takes time to build up the courage to follow through on those plans. And it takes an awful lot of effort, effort that is not easy when my depression is strong." And so knowing this, Scholtes, a Lutheran pastor, made sure that a quick, effortless suicide is not available to him. Scholtes doesn't own a gun, and this decision for him is purely about self-preservation. "If I had a gun and ammunition at my disposal?" he muses. "So much less time. So much less effort. So much less time to change my mind, and so much less chance of a failing attempt."

Friends of the country singer Mindy McCready thought those same kinds of things when she finally took her life in 2013. Before her eventual death at age thirty-seven, McCready had made four previous suicide attempts, each time intentionally overdosing on prescription pills or slitting her wrists. She survived those attempts, and in between, though McCready continued to struggle with mental illness and addiction, she always seemed close to turning the corner. In fact, in the days leading up to her final attempt, she was reportedly working on a project to raise awareness about the danger of suicidal behavior. But on her fifth and last suicide attempt, she used a different method. Mindy McCready pointed a gun at herself, and with one quick pull of the trigger, her life was over.

Suicidal thoughts are dark, curious creatures. For most individuals who have them, they are temporary and passing, like the ones Michael Scholtes describes. One study of young people who had survived a suicide attempt found that more than half of them waited less than twenty minutes to make the attempt after the first suicidal thought entered their mind. And so the most important task for someone who experiences one of these moments is to simply wait it out. Nine of ten people who survive their first suicidal impulse never end up taking their life.

But getting through those dark moments is more difficult when quick, easy lethal violence is right at hand for the suicidal thinker. Guns are used in 5 percent of all suicide attempts, but 55 percent of successful suicide attempts. Not surprising, right? When you shoot a gun into your temple, it does what it's intended to. That's why 85 percent of suicide attempts with a firearm are lethal. Guess how many suicide attempts by drug overdose are successful? Three percent.

Now, before we leap to a simplistic explanation of suicide, it is important to note that global suicide statistics cast doubt on blaming our self-harm epidemic on guns alone. If gun availability was the primary driver of suicides, then would a country like Japan, a nation with almost no private gun ownership, have a higher suicide rate than the United States?

There is, however, plenty of data to suggest that the American suicide rate would be much lower—maybe a global outlier at the *bottom* end of the chart—if we didn't have so many weapons lying around. A landmark National Institutes of Health–funded study in 2018 found a strong correlation between communities with high rates of gun ownership and high suicide rates. This could be a contributing factor to the high rates of both rural and white male suicide, since gun ownership rates are much higher in rural areas than in cities, and among white men compared to African American men. Ralph Demicco sells a lot of guns at Riley's Sport Shop, and New Hampshire's high gun ownership rate contributes to that state's suicide crisis. The NIH study also confirmed the finding of other research showing that the stronger a state's gun laws, the less likely the state is to have a high suicide rate. Universal background checks, locally issued gun permits, and waiting periods—policies that put time between a decision to purchase a gun and its receipt—all lead to fewer successfully attempted suicides.

There's even more interesting data to demonstrate that controlling the means of self-harm is an effective way to limit successful self-harm attempts. Consider the decision by the Israeli army to stop allowing soldiers to take their firearms home over weekends. That one action led to a 40 percent reduction in soldier suicides, driven by—you guessed it—a dramatic reduction of firearm suicides on weekends. Or what about the massive gun buyback program in Australia that took one-fifth of all guns out of private hands, which was followed by a 74 percent reduction in firearm suicides, without affecting non-firearm suicide rates at all? And finally, we can go back to 1950s England to find a dramatic drop in successful suicides after the primary means of self-harm, diverted domestic gas, was purged of the carbon monoxide that made it lethal. Reducing the ease of access to the deadliest means of violence matters when the goal is to help someone survive what may well be just a fleeting instinct for self-harm. Says Harvard suicide researcher Matthew Miller, "If you save a life in the short run, you likely save a life in the long run."

THE VIOLENCE AT HOME

The manhunt for Scott Gellatly lasted six hours. State and local police used helicopters and thermal scanners to search every avenue, parking lot, and alleyway in western Connecticut, looking for the car he had stolen from his estranged wife, Lori, on the morning of May 7, 2014. Gellatly was considered armed and dangerous, and so schools all over the area were placed on lockdown, and law enforcement departments all the way south to Florida were alerted to the possibility that the forty-six-year-old Gellatly may have fled the state. He made it only forty miles north. Police found him in an abandoned KFC parking lot, in a truck he stole after dumping Lori's car, and apprehended him as he was trying to kill himself by pumping exhaust fumes into the cab of the vehicle.

Two weeks earlier, Gellatly's thirty-two-year-old wife, Lori, the mother to the couple's toddler twins, had filed a restraining order against her husband and fled their home with the children to live with her parents. Scott Gellatly had always had a temper, but his moods had become more unstable in the spring of 2014. He suspected her of infidelity, and Lori Gellatly described how her husband grabbed her and screamed at her during a recent fight. She wrote in the application for a restraining order that "he acts out very violently and I'm afraid for my kids and myself." Once ensconced at her parents' house, Lori Gellatly took precautions that confirmed how afraid she still was of her husband. Her parents installed a new alarm system in the house, and she clipped a personal alarm to her nightgown and wore it to bed each night.

The alarm didn't save Lori. Early on the morning of May 7, Scott Gellatly broke into his in-laws' home, triggering the alarm systems. His assault on his wife and mother-in-law happened too quickly for the authorities to act. Enraged at Lori's decision to leave him, Scott Gellatly shot his wife four times in the torso and head, and shot Lori's mother, Merry Jackson, in the head as well. The twins were unharmed. Scott sped off in Lori's car, and Lori and her mother were eventually rushed to the hospital. Merry would survive her injuries. Lori would not.

Lori Gellatly had done everything right. She had fled an abusive spouse. She'd gone to court to file a restraining order. She'd secured her new home as best she could. And yet, it was not enough. She would become one of approximately one thousand women across America who die each year at the hands of a spouse or a domestic partner.

Of course, domestic homicides are only the most devastating of the ways that men use violence in relationships and within families. Much of it goes unreported, as large portions of Americans are still reluctant to bring charges against a spouse or even to discuss with friends what's happening in the relationship. And violence in the home is not just directed at partners; children in the United States are routinely the victims of abuse and neglect as well. The acceptability of violence as a method of control and domination by men in American homes has changed over the decades, but it is still standard practice in many households. It remains a substantial aspect of the narrative of American violence.

.   .   .

The biggest laugh in the legendary 1950s television show *The Honeymooners* came when bus driver and frustrated husband Ralph Kramden would threaten his wife with brutal assault. "One of these days, Alice, *pow*! Right in the kisser!" he would roar, and the audience would roar back in laughter and applause. Kramden's inference that he had never hit Alice before was likely a reflection of a growing sensibility that domestic violence was beginning to feel a bit taboo, and most Americans at that time viewed male violence against a spouse or partner to be a private, not public matter. This view was undergirded by law, since for most of the 1900s the law treated women as property of their husbands. Men could avoid jail time if they killed an adulterous wife. They could legally confine women to the home. And there existed in many places a crime called "harboring," which prevented anyone from providing sanctuary to a wife fleeing an abusive spouse. While these laws began to change in the 1970s, a 1987 survey of Americans found that only half of all respondents still thought it was wrong for a man to strike his wife with a belt or stick.

Before going further, it's important to recognize the two different types of domestic violence. Statistically, women commit as many acts of violence against men as men commit against women. That may come as a surprise, but most of the examples of women-initiated violence are relatively low-intensity violent outbursts—short rushes of anger as a result of a verbal disagreement. A different kind of domestic violence, one that is disproportionately carried out by men, is what is called "coercive violence," described by Steven Pinker as the "systematic intimidation and coercion of one partner by another."

Biologists suggest that this sort of violence is often used as part of a broader animal phenomenon called "mate guarding," where males use violence and the threat of it to maintain a sexual monopoly on a particular partner (thus the centuries of law making a woman the property of her husband). Pinker points out that many common American social practices, like chaperoning and segregation by sex, are culturally sanctioned mate guarding. "Domestic violence is the backstop" of this list of practices to control the sexual freedom of partners, Pinker argues. Other times, men harm or threaten to harm women as a simple mechanism to maintain a dominant role in the relationship, regardless of sexual jealousies.

Whatever the purpose of the coercive aggression, it has become the stickiest of all categories of violence. In 1951, Finnish criminologist Veli Verkko noticed that when violence rates drop precipitously in any society, it is normally only male-on-male violence that moves fast, with male-on-female rates declining at a much lower pace. Dubbed "Verkko's law," this finding, which has held up over time, suggests that the biological instinct to commit violence, and the lingering cultural acceptability of domestic abuse (by 1995, a stubborn 15 percent of American men still felt it was acceptable for a husband to slap his wife), continues to make this type of violence more impervious to social and legal interventions.

So now let's come back to a question we have asked over and over again when considering different forms of American violence: How does the United States rank globally when it comes to this issue? Like suicide rates, the United States has one of the highest domestic violence rates in the world, though, also like suicides, we are not as much of an outlier as we are on other forms of violence. New Zealand, Australia, and Britain report higher rates of domestic violence, while rates are lower in the southern European countries of Italy, Spain, and Greece.

Where the break occurs on domestic violence rates is between high-income nations and low-income nations, a disparity that is larger for spousal abuse than for any other form of physical harm. Even in New Zealand, the OECD nation with the highest level of reported domestic violence, less than 3 percent of all women report that their spouse assaulted them in the previous year. Compare that rate to 27 percent in Nicaragua or 52 percent for Palestinians. Only 1 percent of

New Zealanders say it's okay for a husband to beat a wife who disobeys him, but that number skyrockets to 78 percent for men living in rural Egypt and 50 percent in parts of rural India.

This brings us, once again, to the connection between violence and poverty, because even in the United States, there is a clear correlation between a man's propensity to assault his wife and his family's income security. In a household where one spouse is unemployed, a woman is four times more likely to be the victim of spousal abuse than in a house where neither spouse is unwillingly unemployed. Women in low-income neighborhoods are nearly three times as likely as women living in high-income neighborhoods to report domestic assault.

I theorized that homicides in low-income areas are a result of violence becoming a last resort to secure economic gain, when all the nonviolent means of advancement have been emptied out of these neighborhoods. But domestic crime isn't about economic survival; it's about domination and control. So why does it rise as economic opportunity goes down? Likely, this phenomenon stems from the stresses and tensions that build inside individuals as their poverty increases, and the lack of available resources to deal with the mental illnesses and addictions that often serve as the fuel for domestic rage.

·　　·　　·

In 2018, The Trace, a website dedicated to chronicling the cost of gun violence in America, published the story of a young woman in suburban Illinois whom the authors named Sophie. In her twenties, she had moved into her boyfriend's house. He was her high school sweetheart, and she was thrilled to finally be living in the same place with him. Shortly after she moved in, her boyfriend bought a gun, which Sophie thought was odd, since he didn't have guns in his home growing up. But he took gun ownership seriously—he got a permit, kept the gun in a locked safe, and stored the bullets somewhere else. She trusted him, and so she thought little of it.

Then, suddenly, the gun became a part of their lives. When her boyfriend would drink and they would argue, he would head into the bedroom, open the safe, and get his gun. At first, he wouldn't point it at her or threaten to shoot her. It was normally just out on the kitchen table, or in his hands. But her boyfriend had taken the gun out of the safe for a reason, and Sophie knew it. Soon, he bought more guns, and the threatening behavior escalated. He would fire an unloaded gun at the ceiling. He would point the gun at her or himself. All the time they lived together, he never touched or assaulted Sophie; he never actually pulled the trigger of a loaded weapon. But Sophie knew the score. Whenever the gun came out, she would acquiesce and do whatever he wanted her to do.

"It was almost like being held captive," she told The Trace. "In a physical fight, I'd at least have a chance. I could poke him in the eye or knee him in the groin. But when there's a gun involved, it's not a level playing field."

For every Lori Gellatly, there are far more Sophies. At least 1,000 women are killed each year by a partner, but as many as 4.5 million women living across the country today have been menaced by a domestic partner with a gun at one time (another one million have been shot or shot at and survived). One study of domestic violence victims in Pennsylvania found that one-third lived in a house with a gun, and in 74 percent of those cases, the male had used the gun to threaten or coerce the woman. Guns are a reliable tool of the coercer, and because the act of routinely placing a gun on the kitchen table while arguing with your girlfriend is not a clearly criminal offense, there is no way to accurately gauge how often women are terrorized by firearms. But it's a uniquely American aspect of the global phenomenon of domestic abuse.

The gun, though, does not always remain on the kitchen table. In 2016, 57 percent of domestic homicides were committed with a firearm. Gun industry allies suggest that this statistic is immaterial—when a domestic abuser decides to kill, he will find a way to kill regardless of whether he owns a gun, they argue. But the data tells a totally different story.

Studies show that women in abusive relationships are five times more likely to be killed if there is a gun in the house. If there was already a report of a previous assault, the presence of a gun in the house makes the woman forty-one times more likely to be murdered than those that reported abuse but live in homes without guns. And how about this: In states that make it harder for men with felony abuse histories to get guns (states that have truly universal background check laws), domestic homicides are 40 percent lower than in states without background checks. Without so many guns in American households, the data tells us, American domestic violence homicides would be close to the bottom of the global pack.

. . .

No one circumstance nor any single event of Shane Oliver's life adequately explains why this young man of such promise did not live past the age of twenty. There is no shortcut to understand why a simple argument over a girl ended a life that day. But the search for why their family's experience in the north end of Hartford was so different from those in nearby communities, or those in other nations, still consumes Sam and Janet. Why did the people in charge allow for the kind of racial and economic segregation that gave their family such limited possibilities? Why did no one notice the daily threat of violence that changed the chemistry inside their children's brains? Why did a ten-year-old kid have to be out on the streets selling water in order to avoid being swept up into a life of crime? Why wasn't college even a consideration for a young boy who showed so much initiative and drive? Why was stripping and reselling cars the best that Shane could do? And, maybe most important, why were there so many illegal guns in their neighborhood that one found its way in the back seat of the car of Luis Rodriguez?

The artificial, crippling limits placed on Shane Oliver's life—he died at the exact place where he took his first steps as a child—are much of what explains his untimely death. Shane was trapped in a cycle of poverty and low expectations, a result of decades of purposeful exclusion of young African American men from the mainstream economic opportunities available to kids like me, who grew up just blocks away in a different kind of place. I knew violent death was not my destiny. Shane knew it might likely be his. And it was. But the garden-variety argument that led to Shane's murder became deadly because of a weapon that rests in the front seat of no young man's car in Britain or Italy or Japan. America has made choices, over and over, to spread weapons like the one that killed Shane far and wide, and to put them in the hands of knowingly dangerous people.

"It's too soon! It's too soon!" Shane cried into the arms of his girlfriend, as his mother stood helplessly frozen on the other side of the door in the emergency room. Minutes later, he was the twentieth victim of homicide in one of America's smallest cities, another anonymous casualty in the cavalcade of violence that is the United States of America. The murders on our city streets, the suicides in our vast countryside, the beatings that occur behind closed doors in thousands of our homes—these are regular, everyday, and persistent. And I should have cared, long before Sandy Hook. I should have noticed what was happening right up the road from my childhood home. I should not have taken for granted the serene safety of my upbringing, when nearby children were disappearing off their bicycles—with no one noticing or caring—just a few miles away.

In December 2012, I came to know all about the short but wonderful lives of Charlotte and Allison, Daniel and Ben, Olivia and Avielle, Josephine and Jessica, Dylan and Caroline, Madeleine and Noah, Catherine and Jack, Chase and Emilie, Jesse and Grace, and Ana and James. Their deaths—and their beautiful, far-too-short lives—changed my own life in an instant.

But I should have known about Shane Oliver first.

6

THE VIOLENCE WE EXPORT

It is likely that no American ever exported more violence from our shores onto foreign soil than Dwight D. Eisenhower. In the first three days of the invasion of Normandy beginning on June 6, 1944, and overseen by Eisenhower, then the commander of Allied Forces in Europe, 1,213 naval combat ships, supported by 4,126 landing craft carrying 156,115 men (73,000 of them Americans), 20,000 vehicles, and 347 minesweepers landed on French beaches. It constituted the biggest seaborne invasion in recorded human history and resulted in a stunning 425,000 troops on both sides being killed or seriously injured. It was the beginning of the end of World War II, the most horrific six-year cacophony of violence in the history of the world by the time the conflict was finished.

Once president, Eisenhower, the general who witnessed such unprecedented carnage up close, set about ordering postwar America to discourage another march to war. He worried mostly about what to do with the weapons industry that had, virtually overnight during the 1940s, become a substantial component of the American economy, employing millions in factories across the country. The dizzying array of new weapons technology now available to the United States and its allies—from the atomic bomb to nerve gas to cluster bombs—threatened to turn even the smallest skirmishes into human annihilations, not unlike what Colt's revolver had done for previously innocuous sidewalk arguments.

Eisenhower knew that the United States, the most powerful military nation in the world in 1952, could take steps to harness and limit the destructive capability of military weaponry, and he set about warning the nation and the world about the danger of a global arms race. While his most famous remarks on the subject were reserved for his farewell speech, when he cautioned the nation against the dangers of allowing an amorphous entity he dubbed the "military-industrial complex" from dominating policy decisions in Washington, the Eisenhower speech I admire most was delivered just a few months after his first inauguration in 1953.

In his "Chance for Peace" speech, delivered to the American Society of Newspaper Editors shortly after Joseph Stalin's death, Eisenhower forcefully argued against a world armed to the hilt in constant preparation for the next round of hostilities. He proposed a massive global disarmament campaign, with the savings put into an account to fight poverty and hunger. Said Ike that day:

> This world in arms is not spending money alone. It is spending the sweat of its laborers, the genius of its scientists, the hopes of its children. The cost of one modern heavy bomber is this: a modern brick school in more than 30 cities. It is two electric power plants, each serving a town of 60,000 population. . . . We pay for a single fighter with a half-million bushels of wheat. We pay for a single destroyer with new homes that could have housed more than 8,000 people. . . . This is not a way of life at all, in any true sense. Under the cloud of threatening war, it is humanity hanging from a cross of iron.

Eisenhower had seen the good that nonmilitary investment could do in war-torn territory, having advocated for the Marshall Plan, America's mammoth investment in rebuilding the economies and democracies of the European and Asian nations torn apart by world war. And he knew that the defense and weapons companies, by then holding substantial economic power in 1950s America, would push for policies that would add to their profit margins, though not necessarily to the national security of the country or the world.

Despite the relative domestic tranquility of the 1950s, a decade wedged in between World War II and the violence spike of the 1960s, Ike knew that America's penchant for violence had not simply disappeared. He knew that, uncontrolled, it was a flip of a coin as to whether America's newfound dominant military would stabilize or destabilize the rest of the world.

In the decades since the "Chance for Peace" speech, the world has seen both sides of that coin. The notion that American military hegemony brings "peace through strength" is not untrue. Wars between nation-states, a regular occurrence before the ascendancy of postwar America, are now rare, due largely to the mutual defense treaties—like NATO—that the United States has signed with other nations, and the international associations—like the United Nations—that the United States underwrites. Countless lives have been saved in the post–World War II era by a strong American military that offers its protection to others and helps bring warring parties together in a way that no other nation can or is willing to do.

But, increasingly, it seems America is forgetting the lessons we learned in the aftermath of the Second World War and is relying instead on brute force and the proliferation of dangerous weapons to advance our national security goals. Today, America spends eighteen times as much money on its military as it does on other, nonmilitary means of projecting power around the world. Our war-making operation comprises approximately one-third of total global military resources. Our firearms industry works in tandem with foreign policy makers to export guns all over the globe. And that military-industrial complex that Eisenhower warned against is distributing arms at a record-setting pace, having increased weapons sales to other countries in 2018 by a whopping 33 percent over 2017, for a total of $55 billion in total exports.

Violence is one of America's most important modern export products, and in this chapter we will survey how the same profit motivation that led America to become populated by more guns than citizens also led to a foreign policy where American military might and American weapons end up making dangerous places more dangerous. As we've learned, America, by definition, was always going to be a violent place. The guns just made the intensity of our carnage much, much worse. The same can be said for the way in which America has come to throw its military weight and armaments cache around the globe. And so a survey of American violence cannot be complete unless we count the ways that our nation acts to make places far away from our shores less safe. We didn't light many of the fires currently burning in places like the Middle East or Central America, but our soldiers and ubiquitous guns have inadvertently fueled those flames. This chapter tells that story.

BAGRAM

When you fly on a Blackhawk helicopter into Bagram Airfield Base, you are awed by the overwhelming scope and sprawl of the American presence in Afghanistan. In the span of a few years, the U.S. military built the equivalent of a small American city in the middle of the Afghan desert. As the helicopter descent begins, you look over a settlement covering six square miles, capable of housing more than forty thousand military personnel, with its own electrical grid, sewer system, and cellphone network—perhaps the most impressive testament to the logistical power of the U.S. military and its partners.

I went there in the spring of 2011 to review the progress of an American occupation that was approaching a decade in duration. It was my third trip to Afghanistan in six years, and meeting with the American generals was starting to feel like Groundhog Day. Congressional trips into war zones are often military marketing exercises. U.S. military hosts control what members of Congress see and who we meet, and what we don't see and who we don't meet. Every officer and soldier we encounter is impressive, capable, and earnest, and makes you proud to be an American. Generals all have impressive PowerPoint presentations detailing how they are on the verge of securing the country from the enemy and ridding the fledgling democracy of corruption. And I've sat with many representatives and senators who are so awestruck with the quality of the generals and colonels (and they *are* impressive) and the sincerity of the presentations that they miss the fact that, year after year, the hype rarely pans out. The corruption doesn't get better. Our military partners don't get any closer to being able to handle the fight themselves. And the enemy just seems to adapt and grow in numbers.

I had run for Congress in 2006 as an opponent of the Iraq War, but it wasn't until I visited both Iraq and Afghanistan that I fully understood the futility of our missions in both places. We had no choice but to invade Afghanistan; having been attacked by al-Qaeda, a terrorist group given protection by the Taliban government in Kabul, the United States needed to respond proportionally. And that meant removing the Taliban government by force. But instead of installing a new government and then packing up and leaving, with notice to all parties that American troops would quickly return if al-Qaeda ever returned, we set about the impossible work of trying to police the country and nurse a democracy to health in a place where tribal-based social and political systems meshed horribly with American-style democracy.

My impression, during those early visits, was that the open-ended nature of the American occupation of both countries was creating more violence, perpetuating more conflict, and giving millions of dollars to the companies and industries that profited off of never-ending war. But I had to hand it to the military brass—they were great at putting on a good presentation for visitors, and in the spring of 2011 in Afghanistan, an extraordinary admiral named William McRaven was eager to wow us with some new weaponry that was transforming American combat operations across the world.

Late on the night of April 29, 2011, our delegation of four Republican and two Democratic House members shuffled into the headquarters of an elite unit of terrorist hunters run by McRaven called the Joint Special Operations Command ("JSOC" in military parlance) to get an update on the unit's progress on tracking Taliban leaders and lingering al-Qaeda elements in and around Afghanistan. The inside of the JSOC building at Bagram, even back in 2011, was as close to a Marvel superhero movie set as you will find in the world. Intelligence officers, drone specialists, and counterterrorism experts sit in a stadium-style room, with tiers of desks looking across at a colossal wall of screens piping in footage from an array of drones, cameras, and spy planes scouring Afghanistan for enemy combatants. On the wall was a series of "Most Wanted" posters detailing JSOC's most highly sought enemy targets. In the middle of the arrangement was the poster of America's enemy number one: Osama bin Laden.

McRaven, lean and dashing with a quick, knowing smile, was easy to trust. He explained that each screen represented a different surveillance operation, drones equipped with Hellfire missiles patiently circling above enemy targets, waiting for the marks to reveal themselves. But I was immediately confused. Several of the screens showed targets in Afghanistan, but several other screens depicted surveillance operations in countries in which the United States was definitely not legally at war.

I leaned over to Congressman Cedric Richmond from New Orleans and cupped my hand over my mouth. "Cedric, are we about to drop a bomb on someone in Somalia? Did we declare war on Somalia?"

"If we did, I missed it," Richmond whispered back.

McRaven was jumping with energy as he explained that these weaponized drones, called Reapers, were the future of warfare. They were both hunters and killers, able to locate enemy leaders with their revolutionary surveillance cameras and then wipe them off the face of the planet with a small but powerful missile that kills anyone or anything within fifty feet of its detonation spot. America could now find and destroy bad guys without risking the life of one single American soldier.

The admiral and his team delighted in pulling up footage of the previous day's successful drone strike on a suspected Taliban leader.

We watched in awe as satellite footage showed a few adult males in white robes milling about a complex of buildings, followed by a blinding flash of light, clouds of smoke billowing out from the buildings, and then, *nothing*. In an instant, a robot in the sky had obliterated a person who, from grainy images taken from a thousand feet above, McRaven and his team believed to be a threat to the United States and our partners. Members of our delegation *ooh*ed and *ahh*ed at the explosions.

The admiral's deputies explained to us that the Taliban and its affiliates were getting worn down by the constant pursuit of Reaper drones. It was just a matter of time before this new technology overwhelmed the enemy and forced them to sue for peace. As McRaven escorted us out of the building, the former history major inside me recalled that Robert McNamara used the same argument repeatedly to justify Operation Rolling Thunder during the early stages of Vietnam. His theory of the case was simple: Just keep bombing North Vietnam and eventually the Vietcong will see the light and back down.

. . .

The first kill by an armed, unmanned drone was tallied in Yemen in 2002, when the CIA used a Predator drone, the precursor to the Reaper, to wipe out an al-Qaeda member suspected of being involved in the bombing of the USS *Cole* two years before. No declaration of war in Yemen had been passed by Congress. In 2004, President George W. Bush ordered another strike, again by the CIA, but this time in Pakistan, another country for which no declaration of war existed. The target this time was the Taliban-aligned Pashtun military leader Nek Muhammad Wazir, who was killed along with two children. It's hard to know how many more times Bush ordered Predator strikes—incredibly, even most senators don't have access to this information—but reports suggest Bush used this technology sparingly, perhaps authorizing fewer than ten kills over the rest of his presidency.

When President Obama was sworn in, he arrived at the West Wing with a promise to end the wars in both Iraq and Afghanistan. Like me, Obama was deeply skeptical of the power of the U.S. military to cure vexing political conflicts on the other side of the globe, and he went looking for a way to keep terrorists at bay without the deployment of hundreds of thousands of American troops. He found it in the Reaper. In Obama's first year in office, he ordered more drone strikes than Bush did in eight years. In Pakistan alone, Obama signed off on 54 strikes, which reports suggest killed somewhere between 370 and 725 people, and in 2010, Obama ordered 128 more strikes in Pakistan.

The Obama administration regularly testified to the effectiveness of these strikes, if never openly admitting to the scope of the clandestine, largely CIA-run bombing campaign. In 2011, Obama's capable top counterterrorism official, John Brennan, claimed that not a single civilian had been killed by the drone attacks "because of the exceptional proficiency, precision and capabilities we've been able to develop." Whether he knew it or not, Brennan was not telling the truth. Not even close.

A nonprofit watchdog group, the Bureau of Investigative Journalism, collected as much information as they could find about the impact of the drone strikes inside Pakistan during Obama's first term and concluded that at least 390 innocent civilians (and as many as 780) had been killed in collateral damage from the strikes. A later report by *The Intercept*, citing classified data on drone strikes in northern Afghanistan in 2012 and 2013, came to an even more startling conclusion: A stunning 90 percent of strikes did not hit the intended target. Two hundred people were killed during this period by drones, and only 35 of them were the bad guys.

It wasn't hard to guess why so many mistakes were being made. If the handgun, by allowing a human being to kill another from a great distance with a simple flick of a finger, was the first invention to substantially depersonalize violence, then the Predator and the Reaper almost completely removed the individual from the act of killing altogether. Suddenly, a technician sitting in a darkened room in the American Midwest could use a joystick to maneuver an armed robot plane flying over a home seven thousand miles away and, with the touch of a button, kill another human being. The moral cost of killing another person was virtually eliminated for everyone in the decision-making tree, especially because from a thousand feet up, who could really tell if the blurry figures being obliterated were the guys you meant to kill or an innocent bystander? Strikes were clearly ordered without full knowledge of the consequences.

Just as troubling was the effect the drone campaign seemed to have on the various enemies we were seeking to defeat. There is no doubt that despite their reported inaccuracy, Predator strikes successfully eliminated many important Taliban and al-Qaeda figures. But one must wonder whether the strategy of cutting the head off the snake has actually killed the snake, when more than a decade and a half after American troops first entered Afghanistan and Iraq, we're still there. In fact, our position in Afghanistan, where the bulk of the strikes have occurred, has gotten steadily worse. In 2014, NATO estimated that there were 20,000 Taliban fighters in the country. Today, the estimates range from 30,000 to 75,000. We may be killing the enemy's top brass, but a hundred more seem to join for each one we blow up. Why?

A 2016 Georgetown study overlaid maps of terrorist activity and drone strikes in Pakistan from 2006 to 2012 and found that terrorist activity increased in places where the strikes were most frequent. Maybe the drone strikes are drawing more recruits into terrorist organizations, as the American hunter/killer robots in the sky breed more and more hatred for the United States. In 2013, retired general Stanley McChrystal, the man who created the U.S. counterinsurgency campaign in Afghanistan, sounded the alarm about this possibility. "The resentment created by American use of unmanned strikes . . . is much greater than the average American appreciates," he said. "They are hated on a visceral level, even by people who've never seen one or seen the effects of one."

It gets worse. Inevitably, technology slips the bonds of its originators. Killer drones may have been invented by the American military, but soon others got in the game, possibly aided by Predators and Reapers that were shot out of the sky and seized by enemy forces. Sometimes, military leaders decide against deploying a technology because they fear that once the genie is let out of the bottle, it cannot be forced back in. That logic is part of the reason why the American military refuses to use certain weapons, including cluster bombs or poisonous gas, that pose too great a risk to noncombatants. I'm sure these conversations happened in the Bush and Obama administrations, but the reward of killer robots apparently outstripped the risk.

Now ISIS has them. The Yemeni Houthis have them. So do the pro-Russian Ukrainian militias. They threaten U.S. troops and U.S. allies everywhere. While our adversaries' technology is still light-years away from the Reaper, just give them time, and they'll catch up. And here at home, anti-terrorism planners believe it's inevitable that a bomb- or missile-equipped drone will eventually target civilians or a government installation in America. Weaponized drones, as it turns out, are a nightmare.

· · ·

There is another important player in this story that may help explain why the U.S. government rushed headlong into a weapons system that we may soon regret having legitimized. Eisenhower's farewell speech warning about the defense industry's ulterior motives were rooted in his belief that the U.S. government had to ward off the temptation to let industry profits, rather than clearheaded national security considerations, drive defense policy. Since the beginning of time, war has been big business. Those who profit from selling things to the war makers are always going to trump up the benefits and minimize the risks of developing and buying more and more weapons.

When it came to the future of weaponized flying robots, the swashbuckling brothers Linden and Neal Blue saw only upside. Today, the octogenarian billionaire Blue brothers are probably the two most interesting Americans you've never heard of. They hide from the public eye in their twin mansions in a gated community outside of San Diego, but sixty years ago, the boys, then Yale students, made the cover of *Life* magazine in a story that recounted their daredevil journey in a small plane flying from New Haven to the Colombian Andes and back. Along the way, they somehow befriended the Somoza family in Nicaragua, whose brutal rule of that country lasted more than forty years.

After college, the Blues went into business with the Somozas, helping to run banana and cocoa plantations. Given the Blues' strange choice of postcollege careers, friends figured they might be undercover CIA operatives, and the various regular adventures of the brothers just fueled those rumors. One example was Linden Blue's decision to fly his plane to the site of the Bay of Pigs training operations two weeks before the invasion was launched (coincidence!). When the Cubans detected his plane, he was forced down by their air force and held for twelve days in a secret police prison. Eventually, the boys came back to do business in the United States, and, still attracted to risk and controversy, they bought General Atomics, a failing uranium company based in San Diego. They kept a leaky processing facility in Oklahoma running despite knowing that it was contaminating the local water supply, agreeing to shut it down only after the radioactivity of nearby wells was found to be thirty-five thousand times the acceptable level.

The brothers' continued friendship with the Somoza family ultimately led to an interest in weaponized drones. In the 1980s, the Soviet-backed Sandinistas had toppled the Somoza dynasty, and the brothers (and, covertly, the Reagan administration) were backing the vicious Contra rebel campaign against them. Linden and Neal figured that the easiest way for the United States to help was to destroy the Sandinistas' fuel supply by flying unmanned, undetectable planes over the fuel tanks and dropping small but lethal bombs from above. The ability to avoid responsibility interested Neal most.

"You could launch them right from behind the line of sight," he told *Fortune* magazine years later, "so you would have total deniability." The brothers' new company partnered with an experienced Israeli drone maker, and soon they had a workable prototype of the first Predator. But they had one problem: The U.S. Department of Defense wasn't interested.

The Blue brothers decided that they needed to get creative and find a way around the indifferent bureaucrats at the Pentagon. And so General Atomics, a small, struggling defense company in the southwest corner of the continental United States, became, virtually overnight, one of the most prolific lobbying forces in Washington, D.C. Starting in the late 1990s, the Blues blanketed Capitol Hill with lobbyists, eventually spending $2.5 million a year—an impressive sum for a bit player in the defense industrial complex.

They got what they paid for, as something now called the Unmanned Systems Caucus was formed by a group of mostly hawkish Republican congressmen who advocated loudly for the defense budget to include money to purchase General Atomics' drones. While campaign contributions rarely produce explicit quid pro quos in Congress (contrary to popular belief), the Blue brothers spread around eye-popping sums to the key legislators' campaigns through the 2000s: $80,000 to Armed Services Committee chairman Duncan Hunter, Sr., and $65,000 to Appropriations Committee chairman Jerry Lewis, to name just two examples.

But the Blue brothers got even more creative. They exploited a loophole in the congressional gift rules that allows contractors to pay for lavish overseas trips for key staff members if there is an "educational value" to the junkets. In the defense appropriations world, congressional staff are often more important and influential than their bosses. The military budget is too dense and too technical for any modern member of Congress to master. So, regrettably, staff end up making many of the key decisions on what gets funded and what doesn't. The Blues knew this, and a 2006 Center for Public Integrity study found that General Atomics spent fifty times what other, much larger, defense companies spent on congressional staff travel. Convicted California congressman Duke Cunningham was one of General Atomics' most fervent backers. Not coincidentally, from 2002 to 2006, the company jetted Cunningham's top legislative staffer all around the world—ten days in Germany, ten days in Italy, eight days in Turkey, a trip to Australia.

Today, General Atomics is a billion-dollar business—the biggest player in the fast-growing world of weaponized drones, with one-quarter of the international market. It is impossible to say with certainty if their lobbying campaign compromised the decisions made by Bush, Obama, the Department of Defense, and congressional appropriators. But the Blue brothers are smart businessmen. They wouldn't have kept making the investment in Congress unless they thought they were getting a return. This is, of course, Eisenhower's warning come to life: Powerful, cash-rich defense companies using their clout to push America into national security decisions that are good for industry, but questionable for the country's long-term security. Weaponized drones made the Blues billionaires. The jury is still out as to how much damage has been done by the violence their robots have exported to the rest of the world.

GUN RUNNERS

One sweltering summer afternoon in 2017, I found myself at the center of the American immigration debate, which at that moment happened to be in the basement of Iglesia de Dios Pentecostal Church in New Haven, Connecticut. Less than twenty-four hours earlier, a young mother of four named Nury Chavarria had defied a deportation order from President Trump's Immigration and Customs Enforcement (ICE) office and instead taken sanctuary in the basement of Pastor Hector Luis Otero's small Fair Haven neighborhood church. As she was one of the first undocumented immigrants to publicly refuse her deportation order, her case immediately attracted national attention, and as I huddled with Nury and her lawyer inside, a dozen television cameras waited outside for the latest update on her stunning act of civil disobedience.

Nury hadn't slept the night before, still unsure whether she had made the right decision. She was exhausted and weak when I met with her and an interpreter. "I can't go back," Nury told me, wearily. "My kids won't survive."

Nury had escaped the violence that surrounded her in Guatemala twenty-four years earlier when she was nineteen years old. In the United States, she got work as a housekeeper, became a model member of the New Haven community, and raised four children, including one with cerebral palsy. She never hid herself from the authorities—she checked in with ICE every year. But the election of Donald Trump changed her life. Convinced that immigrants presented a threat of violence to natural-born Americans—the same drivel used over the years by weapons makers to sell more handguns—Trump ordered ICE to crack down on undocumented workers and start issuing deportation orders even if the individual, like Nury, had minor children who were U.S. citizens and no history of legal trouble.

As I spoke with Nury, her petrified nine-year-old daughter held a sign on her lap decorated with hearts and exclamation points: LET MY MOM STAY. PLEASE. Going back to Guatemala alone was not an option for Nury—there was no way she could turn her children into wards of the state. But taking her kids with her to a country with a murder rate five times higher than that of the United States, where children are regularly recruited into lives of crime and violence, was no more viable. Taking them to Guatemala was a death sentence, she believed. And so for now, she wasn't leaving that church.

A few days later, a federal court intervened and suspended the deportation proceedings, allowing Nury to leave the church. For the time being, she is safe in Connecticut, but there is no telling how long that will last.

. . .

Outside of active war zones, the most violent place on the entire planet might be the city of San Pedro Sula in northern Honduras. Here, children choose to become criminals like they choose to breathe—you do it, or you don't live very long.

"Our greatest challenge here is to stay alive," sixteen-year-old Edwin Vásquez told *The Atlantic*. Edwin narrowly dodged an assassination attempt by a gang that targeted him simply because he lived in a rival group's territory. According to Edwin, the main objective for him and his friends was "to be together with your mom, your family, and make it to eighteen or twenty-two." Edwin survived and even attempted to flee to the United States before being returned to his town by Mexican authorities.

But down the road, in another San Pedro Sula neighborhood, thirteen-year-old Anthony Castellanos was not so lucky. He had been drafted into the city's lethal 18th Street gang as a lookout, but he wanted out. So he told the group's leaders he was quitting. But there is no "out" in San Pedro Sula: The gang members shot Anthony and a young friend in the head. To send an additional message to any other young boys who were considering trying to quit their lookout positions, when Anthony's seven-year-old brother, Kenneth, hopped on his green bicycle and went looking for his missing older brother, the gang members murdered him, too, but not before torturing him—a boy who never even reached four feet tall—by beating him with sticks and rocks.

Farther north in Mexico, many parents would feel lucky to find the bodies of their dead sons or daughters. Thirty-seven thousand people have been deemed "missing" by the Mexican government, casualties of the warfare between drug cartels that is spiraling out of control. Mothers of the missing are reduced to spending their days digging in muddy fields, acting on tips about where the cartels have buried bodies.

"This is my life," said Mirna Medina as she scoured a field in El Fuerte near the Pacific coast. "Digging up holes."

In Acapulco, the heady resort town days are long gone—last year, in a town of about three-quarters of a million people, 953 individuals were murdered. That means that if you live in Acapulco, you have a 1 in 1,000 chance of being murdered this year alone. With statistics like this, it is no surprise that today Latin America is the most murderous place in the world. It is no surprise that Nury refused to introduce her children into this bloodbath. Eight percent of the global population lives in the countries of Central and South America, and 33 percent of the world's homicides happen here.

And most of the dead are being killed by American guns.

·　　·　　·

"I fished with Hugh back in the 2000s," noted one August 2010 post on the popular fishing website BassResource.com. "Great guide and overall nice guy, was surprised to find out he was part of a gun trafficking ring. Anyone else here fish with him?"

Hugh Crumpler was indeed a beloved bass fishing guide in central

Florida. Locals said no one had spent more time with a line in the water at Stick Marsh in Melbourne than Hugh. "Legend has it Hugh has some of the big ones named and trained," Probass.net noted of him. So it was a big shock to his clients and fishing industry friends when he was arrested and charged with being at the center of an illegal firearms trafficking operation that smuggled more than one thousand high-powered weapons, including Glocks and AR-15s, from the United States to Mexico, Honduras, and Colombia.

What had started out as a side hustle for Crumpler soon became a profitable business and an important conduit of guns to criminal syndicates in Latin America. Crumpler was a prototypical "straw man" purchaser. He bought the guns mostly at unregulated gun shows, where he would not be required to go through a background check and would not be asked questions about the end user of the weapons. He then transferred them to his Honduran buyers who sold them to gangs in Central and South America.

Gun running is a lucrative business. Markups on trafficked AR-15s and semiautomatic pistols—guns that cannot be bought legally in a place like Mexico—can sometimes run 200 to 300 percent. Crumpler's ability to procure hundreds of high-powered weapons made him a serious player. "I developed a group of customers," he explained in an interview with Univision. "And it dawned on me one day that they were all Hondurans, and that they all seemed to want the same type of guns, and they all seemed to want more and more."

Illegal guns are one of America's most profitable exports, and Crumpler and thousands of straw men like him are indispensable to the criminal organizations of Latin America. The guns that are being used to terrorize the people of Mexico and Guatemala do not come from Mexico or Guatemala (Mexico, for instance, has only one gun store—and it's run by the military). Every year, more than two hundred thousand guns are illegally trafficked over the U.S.-Mexican border. Pretty much all the guns used in crimes in Mexico come from the United States. In a survey of firearms crimes from 2002 to 2006, an incredible 70 percent of the weapons could be traced back to an American-licensed gun dealer (and that number is likely much higher

because many of the guns were untraceable). Maybe even more troubling, 2 percent of all gun sales in the United States end up in the illegal
Latin American trade, representing a $127 million business to U.S. fire-
arms sellers. And those numbers are escalating dramatically. From
1997 to 1999, the illegal gun market in the United States was only $32
million.

It is, of course, hard to know whether the increase in the movement of weapons from the United States to Mexico was the cause or
the effect of the dramatic rise in violence in Latin America over the
past decade. The battle for control of the illegal drug trade and its
transport to the lucrative American market is behind much of the carnage. Corrupt political leaders and law enforcement—who often take
part in the bloodshed—contribute to the problem, but statistical evidence suggests that American weapons have made the violence much
worse. The homicide rate in Mexico is now at a twenty-year high, and
while guns were used in only 15 percent of murders in 1997 (when the
U.S.-to-Mexico gun trade was relatively small), today guns are a factor
in 66 percent of homicides.

American military-style weapons allow the drug cartels to flourish
in Central America because they have more firepower than the authorities that are trying to chase them. Ioan Grillo, a long-time crime
reporter in Mexico, argues that this supremacy is achieved in part because of guns that are legal in America but almost nowhere else:

> The availability of . . . potent weapons gives Mexican mobsters the
> ability to overwhelm security forces. Cartels buy .50 caliber sniper
> rifles which are amazingly on sale in America, and have repeatedly
> used them to attack police and military vehicles from a distance. Hit-
> men wield Kalashnikovs made in China and the Czech Republic and
> sold in the United States to murder in Mexico. Cartels have work-
> shops where they convert semiautomatic AR-15s into fully auto-
> matic weapons.

·   ·   ·

In 2008, Rogelio Barajas was arrested for smuggling up to one hundred guns from Illinois to Mexico. He had, it seemed, made a practice of going into a gun store near Chicago and buying guns that he then packed in his luggage and transported to Mexico. He told the salespeople at the gun store he was starting a hunting business. The gun store clerks were skeptical but sold the weapons to him anyway. The ATF became suspicious after a gun he had bought was found in an abandoned car in Mexico.

Barajas was not the only gun trafficker who had drawn the ATF's attention. A cluster of nine gun traffickers bought their guns from the same store. Worse still, the store was flagged by the Chicago mayor's office as a top source for guns used to commit crimes in the city. Barajas pleaded guilty to his crime and was sent to prison. But the federal government is virtually powerless to crack down on gun stores like this. And the legendary congressman John Dingell was one of the reasons why.

I consider myself lucky that I got to know John Dingell. No one ever served in the House of Representatives longer than John. His fifty-nine-year career was bracketed by the passage of the Medicare Act, which he gaveled into law as the presiding officer on the day of its passage, and the passage of the Affordable Care Act, which he helped author as a senior member of the Energy and Commerce Committee. No one fought harder during those six decades for the principle of universal healthcare than John Dingell, and I got to spend hours by his side during my six years in the House as he regaled me with stories from the front lines of his long fight for healthcare reform.

But if I had met John after my life and priorities changed in 2012, instead of six years earlier, we probably would have been at each other's throats. Because in addition to fighting for universal healthcare, John's other passion in Congress was working to fight attempts to tighten America's gun laws. Most notably, Dingell was the NRA's chief Democratic ally in passing the 1986 legislation that neutered the ATF's ability to crack down on illegal gun sales by limiting reports on those sales (thereby making illegal gun tracing a labor-intensive chore) and

by limiting inspections of gun stores to one per year (effectively grant-
ing enforcement immunity to any store once their annual inspection
has taken place). Howled John in a 1981 NRA-produced video, "If I
were to select a jackbooted group of fascists who are perhaps as large
a danger to American society as I could pick today, I would pick ATF."

Congress was not done after the 1986 law. Once Republicans took
over Congress in 1994, the assault on the ATF got even more intense.
The most damaging change was a prohibition on the bureau sharing
any information on weapons it traces with the public, thus making the
agency opaque to the press and researchers. Then, Congress stripped
the ATF out of the Department of the Treasury and made the ATF
director subject to separate confirmation by the Senate, essentially giving the gun lobby veto power over the head of firearms enforcement.
Since this change, the ATF has never had a Senate-confirmed director,
making it a permanently leaderless (and thus toothless) enforcement
operation. Today, the annual appropriations statute for the ATF de-
votes eleven lines to describing the agency's authorities, and seventy-
six lines to restrictions on that authority.

With the gun lobby having rendered the ATF impotent, there is
little the agency can do to stem the tide of illegal weapons into Latin
America. To trace a gun without data from gun stores, the ATF is
forced to work backward, a process that is time-consuming and filled
with dead ends. First, the ATF must find the serial number on the gun,
which allows them to trace the gun back to its manufacturer. The
manufacturer can identify the wholesaler that the gun was sold to, and
then the wholesaler can theoretically track down the retail location
where the gun was actually sold. This process, which could take minutes with an online database of sales (which the gun lobby's allies in
Congress made illegal), today takes days or weeks, often making the
information useless in a crime investigation, where trails grow cold
after a few days. And without a director, there is no one to advocate for
additional resources to fulfill the agency's mission. The ATF may be
limited to only one inspection of a gun store a year, but for 90 percent
of gun shops, they don't even get an annual visit because the bureau's
budget has remained unchanged over the past decade, despite the

surge in annual gun sales in America. Even when the ATF does have evidence that something fishy is going on, they rarely have the bandwidth or willingness to take action.

. . .

Perhaps the most egregious loophole that facilitates the flood of weapons to the gun-thirsty Latin American markets is the one that allows gun buyers to avoid background checks by purchasing their weapons at gun shows. The past few decades have witnessed an explosion of these time-limited events, where various licensed and unlicensed gun dealers sell weapons from tables to willing buyers. In 2019, in Texas—from Abilene to Dallas to Houston—there were twenty-two gun shows in January alone, making it wildly convenient for criminals trying to avoid detection to get their hands on any type of weapon legally available.

Luis Pina Romano was one such criminal. From 2009 to 2013, Romano crisscrossed Texas, hitting as many gun shows as possible and seeking out the dealers at those shows who did not require him to submit to a criminal background check to buy a gun. A typical trip would be like his May 2013 visit to the Original Fort Worth Gun Show at the Will Rogers Memorial Center, where Romano spent $10,000 and bought sixteen guns and a handsome supply of ammunition. Romano's buyers were most interested in AR-15-style semiautomatic rifles, and though it's impossible to know how many rifles he sold to smugglers during his time as a straw purchaser, the authorities know of at least sixty—each making Romano a $500 profit—that he purchased at gun shows without any background check.

Another gun trafficker who told his story to *The New York Times* did better than Romano, marking up the semiautomatic rifles he bought at Texas gun shows 500 percent before reselling them in Mexico. He became rich, using his smuggling profits to buy a house, new trucks, and motorcycles. "At the beginning I felt bad, but you get used to it," he explained. "You sell weapons, you earn money and you have fun."

In 1999, after the Columbine massacre, the NRA launched a public relations campaign entitled "Be Reasonable." It took out a full-page ad in *USA Today*, stating, in part: "We believe it's reasonable to provide for instant background checks at gun shows, just like gun stores and pawn shops." But by 2013, the gun lobby had done a 180-degree turn, and now forcefully lobbied against the need to close the gun show loophole. In testimony before Congress in February of that year, Wayne LaPierre dodged and weaved when asked why his organization had changed its position, and only under duress admitted that its opposition to this particular loophole was simply an extension of their newfound belief that the entire background checks system was illegitimate. When the NRA succeeded in defeating the 2013 background checks bill, they kept alive a font of profits for both gun smugglers and the American gun industry.

NAILS AND HAMMERS

At the end of 2018, Senator Lindsey Graham sauntered up to the clerk's desk in the well of the Senate, ready to cast his vote as the body considered a motion to begin debate on an unprecedented resolution to pull the United States out of a war overseas.

"No," he said confidently, pointing toward the carpet with his right thumb. I gave him my best death stare. Dirty looks really aren't in my arsenal, so I'm sure whatever facial contortion I mustered probably looked ridiculous. But it did the trick, and Lindsey made a beeline in my direction.

"You voted no?" I asked incredulously. "I thought we're finally on the same team on this, Lindsey. What are you doing?"

"We are. I just don't agree that this resolution is the right way to get what we want done, Chris. We're going to work together on this, but I just can't be with you today."

I reconjured the death stare. I shook my head and said nothing. He got the hint.

"Okay, let's sit down and talk this out," he said, motioning to two open seats right behind Majority Leader McConnell's desk.

I was astonished that Graham had voted against me, because I was sure that I finally had the hawkish Republican in my corner on an issue that, three years ago, scarcely anyone but me knew anything about. In 2015, I had come to the Senate floor to give the first speech in the chamber on a conflict in the Middle East that barely anyone in Congress had heard of then. For years, the government of Yemen, made up of Sunni Muslims tightly aligned with the royal family of Saudi Arabia, had waged war against a tiny group of Yemenis from the northwest corner of the country called the Houthis, named after their group's founding family. The Yemeni government and their Saudi patrons saw the Houthis as possible allies of Iran and tried to stamp out their religion through the aggressive spread of Saudi Arabia's preferred version of Islam. When that tactic didn't work, they fought six wars to try effectively to exterminate the Houthis.

The Houthi threat was largely imaginary. The Houthis were not militarily allied with Iran when the Saudi onslaught began (they are today by necessity), and when the United States agreed to support the Yemeni government's efforts to hunt down al-Qaeda members, our assistance came with the specific condition that none of our resources be used to fight the Houthis. But the Yemeni government, pushed by the Saudis, created the problem they were seeking to solve.

The conversion campaigns and military attacks hardened Houthi resolve, swelled their ranks, and, eventually, when the chaos of the Arab Spring created a vacuum of power in the Middle East, the Houthis rushed in and captured Sanaa, the Yemeni capital, and much of the rest of the country's vast territory. The Houthis were aided by citizens who had tired of a Saudi-backed regime that was regularly cited as one of the most corrupt in the world and that presided over an economy in shambles, making Yemen the poorest country in the Middle East.

The Houthi takeover shocked the Saudi royal family, and a new quick-tempered, hawkish defense minister named Mohammed bin Salman (colloquially called by his initials, "MBS") ordered the long-dormant Saudi Arabian air force to climb aboard their American-made planes with their American-made bombs and start hitting the Houthis hard. Over and over again, Saudi bombs hit civilians and civilian targets: highways, bridges, hospitals, churches, schools, and wedding parties. Worst of all were the water treatment facilities destroyed by

American-made bombs, turning much of Yemen into a cesspool of untreated human waste and setting into motion a cholera epidemic that would, by 2017, become the worst in recorded history. Tens of thousands of children under the age of five died of starvation and disease. Thousands more were killed in the crossfire between the Saudis and the Houthis.

Adding insult to misery, extremist groups like ISIS and al-Qaeda in the Arabian Peninsula (AQAP), the arm of the terrorist group with the clearest intention and capability of targeting the United States, took advantage of the chaos and gobbled up territory left ungoverned in the civil conflict. At AQAP's height, they controlled more than three hundred coastal miles in southern Yemen, including the lucrative port city of Mukalla, with a population of a half million.

Yemen had become a humanitarian and national security disaster, and what made the situation completely unconscionable was that the United States was not just an innocent bystander. No, as it turns out, we helped make the whole thing happen. For decades, the Saudis had been our strongest ally in the Middle East. Based mainly on our reliance on their oil, our alliance had more recently shifted to a military codependence as the Saudis eagerly signed American defense contracts pushed by the same interests that led to the explosion of the American drone program.

Over decades, we sold the Saudis billions of dollars' worth of expensive, complicated weaponry, though under the implicit agreement that the Saudis would use them only for defensive purposes. Then we looked the other way as the Saudi royal family intensified its campaign to spread its version of Salafi Islam to every conceivable corner of the world, trying to outflank the Shia Iranians for supremacy in the Muslim world.

When the Saudis put our weapons systems into operation against the Houthis, they also asked the United States to directly intervene against the Houthis. We obliged, helping the Saudis pick targets inside Yemen, refueling Saudi jets in midair, and stepping up our military sales, including new precision-guided missiles for the Saudi jets. The United States had become a full partner in Saudi Arabia's campaign of terror inside Yemen. There is no doubt that the American government is culpable in the expansion of ISIS and AQAP, and the deaths of the eighty-five thousand children who have died of starvation or disease, and the ten thousand civilians who have perished in the crossfire of the war.

The most horrific incident of this disastrous war occurred in early 2018, when the Saudis intentionally bombed a school bus carrying schoolchildren in northern Yemen. Forty-four boys, ages six to eleven, were killed on a field trip to a local graveyard, one of the last green spaces in the Saada province. As the families held a makeshift funeral in front of dozens of small, rudimentary wooden caskets covered in pictures of the dead children, the claims by the Saudis that the bus was a "legitimate military target" simply stiffened the spines of the weary Houthi fighters, making any peace agreement substantially less likely. Yemeni journalist Ahmad Algohbary tweeted a picture of a fragment of the bomb, made by American defense contractor Lockheed Martin, exclaiming, "America has its hands stained with Yemen kids' blood!" For years, both Obama and Trump administration officials claimed without evidence that U.S. assistance was making Saudi targeting more responsible. For years, we were told that without the United States, civilian casualties would be worse.

Finally, in December 2018, with the help of Senator Bernie Sanders, I was on the verge of a breakthrough. We had introduced a resolution to pull the United States out of the Yemen war, and as the vote approached, it looked like we might finally prevail. Two days before the final vote, I was talking with background checks hero Joe Manchin as we walked out of a classified briefing on Yemen from Secretary of State Mike Pompeo and Defense Secretary Jim Mattis, who once again made the *it could be worse without us* argument. Manchin, the Trump administration's most reliable vote in the Democratic caucus and a normal ally of the Saudis, was at his wits' end. "Eighty-five thousand kids have died? How do they expect me to explain to folks in West Virginia *it could be worse than eighty-five thousand dead kids?*"

·   ·   ·

I began to pay attention to the U.S. role in the Yemen civil war before anyone else in Congress because the crisis seemed the perfect distillation of America's obsession with using violence to solve crises overseas that would be better met with nonmilitary tools. The hostilities in Yemen exploded because a place of intense poverty and corruption, already fertile for rebellion, became the battlefield in a proxy war between two regional powers who sought to influence the future of the Muslim religion throughout the Middle East and the world. The United States, upon being asked to help solve the bloody conflict, reacted by providing massive military assistance to one side of the proxy war, essentially trying to end a campaign of violence with more violence.

This theory of conflict resolution—confront an application of force with an even more overwhelming application of force—is what won America two world wars. We had more soldiers, more planes, more tanks, and, eventually, more advanced bombs, and we beat our enemies into retreat, submission, and surrender. This was the era when nations fought nations, armies marched against armies in open battlefields with trenches defining discrete battle lines, and wars were tidily concluded with peace treaties that everyone dutifully signed. But in the seventy-five years since the unconditional surrender of Germany and Japan, the nature of war itself has been utterly transformed.

The war on terror, launched by President Bush on September 12, 2001, has no end. Eighteen years later, thousands of U.S. troops are still fighting overseas under the war authorization Congress passed two days after the planes hit the towers. We are now engaged in a war with no end against not a great power, but a stateless ideology. And as our drone wars proved, for each bad guy we kill with force, two more seem to join up. More planes and more soldiers and more bombs don't seem to work the same way they did seventy-five years ago.

The challenges America faces today are largely immune from conventional military force. To beat an energy rich petro-dictator like Vladimir Putin you must cut off the demand for his product by making more of his customers energy independent of Russia. To beat online terrorist recruiters you need to have a nimble counter-propaganda operation that shuts down the online pathways for extremist networks. To stop pandemic disease, you need to coordinate global prevention and public health programming across dozens of countries. To combat climate change, developed nations need to find ways to help developing nations grow with lower carbon footprints. But today, America possesses few, if any, of these capacities. What we have are the tools of violence—the tools provided, gladly, by the military-industrial complex. But these weapons are inept, to say the least, at solving this panoply of nonmilitary challenges.

.   .   .

The day after our visit to Bagram in 2011, our delegation traveled by cargo plane and helicopter to Parmakan, a small town in Herat province on the Afghan border with Iran. The location was chosen by the army to show off the positive effects of the increase in the American presence in Afghanistan, which had allowed for U.S. troops to spread out farther from the major cities to guard against a newly resurgent Taliban. The local tribal leaders were grateful for the newly arrived protection from the Taliban raiders, and they took us for a walk along the dusty roads that connect the small farms that were the basis of the town's economy. The landscape was stunning—as far as the eye could see, endless meadows of bright, colorful flowers spanned the countryside.

"What are you growing in these fields?" Republican congressman Adam Kinzinger asked one of the farmers.

He looked at us disbelievingly. Did we really not know? "Poppy," he said, without hesitation.

I squinted my eyes at Kinzinger, a former air force pilot, not clear why the U.S. Army would purposely bring us to a town whose major crop was heroin. But it was about to get worse. "Who do you sell the poppy to?" I asked the farmer.

Through a translator, the man explained to Kinzinger and me that before the Americans came to Parmakan, the Taliban would arrive at harvest time to collect the poppy, and sometimes the farmers would get paid and sometimes the insurgents would just take their crop. But now that the Americans had arrived, the poppy trade was working much more efficiently. The Taliban were now reliable, paying customers, and the town's farms were thriving.

I turned to Kinzinger and whispered, "So we're basically here protecting the poppy trade that provides the Taliban with an income to continue the insurgency that we are supposed to be fighting?"

There's an old adage, *Everything looks like a nail, if the only tool you have is a hammer.* That is essentially what happened to the United States in both Yemen and Afghanistan. In Yemen, had the United States drawn an early line with Saudi Arabia and made clear that our military support for them would be at risk if they continued pushing their version of Islam on a small, minority religious group that posed no existential danger to the royal family, the entire disaster may have been averted. Or had we spent the money we dedicate to Saudi military assistance on helping build a sustainable Yemeni economy, maybe the country would have never been so vulnerable to civil conflict. During the 2000s, America did spend economic development money in Yemen, seeing the potential future risk of AQAP's home base becoming even more unstable, but the millions spent in development pales in comparison to the billions spent on the Yemen war.

In Parmakan, the prescription was even simpler. Why send a detachment of highly trained army commandos when we could just help the Afghans learn to produce a crop that could be sold into a legitimate market, instead of black-market poppy, which only the Taliban was willing to purchase? The answer, of course, is simple. The United States can't deploy technical experts from the Department of Agriculture to Herat province. We don't do that. But we can send commandos, who are wonderful fighters, but (generally) pretty feeble farmers. So Parmakan gets twenty-one-year-olds with guns, and they do what they are best at doing—guarding people and things and scaring off the enemy. Nothing really changes, except for the corrupt system being able to work just like before, just now without the threat of outside attack.

Rosa Brooks is a former defense official who wrote a wonderful book about this problem, called *How Everything Became War and the*

Military Became Everything. Brooks recalled one development expert complaining to her, "You've got these *kids,* these thirty-year-old captains who've spent their lives learning to drive tanks and shoot people, and they think they know how to end poverty in Afghanistan, in six months."

      •   •   •

Lindsey Graham was the most vocal Saudi champion in the Senate, and so I worked him hard on Yemen. *For two straight years.* First, I teamed up with a strange bedfellow, Senator Rand Paul, to force two votes on the Senate floor objecting to arms sales to Saudi Arabia, requiring Graham to stand on the floor and defend the Saudis' bombing campaign. Then I drafted amendments to budget bills to strip out any funding for the Yemen war. And when Graham and I were in hearings together, I would use my question time to probe witnesses about the wisdom of U.S. support for the Saudi offensive. I knew that if I was able to wear Graham down, I had a chance to get enough Republican support to pull the United States out of the coalition.

Eventually, in mid-2018, Graham agreed to organize a small dinner with a group of senators and the crown prince's brother, a key member of the royal family. At the dinner, Graham pressed the Saudi leader hard about why so many American-made bombs had ended up killing so many civilians. The Saudi delegation assured us that these were simply mistakes, and that they were taking steps to ensure that buses and churches and weddings would no longer be on the receiving end of American munitions.

But then, a few months later, all hell broke loose. A prominent critic of the royal family named Jamal Khashoggi, living in the United States because he feared for his life in Saudi Arabia, walked into a Saudi consulate in Turkey and never walked out. The Turkish authorities claimed that they had audiotapes detailing the murder and dismemberment of Khashoggi. Graham was livid, knowing that the Saudis were lying about the journalist's fate, and wondering whether the Saudis had been lying to him about other misdeeds, like the targeting of civilians in Yemen.

"I feel used and abused," Graham fumed during a *Fox & Friends* interview. "I was on the floor every time defending Saudi Arabia." Watching this filled me with a weird pride, knowing that I was the one who had forced Graham into going out on a limb for the Saudis over and over.

So, finally, Lindsey was ready to cut off arms sales and military support to the Saudis, but as we sat down to chat in the back of the Senate chamber, he was hesitating. He wanted to send a message to the royal family, but he wondered whether our resolution to cut off all military support was the right means to that end. I think, perhaps, he was just wary of getting behind anything with Bernie Sanders's name plastered all over it.

"Lindsey, they're killing kids and lying to us, just like they killed Khashoggi and lied to us," I implored, knowing that time was running out on the vote.

"I'm with you on this, Chris. I am," he replied. "But I hate the way you guys are doing it. Let's find another way to work together on this."

"Lindsey, there isn't another train pulling up to the station. This is the only vote we are going to take this year, and if you vote no, given all you've said in the last few days, it will look . . ." I couldn't find the right, somber enough word. So I settled. "It will look goofy, Lindsey."

He knew I was right. He knew this was our best chance to let Saudi Arabia know that the U.S. Senate did not condone the reflexive use of violence as a means of quelling dissidence internally, like they did with Jamal Khashoggi, or externally, like they were doing with the Houthis in Yemen.

He walked back down to the well of the Senate with me, giving his vote a long hard think along the way. He caught the attention again of the Senate clerk. "Aye," he said.

"Senator Graham. Aye," repeated the clerk.

CNN reporter Phil Mattingly, sitting in the gallery, immediately tweeted, "Lindsey Graham just switched his vote on the motion to discharge the Yemen resolution. And then gave Chris Murphy a big handshake."

In the end, Trump vetoed our war powers legislation, but my work on Yemen taught me that with sustained effort and reasoned argument it is occasionally possible to get even the most notorious hawks to realize that when you export violence you will inevitably reach a point of diminishing returns, and discover that many of the crises you are managing are actually catastrophes of your own creation. We are strong enough to be honest about this—and it ought not be controversial to hold a position that the U.S. military shouldn't create more misery in the world than it alleviates.

. . .

The violence America exports to the world comes in many forms: Lethal hardware pushed by profit-motivated military-industrial companies mostly unconcerned about the consequences. Military-grade firearms that are vacuumed out of America and delivered to the most dangerous countries in the world as fast as smugglers can export them from unregulated American gun shows. An American foreign policy that seeks to quell violence with more violence, simply because of a lack of a more effective tool kit. As much damage as Americans do to ourselves, our addiction to violence arguably does even more harm overseas.

Our country has not yet heeded Eisenhower's repeated warnings about the danger of an overly militant foreign policy. But, then again, neither did Eisenhower.

In Ike's first year in the White House, Iranian prime minister Mohammad Mosaddegh was giving him all sorts of fits. He was in the process of nationalizing Iran's vast oil reserves, eliminating Britain's colonial monopoly and setting a dangerous precedent that other Middle Eastern governments might follow (jeopardizing American corporate monopolies in other nations). Further, Communist agitators were growing in strength, and Eisenhower worried the weakness of the Mosaddegh government might allow the Soviets to gain a foothold in the Middle East. In the summer of 1953, Eisenhower ordered the CIA to organize a violent coup d'état of the democratically elected government, restoring power to Iran's monarch, popularly called the Shah.

Eisenhower had other options. He could have used increased foreign aid to bolster and strengthen the Mosaddegh government and stabilize it from Communist attacks (which were greatly overhyped and likely would never have been serious enough to topple the government). He could have broken with Britain and acquiesced to the nationalization of the oil fields. Or he could have simply done nothing and let the chips fall where they may. Often, doing nothing is actually pretty wise foreign policy.

But inaction is unnatural when you have massive military power and covert capabilities built to *do things*. Why possess a military bigger than all the world's others combined if it's just going to sit around and do nothing? Why have spies all over the world if all they are going to do is report on what other people are up to? In 1953, smart CIA analysts wrote a script that sounded plausible, and Eisenhower bit.

The United States hired Middle Eastern mobsters to prowl the streets to create trouble for Mosaddegh. Protestors and agitators, paid for by the CIA, were shipped in to foment unrest. America (and our British allies) set ablaze a violent revolution that left hundreds dead, Mosaddegh jailed for life, many of his allies executed, and the Shah in power with a new autocratic regime backed by force. Equipped with unparalleled means of violence, the United States couldn't help but use its capability to depose a democratically elected government in a deeply volatile part of the world.

In retrospect, the 1953 coup d'état was a watershed moment in American foreign policy. The Iranian republic, which could have become a model for democratic governance in the Middle East, was gone. America replaced a democracy with an autocracy in order to protect its oil interests and to keep the Soviets at bay. The signal was received loud and clear by other conservative monarchies in the region, which were subsequently given a pass on domestic abuses by the Americans so long as they kept the oil flowing and the Soviets out.

Inside Iran, the misrule of the repressive Shah government, propped up by the United States, eventually led to the Iranian Revolution of 1979, creating a fundamentalist regime in Tehran that would spend the next thirty-five years trying to undermine the United States and our allies all over the region. Finally, the short-term "success" of the coup greatly empowered the CIA, and it began to plan and execute other secret violent rebellions all over the world, including a successful coup in Guatemala the next year, a failed coup of the Syrian president in 1957, and the embarrassing Bay of Pigs debacle in 1961.

Eisenhower's green-lighting of a violent operation, despite his misgivings about the use of force, is testament to how seductive U.S. military power is as a way to *do something* when events overseas start to spiral out of America's control, especially when American leaders don't have other options available. Just like early humans had a wretched time controlling their aggression once they discovered the ability to use physical force in the face of real and potential conflict, so has the young nation of the United States found it difficult to hold back the export of a kind of violence that only America and its military-industrial weapons industry can deliver to the rest of the world. America's violence problem isn't just at home. We ship it overseas now, too.

7

CURBING THE MEANS OF VIOLENCE

I typed out my first tweet ever to go viral on December 2, 2015, as I sat in the passenger seat of my car while a staffer drove me to an evening fundraiser. Earlier that day, fourteen people had been killed by a pair of assassins in San Bernardino, once again using the mass execution-er's weapon of choice, the AR-15. All day, various Republicans—the same ones who looked the Sandy Hook parents in the eye and told them they were prepared to do nothing about gun violence in America—hustled to dispense empty words of apology and sorrow for the victims. I was furious, and for the first time I violated my rule of waiting for thirty minutes to allow for a cooling-off period before hit-ting "send" on angry posts. I came in hot and wrote: "Your 'thoughts' should be of steps to take to stop this carnage. Your 'prayers' should be for forgiveness if you do nothing—again."

It was one of the first instances of a national political figure chal-lenging the idea that mere expressions of grief were insufficient—counterproductive, even—in the wake of an act of mass tragedy. I spent the next two days on the phone trying to explain my position to journalists and pundits, many of whom were astounded by what was labeled my "prayer shaming."

"Prayers are wonderful," I told one reporter, "but God isn't coming to the rescue here. We are."

.　　.　　.

You've reached the fulcrum where we transition from diagnosing the problem to treating it.

We have learned that violence—no matter its connection to our DNA, our history, our prejudices, our politics, our economy, or our foreign policy—does not have to be our destiny. Time and time again, humans have proved that we have the power to make behavior-governing rules that reduce the likelihood of acts of violence between individuals. Maybe we can't legislate away all violence, as Governor Bevin of Kentucky scolded after the Las Vegas shootings, but centuries of declining rates of violence across the globe, and periods of relative calm in the United States, are testimony to the power of public sector policy and private sector norms of behavior to make our communities less harm-filled places. Over the course of the final three chapters, we will take a journey through the policies that promote nonviolence, and how Americans can collectively engineer a movement to enact those policies.

We start with the easiest way to reduce American violence—making small adjustments in our nation's firearms laws that make sure only the right people have these deadly weapons, and that the most lethal guns remain out of the hands of potential killers. Then, in the next chapter, we will turn to the tougher question of how to address the two deepest root systems of American violence: poverty and racism.

We start with the outlaw Jesse James.

BUSHWHACKERS

During the Civil War, there weren't many more chaotic, bloodstained regions of the United States than the western counties of Missouri. Missouri was a Union state, but neither firmly nor happily. In fact, two rival state governments set up operation in the state, and they sent representatives to Washington, D.C., and Richmond, Virginia, where the Confederate States Congress was based. The open, violent conflict between pro-slavery and anti-slavery groups in Missouri that preceded and likely helped instigate the Civil War didn't end with the South's secession, as the Confederacy passed legislation encouraging small bands of men living in the northern territory to organize themselves into militia units to fight unionists.

In Missouri, thousands of young men took up the offer, and overnight a massive, semi-organized guerrilla force took shape in the rugged backcountry and forests of the sparsely populated swaths of the state's western counties. Calling themselves the Bushwhackers, they developed into a subculture that captured America's attention. Mostly illiterate young males, they wore their hair long and beards untrimmed, and styled themselves in fancy hunting shirts with custom embroidery sewed by wives and girlfriends.

Their insurgent tactics foreshadowed modern warfare in Vietnam and Afghanistan, as the Bushwhackers rarely openly confronted Union army units and focused instead on small raids and ambushes. But they gained a reputation as ferocious fighters, and few were ever taken alive. Eventually Union soldiers adopted a practice of simply shooting Bushwhackers on sight and executing the rare prisoner they could capture. When that didn't work, the Union began to imprison anyone in the backcountry who supported the insurgency, jailing the spouses and children of the Bushwhackers to get them to put down their arms. Eventually, sixty thousand Union troops and the forcible removal of twenty thousand people from the western counties put down the rebellion.

Most insurgents were killed during the conflict, but a few of the most ruthless Bushwhackers survived and refused to put down their arms as postbellum Missouri tried to put the pieces back together. Two of them were the infamous James brothers: Jesse and Frank. They spent the ten years after the Civil War terrorizing Missouri—robbing banks, stagecoaches, and trains—and using the local media to add a political flair to their crime spree by writing letters attacking Republicans and playing up their Confederate sympathies.

The Missouri state legislature did not stand by idly. Citizens demanded that the state's political leadership pass laws to crack down on the surge in vigilantism, and the legislature quickly went to work. In 1874, Missouri passed a ban on concealed weapons in certain public locations, and a year later made the ban complete. The Missouri constitution was amended to make clear that the state government had the power to continue to limit gun ownership. And then that's exactly what it did, making Missouri's gun laws among the strongest in the nation. The laws helped, as did more vigorous law enforcement, and eventually the Missouri frontier settled down just like the frontier towns that passed strong gun laws in the heyday of the Wild West. Among the basket of laws passed in Missouri during these years was a noncontroversial provision requiring handgun permits issued by local authorities.

After the hardliner takeover of the NRA in 1977, the organization turned its sights first on state legislatures, and Missouri, a rare southern state with strict gun laws, quickly became a mark. In 1999, as the gun industry sought to regroup after the passage of the Brady bill, the NRA pushed all its chips to the middle of the table in Missouri, putting $3.8 million behind a referendum ending any restrictions on carrying concealed weapons. Democratic governor Mel Carnahan was a fierce gun lobby opponent, and the NRA-backed initiative failed in a close vote, 52 to 48 percent.

But the gun lobby had established a powerful grassroots base in Missouri and helped elect more and more anti–gun control state legislators. In 2003, the NRA was able to pass concealed carry legislation through the legislature. But another Democratic governor, this time Bob Holden, vetoed the legislation. The governorship being the last obstacle to NRA political dominance in Missouri, the group helped elect Republican Matt Blunt (son of my present colleague and friend Senator Roy Blunt) in 2004, and after giving the new governor a few years to get his feet underneath him, targeted 2007 as the year they would sweep Missouri's tough gun laws away forever.

The April 2007 national NRA convention in St. Louis was its biggest to date: Sixty-four thousand members descended upon Missouri's largest city. While there, the top five hundred NRA leaders were treated to a feast on the Budweiser estate, featuring a live auction stocked with collector-grade guns donated by various major firearms manufacturers. Blunt was the featured guest, and a few months later, on the third day of July, he invited a top NRA executive, Christopher Cox, back to the state to stand with him as he signed into law a package of bills laying waste to most of Missouri's restrictions on gun ownership. "I can't think of a better early celebration of the Fourth of July," gloated Cox.

Among the least noticed of the changes made in the 2007 bill was a repeal of that Jesse James–era requirement that gun owners apply for and receive a county gun permit before possessing any handgun. Because a federal background check still was required to get a permit from licensed dealers, the primary effect of repealing the county permit was to allow people to buy guns through private sales, the Internet, and gun shows without a check.

Though other provisions of the bill were viewed by its opponents as more dangerous, there was widespread praise from gun advocates for the repeal of the permit requirement. Explained one county sheriff: "It's been a good thing because we historically have issued from 300 to 400 permits a month. It's a job that takes up quite a bit of time." Local gun dealers agreed. "It's an advantage to the gun buyer," said one gun store owner. "No longer does he have to wait five to seven days to buy a pistol."

Then a funny thing started to happen in Missouri. From 2008 through 2012, as gun murders across the United States were in the middle of a precipitous decline, in Missouri, as soon as the permit law was repealed, gun murders started to increase at startling rates. In the decade leading up to the passage of the NRA-backed measure, the gun homicide rate in Missouri was relatively stable from year to year—about 4.6 deaths per 100,000. And then, in the first year after the law changed, the rate jumped by a third, to 6.2 per 100,000. The rate stayed higher for the next several years, and Missouri—all of a sudden—became this curious American outlier on gun homicides.

Johns Hopkins researcher Daniel Webster decided to jump into the data to see whether the gun law changes were responsible or whether the spike in violence could be attributed to chance or some other factor. By way of comparison, Webster decided to study a state that had made the opposite decision from Missouri—my state of Connecticut. In 1995, Connecticut decided to plug the holes in the national background check law by requiring a similar permit to the one that Missouri repealed. Connecticut made sure that even guns bought through unlicensed sales were subject to a check.

What Webster found was groundbreaking. The repeal of the requirement that all gun purchasers obtain a permit led to an additional 49 to 68 murders per year in Missouri from 2008 to 2012—a 25 percent increase over what he predicted would have occurred if county permits had still been required. The addition of a similar requirement in Connecticut had led to a 40 percent reduction in our state's gun homicides. Webster found all sorts of supporting data to show how this one change in law, largely unheralded at the time of passage, had led to the dramatic increase in Missouri murders. He noted that nonfirearm homicides didn't increase after the law's passage, suggesting an absence of a broader upward movement in societal violence. The number of guns used in crimes shortly after purchase from in-state sources doubled after the law was passed, while the number of Missouri guns trafficked out to neighboring states increased by 37 percent.

For 150 years after the James brothers and thousands of other Confederate-aligned guerrillas plunged Missouri into violent chaos, the state had demonstrated that discerning who were the right and wrong people to own guns was a meaningful way to keep the violence of the Civil War era from returning. And then the NRA showed up in Jefferson City, and 150 years of conventional wisdom on firearm regulation came crashing down. The result was at least four dozen more

Missourians murdered each year, and thousands of mothers, fathers, brothers, and sisters having their lives upended, overnight, with trauma that ripples forever.

.   .   .

As we have learned over and over, guns are not at the foundation of every American murder or suicide. There are factors, some unique to America, some universal, that lay the groundwork for lethal violence. But the presence of so many guns in our nation—dangerous guns, many in the hands of people who common sense would dictate should not have them—could end up doubling the number of people who have been killed by an act of human physical force over the course of our nation's short history. And the experience of how one single change in law, in Missouri and Connecticut, could have such a monumental effect on the number of murders in each place, altering the trajectory of thousands of lives in these two states, points us to gun laws as the quickest, most impactful way to change the story of violence in America.

America was going to be a violent place without the guns, but once Samuel Colt's invention allowed a back-alley argument between neighbors to become a lethal flashpoint, the way people get guns—and what kind of guns they get—became a big part of the story of how America manages our violence. The flood of guns into an already violent nation had the effect of purposefully throwing kerosene onto a smoldering fire. And so that's why we start our exploration of policy and politics here—because the shortest route to lower rates of American violence is to simply make sure that fewer arguments, fewer contests over drug turf, fewer episodes of domestic abuse, and fewer suicidal thoughts end in a life being extinguished, in an instant, from this earth, and all the trauma that tumbles forth from that.

.   .   .

Here are the two headlines, and there's no uncertainty to the claims: First, states with tougher firearms laws have way fewer gun homicides and suicides than states with weak gun laws; and second, states with fewer firearms have fewer gun homicides and suicides than states with more heavily armed populations.

A 2013 study from Harvard and the Boston Children's Hospital scored every state's gun laws, giving higher marks to states with universal background checks, restrictions on concealed weapons permits, bans on assault weapons, and bans on guns in public places. The results showed that the states with the toughest laws experienced 42 percent fewer gun deaths than states with the least restrictive laws.

As I regularly remind people, just take two states that have probably had the highest profile experiences with mass shootings, Connecticut and Florida, which also happen to be on the opposite ends of the spectrum when it comes to strict firearms laws. The difference in the gun death rate between my state and Florida is not 42 percent—it's 240 percent. Now, it's entirely possible that there are mitigating factors that help to explain the differences between very violent and less violent states, but the data on the effect of gun laws is overwhelming. And the Missouri and Connecticut experiences demonstrate that things can go right and wrong super quickly after states pass good and bad laws. If you pass a law that works, you don't have to wait decades to save lives.

So, then, what are the best gun laws—the ones that get the biggest return on enactment?

It's not that complicated, as it turns out. Daniel Webster from Johns Hopkins was onto something: Plugging the holes in the federal system of background checks, like Connecticut did in 1995, is the quickest way states can reduce lethal violence and save lives. One analysis of all fifty states' background checks laws showed that states with universal background checks had an average gun homicide rate of 3.3 per 100,000. States where citizens could buy guns online or at gun shows without a check had a firearm homicide rate of 4.3 per 100,000. For a state the size of Texas, that difference extrapolates to 280 extra deaths per year because of weak background check requirements.

Why does making every gun buyer pass a background check save so many lives? After all, wasn't the gun Adam Lanza used purchased with a background check? Yes, but on balance, background checks tend to stop lots of people from buying guns who are more likely than others to use the gun for malevolent purposes. By and large, that's a good thing.

A survey of gun purchases in Washington State from 1998 to 2014 found that in that medium-sized state alone, more than forty thousand felons had been stopped from buying guns because they failed a background check. Now, of course, most individuals with prior felony records pose no threat of harm to anyone, but these denied purchases represent the felons who went to the gun store and filled out a background check form, knowing that they were likely to be stopped from buying a gun, hinting at some possibility of malevolent intent. Further, in states that require background checks, gun trafficking becomes more cumbersome. States with universal checks force traffickers with criminal records to go out of state to buy guns, creating a meaningful barrier to the resale of these weapons in these states.

State-by-state data cannot, of course, fully predict the impact of the background check system becoming truly national. As discussed earlier, the iron pipeline runs guns from states without universal background check laws (where felonious gun traffickers can purchase weapons at gun shows or on the Internet without having to reveal their criminal past) to states with tougher laws. The only way to shut down this trafficking route is to close the background check loopholes everywhere. Thus, when a national background check law passes, gun crime will drop not only in the states where the loopholes exist today, but also in the states with tougher gun laws that cannot keep out guns coming from states with weaker laws.

. . .

The research surrounding bans on certain firearms and associated technology is not as robust as the data on the efficacy of background checks, but the simplest articulation of the data is the most persuasive. In the ten years after the national assault weapons ban (which included a ban on high-capacity magazines) was passed in 1994, there were 37 percent fewer murders of six or more people than in the ten years before it was passed. And then, during the ten years after the national ban expired in 2004, mass murders in America increased by 183 percent. This upside-down bell curve of mass murder, with a giant dip occurring during the ten years when assault weapons and high-capacity magazines were not sold anywhere in the United States, is not coincidental. Another study found that the number of semiautomatic weapons used in crimes increased dramatically after the expiration of the ban, and many local jurisdictions report that high-capacity magazines are now in regular usage. From 2012 to 2014, 21 percent of all gun crimes in Baltimore involved a firearm with a high-capacity magazine. In Hartford, during a similar time period, the number was 30 percent.

For the survivors and relatives of those lost in mass shootings, data is unnecessary to explain the danger of assault weapons. The slaughter surrounding the shooting of Congresswoman Gabby Giffords would have continued if not for the shooter fumbling during an exchange of cartridges. Gabby's husband, Mark Kelly, wonders frequently whether the shooting would have ended much earlier had the killer had to reload after every ten rounds, not thirty. The same question is asked frequently in Sandy Hook, where authorities believe six children are alive today because, as Lanza had similar difficulty changing magazines, the children were able to escape his gaze and run out of the classroom. How many more children would have escaped if Lanza had had to perform that exchange three times more often?

Recently, several other promising policy avenues have begun to find favor in state legislatures throughout the country. First, several states have passed legislation authorizing court-ordered "extreme risk protection orders." These are legal mechanisms to allow police to take guns away from individuals who have acted in ways that demonstrate they pose a potential immediate threat to themselves or others. California passed their version of the law in response to the mass shooting in Isla Vista by twenty-two-year-old Elliot Rodger, who had displayed clear signs of unstable behavior at the very time he was acquiring the weapons that he would use to shoot seven people, four fatally, including himself. Recent studies of similar laws passed in Connecticut and Indiana show that these laws can reduce suicide rates by allowing family members to take guns away from loved ones showing signs of suicidal behavior.

Second, a movement has been gaining steam to require gun owners to more responsibly store their weapons. Properly locking guns away can reduce suicides, homicides, and accidental deaths. In early 2018, high school freshman Ethan Song was at his friend's house in Guilford, Connecticut, when they decided to play with his friend's father's handgun the teenagers believed was not loaded. The result was Ethan Song becoming one of approximately five hundred Americans who die each year from accidental gun discharges. Ethan's heroic parents, Kristin and Mark, immediately went to work to pass state legislation that requires, under penalty of law, all owners of firearms to keep guns locked away if children live in the house. A similar bill has been introduced in Congress, and hopes abound that safe storage legislation might end up drawing the support of gun owners who see this approach as less threatening than bills to curtail particular kinds of gun sales.

All of these measures, though, fall into the same general category of policy interventions. If you make sure that only responsible people own and handle guns, and you pull back the most lethal weapons from the market, research tells us that we can demonstrably bring down rates of violence. Thus, while the data is less comprehensive on some of these newer approaches, we can safely conclude that gun registration laws, requirements to undergo training before purchasing a gun, waiting periods, expansions of background checks laws to include more prohibited purchasers, and bans on technologies that make semi-automatic rifles fire even faster are likely to get positive returns on gun violence rates.

. . .

One day, shortly after I gave a speech on the Senate floor on gun violence, Republican senator Ben Sasse of Nebraska, who was presiding over the Senate at the time, beckoned me up to the dais. "You should check out John Lott's research. He comes to the exact opposite conclusion you do," recommended Sasse. The title of Lott's wildly influential 1998 book, *More Guns, Less Crime*, forms the backbone of the conservative argument regarding gun control. Lott argues that states that allow carrying concealed weapons experience less crime because of the fear struck into the hearts of potential miscreants by cadres of armed citizens lying in wait to frustrate crime. This argument, backed up by piles of Hollywood action movie scripts, makes the NRA salivate—recall Wayne LaPierre's claim a week after Sandy Hook that "the only thing that stops a bad guy with a gun is a good guy with a gun." The problem is that the claim, and many of the other protests by the gun lobby, are just not true.

Before the sun rose on the morning of November 2, 2013, Theodore Wafer jumped out of his bed at the sound of pounding at his door. Unable to find his phone in order to call the police, he instead picked up his shotgun and headed for the door. Behind the screen door he saw a shadowy figure he interpreted as an intruder and let fly a single shot from his gun. The blast killed the nineteen-year-old girl standing on his doorstep, who had just been looking for help after an auto accident nearby.

Wafer's experience is not the exception—it's the rule. An industry has developed dedicated to debunking Lott's "research" and his bizarre and irresponsible methods of analysis. It turns out that if you have a gun in your home, it is six times more likely to be used in a crime than it is in a legitimate instance of self-defense. Research shows that running away from a threat, or even doing nothing, is statistically more effective than trying to fire a weapon at an assailant. Despite the rapid increase in gun ownership by women (prompted in part by a public relations campaign by the NRA), a study in 2006 of 1,119 sexual assaults found that only a single one had been stopped by a victim brandishing a firearm.

And perhaps the simplest analysis is the most persuasive: If more guns led to less crime, America would be the safest place on earth. We are not—in fact, America is the most homicidal country in the high-income world—and that, the data clearly demonstrates, is because countries and states with higher rates of gun ownership have more murders than countries and states with fewer firearms per capita. More guns actually means more lethal crime.

.   .   .

The gun lobby also spends a lot of time complaining about what it re-
gards as the arbitrary definitions used in gun laws. This grievance goes
all the way back to the 1968 law, which galvanized the growing radical
wing of the NRA, which felt the definition of banned automatic weapons was overly broad. Today, the gun lobby makes sensible arguments
regarding the kinds of weapons gun control advocates want to ban and
those that would remain legal. In a widely viewed CNN town hall
meeting after the Parkland shooting, Florida's senator Marco Rubio
argued that while a ban on so-called assault weapons is popular, a total
ban on all semiautomatic rifles would not be. His point was that the
definition of assault weapons in the 1994 law is somewhat arbitrary,
built around the physical characteristics of the gun, like a pistol grip or
a folding stock, that allow it to be more easily handled and hidden by
amateur shooters.

Other critics ask why a "high-capacity magazine" is defined as
eleven bullets. What's the science behind that number? The truth is,
there are always arbitrary distinctions made in law between what is
allowed and what is not. Some have suggested, for instance, that the
definition of an assault weapon should be tied to the muzzle velocity
of the gun (which would likely ban many pistols as well as rifles) since
the speed of the bullet has significant correlation to the chance that a
shot will be lethal.

The definition of what qualifies as a weapon acceptable for commercial sale will never be easy, and those of us who support these bans
should always be open to accepting a better definition of what weapons are too efficiently deadly to remain legal. But weapons like the
AR-15 that were specifically designed to kill as many humans as possible, and that have features designed not for single shot accuracy but for
mass casualty, should not be sold to the public, and if the definition
happens to capture a few guns that were not built for this purpose,
then that is an acceptable unintended consequence.

Gun company lobbyists also protest that background checks, too
broadly applied, end up prohibiting many Americans who present no

threat to others. This claim *is* true, and the complaint will find little pushback from me. In fact, in 2017, I found myself locked in a deeply distasteful legislative spat with the National Alliance on Mental Illness, a group that had been one of my most trusted allies for close to a decade, over whether gun purchases should be prohibited to people whose mental function had deteriorated such that they needed a conservator appointed to handle their fiscal affairs. President Obama had added this population of Social Security recipients to the list of those who should fail a firearms background check, and the mental health advocacy community rightly worried that this would further stigmatize those with mental illness as being inherently prone to violence. A year earlier, the ACLU had objected to adding those on the terrorist watch list to the same list, arguing that the late senator Ted Kennedy's temporary inclusion on the list was evidence that the wrong people often get swept up in less-than-perfect lists of Americans with supposed connections to extremist groups.

All these objections to expanded background checks and bigger lists of prohibited purchases have merit, but when the wrong person gets their hands on a gun and fires it at another human being, the damage done is permanent. On the other hand, there are processes to allow individuals wrongfully included in the NICS system to expunge their record, making this inconvenience temporary.

Yes, there are many harmless people with felony records who will not be able to have their gun rights restored. And if the data on the number of lives saved by keeping the harm-prone individuals from owning guns was less persuasive (if, say, universal background checks decreased crime by only a few percentage points) then the civil liberty concerns would be more convincing. But when weighed against the thousands of lives saved (and tens of thousands of resulting trauma cases prevented), the injustice of a handful of Americans losing their ability to own a gun is, in my opinion, not a close call.

. . .

One sweltering summer day in 2017, I was attending a veterans' recognition ceremony in Meriden, Connecticut, when an older man caught my eye as I was descending from the podium at the conclusion of the program.

His scowl predicted his opening line. "I'm one of those deplorables," he told me gruffly.

"Well, I wouldn't call you that, sir. I don't agree with President Trump on much, but you have every right to support him," I replied, hoping I could keep the conversation short enough to avoid a messy confrontation. But he wasn't done.

"He's a good man, Trump is," the man said to me. "And he'd be able to do what he needs to do if you'd stop opposing him on everything."

I remained in listening mode, figuring that more was on its way. And it was. "What I know is that Donald Trump is protecting my guns from people like you who want to take them away," he continued. "As long as there are people like you around, then I need people like Trump."

I sensed my opportunity. "Let me ask you this—do you think somebody should have to get a background check before they buy a gun?"

His disposition immediately changed. His eyes opened wider and he said confidently, "Well, of course. I don't want criminals buying guns. I'm for *that*."

"And you probably went through background checks to buy your guns, right? Probably wasn't too much of a hassle for someone law-abiding like you."

"Took ten minutes. Easy."

"But *that's* what I'm for. I don't want to take your guns away. That's what people want you to believe—that people like me have a secret agenda. But we don't. We just think some people are too dangerous to own a gun, and there are a few guns too dangerous for anyone to own. And frankly, most gun owners I talk to you—like you—think the same thing."

Today, gun rights proponents and anti–gun violence advocates spend far too much time talking past one another when, unbeknownst to most activists on both sides, there exists far more common ground than conflict. Polls consistently show that 90 percent of Americans support the passage of national universal background checks, with more than 80 percent of gun owners supporting the policy. A 2013 poll noted that support for background checks registered higher than support for apple pie (81 percent), kittens (76 percent), and laws banning child labor (71 percent). And assault weapons regulation isn't much less popular. By a two to one margin, Americans support banning certain weapons, like AR-15s, that are designed for mass slaughter.

The problem, however, is that both sides ascribe positions to the other that are not accurate. My friends often believe that the people driving pickup trucks with NRA stickers on the back don't support some tougher gun laws. They do. And many of those pickup truck drivers assume that people like me want to confiscate people's weapons. We don't. That's why I think anti–gun violence advocates need to make clear that we believe that there existed at the founding of this nation a common-law right to private-sector gun ownership, and that the Second Amendment, while bizarrely worded, protects that right. But just like all other constitutional rights, it is not absolute. And if my side concedes that the Constitution forbids the prohibition of an individual's right to own a gun, then gun rights advocates should be more willing to openly support measures like universal background checks, confident that the law isn't just a camel's-nose effort to obtain more draconian policies. A more sensible conversation is possible, but only if we all stop believing the worst stereotypes about people with whom we don't agree.

MOTHERS AND CHILDREN OF THE MOVEMENT

The afternoon of February 14, 2018, I was riding the underground subway that connects the Senate office buildings to the U.S. Capitol, checking my notes one last time before giving a speech on immigration on the Senate floor. A flurry of familiar messages started to crowd the in-box on my phone. By then, the near-weekly notifications from my staff of yet another school or workplace shooting were becoming an almost unremarkable routine. This time, it was a school shooting in a place I had never heard of: Parkland, Florida. Details were sketchy, but early reports suggested that the scene was grisly.

My hesitance to talk about gun laws in the wake of tragedy— something I felt keenly in the hours and days following Sandy Hook— had long since vanished. I had become convinced that the claim from gun industry allies that speaking about gun laws in the hours or days after a mass shooting was "politicizing the tragedy" was simply a cold-blooded tactic to stamp out any talk of tightening gun laws at the very moments when the entire country was tuned in to the issue. My staff wasn't convinced, and some cringed when a profile piece on me in *The Washington Post* was titled "What's Wrong with Politicizing a Tragedy? For Chris Murphy, Nothing at All." But I was undeterred; detectives don't wait forty-eight hours to start solving a crime, so why should senators not be able to talk about changing the laws that allow for this slaughter after another massacre occurs?

"As we speak, there is another horrific tragedy playing out in a high school in south Florida," I began, my pace slow and purposeful. "Turn on your television right now and you will see scenes of children running for their lives." I don't write most of the speeches I give on the Senate floor, but most of the time, I at least have a rough idea in my head of what I will say. Not that day. I was winging it, and getting angrier and louder as I went.

"This happens nowhere else other than the United States of America, this epidemic of mass slaughter, this scourge of school shooting after school shooting," I continued. "It only happens here, not because of coincidence, not because of bad luck, but as a consequence of our inaction. We are responsible. . . ."

The short, impromptu speech was replayed on cable and online news thousands of times over the next few days, and though it attracted the familiar complaints by those in the gun lobby's orbit who still clung to a "no policy discussion waiting period," the response was almost universally positive. *The New Yorker* ran an article entitled "Chris Murphy and the Accelerating Politics of Mass Shootings," and our office was barraged with phone calls from people all across America who were hungry to hear voices of change in the wake of these now regular mass slaughters.

In the years since Sandy Hook, and especially in the years between the 2015 San Bernardino shooting and the events in Parkland that I was just learning about that Wednesday morning, America had changed—although most politicians had been slow to catch on. A popular online frame for thinking of the politics of the gun debate in the wake of Sandy Hook was perfectly encapsulated by columnist Dan Hodges, who wrote in 2015, "In retrospect, Sandy Hook marked the end of the US gun control debate. Once America decided killing children was bearable, it was over." His argument was persuasive: If the murder of twenty first graders didn't convince Congress to change the laws of the nation to protect against gun violence, what else could? And that is certainly what I thought in the immediate moments after the failure of the 2013 post–Sandy Hook drive to pass comprehensive federal background check requirements. I wondered, what more motivation could my colleagues need than this?

But I soon realized that we hadn't lost the argument in the Senate on the merits that spring, nor had we failed to convince the majority of the American voting public that our position was the right one. Our only deficit—and the only deficit that matters in politics—was of political muscle and organization. The gun lobby had loads of it in 2013. We had virtually none.

"They were ready—the gun lobby was—for those parents," I told NPR in 2017. "And they took them down. Every single vote failed because they had more political power than we did. Since Sandy Hook, we have been gradually, year by year, accumulating more and more political power, more activists, more money. I don't think there's going to be a tipping point where one shooting changes the debate. . . . This is just a matter of political power dynamics. We need more power. We'll get it, and we'll eventually be as strong as the gun lobby."

I had concluded that our movement must not allow any space between the headline-grabbing mass shootings and political action. If we were to grow our power, we needed to harness the emotion that erupts from mass murder and turn it into a high-powered grassroots engine. There was no shame in that kind of seamlessness—this was how we would save lives. And that same day, as I sustained more criticism for "politicizing" this latest mass shooting in a high school in south Florida, a group of unafraid, brilliantly mouthy high school kids from Parkland were arriving at the same conclusion.

.   .   .

I'm grateful for the foundation that legacy gun violence prevention groups like the Brady Campaign laid down in the decades leading up to the Sandy Hook shootings. Their success in passing the 1990s gun bills, and keeping the torch lit during the dark days of the 2000s, is heroic, but the modern anti–gun violence movement began on December 13, 2012. That day, a forty-one-year-old stay-at-home mother of five hastily set up a Facebook page entitled "One Million Moms for Gun Control." So many moms had the same idea that day, Shannon Watts remembered, "it was like lightning in a bottle." The page garnered thousands and thousands of likes, and then a few days later, three mothers in Brooklyn, with an idea to turn Watts's social media campaign into an organization, asked to talk to the Indianapolis mother on Skype. After the call, the New York moms established the first chapter of what was eventually called Moms Demand Action, and within a single year, the group would have one hundred thousand members and chapters in every single state.

In Tucson, Arizona, former congresswoman Gabby Giffords was in the middle of her grueling recovery from the bullet wound that shattered her skull and pierced her brain when news of Sandy Hook reached her and her husband, Mark Kelly. I remembered my friend Gabby, my freshman-term neighbor on the fifth floor of the Cannon House Office Building, as a supporter of gun rights. She was a proud gun owner and an enthusiastic signer of the Supreme Court amicus brief in support of the NRA's position on the *Heller* case in 2008. She wasn't a consistent vote for the NRA, but she was a better ally to the gun industry than most other Democrats during her three terms in

Congress. And in the two years after her shooting, she and Kelly had stayed out of the political fray, focused instead on Gabby's long road back from near death.

Sandy Hook jarred the couple from their political hiatus. Shortly thereafter, they launched a new political action committee dedicated to ousting members of Congress who refused to vote for common-sense gun reform. Within six months, the organization had five hundred thousand members, seventy-two thousand donors, and $6.5 million in the bank.

In those early years, I did all I could to support the growing movement. In addition to my regular calls for action in the immediate wake of high-profile incidents, I showed up at every press conference, I went to every rally, I joined every organizing conference call. I put myself as close to the center of the movement as possible. And I began a relentless series of speeches on the Senate floor, every week or two, telling the personal stories of the individuals lost to gun violence in America. The effort, called "Voice of Victims," was designed to keep up a drumbeat of shame on my inactive colleagues. When my new chief of staff convened her first all-staff retreat in 2014, we drafted our top three priorities for the rest of our first term. First on the list was "Eat, sleep, breathe anti–gun violence." I tried to fulfill this maxim as best I could.

Time and time again, I would have to remind weary activists, who couldn't understand why Congress refused to budge, why we could not give up. The speech, to crowds of skeptical, angry anti–gun violence activists, was always some version of the same theme:

Great social change movements are not defined by their immediate successes. They are defined by their early failures and how they respond to those defeats. The reform campaigns that give up when they hit their first obstacles are the ones you never read about. The efforts that persevere, through gut-wrenching loss after gut-wrenching loss, confident in the righteousness of the cause and the eventual downfall of the status quo, are those that make the history books.

In those first five years, I gave this speech hundreds of times, and most of the time, I believed it.

I believed it, because despite our lack of legislative success, and the shellacking of Democrats in the 2014 midterms (including a lot of senators who had voted for the 2013 background checks measure), I began to notice that all across the country, our numbers were slowly and steadily growing, and the manpower of the gun lobby seemed to be slowly withering. As I suspected, it was depressingly cataclysmic events that spurred growth of the movement. The 2016 Orlando shooting was the first.

I can't really pinpoint why Orlando is, in retrospect, a before-and-after moment in the movement, but my guess is that the shooting, which was at the time the worst in American history, was the final proof for many Americans that this epidemic was not going away. The parade of tragic events from Sandy Hook through the summer of 2016 had put many Americans at a breaking point, and Orlando pushed them over. The subsequent legislative debate, in which the Republican Congress refused to prevent even individuals on the terrorist watch list from buying guns, was a second insult—a clear sign that Congress was still so compromised by the power of the gun lobby that it was willing to endanger American lives.

That fall, I took trips to Florida and Ohio to campaign for Hillary Clinton, and I was amazed at each campaign headquarters to see that the issue motivating the most people to volunteer was guns. I got used to seeing legions of red Moms Demand Action T-shirt–wearing volunteers at every event at which I appeared. And polling began to finally show that gun issues were inching up among the priorities of swing voters. In the key 2016 battleground Senate race in New Hampshire, incumbent Republican Kelly Ayotte's first ads were dedicated to explaining why despite voting against the 2013 Manchin-Toomey bill on universal background checks, she was truly, strongly in favor of gun reform legislation. That was an ad that no New Hampshire Republican would have had to run just two years earlier.

And then, the second watershed moment: the day the world met Emma González. Shortly after the Parkland shootings, I departed

Washington for a long-planned vacation with my extended family to, coincidentally, Fort Lauderdale. I desperately wanted to contact the students who were lighting up social media in the days after the massacre, pleading for leadership. "I don't want your condolences you fucking piece of shit," tweeted sixteen-year-old Sarah Chadwick at the president. "My friends and teachers were shot. Multiple of my fellow classmates are dead. Do something instead of sending prayers. Prayers won't fix this. But gun control will prevent it from happening again." But I knew that interference from anyone inside the political mainstream would just pollute what was emerging as the most authentic, impassioned call for change in the movement's history. So I watched it unfold on television, along with the rest of the world.

At around one-forty in the afternoon, three days after the Parkland killing, seventeen-year-old high school senior Emma González, nervous and fighting back tears, stepped to the microphone at a hurriedly arranged rally just down the street from where my family was staying in Fort Lauderdale. As she repeatedly brushed back tears with the open palm of her hand, González levied a remarkable broadside at cowardly politicians who chose the gun lobby over the safety of children. And she called out the NRA, by name, over and over.

"To every politician who is taking donations from the NRA, shame on you," she yelled, her voice cracking with emotion. The crowd of thousands chanted back, *"Shame on you! Shame on you! Shame on you!"* Every word of González's seven-minute speech was dripping with a combination of fear for her own life and fury at those who had let her and her friends down. The raw power of this captivating combination of emotions transfixed those who watched it, and clips of her speech became mandatory viewing across America.

Sometimes it's hard to notice historic moments when they happen. But as I watched that speech on that day, I knew, immediately, that everything had changed. Because these kids, and their energy—layered upon the foundation we had built during the prior five years—would be unstoppable. The Sandy Hook first graders who survived couldn't speak for themselves. But these kids could. I only watched González's speech that day, but I knew that she and her friends would inspire thousands of other students like her to join the movement. And I remembered from my high school history classes that virtually every great social change movement in history, from the French Revolution to the civil rights movement, was led not by seasoned adults, but by young people. And now, right before my eyes, inside the cauldron of yet another tragedy, our movement was being handed to children. Just as it should be.

Within days, dominoes began to fall. Major companies began to end business arrangements with the NRA. Polls began to show that for the first time ever, more people disapproved of the gun rights organization than approved of it. González, virtually overnight, had more social media followers than the NRA. I was on the phone all week, trying to make sure legislators in Washington were ready to assist these kids as they began to build their collective voice. It turns out they didn't need our help.

"We need to make sure they come to Washington," I suggested to John Feinblatt, the president of Michael Bloomberg's group Everytown for Gun Safety. "Like soon. They could change the world with a massive rally."

"They're already planning it. And we're going to fund whatever they choose to do," he replied.

. . .

A week after Parkland, President Trump invited a handful of senators and congresspeople, including me, to the White House for a televised, reality show–inspired conversation about gun violence. The night before, I went to the West Wing to see Trump's director of legislative affairs, to talk about what could be accomplished at the meeting. "Ask him about background checks," he said. "I don't know what he'll say, but I'd suggest getting the conversation there as quickly as possible." He repeated versions of this suggestion a few more times during our meeting, and it occurred to me that maybe some in the White House had their own agenda and were hoping to use me as a way to steer the president into a policy direction others in the White House might warn Trump against. I thought to myself, How fucked up is this White

House that the president's top advisers are using Democratic senators to try to influence the president on live TV?

The meeting was, predictably, a fiasco. Pro-NRA Republicans at the meeting cringed in a mix of horror and confusion as Trump appeared to endorse every priority of the anti–gun violence movement, even coming close to sending Dianne Feinstein into cardiac arrest when he suggested he might support her legislation to re-impose the ban on assault weapons and high-capacity magazines. I reminded Trump that the only way any progress would be made on gun policy was for him to clearly and forcefully stand up to the gun lobby and force-walk Republicans into negotiations.

As we departed the meeting, I turned to Ted Deutch, the congressman from Parkland. "That was all bullshit, right? Like, every word."

"I think so," he said. "Just a matter of time before the NRA gets to him."

It took a whole day. The next evening, Christopher Cox, the group's chief lobbyist, met with Trump at the White House and easily secured a commitment from the president to back off supporting background checks or weapons bans. A triumphant Cox tweeted after the meeting: "I had a great meeting tonight w @realDonaldTrump and @VP. We all want safe schools, mental health reform and to keep guns away from dangerous people. POTUS and VPOTUS support the Second Amendment, support strong due process and don't want gun control. #NRA #MAGA."

But it was too late to save the gun lobby. Trump's attacks on the NRA at the televised meeting (at one point he chided Senator Pat Toomey, the author of the NRA-opposed 2013 background checks bill, for being afraid of the gun lobby), piled on top of the Parkland kids' assault on the gun lobby, gave permission for even hardened Republican voters to rethink their traditional opposition to new gun laws, and for moderate gun owners to drop their NRA membership. In the year after Parkland, members fled the NRA, and their dues income dropped a remarkable 22 percent.

· · ·

Retired flight attendant Lucy McBath was in her suburban Georgia home watching the White House meeting on her television, bursting with anger at what she knew to be Trump's hypocrisy. But her fury wasn't directed at only Trump. "I didn't know why all these congressmen weren't standing up to him and saying what we all knew, that he was lying!" she told me a year later, as I tried not to take her anger personally. Tearing her hair out, listening to the president of the United States make promises she knew he wouldn't keep and congressmen who were acting far too polite for her taste, she made a decision on the spot. She was going to run for the U.S. Congress.

McBath had a personal stake in the discussion at the White House that day. Just over five years before, her son Jordan Davis had pulled up to a gas station in Jacksonville, Florida, with three other friends in their sport utility vehicle. Like a lot of teens, Jordan and friends played their music loud, and when Michael Dunn, a white customer at the same gas station, complained about the teens' "thug music," an argument broke out. It was the kind of argument between a teenager and adult that occurs every hour of every day in every country across the world. But only in America does someone regularly end up getting killed.

Dunn, a Florida concealed weapons permit holder, decided that he needed to teach a lesson to this young African American teenager who wouldn't follow a stranger's directions and turn down his music. "You aren't going to talk to me like that," exclaimed Dunn as he pulled a handgun out of his car's glove compartment before firing at Davis, hitting him in the liver, lungs, and aorta. As the driver of the teenagers' car desperately tried to back out of the kill zone, Dunn focused and continued firing at the car. When Dunn's girlfriend emerged from the gas station, they drove to their hotel room and ordered a pizza. He never called the police; the next day Dunn was arrested based on eyewitness reports of his license plate.

Jordan's death catapulted his mother into the anti–gun violence movement, eventually landing Lucy McBath the job of national spokesperson for Moms Demand Action. But McBath's decision to run for Congress seemed destructively impulsive to her friends and the network of victims' parents, otherwise known as the "mothers of the movement." Even up to the last minute, some tried to convince her not to run for the seat, which had been reliably held by Republicans since 1979. Pundits wrote her campaign off.

Just a year earlier, the entire national progressive movement had descended upon this very district when it became the first high-profile open seat after Trump's election. In that special election Democrats got behind a handsome, charismatic young candidate named Jon Ossoff, who ran a perfect race, sticking with the time-honored Democratic tradition of avoiding the issue of guns in competitive races. Politico ran a story during the special election entitled "The Issue Democrats Wish Would Go Away," suggesting that Ossoff would lose his race because just being quiet on guns was not sufficiently conservative in a swing district like Georgia's Sixth District. You couldn't win in a place like that without being endorsed by the NRA, held the lingering conventional wisdom.

When McBath told me the story of her journey to Congress, we were sitting in her congressional office, just after she was sworn in as the first Democrat to represent that Georgia district in forty years. So what happened?

First, the political infrastructure around the movement had gotten much stronger in less than two years. Gabby Giffords's PAC was able to raise more money to target more NRA-friendly incumbents. In the wake of Parkland, the volunteer base of Moms Demand Action tripled. The March for Our Lives, held on March 24, 2018, less than six weeks after the Parkland shootings, drew two million people to protests all over the country, and Students Demand Action chapters were created in hundreds of high schools. Congressional town hall meetings were overflowing with anti–gun violence activists, and gun rights activists were in retrenchment.

Second, voters started to elevate the issue of gun violence to their priority list. Increasingly, they couldn't understand why interventions that enjoyed more than 90 percent public support, like closing the gun show and Internet loopholes in the nation's background checks system, couldn't even get a hearing in Washington.

But there was another phenomenon that possibly had an even

greater effect on voters than any one single shooting. One evening, sitting at our family's dining table, I asked Rider, in kindergarten at the time, if anything interesting had happened in school that day. He explained to me that they had practiced something called "shelter in place," just in case, he told me, "somebody gets into the school that's not supposed to be there." He went on to describe the twenty-five children in his class being packed like sardines, shoulder to shoulder, into their public school classroom's little one-toilet bathroom, and told by their teacher to remain quiet for as long as possible. Rider didn't know enough to understand that what he had participated in was one of thousands of active shooter drills that are routinely practiced by schools all across America. But he knew enough to tell me how he felt.

Dropping his voice to a whisper, he leaned forward at the table. "Daddy, *I didn't like it.*"

My heart sank, as I thought about the fear and confusion that must have been racing through those five- and six-year-old children as they wondered what stranger could be so scary as to force their teacher to pack twenty-five of them into a tiny bathroom.

Millions of parents heard stories like that from their elementary age schoolchildren from 2013 to 2018, and all of a sudden, no one could escape the trauma of gun violence.

In the 2017 governor's race in Virginia, exit polls showed that guns was the second most important issue to both Democrats and Republicans, and Ralph Northam, who ran unapologetically on universal background checks and an assault weapons ban, won handily. And then, in early 2018, as Lucy McBath was declaring her candidacy, so were hundreds of other candidates, many of whom cut their political teeth in the anti–gun violence movement, and who planned to make the issue a centerpiece of their campaigns.

I launched a campaign to raise money for eight congressional races where an anti–gun violence candidate was running to replace an NRA A-rated Republican incumbent, and in about forty-eight hours we raised nearly $1 million. Then, on Election Day, the movement scored its first major victory. Twenty-seven NRA A-rated Republican incum-

bents were swept out of Congress, replaced by anti–gun violence activists. All eight of the candidates for whom I raised money won.

Polls showed that of those voting for Democrats, once again guns
was the second most important issue (again, as in Virginia, trailing
only healthcare), and, most remarkably, of the voters who said guns
was their top issue, seven of ten were voting for Democrats. As it turns
out, by 2018 the conventional wisdom on guns had finally been flipped
on its head: Lucy McBath won because she ran strongly on strengthen-
ing the nation's gun laws. Jon Ossoff, despite all of his strengths, had
lost because he stayed silent about an issue on which winning candidates could no longer afford to be quiet. McBath knew this before others did. And that's why she ran. "If I really wanted to be a mother of
the movement," McBath told me, "then I had to mother the movement."

8

PULLING OUT THE ROOTS OF VIOLENCE

ANSWERING THE SOS CALL

The kind of offer that Shane Oliver received at the age of ten—the one to stand lookout for a local drug gang—is often the only tangible opportunity for advancement young men get in cities like Hartford. Shane had the good sense to turn it down, and with help from his father set up his stand selling water instead. But his limited options frame the economic trap that clamps down on the urban poor—especially those who are African American and Hispanic. I grew up just a few streets away from Shane, but the drug gangs of Hartford seemed a million miles away. My teenage options were bountiful, and my ability to get a job during the summers teaching tennis at a local private club was a by-product of my family's connections and my immense privilege. Shane and poor children like him enjoyed no such privilege. As the young man in Baltimore told me, "If I can't find a job, then I gotta do something else. I gotta steal, I gotta rob, or I gotta deal."

Yes, changing gun laws gets you the most immediate return on policy change with respect to violence rates in America, and that's why it's where policy makers should start. But at the basement level, American violence is often a symptom of a much deeper rending of our social fabric. Violence, as we've seen, thrives on both poverty and the intentional policy of putting a disproportionate number of people of color into poverty. There is nothing automatic or preordained about poverty's attachment to violence—99 percent of poor people never perpetrate an act of life-ending violence—but poverty is a condition in which violence can flourish. And violence is often the means by which in-groups keep out-groups in check.

In the previous chapter I outlined a framework for the changes in gun laws that provide the biggest returns on reducing violence. But an appropriate discussion of how to tackle the economic collapse of so many American communities and the reliance on violence by in-groups to dominate out-groups would be sprawling in scope, and this book is long enough already. For now, I simply want you to understand that we cannot fully address America's violence obsession without both changing American firearms laws *and* addressing these root causes, and so what you will find in this chapter is just a teaser—a suggestion for a few paths forward to serve as guideposts for your own more in-depth study. And then I need to bring you back to U.S. foreign policy, and explain the commonsense moves we can make abroad to export more American values and less American violence.

. . .

In 1899, the Democratic slate in Baltimore's municipal elections ran on a simple, catchy slogan: "This Is a White Man's City." The campaign's closing argument was straightforward—Baltimore's city government should be run in a manner that gave every possible advantage to its white citizens, the Fourteenth Amendment be damned. The Democrats' overt, unapologetic paean to prejudice and discrimination carried the day, and the slate was elected. Eight years later, Democratic mayor Barry Mahool, a self-proclaimed progressive reformer, got word that George McMechen, a prominent Yale-trained African American lawyer in the city, was planning to move into one of the city's exclusively white neighborhoods. Mahool and the city council responded by passing an ordinance that prohibited any African American from living on a block where the majority of residents were white, and further required home builders constructing new city blocks to designate ahead of time whether they were building a "white block" or a "black block." Said Mahool in defense of the ordinance: "Blacks should be quarantined in isolated slums in order to reduce the incidence of civil disturbance, to prevent the spread of communicable disease into the nearby White neighborhoods, and to protect property values among the White majority."

Racial zoning laws were struck down by the Supreme Court a few years later, but that didn't stop local, state, and federal leaders from continuing their crusade to marginalize communities of color. In the 1920s, white city landowners began a campaign to place racially restrictive covenants on their property deeds to make sure homes in white neighborhoods couldn't be sold to families of color. In the 1930s, the creation of the Federal Housing Administration made available low-rate mortgage loans in white neighborhoods and not in majority African American or Hispanic neighborhoods. In the 1950s and 1960s, the construction of highways, many straight through African American neighborhoods, facilitated the flight of white families out of the city altogether. In the 1990s, the government tore down most of the city's public housing and replaced it with nothing, pushing the mostly African American and Hispanic residents into higher-rent, unaffordable units. Many of those private-sector units were polluted with lead paint, and today, the refusal of the federal, state, and city governments to alleviate those high lead levels has created a public health epidemic for the kids who live in those toxic apartments.

As reporter Emily Badger has explained in *The Washington Post*, what happened in Baltimore over the past one hundred years, to African Americans in particular, happened in American city after American city:

> Each of these shocks further diminished the capacity of low-income urban black communities to recover from the one that came next. It's an irony, a fundamental urban inequality, created over the years

by active decisions and government policies that have undermined the same people and sapped them of their ability to rebuild, that have again and again dismantled the same communities, each time making them socially, economically, and politically weaker.

There is no way to explain this unyielding assault on poor Americans living in urban environments other than through the prism of racism and intentional discrimination. And so any conversation about how to pull out the roots of violence must begin with an honest conversation about policies that seek to address America's long history of racism and discrimination.

. . .

In the moments when I am struggling with the question of why I didn't work on the issue of gun violence prior to Sandy Hook, during my time in the U.S. House of Representatives, I rationalize that this decision was because the one major city in my congressional district, Waterbury, had very few gun homicides. Despite being only slightly smaller than Connecticut's other major cities, Waterbury was mysteriously immune to the gun violence epidemic plaguing other municipalities when I arrived in Congress. My first year in Washington, only three people were murdered in Waterbury, while just a few miles down Route 8, in Bridgeport, fourteen people were killed. The explanation for this extreme difference was not rates of poverty—Waterbury's per capita income levels are similar to those of other cities in Connecticut. But Waterbury does have something that other, more violence-prone cities don't: Neil O'Leary.

I came to know the genial Waterbury native during my first term in Congress, when he was serving his third year as the city's police chief. Twenty-four years a Waterbury cop before being named chief, O'Leary looks like an officer out of a Norman Rockwell painting, with his Irish complexion, ruddy cheeks, round nose, and close-cropped hair. O'Leary arrived in the chief's office with a reputation for doggedly pursuing every case as a detective, even the ones others in the department couldn't crack.

As a young detective, he was featured on NBC's *Dateline* for solving a high-profile rape case that had gone cold in the hands of other officers after seven months of dead ends. As chief, O'Leary was relentless in learning from his department's mistakes, and never shy to admit when the time-honored practices of his officers weren't in the best interests of crime victims. In one case, his department didn't take seriously a report that a man had gone missing, believing that he had just skipped town. Later, after they learned that the man had likely been abducted and killed, O'Leary undertook a top-down reform of how his department responds to the concerns of the public. Victims of crime—most important, African American and Hispanic victims—knew in Waterbury that if there was justice to be served, O'Leary would turn over every stone to get the job done. This meant that the self-help mechanism that causes many poor urban residents in America to pursue their own private justice did not exist, by and large, in Waterbury. And so the cycle of violence that often spills out from this system of private vengeance was largely absent from Waterbury as well.

O'Leary also made a massive commitment to solving the breach in trust between the police and the communities of color they serve. He decided to supercharge the city's Police Athletic League (PAL) and raised significant private dollars to build a new gym and classroom space for PAL's programming (a fund-raising project that would be unnecessary if government collected enough revenue to fund such a worthwhile project). Though it wasn't technically in their job description, Waterbury officers knew that they were expected to volunteer to coach teams, referee, or organize PAL events to serve the children of Waterbury. This meant that the police officer who showed up at your house to break up a fight or investigate a noise complaint likely had coached your kids in football or basketball. PAL ensured that many police officers who walked the beat in Waterbury were part of the fabric of the communities they patrolled, even after hours.

And O'Leary went even further—he created a unique partnership with the city's school system, through which his coaches would be sent notices of student truancy so that when a child showed up for a game or a club meeting, the coach or adviser could talk to him or her about the reason for school absences. This way his officers could identify children at risk of delinquent behaviors early and use the child's extracurricular interests to change behavior. Through PAL, O'Leary created a seamless connection between his department and the community, and the legitimacy of law enforcement became largely unquestioned. Unlike in Baltimore, Waterbury citizens trusted the police, and frictions between Waterbury in-groups (like the police) and out-groups (like the low-income communities they patrolled) eased.

What O'Leary proved was that the legitimacy of law enforcement—the belief among communities of color that the police exist for their protection and benefit rather than to prey upon African Americans and Hispanics—reduces the instinct for self-help systems of justice and private retribution. But O'Leary's investment in PAL also proved that building systems of support, and true pathways to success and accomplishment, for low-income families can result in a big payback as well.

All over America today, government and law enforcement leaders are implementing a more targeted version of O'Leary's model, called "focused deterrence," and it is demonstrating very promising results. This approach, pioneered by Harvard criminologist David Kennedy, seeks to identify the small handful of (mostly) young men who are committing violent crimes, or those who have risk factors that indicate they may commit violent crimes. The approach wraps interventions and services (like mentoring, job skills, and mental health and addiction counseling) around this relatively small coterie of young men, seeking to interrupt the cycle of retributive violence that plagues many low-income communities of color. The theory is simple: After decades of disinvestment in these neighborhoods, what might happen if an infusion of funding and services was pumped into the areas most affected by the multiple "shocks" delivered to these communities over the last century?

Many of these initiatives have been plagued by inconsistent commitment from political leaders and lapses in funding, but those communities with a more sustained commitment show remarkable results. Before Project Longevity, the focused deterrence project in three Connecticut cities, was sapped of its funding in 2017, its five-year run had resulted in a 73 percent decrease in homicides in New Haven, Bridgeport, and Hartford. Oakland, California, launched its own version of the program in 2012, and in the five years since its launch the city has seen a 50 percent reduction in shootings and a 42 percent decrease in homicides. Philadelphia, New Orleans, and Lowell, Massachusetts, have also seen significant declines in gun homicides when implementing this approach. Other interventions show significant promise as well. When I told my friend Dr. Pamela Cantor, a child psychiatrist and founder of the nonprofit Turnaround for Children, that I was going to write about the cycles of trauma that weigh down communities of color, she wrote to me with a worry. "If you speak to only the negative effects of trauma, you are really only speaking to one half of the scientific and human story," she counseled. "But there is a whole other half to the story—if we provide healthy environments to our children and families, with economic security and opportunity, mobility, real safety guarantees, and above all, a chance at a real education, we could literally change the biological and evolutionary game."

Cantor's program is trying to prove this hypothesis. The core insight underpinning Turnaround for Children's work has been that adversity doesn't just happen *to* children, it happens *inside* their brains and bodies due to the biological effects of stress and an excess of cortisol, the "fight or flight" hormone we talked about in chapter 5. Cantor's work has discovered that just as negative traumas can change the biology of children, so can positive interventions. Strong relationships that build trust in the institutions and individuals that look after children increase brain levels of oxytocin, a hormone that can help children offset the negative effects of high cortisol exposure. Children with fewer trauma impacts are more likely to build positive relationships and less likely to resort to aggressive behaviors to settle differences or resolve conflicts. To help stimulate this biological repair work in children, Turnaround works with schools to build a set of tools, services, and practices that can build oxytocin levels in students. Early results suggest that these programs can in fact ignite resilient developmental forces inside children and counteract the effects of trauma.

It turns out that if you spend resources in places where the consequences of a century of racial discrimination and economic marginalization have been the worst, on quality programming like focused deterrence or trauma intervention, you can make those places safer and interrupt the downward spiral of marginality.

.   .   .

One October afternoon in 2006, a few weeks before the end of my first campaign for Congress, I received a call from a reporter friend at one of the local television stations. "I just saw an attack ad that was delivered to the station this morning. It's going on the air tonight and it's awful. I felt like I had to give you the heads-up," she explained in a hushed voice. "There's an actor playing you, going door to door, and at the last home he visits, he's welcomed in by a bunch of drug dealers who say they're excited that you voted to lower penalties for selling drugs."

The ad, it turned out, completely backfired on the twenty-four-year incumbent congresswoman, Nancy Johnson, whom a few weeks later I would beat by a remarkable twelve-point margin. It was over the top in its negativity (the final scene portrays a young man with a marijuana blunt tucked into his hat opening their door and exclaiming, "Murphy! You wanna weaken penalties for drug dealers. That's so cool! C'mon in! You guys, Murphy's here!"), and it ended up just reinforcing my reputation as a door-to-door campaigner who was willing to work for every single vote. But the "soft on drugs" charge had us worried when we heard about it that afternoon, and my campaign went to work to find out what vote the attack ad was referencing.

We quickly came to the conclusion that the reference was to a vote I had taken in the state legislature to equalize the prison sentences for the sale and possession of powder cocaine and crack cocaine by increasing the former and decreasing the latter. It was a vote for which I was deeply proud, and I finished the campaign by confidently explaining why decreasing the prison terms for people convicted of drug possession was one of the most important things I had done since I entered politics. But the attack ad reinforced how powerful a motivating force the mass incarceration of people of color can be in American politics—my opponent thought she would win the election by accusing me of letting drug offenders (largely African American and Hispanic) out of prison. Luckily, she was wrong.

The war on drugs, begun by President Nixon and carried on by multiple Republican and Democratic administrations, can more accurately be called a war on people of color, because both the laws and the enforcement of the laws were designed to lock up African Americans and Hispanics, while giving whites a broad immunity from persecution and prosecution. This created the closed circuit of marginality we discussed earlier. Nowhere was that more evident than in the unbalanced penalties for the possession and sale of crack cocaine (perceived as largely used in communities of color) and powder cocaine (perceived as largely a habit of whites).

The examples of how this wayward policy ruined lives are endless, but here is one: In February 2001, Eugenia Jennings, a twenty-three-year-old African American who was abandoned by her parents, sexually abused, and addicted to drugs by age fifteen, was sentenced to 262 months in prison and eight years of supervised release for selling an amount of crack cocaine that weighed about as much as seven packets of sugar. She had sold the crack to undercover officers near East St. Louis, Missouri, in exchange for clothing for her three children. *Twenty-one years* in prison for selling a tiny amount of drugs so she could clothe her kids. During the ten years she was in prison, until President Obama commuted her sentence, her young children were able to see their mother only once. Eugenia's story was not an exception—it was the rule for thousands of African Americans who, by the time I ran for Congress in 2006, were serving average prison terms for nonviolent drug offenses that equaled the terms being served by white offenders convicted of truly violent crimes.

To combat the closed circuit of marginality that has been created by the epidemic rate of imprisonment of people of color, major reform is needed at the state and local level. Over the past decade, my state has been an example of the anti–gun violence gains that can be achieved by tackling criminal justice reform. Across the state, starting in 2010, Connecticut's violent crime rates began a remarkable decline. Violent crime in the rest of the country during this same post-2010 period remained fairly stable, so Connecticut was clearly doing something different, innovative, and positive. If you ask Neil O'Leary what made the difference, he will point to then-governor Dan Malloy's decision, shortly after 2010, to push forward a series of criminal justice reforms to severely limit the number of people sentenced to prison for nonviolent crimes.

Malloy and the state legislature carried out a methodical campaign of reform, decriminalizing the possession of small quantities of marijuana, making reforms to the bail system to lower the rate of bail violations, allowing more people with nonviolent records to apply for parole and pardons, and reducing the prison sentences for other kinds of drug possession charges. Unsurprisingly, by 2018, Connecticut's prison population was the lowest since the federal 1994 crime bill was signed into law, and arrests had dropped 26 percent compared with a decade earlier. The effect was that many fewer poor people, and many fewer African American men, were incarcerated, thus creating a substantial break in the closed circuit of marginality and violence. Mass incarceration can have a *temporary* positive effect on violence rates (the increases in mandatory minimum sentences in the 1994 crime bill are given partial credit—along with the gun law reforms—for the rapid decrease in the U.S. homicide rate that followed its passage), but the long-term effect is to depress the economic fortunes of the communities targeted by the roundups and to perpetuate an in-group (white jailers)/out-group (African American prisoners) dynamic that incentivizes future violence (think police brutality or the 1967 urban riots). Connecticut's experiment with mass de-incarceration from 2010 to 2018 proves that locking fewer people up can lead to less violence.

While most of the tools to end the cycle of marginality for people of color are found at the state level (of the 2.4 million people who are in prison in the United States today, 2.2 million are locked up in connection with state law violations), there are plenty of changes in federal law that could also poke some significant holes in this circuit. Luckily, there are growing numbers of Republicans and Democrats interested in this project. Billionaire Republican kingmakers Charles and the late David Koch reportedly sunk hundreds of millions of dollars into criminal justice reform efforts in 2018, resulting in a modest but important reform bill passing Congress and being signed into law at the end of that year. The legislation addressed the different treatment for crack and cocaine possession, unbound judges from the requirement to impose mandatory minimum sentences, and improved opportunities for prisoners to be released early if they engage in certain behaviors or programs. Other pending legislation could have just as big an impact, like a bill to end the practice of public employers automatically disqualifying those with criminal records from the hiring process. Connecticut proved that justice reforms can reduce violence, and there has never been more interest in this work in Washington than right now.

.   .   .

The year John F. Kennedy was elected president of the United States, East Baltimore was a thriving place to work and live. The neighborhood's biggest employer was Bethlehem Steel, which at the time cut checks to thirty-five thousand workers, paying experienced laborers the modern equivalent of $25 an hour with paid vacation time, healthcare benefits, and a defined-benefit pension plan. Baltimore was building new infrastructure, schools, and affordable housing, in part due to a 91 percent marginal federal tax rate for the highest income earners. Those steelworkers were "blue-collar aristocrats," as Nobel Prize–winning economist Angus Deaton described them—men who could work one forty-hour-a-week job and earn a stable, reliable living wage for their families. But by 2003, Bethlehem Steel was bankrupt, and the plant was down to a few thousand employees. Johns Hopkins University was a neighborhood anchor, but many other companies had fled to the suburbs. And redlining had made investment in the declining neighborhood almost impossible.

In 2002, three major players in Baltimore put together a very big idea designed to bring the neighborhood back to its former glory. The neighborhoods of East Baltimore suffered some of the highest violence rates in the state, and city leaders knew all the data that linked poverty to crime. So Johns Hopkins University, East Baltimore's biggest employer, joined with the city of Baltimore and the Annie E. Casey Foundation to tear down two thousand dilapidated row houses over an eighty-eight-acre site and built in their place a mixed-income neighborhood with a new biotech innovation hub to help spur economic growth in the neighborhood. In 2010, the initiative took off, with major infusions of funding, and work began to revitalize the area.

Four billion dollars has flowed into what is known as the East Baltimore Development Initiative, and new housing developments now dot the landscape, parks and gardens look greener, and glistening new schools now educate the neighborhood's children. The Johns Hopkins researcher Daniel Webster studied what happened to violence rates in East Baltimore, before and after his employer undertook the initiative, and found that the redevelopment was associated with reductions in homicides of up to 25 percent and a reduction in nonfatal shootings of 30 percent. That's a sure sign that concentrated redevelopment of blighted, low-income neighborhoods can make a meaningful impact on violence rates, right? Well, as it turns out, like a lot of the ground we've covered in this book, it's a little more complicated than that.

Of the hundreds of East Baltimore residents who were displaced when the ramshackle row houses were demolished, few were able to afford to stay in the neighborhood. Johns Hopkins, in a well-meaning effort to keep more of its middle-class employees in the area, offered $36,000 bonuses to those who would purchase the new apartments being built. The incomes of those living in East Baltimore increased, but critics of the project say that this was simply the result of poor families being displaced and more affluent families moving in.

"This is gentrification," said Lawrence Brown, a professor at Baltimore's historically African American university Morgan State. "A big institution pushing out a vulnerable community for its benefit." Warned Marisela Gomez, an activist physician from the neighborhood, "Every community that's black or brown and low-income in Baltimore is at risk."

The controversy over the East Baltimore Development Initiative is a reminder that certain *neighborhoods* aren't more violent than other neighborhoods—it is the *circumstances* under which people live in those neighborhoods that create the conditions of violence. Simply fixing up the houses in a neighborhood while doing little to systemically change all the other factors (stagnant wage growth, prejudice in employment, generational poverty, mass-scale incarceration, police impropriety, and so on) that cause individuals to fall into economic desperation, and thus become more susceptible to violence, is insufficient. Moving poor, oppressed individuals from one place to another doesn't lead to less violence; it often just moves the violence to another spot.

A better way to solve segregation by race and income in America, and the violence that it leads to, is to attack the problem through the schools. In this book, I cannot do justice to the complicated, nuanced debate over the future of American education, but it's an area of reform that is essential to any serious effort to tackle racial bias. University of California professor Rucker Johnson, in his book *Children of the Dream: Why School Integration Works*, argues that for every five years an African American child spends in a racially integrated rather than segregated school, that student's earnings as an adult increase by 25 percent. This shouldn't be surprising, since other research also shows that companies with racially diverse workforces perform better than those with homogeneous employee pools. Diverse environments are intellectually stimulating environments, whether in a workplace or a high school. Perhaps more interesting is that those same five years in an integrated school increase the child's life expectancy by an incredible seven years. Of course, the two findings are related, because the higher the income, the lower the likelihood of premature, violent death. In Congress, I have written legislation, first championed by President Obama's second secretary of education, John King, Jr., that establishes a new fund to support states and school districts that implement voluntary desegregation plans, like Connecticut's magnet school model. Magnet schools, which draw students from multiple school districts, tend to be more racially and economically diverse, with higher test scores than conventional neighborhood-based schools.

Another promising avenue is the growing community of advocates arguing for a more just form of school finance. As we discussed in chapter 5, as white families moved out of America's cities in the middle of the twentieth century, white-dominated state governments created funding mechanisms to make sure the suburban schools were better funded than the city schools. In Connecticut, for instance, wealthy (and almost exclusively white) New Canaan spends $7,500 per student. In urban Bridgeport, only twenty minutes away, each student is allocated only $3,900. This disparity is made all the more unconscionable considering that Bridgeport educators need to deal with all the trauma experienced by kids who live in a city where 40 percent of them live in households with less than $20,000 in annual income, and where gun homicides and gang crime are a regular occurrence. Federal and state interventions to even out this funding unfairness could make an enormous difference in the quality of education urban children receive, and, like access to integrated schools, increase both their economic prospects and life expectancy. I feel proud and lucky that my wife, Cathy, in her work as an educational policy expert, is helping to organize a national effort to push school finance reform, and I hang on her every update as proof that the national will to increase school funding for low-income kids is increasing.

School desegregation and school finance are but two areas of policy that could make a big difference in changing the reality of poor children of color throughout America, who labor under the weight of poverty, discrimination, and the accompanying increased risk of violence. The truth is that place-based approaches (at the expense of broad policy reform) are often a convenient way for those with power and wealth to paper over the two intractable problems that restrain the mobility of people without power or wealth. Until the rules that intentionally transfer wealth from the permanently poor to the permanently rich change, and until the rules that rob persons of color of the chance to grab hold of the economic and political levers change, no redevelopment plan or Promise Zone designation will rescue these chronically poor, overly violent places.

Place-based approaches, while mostly well-meaning, are often reliant on private-sector and philanthropic gifts, which means that the economically powerful get to control where and when they spend their economic winnings to benefit the poor and disadvantaged. This makes it appear as if America has a strategy to combat poverty and discrimination without actually changing any of the broadly applicable rules that are still stacked in favor of those who currently possess, and will continue to possess, all the money and power. What America needs to do is radically change the rules of the game in order to seriously attack racism and discrimination and to even out the economic playing field everywhere, not just the places where the powerful decide to place a redevelopment zone.

.   .   .

The roots of violence run through more than just America's racist past and present. Remember that poor whites are just as likely to be the victims of crime as poor African Americans. Recall that low-income white men are three times more likely to turn a gun on themselves than a low-income African American. The year 2018 was the first in which the rate of rural violent crime in America eclipsed the overall national rate of violent crime. There isn't a mechanistic connection between poverty and violence—the former does not automatically cause the latter—but over and over, since the beginning of time, we see that economic desperation is a condition that increases one's risk of becoming a victim of violence. So we also need to think about how to reorganize the rules of our economy more broadly to rebuild the blue-collar aristocracy.

First, let's understand how badly we've screwed up the current balance of economic power. Today, 90 percent of Americans control only 23 percent of American wealth, leaving the wealthiest 10 percent of Americans with the other three-quarters. Today, perhaps the clearest statistic demonstrating the scope of the massive economic underclass we have built is this: Right now, a full 40 percent of Americans cannot pay for a $400 emergency (an illness with a high deductible, a broken-down car) without borrowing money or selling something. Two-fifths of Americans live either in poverty or on the brink of it.

That kind of desperation filters into daily life. The need to spend all the hours of the day engaging in simple survival breeds violence—both the kind perpetuated by one against another and the deaths of despair that come from personal collapse amid overwhelming stress and illness. That's why we cannot holistically confront violence in America without tackling the massive transfer of wealth that has occurred from workers to economic elites over the past fifty years.

This yawning gap between the haves and the have-nots did not happen by accident. Policies have been purposely put into place to keep poor people poor, so that the relatively reasonable wages an average worker made fifty years ago could be redistributed to make the super-wealthy even wealthier. No policy maker or hedge fund manager really wakes up every day with a mission to make more people poor. I'm not suggesting that the campaign to create more and more have-nots is that intentional. But there is no way to study the decisions made over the past fifty years regarding educational, tax, and labor policy without viewing a quilt of policy decisions that lawmakers must have known would push more money to those who already had lots, and make it much harder for those with little to get more.

The first of these decisions happened like a slow-motion car crash, as America decided to rupture its century-old commitment to American workers to provide enough free public education that those workers could land jobs with livable wages. America's blue-collar aristocracy was built on the simple truth that at the turn of the twentieth century a twelfth-grade education was more than enough for an American to avoid being poor. But the economy began to change in the late twentieth century, and the jobs requiring only a high school diploma moved to Mexico and China, effectively wiping out millions of blue-collar aristocrats.

Service-sector jobs replaced factory jobs as a white-collar aristocracy arose. Entrance into that club required more than a high school degree, yet policy makers refused to update the guarantee, and the amount of free education available in America in 2019 is the exact same amount that was available in 1919. To add insult to injury, policy makers allowed for colleges to increase their costs astronomically. From the time I was born until today, the cost of college has almost tripled, even adjusted for inflation.

So today, America no longer helps its citizens get enough education to attain middle-class status. Rather, we make sure that the cost of the extra education one needs to avoid poverty is out of reach for most without means. This makes no sense, especially since a new commitment to update the guarantee would not break the bank (federal education expenditures today account for only 2 percent of the entire budget). But when Senator Bernie Sanders in 2016 called for the United States to adopt a program of "free college," American elites scoffed at the prospect of a new $75 billion–per–year commitment to education as fiscally extravagant, pie-in-the-sky naïveté. Many of these naysayers were the same people who cheered a massive tax cut for the wealthy that cost taxpayers far more than any free college plan would. Whether or not Sanders's specific plan is the best path forward, it's clear that without a new education guarantee, there is simply no way to provide poor people avenues out of economic desperation other than violence, or activities that bring along the risk of violence.

Second, the American revenue collection system badly exacerbates both extreme wealth and extreme poverty. It's true—the American income tax system is "progressive." This means that your tax rate increases the more money you make. But the rates stop increasing at about a half-million dollars in income, so that someone making $500,000 a year is paying the same rate as someone making $500 million. Adding insult to injury, those with big bank accounts usually make almost all of their take-home cash from investments, and that income is taxed at much lower rates than the money I make on my federal salary.

Poor and middle-class Americans may technically pay a lower income tax rate, but they rarely have moneymaking investments, so they pay the higher ordinary income tax rate. And even worse, all the other taxes poorer Americans pay—like sales, property, fuel, and payroll taxes—aren't progressive. So today, taxpayers making less than $15,000 a year are still paying 20 percent of their income in taxes (compared to about 33 percent for the top quintile of earners). Someone making $1 million will still have enough left over to live on after paying a 33 percent rate. But if you're starting with $15,000, the $3,000 that goes for taxes is likely the difference between two and three meals a day.

To make matters worse, the 2017 tax reform bill took another large bite out of the federal inheritance tax, further encouraging the wealthiest Americans to hoard their money to be able to pass it down to subsequent generations. Today, the richest 1 percent of Americans, who control 40 percent of all the nation's wealth, are saving almost 40 percent of their available resources. This may be a sound, frugal decision for each wealthy taxpayer individually, but the withdrawal of such immense amounts of money from the economy means that no one else has a chance to gain the benefit of the "trickle down" effect. The American tax system isn't as progressive as you think, and the prejudice against salary or hourly income versus investment income cements the gap between rich and poor; the ability to pass this wealth down to future generations further handcuffs poor people to their economic station by robbing them of the ability to compete for all of this cash, which is just sitting in index funds waiting to be accessed by the sons and daughters of rich parents.

Cutting taxes for poor Americans is a good policy start, but by raising revenue from the very richest among us (for instance, those who have personal wealth above $10 million), we could finally begin to make the investments in public housing, broken infrastructure, and higher education that sustained vibrant middle-class cities like Baltimore a half century ago.

Finally, let's think about the most important tool American workers used to climb out of poverty in the first half of the twentieth century: labor unions. Gradually, through the early and middle part of the 1900s, more and more Americans became members of organized labor unions, and—not coincidentally—more and more of the nation's wealth found its way into the hands of these workers.

In 1950, when more than 30 percent of Americans were able to jointly negotiate with their company's leadership, the ratio of American CEO pay to the average worker's pay was 20 to 1. Today, with only 10 percent of workers using collective bargaining, that ratio has skyrocketed to 287 to 1. A 2011 study from researchers at the University of Washington and Harvard found that nearly one-third of the increase in income inequality since the 1970s can be attributed to the decline in union enrollment. As workers increasingly have been left to bargain against giant employers with almost no leverage, it should be no shock that average worker wages have remained flat.

The declining membership in unions did not happen by accident. Over decades, Congress stood by and refused to update the National Labor Relations Act as employers sharpened and modernized their union-busting tactics. And conservatives packed the U.S. Supreme Court with anti-union justices, most recently securing a landmark decision devastating the ability of public employee unions to raise funds. Restoring the ability of workers to collectively bargain would give an enormous boost to wage growth.

To save poor people from the closed circuit of marginalization and violence, we must have an honest conversation about race, and push forward real breakthrough policies to lift up people of color. But we must also end the economic crusade that has been waged against poor people of all races, and enact policies that return stolen wealth to hardworking families. Fixing up a few streets or apartment buildings in a handful of targeted neighborhoods won't do the trick if nobody can afford the fancy new units. Until we are honest about the ways in which discrimination and poverty relegate millions of Americans to lives on the margins of society, some Americans will be forced to turn to the desperate last resort of violence as their only means of survival.

BUTTER OR GUNS

There is no need for America to answer for all episodes of violence that occur overseas. The overreliance of American foreign policy on military intervention, complicated weaponry, and arms export does not explain most of the violence that plagues many parts of the globe. But it is time for American policy makers to figure out that a strong military is not the only way to protect our nation from attack. In fact, the evidence says that plenty of nonmilitary tools are far more effective at curing global violence and securing our homeland. To tell that story, let's start, perhaps surprisingly, with the presidency of George W. Bush.

In 2001, shortly after being sworn in as America's sixty-fifth secretary of state, Colin Powell began to hear troubling reports about the quickening pace of the HIV-AIDS epidemic in sub-Saharan Africa. The disease was threatening to wipe out the entire childbearing populations of certain nations, like Zimbabwe, where in 2000 a full quarter of the population aged fifteen to forty-nine were HIV-positive. In nearby Kenya, 10 percent of the population was infected, and over one hundred thousand more were added to the rolls each year.

Powell's years in the military had taught him that economic and health instability go hand in hand with outbreaks of violence. Two weeks into his new job, Powell called the equally green secretary of health and human services, Tommy Thompson, to express his fears that outbreaks of violence in AIDS-ravaged African countries could create a political vacuum that enemies of the United States could exploit. "Tommy, this is not just a health matter," he warned his fellow cabinet member. "This is a national security matter."

President Bush had shown some interest in Africa before coming to the White House, having traveled to the region with his wife, Laura, where he witnessed firsthand the consequences of the continent's nineteenth-century public health infrastructure. Yet as a candidate in 2000, he'd advertised a general weariness toward expanding the reach of U.S. international aid programs. He talked, specifically, of letting "Africa solve Africa's problems."

But Powell's concern, and the growth of the Christian conservative focus on the overseas epidemic, began to pique Bush's prior interest in Africa. So in 2002, Bush sent Thompson and a senior official from the U.S. Centers for Disease Control and Prevention to Africa on a fact-finding trip, and when they returned recommending a $500 million assistance commitment, Bush told them to think bigger, putting Deputy Chief of Staff Josh Bolten in charge of a working group to give him options.

Bush's 2003 State of the Union speech is rightly remembered for the infamous sixteen words of faulty intelligence ("The British government has learned that Saddam Hussein recently sought significant quantities of uranium from Africa") that helped set the stage for the disastrous and history-changing invasion of Iraq. But buried inside that speech and barely noticed at the time was a proposal to create a massive $15 billion account to fight the spread of AIDS in Africa. It was included in the speech at the specific direction of Bush, who had become a convert to using the massive spending power of the U.S. government to reverse the trajectory of the AIDS crisis in Africa.

It helped that Powell and National Security Adviser Condoleezza Rice were pushing Bush in this direction; both of them understood the risk of civil conflict if the pandemic continued to rage unchecked. But others inside the White House were worried about the political implications of the program. Michael Gerson, Bush's speechwriter, remembers Bush overruling a last-minute attempt by some advisers to expunge this section of the speech, believing it "problematic to be announcing a lot of money for foreigners." The announcement stayed in, and within five years, Congress had enthusiastically appropriated $19 billion for what would become known as the PEPFAR, the President's Emergency Plan for AIDS Relief.

PEPFAR is arguably the most successful American foreign policy project in history. Before you roll your eyes at this claim, consider this: The drugs PEPFAR has dispensed, the clinics it has funded, and the prevention programs it has sustained have saved approximately seventeen million lives around the world. That's right—seventeen million. Global annual AIDS deaths today are half what they were just over a decade ago—an extraordinarily rapid decline. In Kenya, 210,000 people were newly infected in 1994. Last year, that number was expected to be 53,000. Granted, the efficacy of the treatments has improved greatly since PEPFAR was announced, but that's still an impressive return on investment.

．　　．　　．

In 1996, *New York Times* columnist Thomas Friedman famously posited his Golden Arches Theory of Conflict Prevention, noting that no two countries with McDonald's franchises have ever gone to war with each other. People who have access to McDonald's "don't like to fight wars. They like to wait in line for burgers." He theorized that "countries with middle classes large enough to sustain a McDonald's have reached a level of prosperity and global integration that makes warmongering risky and unpalatable to its people."

Even Harvard psychologist Steven Pinker, who generally questions the connection between poverty and violence, admits that "the likelihood that a country will be torn by violent civil unrest . . . starts to soar as its annual per capita domestic product falls below $1,000." The connection between a country's economic security and its propensity to commit itself to violent conflict is, of course, not a new idea. Recall the sociologist Norbert Elias's case that a large component of the civilizing process of the late Middle Ages was the establishment of an economic rule of law that made it possible for individuals to provide for their families without using violence to take wealth from others. The easier your life is economically, the less you need to rely on violence to survive. Makes sense, right?

That's why in Africa, seventeen million lives saved is just the beginning of the story. The success of PEPFAR is much more than the individuals who would have died of AIDS who are alive today. No, the story of President Bush's program is also about all the other lives that were likely saved by this multibillion-dollar investment in the political and economic stability of these fifteen African nations. A 2018 comparative study of countries with little or no PEPFAR investment versus those nations with high levels of PEPFAR money showed worker productivity increased by around 20 percent in PEPFAR countries during the same period that productivity dropped slightly in non-PEPFAR countries.

Another study posed an explanation for why PEPFAR nations became more politically stable in the wake of the American investment. In Africa, orphaned children often swell the ranks of criminal gangs, terrorist organizations, and guerrilla armies. "HIV/AIDS and child soldiering are thoroughly intertwined problems that exert reciprocal influences on each other," noted one researcher. With fewer parents dying of AIDS, there were fewer unattached children to serve as recruits for organizations that perpetuate violence against civilians. Today, civil conflicts still rage across the African continent—some in

PEPFAR priority countries like Nigeria. Improving health outcomes is certainly not a total prophylactic against violence. But it doesn't take a leap of imagination to understand why the data suggests that both the economy and safety of countries in the PEPFAR program improved, on balance, when the crisis of thousands of people needlessly dying each and every month abated.

And these African nations aren't the only examples of U.S. foreign assistance quelling violence abroad and preventing the development of threats to our security. After sixty-eight thousand minor children fleeing violence in Central America presented themselves at the U.S. border with Mexico during the summer of 2014, President Obama pushed Congress to send $750 million in emergency aid to Guatemala, Honduras, and El Salvador (referred to as the "Northern Triangle") to try to curb the violence.

As usual, causation and correlation are hard to differentiate, and the Central American violence problem is as complex and deep-seated as America's. But within two years, the partnerships that the emergency aid established looked like they were reaping significant rewards. By the end of the Obama administration, the murder rate in Honduras had dropped by a third, Guatemala had made significant anti-corruption reforms, and El Salvador had started finding success cutting off the funding streams for the criminal organizations that dominated the small nation's streets. When President Trump came into office and turned a blind eye to the crisis in the Northern Triangle, eventually cutting off Obama-era funding out of spite, it is no coincidence that migration numbers to America's southern boundary began once again to spike.

. . .

"The Balkans," goes a saying reportedly first uttered by Winston Churchill, "generates more history than it can locally consume." Students of history know, of course, that the clutch of countries nestled in between Europe and the Middle East is the place where world wars start. For millennia, it has been "the crossroads of empires and religions, riven by ethnic tribalism and the meddling of outside powers."

For a decade, it has been a personal fascination of mine, in part due to the large number of refugees from the region that settled in Waterbury and throughout Connecticut during and after the Balkan wars of the 1990s. In 2014, I journeyed to the region for the first time, as the top Democrat on the Foreign Relations Subcommittee on Europe, to demonstrate Congress's support for the continued democratic and economic reforms under way in the region.

As I got off the plane in Belgrade after a nearly twenty-four-hour journey, I was hustled off to a dinner to meet with a group of Serbian political and civic leaders. In the middle of our meal, I noticed everyone at the table beginning to turn their attention away from the discussion and toward their laps, where their smartphones buzzed with incoming messages and calls. Our ambassador, the studious career diplomat Michael Kirby, was standing in the corner of the room, clearly taking a phone call regarding whatever crisis had interrupted our meal.

He dropped his phone back into his pocket and sat down in the seat next to me. "Did you know that there's a big football match here tonight between Serbia and Albania?" he asked. I had heard some vague talk of it on my way to the restaurant. "Well, apparently somebody flew a drone over the match with a map of greater Albania," he continued. "Lowered the thing right into the stadium in the middle of the match, and almost started a riot between the players."

I knew just enough about the history of the Balkans to know why this act was so worrying to the political leaders at our table. Ethnic Albanians are scattered all over the ten or so countries that call themselves part of the Balkan region. There is only one Albania, but there are hundreds of thousands of people who call themselves Albanians who live in other countries. The most fervent among them yearn for the establishment of an Albanian state that incorporates all the places where Albanians live. They want this future because much of the bloodshed over the years in the region has been due to the treatment of Albanians by non-Albanians.

In the wake of the flag incident, relations between Serbia and Albania took an ugly turn. Edi Rama, the Albanian prime minister, canceled his planned history-making visit to Belgrade, in part because the

Serbian authorities began to circulate wild rumors that Rama's brother had piloted the drone into the stadium. A war of words erupted between the two countries' leaders on social media.

"A normal Serbia might be possible only if the Real Serbia will understand that Greater Albania is their nightmare not our project!" tweeted Rama. Aleksandar Vucic, Serbia's young prime minister, tweeted back, "It is not only our nightmare, it is a European nightmare, it is mankind's nightmare, and we will do our best to prevent world getting that nightmare." Yikes, I thought, as I finished off dinner and dragged my tired body to the hotel. What a mess I had been parachuted into.

The next day, I went to see Vucic, and we sat in his big office talking for almost two hours. He registered his complaints about the previous night's events, but he really wanted to talk to me about something else: Poland. In 2003, right before Poland joined the European Union, it had been an economic backwater. Journalist Jan Cienski remembers *nie ma* ("we don't have it") being the phrase heard most often by tourists visiting pre-EU Poland. "They heard it in shops when they tried to buy meat or wine. They heard it in kiosks when trying to buy luxuries like soap and razor blades," Cienski wrote. "They heard it fired at them by surly waiters indicating a lack of almost every item on the menu." All that changed when the European Union came calling. Now seamlessly connected to the rest of Europe, Poland took off, economically, culturally, and politically. As £56 billion in EU development funds poured into the country during the first ten years of EU membership, and goods and workers moved back and forth to the western edges of the continent, Polish GDP grew from £130 billion to an astounding £305 billion. But something else happened, as well: All those tensions that had erupted decade after decade between Poland and nations on its western and southern borders just vanished, likely as a result of Friedman's Golden Arches Theory of Conflict Prevention.

Vucic wanted Serbia to be the next Poland. And therefore his number one priority was avoiding the old habit of turning a war of words with Albanians into a war of armies. His goal was to join the European

Union. And in order to do that, he needed to quickly patch things up with Rama. Europe would not come calling if there was any hint whatsoever that hostilities could still erupt in the Balkans. I knew that Rama had the exact same dream for his country, and I implored Vucic to quickly reschedule Rama's visit. That's exactly what happened shortly after I left the region, and when they appeared together in a predominantly Albanian section of southern Serbia, Rama proclaimed to the assembled media that his country "does not dream of greater Albania, we dream of great Europe."

For sixteen hundred years after the retreat of the Roman Empire from most of western Europe in the fifth century, Europe could not get along with itself. Perpetual war was the order of the day, century after century, with kings and queens seeing it as a divine responsibility to try to widen their nations' borders by doing battle with anyone who looked temporarily susceptible to pillage. World War II represented the horrific dénouement of this long state of conflict. In eight short years, 9 percent of all Germans, 17 percent of Poles, and more than 6 percent of Greeks vanished from the earth in the most violent conflict in world history.

And then suddenly, after nearly two millennia of near constant war, it all just stopped.

There are many explanations for what brought on this era of European peace (for which we gladly see no end in sight), but the two most important are the creation of the North Atlantic Treaty Organization and the European Union. Defense cooperation and economic interreliance brought the nations of Europe together in common cause. The same phenomenon that Elias noticed was at play here: Local economies reduced the interest in individuals to act out in violence (since it would upset their chances at winning inside that economic system), and European nations came to realize that the mutual benefits of cooperation, inside NATO and the European Union, brought more riches than old-fashioned conquest.

Today, the world generally, and President Trump specifically, seem to be forgetting that the new normal of warless Europe will likely last only if these international associations remain vigorous. President

Trump and his "pro-sovereignty" crowd want to undermine and likely deconstruct both NATO and the EU, seeing it as weakness for any country to outsource to a multilateral organization any function that could be performed in-house. Of course, Trump's base does not have a monopoly on nationalist sentiments—those are growing all over Europe as homogeneous populations predictably fear becoming less homogeneous as the European Union widens and travel between countries increases.

But if the EU or NATO were to fall apart (a faint worry today, but not mere fantasy, either), then not only would existing European countries no longer have as many reasons to refrain from fighting one another, but countries like Serbia and Albania, who keep festering tensions in check in hopes of eventually getting invited to join the club, might see the lid come off the boiling pot. Given the experience of just seventy years ago, it is not hyperbole to say that millions of lives may be at stake.

· · ·

Taking on the means of violence is easier than rooting out its underlying causes. I know that sounds naïve, given how impossible it has been to break the power of the gun lobby and achieve any kind of national reform of our nation's gun laws. But the truth is that the levers that need to be pulled are few, and we know exactly where they are in our statutes and how to pull them.

Tearing out the roots of American violence—the closed circuits of marginality and violence, the centuries-old practice of using violence as a means to control racial minority groups, the overreliance on weapons of war to protect our interests abroad—that's the really tough sledding. And while it requires a much more complicated series of reform initiatives than just making sure everybody passes a background check before buying a weapon, what we've learned so far tells us that the roots are every bit as important, if not more so, than the grass tops.

Why do I say this? Let us finish by going back to the difference in how we compare to the rest of the world in our homicide rates versus our suicide and domestic violence rates. Guns make our suicide and domestic violence rates much worse than they would be without the high rate of American firearm ownership, but the overall rates of both types of violence are not global outliers. There's nothing to celebrate in simply not being the nation with the highest suicide or domestic violence rate, but the numbers would suggest that when it comes to these two categories of violence (which make up the majority of intentional deaths in our country) we have more in common than in contrast with other high-income nations. The conditions that affect the rates of this kind of violence—poverty, mental illness, and addiction, for instance—span national boundaries.

Compare the rates of these kinds of violent deaths to the earlier buckets of violence we surveyed—in-group versus out-group violence, gang-related crime, and sociopathic mass murder. Here we find that the overall rates for our country are wildly outside the global norm. And the fact that these rates are so far outside the norm, while the rates of other kinds of American violence are not, should cause us to conclude that there is something unique happening in America—aside from our high gun ownership rates and loose firearms laws. Don't get me wrong—there is still ample evidence to suggest that the guns drive the rates of every kind of violence way up. But it can't just be the guns, because if it was just about firearms, then all our rates of violence would be outside the world norm, not just the non-domestic homicides.

This reaffirms the case that there are unique American influences connected to our long history of in-group subjugation of out-groups—racism, xenophobia, and the intentional impoverishment of communities of color—that explain why so many kinds of violence in our nation look unlike anything else in the advanced world. Yes, getting rid of the bad guns, and keeping the bad guys away from guns, will save tens of thousands of lives. But sorting through the tougher lot of problems—the roots of American violence—will likely get just as big a return on our investment.

9

WHAT LIES INSIDE US

A GIANT MISTAKE

The Blessing of the Fleet parade in tony Southport, Connecticut, celebrating the opening of sailing season at the Pequot Yacht Club is, unsurprisingly, not a place where you find many liberal Democrats. I was there in June 2016 at the urging of the club's most important member: my father-in-law. I was due to give a short speech, and given the fact that the only time I had been on my in-laws' boat I spent the whole time seasick, I was a little nervous about my ability to connect with the assembled gathering of wealthy yachters.

But as I walked through the crowd, something amazing began to happen. Mothers and fathers, decked out in their New England preppy best, began sheepishly but excitedly approaching me with their kids.

"We watched the entire filibuster, my son and I," said one perfectly coiffed woman. "He's never paid any attention to politics, until you did that."

"We're with you," remarked one man. "My daughter and I stayed up as late as we could. I think it's amazing, what you did."

As I bounced from conversation to conversation, it started to feel like I was at an anti–gun violence rally instead of a yacht club party. I knew that most of the people there were Republicans. It was probable that only a few had voted for me, and even fewer had ever thought to care about the issue of gun violence. But this thing I had just done—three nights earlier on the floor of the U.S. Senate—had touched people in a way that I was just beginning to understand.

·   ·   ·

For me, every breaking news story of another mass shooting is a gut punch. It's a reminder of my inability to enact laws that will change the trajectory of gun violence in America. A reminder of my inability to make good on the promise I made those families in Sandy Hook. A reminder of how continued inaction just multiplies the frustrations and grief felt by Sam Saylor and the Reverend Henry Brown and Merry Jackson.

But for some reason, news of the shooting at the Pulse nightclub in Orlando hurt more than the others. I think it was because I was with my kids when I first learned of the shooting. Owen and Rider were running in and out of a hotel lobby just south of Williamstown, Massachusetts, as I was busy packing the car to head home from the final day of my twenty-year college reunion. As I was turning in the room key, the lobby television was running a chyron across the bottom of the screen: AS MANY AS 45 DEAD AT POPULAR ORLANDO NIGHT CLUB.

The sinking sensation that always accompanies seeing headlines like that felt even deeper that morning. It had been almost four years since Sandy Hook, and though I had made changing the nation's gun laws my personal crusade and thrown the whole weight of my emotional being into the fight, nothing at all had happened. No bills had passed. No laws had changed. And as a consequence, the pace of mass shootings in America wasn't abating—it was getting worse.

I remember one clear thought ripping through me that morning, as I stood there paralyzed, transfixed by the cable news coverage of the massacre's aftermath.

I am a total fucking failure.

As we drove back to Connecticut, the morose, hackneyed script that would play out over the next few days ran through my mind. I knew it well by now. After the statements of thoughts and prayers would come the moments of silence. Next, Democrats would call on Congress to pass legislation, usually a narrowly tailored measure designed only to address the most recent shooting. Democrats would huff and puff, cajole and complain, but business as usual in Washington would proceed until the final act—when the Republicans who control Congress would acquiesce to their gun lobby patrons and refuse to raise a single finger to answer for the deaths of innocents. No legislation. No debate. No committee hearings.

Nothing.

Nada.

Zilch.

I had played my role in this theater piece over and over during the previous four years. I knew the blocking and the choreography by heart. I was *really good* at it by now. But as our kids settled into the back seat and snapped on their headphones to watch cartoons on their tablets, I made a decision.

I wasn't going to play my role anymore. I was going to figure out how to write a new script.

.   .   .

Everybody has that friend who nurtures your riskier impulses—the one you call when you want validation for some crazy idea while all your other friends are telling you to play it safe. For me, in the summer of 2016, that friend was Cory Booker. And so on Monday night, upon returning to Washington, I pulled Booker aside after a vote on the Senate floor. I told him about an idea I had—to commandeer the Senate floor and refuse to give it up until Senate Majority Leader Mitch McConnell agreed to schedule votes on legislation to expand background checks, most importantly to cover people on the terrorist watch list, which we believed held the name of the Orlando shooter. "I'm in," Booker said, without hesitation. "Let's call Schumer tonight and get him on board. Then let's talk about it in caucus tomorrow."

I had expected Booker to put up a little more fight than he did. And I remember feeling petrified that I had just locked myself into something that I hadn't really thought through. A filibuster is really an act of desperation. It's a legislative tactic of last resort, a hostage-taking exercise to get something that you can't get any other, more conventional way. In 2013, we were able to secure a debate on gun policy on the Senate floor because Democrats controlled the Senate, but since Kentucky senator Mitch McConnell had taken control, no amount of political pressure or pleading or cajoling had convinced him to bring any measures to tighten the nation's firearms laws before the Senate.

On the drive back from Williamstown, I had concluded that a filibuster was our only remaining chance to change his mind—a high-risk, high-reward public shaming maneuver to force Senate Republicans into doing something. And unlike prior very long speeches (like Senator Ted Cruz's twenty-one-hour marathon protesting the Affordable Care Act) that were inaccurately labeled filibusters by the press, my speech would actually be a traditional filibuster. That week, we were due to debate the budget for the Justice Department, and amendments to tighten the nation's gun laws would be relevant and germane to that bill. There were also no time limits on debate (for Cruz's speech, a vote was scheduled the next afternoon whether he spoke overnight or not), so I could speak as long as I wanted, until McConnell agreed to call the votes I was demanding, or until I gave up.

Two nights later, MSNBC host and former Senate staffer Lawrence O'Donnell detailed why filibusters rarely happen in the Senate:

> There are three reasons why Senators don't filibuster. One, it's not who they are. They are not disrupters. The second reason . . . is that most of their colleagues will hate them for doing it. And the third and most important reason is that filibusters don't work. . . . Your opponents know that all they have to do is wait for you to give up. . . . The opponents go back to their office or they go home and they wait for you to get tired or sit down, and they give you nothing, absolutely nothing of what you're trying to accomplish. That is the typical outcome of a filibuster. *Absolutely nothing.*

The 2011 version of me would not have given a whiff of consideration to taking a chance like this. But I wasn't the same person that I was before December 14, 2012. I did eat, sleep, and breathe gun violence, as I told my staff would be our office's credo. I did feel a gut-wrenching sense of responsibility to those children, and the parents they left behind, that churned inside me. I thought every day of whether I could live with myself, at the end of my political career, if I hadn't turned over every single stone and taken every available risk to make sure those children did not die in complete vain.

But that didn't mean I had yet made a 180-degree transformation. Inside me somewhere still was that careful, calculating core. And so as the day approached when the parliamentary disposition on the Senate floor would provide an opening for me to take over, I started to get cold feet. I decided Tuesday night that I couldn't do it the old-fashioned way—I couldn't shut down the legislative process for an entire day, making myself the center of attention, without first making sure I wasn't burning a few important bridges. So Wednesday morning, on my commute to the Capitol, I let Booker's office know that before starting my filibuster, I wanted consent from three senators: Dianne Feinstein, the sponsor of the terrorist watch list bill on which I planned to demand a vote; Barbara Mikulski, the author of the pending budget bill on the floor that my filibuster would effectively ruin; and the Democratic leader, the soon-to-retire Harry Reid.

Booker sensed my cold feet, and that maybe I was trying to sabotage my own filibuster before it started, and sent me a text back that I still have saved on my phone to this day:

> Staff briefed me on where we are. Sounds good. I will meet you on
> the floor and be with you for the duration. It may not work out this
> way, but I believe this could be a powerful moment in time. I hope
> that you will err on the side of being daring. America needs that
> now. Don't just think of this through the Senate view, but through
> the lens of what our nation needs amidst a very difficult time and
> ongoing national tragedy. Be that voice—cautious and courageous,
> tactical and bold. Whatever you need, you have me 100% as you

press forward, whether it be for an hour of parliamentary jousting or an epic overnight stand.

It was the push I needed. I called Feinstein. She was thrilled I was pushing her bill for a vote. Mikulski, always spoiling for a fight, said, in her trademark gravelly voice, "Murphy, this is an important bill to me. But dammit, this is more important. You're doing the right thing, and if it kills my bill, I'll deal with it." And finally, I called Harry Reid— lifetime NRA A-rated Harry Reid, who started championing bills the NRA opposed only after Sandy Hook.

"I've had this conversation with a lot of people over the years, Chris," Harry explained. "A lot of people *talk* about filibustering. But nobody goes through with it."

Harry didn't wait for me to respond. He just kept talking, like he had been waiting all morning for me to call. "Chris, I can't tell you what to do. I can't give you permission. That wouldn't be *appropriate*. But here's what I *can* tell you. Stop. Calling. People. If you think this is so important, just go do it."

He paused for a second and a half. I remained silent. "I mean, *right now*," he said sharply. And just like that, he hung up.

I got up from my desk and told my staff that I was heading to the Senate floor. *I was going to do it.* When I arrived at the floor, Senator Roy Blunt of Missouri—father of Matt Blunt, the governor who'd signed the repeal of that state's gun permit system—was finishing an unrelated speech, so I had a few minutes to consider, one last time, whether this was worth it. I started to think of all the ways that a filibuster could go haywire, and one scenario kept playing over and over again in my head. I imagined the horror of taking the floor, announcing my demands, and then . . . nothing. Nobody watches. No one cares. No Democrats join me. McConnell takes one look at this baby-faced, wet-behind-the-ears freshman senator and doesn't even acknowledge my presence or demand. A tree falling in the dense woods, with not a soul there to hear it. I started picturing myself, all alone, trapped on the Senate floor, with no . . . way . . . out. A laughingstock.

Standing at my desk in the front row of the Senate, listening to

Blunt finish his speech, I texted Cathy: "I think I'm about to make a giant mistake. Wish me luck."

.   .   .

When it was all over, fifteen hours later, something amazing had happened. I'd started with only two senators by my side—Booker and my Connecticut colleague Richard Blumenthal. They both stayed on the floor for the entire filibuster, and Booker even committed himself to a "sympathy filibuster." Even though I was the only one required to stand on my feet, in one spot, without a break, for the entire time, Booker also stayed on his feet and inside the Senate chamber for the full fifteen hours. But what I had hoped would happen, did happen.

The filibuster caught fire shortly after I announced my intention to stand on my feet inside the Senate chamber until Senator McConnell agreed to hold votes on universal background checks and closing the terrorist loophole. Cable news networks started covering it live, and it quickly became a top trending topic on social media. Other senators, realizing that a moment was happening that the country was tuned in to, came down to the floor to join me. By the time the evening was finished, forty-one senators had spoken on the floor in support of my filibuster (the rules allow the senator holding the floor to yield the floor temporarily to another senator for the purposes of a question, and, framed the right way, these questions can last a very, very long time, giving the filibustering senator's vocal cords a much-needed break).

As my speech reached its tenth hour, it had become a phenomenon. Booker handed me a note to let me know that it was now the top trending topic on Twitter, and that he had just sent out a tweet providing an update on the filibuster that had been his fastest ever to receive a thousand retweets. My office sent down word that former staff and the parents of existing staff were now crowded into our office, trying to answer as many of the incoming phone calls as possible. When the filibuster had ended, our two-desk front office had handled twelve thousand phone calls of support from all over the world.

It was around midnight, thirteen hours in, when Schumer stepped onto the floor to whisper to me that the negotiations that he and Reid had been engaged in with McConnell were bearing fruit. Schumer explained that if we agreed to end the filibuster, McConnell would commit to allow debate and votes on both of our proposals.

It's a good thing, because my body was starting to quit me. I had been standing in one place with nothing to eat or drink, holding in all my bodily fluids, for thirteen hours. In law school, I had ruptured two discs in my back, and my partially repaired spine was now shooting pains down my legs.

I motioned Booker and Blumenthal over to my desk. "I think it's over," I whispered, "I think we won."

"But we're going to lose these votes, right?" Booker replied.

I knew what the answer was, but I couldn't bring myself to say it out loud. "We'll put people on the record. We'll make Republicans vote against keeping terrorists from getting guns. And even if we lose, we rewrote the script."

.　　.　　.

The filibuster, which reached fifteen hours by its end, set in motion a series of events that would consume Washington for the next two weeks. The two measures McConnell committed to hold votes on both failed, but Republicans, still reeling from the shame brought on them by our effort, organized a new effort to try to find common ground on the terrorist watch list proposal. A compromise between a group of eight Republican and Democratic senators was announced a week later, and though that proposal failed, too, it was the first signal that Republicans now felt significant pressure to act, not just obstruct, on the issue of gun violence.

And then Democrats in the House of Representatives, having watched the success of our filibuster, staged an act of civil disobedience of their own. A handful of them refused to budge from the House floor—literally sitting on the carpet—until Speaker Paul Ryan scheduled votes on the same measures we bargained for in the Senate. Like the filibuster, the House sit-in captured the nation's attention and inspired thousands to join the growing movement.

Parkland and the resulting creation of the March for Our Lives movement is still probably the most significant moment in the short history of the modern anti–gun violence movement, but one could make the argument that the weeks after the 2016 Orlando shooting laid the groundwork for what came after Parkland. For the first time, the anti–gun violence movement was on the offense, refusing to accept the tired pattern of inaction after mass shootings, and showing the gun lobby that we were unafraid and unbowed. It was the moment that our movement got our legs fully underneath us and went toe to toe with the forces of the status quo without flinching. We didn't win any votes. We didn't change any laws. But nothing was really the same after that.

The day after the filibuster, I must have done two dozen press interviews. My day finished with an appearance on *The Rachel Maddow Show,* and by the time I got home, the show following hers, hosted by Lawrence O'Donnell, was playing on the TV screen as our children's babysitter watched. He had begun his monologue with the explanation of the history of filibusters referenced earlier. But now, as I put down my backpack and looked up at the television, he was talking about me. Like he knew me.

Senators, Democrats and Republicans, are mostly very careful people. Their behavior is very careful. They don't take chances. They don't rock the boat. They have spent their lives, most of them, plotting their way to the United States Senate. . . . Most of them are not the kids who get in trouble in high school. They're not the rebels. . . . They were the kids the rebels made fun of.

Chris Murphy has the classic profile of a United States Senator. He was student body president at Wethersfield High School in Connecticut. He carried a briefcase in high school and founded the Young Democrats at his high school. In any high school movie, Chris Murphy would be the predictable square who never has an even slightly interesting moment on screen. Chris Murphy didn't go off into the world seeking adventure and looking for a path in life. He always knew what he was going to do. He was elected State Representative when he was twenty-six. He was elected State Senator when he was thirty. Went to Washington . . . at thirty-four. . . . Along the way, he picked up a wife and two kids. That is the classic Senate résumé.

There was *no clue* in that résumé that Chris Murphy would do what he did last night. That résumé says that Chris Murphy got to the Senate by playing it safe. That résumé says that Chris Murphy is not a rebel. But the single most . . . rebellious thing available to a senator is the filibuster.

·   ·   ·

By the time I got back home to Connecticut and wound my way to the Yacht Club, I was beginning to understand the impact of the filibuster in a more visceral way. These suburban, economically secure mothers and fathers *did* care about the gun violence epidemic. They worried that they were no longer immune from it. And then they watched their senator, who had previously appeared to them averse to risk and controversy, do something so seemingly foolish, and they began to question their own silence. These members of the exclusive Pequot Yacht Club in wealthy Southport, Connecticut, reliable guardians of the status quo, began to wonder whether something more was inside them, too.

There is no joy in your life's work becoming connected to the fight to end the slaughter of innocent children. There is little satisfaction in devoting your career to building a social change movement that will see a hundred failures before a single success. The countless hours I have spent listening to heartbreaking stories of survivors and the family members of those gunned down in cold blood are grueling and taxing on my soul. There are some days, I admit, when I wonder why I couldn't have accepted a different mission, where the pain and the hurt are not so manifest.

But then, on those days, I remember who I was before 2012. And I try to convince myself that maybe, just maybe, I am uniquely suited to this moment. Maybe the emotional hole inside me was meant to be matched with this moment and this fight, and all the overflowing, uncontrollable emotion that comes with it. Maybe this mission is how I find out what lies inside *me*.

ANNIE

Most people fell in love with Dylan Hockley at first sight. His big blue eyes, mop of dark hair, dimples, and infectious giggle were more than enough to melt hearts. Despite his striking looks, in many ways, Dylan was a typical six-year-old. He loved movies, and when he found a flick he liked, he would sit in front of the television replaying his favorite scene over and over until his parents forced him to stop. He devoured spaghetti (plain) and garlic bread. He loved the color purple. And he adored his older brother, Jake, and could spend endless hours jumping on the family's backyard trampoline with him.

But in other ways, Dylan was different from many of his peers. Says his mother: "He was late to develop speech. He was late to learn to crawl, and there was always a little something about him, but we couldn't put our finger on it." Dylan recoiled at loud noises and had a habit of flapping his arms at his sides when excited. Eventually, at the urging of a teacher, the Hockleys got Dylan tested and confirmed that their son was autistic.

School was a struggle for Dylan, but his parents, Nicole and Ian, were determined to give him every chance to keep up with his peers. When the Hockleys were considering settling in Newtown, Nicole and Ian went to Sandy Hook Elementary School to meet with the dynamic principal, Dawn Hochsprung, to talk about their younger son's needs. Hochsprung's assurances "sealed the deal," according to Ian, and the family happily became members of the Sandy Hook community. At the start of his first-grade year, the school arranged for Dylan to have a student mentor so that he could model behavior of other, more socially confident children. He was making friends and becoming more verbal.

But what really made the difference for Dylan, that first-grade year, was a woman named Anne Marie Murphy. Anne Marie, known as

Annie to her family and friends, had devoted her life to children. Originally an art teacher, she took a break from classroom work to raise her own kids. Her daughter Kelly, who followed her mother into teaching, remembers that she and her three siblings never spent much time in front of a television growing up. Their mother organized their free time around so many activities—arts, crafts, games, day trips—that she often seemed more like a camp director than a homemaker.

She went back into teaching when her youngest daughter entered first grade, and she spent nights completing her master's in art education, with the hope of returning to a full-time art teacher's position. But finding a full-time job in art education at a moment when schools were cutting back noncore subject learning was difficult, especially because Annie couldn't stomach a long commute to and from work, lest she miss time with her husband, Michael, and four children. So instead, she took up residence at her hometown elementary school, serving as a teacher's aide at Sandy Hook Elementary School. Eventually, she became one of the school's most experienced and sought-after aides, assigned each year to work with the children who needed the most care and nurturing for their special needs. And so, in the fall of 2012, Annie Murphy was paired up with one of the cutest things she had ever laid her eyes on: precocious Dylan Hockley.

Immediately, Dylan attached himself to Annie. They formed a quick bond, and the Hockleys attributed Dylan's progress that fall to the guidance that his new teacher's aide provided him. Annie had helped teach Dylan how to read, and he beamed with pride every time he read a book to Nicole, Ian, or Jake. Dylan was so proud of his relationship with Mrs. Murphy that he posted a picture of his class on the kitchen refrigerator, and every time he walked by it, he would point to Annie, as if needing to show off to his family his newfound friend. She became his rock that fall, and Nicole and Ian felt a heartening sense of ease sending their autistic, socially limited son off to school each day, knowing that Annie Murphy was there waiting for him.

The morning of December 14, 2012, as Ian and Nicole watched hundreds of children stream into the Sandy Hook firehouse and promptly depart with their panicked parents, they held Jake close as they waited for Dylan to arrive as well. As the minutes turned into hours, and there were only a handful of parents remaining—all parents of children in two first-grade classrooms—a feeling of terror settled upon the Hockleys. Nicole thought to herself that if Dylan was still in that school, then maybe she could find Annie Murphy amid the chaos of the firehouse and ask her what had happened to her son. But then Nicole had a second thought. If something had happened to Dylan, if he really was in danger inside that school, then Annie Murphy—his rock, his friend, his protector—would never, ever leave his side. If Dylan was still inside that classroom, alive or dead, thought Nicole, then so was Annie Murphy.

.   .   .

Our nation's moral core is rotting away to nothing, each and every day that we allow this morbid circus of human carnage to continue unabated. Today, the fact that mass shootings barely hold the national headlines for twenty-four hours is proof of how jaundiced we have become to the new normal of large-scale slaughter. Few bat an eye when over one weekend in Philadelphia or New Orleans or Baltimore, two dozen young people are shot, mostly over trivial disputes over girlfriends or petty grudges. Addiction rates and overdose deaths and suicides spiral into the stratosphere and political leaders throw a few more dollars toward treatment and then go back to their slumber. Hundreds of thousands of people overseas in war-torn areas teeter on the brink of starvation, and America simply offers to send more planes and bombs. Our nation has chosen to anesthetize itself to human-on-human violence like no other country in the world.

We cannot completely escape our history. Ours is a nation founded in violence, and the natural frictions that will exist within a nation made up of so many different subsets of peoples were destined to result in higher levels of violence here than other, more homogeneous places around the world. And our nation's long, complicated history of widespread gun ownership and firearms production was always going to contribute to the perpetuation of American violence—

regardless of how we chose to regulate our weapons. Some of our violence was indeed inevitable.

But most of it—the homicides, the school shootings, the suicides, the domestic violence, and the deaths of despair—is all preventable. And what is most offensive to me and all the families who have lost sons and daughters or brothers and sisters to this uniquely American epidemic, is that today Congress isn't lifting a finger to solve it. It certainly isn't because Congress is blind to the crisis—despite our growing numbness to the mass shootings, the news shows are still filled with scenes from the front lines of the epidemic. And it isn't because Congress doesn't know what to do—the data is clear that keeping guns away from certain people, and keeping the most powerful guns out of private hands, can save thousands and thousands of lives. Just as clear is the research demonstrating the consequences of mixing ubiquitous guns with the toxic mixture of poverty and racism. And the ineffectiveness of our current foreign policy at saving lives abroad is hard to ignore.

What we are missing is simply the courage—the political will—to properly do our jobs.

I dream of the day when Republican lawmakers will realize that democracy dies a little bit when an idea as broadly popular as national universal background checks cannot become law. I wish a thousand wishes that Republicans would stand up to President Trump's racist rants and policies, which further cement the cycle of marginality and violence for millions of African Americans and Hispanic Americans. I am waiting for the GOP to understand the error of a foreign policy weighted so heavily on violence and threat of violence. But democracy is not built on wishes. It is dependent on action. And today, supporters of the status quo—those who continue to vote against the 90 percent of their constituency that wants changes in the nation's gun laws—must pay a political price for their intransigence.

Of all the antiviolence interventions discussed in this book, universal background checks are the most impactful, the most popular, and the most politically possible. And so, for starters, they must be our north star. For decades, the Republican Party and the weapons industry have been in an abusive, codependent relationship with one another. Each believes that it cannot exist without the other. The Republican Party outsources the decision of which of their candidates is a true conservative to the NRA, and believes that the gun lobby's moral power can still carry them over the finish line in conservative-leaning districts and states. The NRA, fast becoming marginalized politically and pushing policies badly out of step with even its own members, attaches itself to the GOP to maintain the group's establishment credentials, even as its agenda finds less and less popular favor.

The gun lobby is right to believe that its future is dependent on its continued favor within the Republican Party. It's the GOP that's wrong—their party, in fact, is destined for long-term obsolescence if it does not realize soon that the public mood on gun violence is shifting quickly, and staying aligned with the gun industry is a disastrous signal to Americans that the party cares more about political allies than the safety of our children.

But for the gun lobby's congressional arm to realize its error, they must pay a political cost with an unmistakable message attached to it.

And that is what we will do. It is what I hope you will do. Because to tip the politics on American violence, we need more voters who will decide never to support a candidate who doesn't support common-sense interventions like universal background checks and assault weapons bans. We need more activists who will demand that Republicans and Democrats find the common ground that is there for the taking on further reform of our racist criminal justice system. And we need more true believers to run for Congress—just like Lucy McBath did—so that we don't just have more people willing to vote correctly in Congress and state legislatures, we have more champions.

But frankly, I have found that trying to discover the precise calibration for action is wasted effort. If you are moved to action by the arguments in this book, just do something. Do not stand idly by while one hundred Americans, every single day, have their lives cut short by a bullet that pierces their skin and rips so violently through their organs that blood and oxygen stop flowing to their brain. Do not let this epidemic of slaughter continue, when the solution lies not in the hands of Congress, but in your hands. The political movement that will eventually dislodge the power of the gun lobby, and make sure Congress abides by the wishes of the vast majority of Americans and does something about gun violence, is yours.

It is mine, too, of course. And at my more self-important moments, I like to think that I've been willing to take the risks necessary to be a leader of it. My experience inside the anti–gun violence movement, and the movement to rethink America's footprint in the world, has changed me. I have an emotional connection to the cause of violence prevention that drives me in a way that nothing else in my professional career has. Inside me, it turns out, was much more than I knew. I just needed a moment—*a moral jolt*—through which I could find things I did not know existed. Being a human being, it turns out, is a tricky business. We are a convoluted mélange of instincts and motivations, and our entire lives are defined, often, by a desire to find out what resides at our core. I am closer than ever before to figuring out my own personal answer to that question.

And the reason, I think, that I chose to tell the story of Annie Murphy in the last six minutes of my fifteen-hour filibuster on June 17, 2016, is that her story, far better than my own, might give us the confidence that something truly good—something that will shake loose our false sense of inevitability about American violence—lies inside all of us.

. . .

No one knows exactly what happened inside Victoria Soto's classroom during those terrifying seconds, when those students and teachers saw a pale, rail-thin boy clad in black with a military-grade rifle walk into the room. But I would guess that Annie Murphy knew what was about to happen. She had heard the rapid-fire, ear-piercing hail of bullets just seconds earlier, in the classroom next door. And I would also imagine that Annie Murphy had a few choices to make, at that life-changing moment. She could have made a run for it. Tried to get to the door before Lanza could hunt her down. She could have hidden. There was a closet and plenty of places under which she could try to find cover. Or she could have simply panicked. No one would have expected anything else under the circumstances.

Hours later, Dylan Hockley's mother, Nicole, stood at the firehouse, just yards away from that classroom, telling herself that Anne Marie Murphy—the teacher that her little boy loved so much that he pointed out her picture on their refrigerator every single day—would not leave Dylan if he was in danger. And Nicole was pretty sure, standing there with nineteen other sets of parents, that Dylan had been confronted with some kind of danger earlier that morning.

When Lanza entered Victoria Soto's classroom, at approximately nine thirty-five that Friday morning, Annie Murphy did not run. She did not hide. She did not panic. Amid the horrifying chaos, she found Dylan Hockley. Or maybe Dylan found her. But however they came together inside that classroom, as Lanza started to spray fire across it, Annie Murphy wrapped her arms around Dylan and embraced this little boy she loved so deeply.

"Do you know why we know that?" I asked a nearly empty Senate chamber, the clock reading 2:35 in the morning, my eyes brimming with tears. I spoke the next sentences slowly, so as to make sure I didn't lose it. "Because when the police entered the classroom, that's how they found Dylan Hockley. Dead. Wrapped in the embrace of Anne Marie Murphy.

"It doesn't take courage to stand here on the floor of the United States Senate for two hours or four hours or fourteen hours," I continued, waving my arms at nonexistent senators who were already home, halfway through their comfortable night's sleep. "It doesn't take courage to stand up to the gun lobby when ninety percent of your constituents want change to happen. It takes courage . . . to look into the eye of a shooter, and instead of running, wrapping your arms around a six-year-old boy, and accepting death as a *trade* for just a tiny, little, itty-bitty piece of increased peace of mind for a little boy under your charge."

Senator Booker stood silent in the well of the Senate, watching me. The normally stoic parliamentarian blotted tears off her cheeks. After fifteen hours, my back was starting to give out. I decided it was time to go home.

"And so I ask you all this question—if Anne Marie Murphy could do *that*, then ask yourself, what can *you* do to make sure that Orlando or Sandy Hook never . . . ever . . . happens again?"

.   .   .

For months after Shane Oliver died, Janet Rice coped with an involuntary reflex that would routinely overcome her in the middle of the night. She would awaken from a deep sleep, put on her clothes, climb into her car, and start driving. Every night she did this, she would arrive at the same location—the corner of South Prospect and Sheldon streets, where her only child had taken his first steps, and where months earlier, she had held him in her arms, as he slowly bled to death from a gunshot wound. A gunshot wound that occurred because of a simple argument over a girl. When Janet would arrive at that place, in the dead of night, she would shift her transmission into park, turn on the high beams, and wait. Sometimes for hours. She would sit in her car, and wait and wait and wait. For her son to come back.

Around that same time, fifty miles away in Sandy Hook, Jackie Barden had figured out one way to give herself a small, temporary reprieve from the all-consuming grief that came with losing a child in a mass shooting. During the day, in the after-school hours, when Jackie needed to get household work done, she would play a game. She would pretend that her little seven-year-old boy, Daniel, was at a playdate, due to be home in a few hours. She would think of him happily running around a neighbor's house, joking with friends, and she would smile as she looked forward to hearing about his exploits when he came home. It worked, for an hour or so at a time, on some days. But eventually, reality would always set back in. Daniel wasn't coming back home. Ever.

For Nicole Hockley, no trick worked. She threw herself into her work—amazing work—building with the Bardens and other Sandy Hook families a multimillion-dollar nonprofit organization teaching children how to combat the kind of social isolation that helped drive

Adam Lanza to shoot her son. But she did find comfort, in those darkest of moments, knowing what really happened in those last minutes inside Dylan's classroom. "To know that he was with her, and that he wasn't alone," said Nicole, "that gives you a huge peace of mind . . . to know that he was loved, even in those last moments."

What Annie Murphy did that morning, inside that classroom, is a monumental act of love, and sacrifice. Annie Murphy, a teacher's aide and a mother of four, didn't look like a hero. But to the Hockleys, that's who she is. Nicole and Ian are able to catch a few more minutes of sleep each night, knowing that their little boy was with someone he loved, deeply, at that moment of deathly peril.

One day I asked Annie's daughter, "Were you surprised when you heard about what happened inside the classroom with Dylan?"

Her answer bore no hesitation. "Nothing my mom did," she said, "surprised any of us."

What Annie Murphy did that morning, in the face of such evil, is proof to me of what truly lives inside all of us. Maybe we are all not capable of the incalculable courage that she demonstrated that day. But we all *do* have the ability to decide our own fate and the fate of our neighbors, and take individual actions that will reduce the likelihood that more mothers and fathers will have to live with the personal destruction that haunts Sam and Janet, and Nicole and Ian, to this day and for every day after. The pace of this slaughter is not inevitable. The story of American violence can be altered.

"If Anne Marie Murphy could do *that*," I asked an empty Senate chamber, "then ask yourself, what can *you* do?"

Violence is a part of us. It is inside us and all around us. But the uniquely American tidal wave of murder and suicide and assault does not have to be our destiny. It is preventable, if we simply decide to make better choices as a nation.

If we choose to rise up and do the small, heroic things of which we know, deep down, we are capable.

If we decide to have the courage to discover what truly lies inside each of us.

ACKNOWLEDGMENTS

Somewhat to my surprise, I thoroughly enjoyed the process of writing this book. It was, on the late nights and weekends and plane and train rides when I could fit in writing sessions, a welcome distraction from the often maddening, demoralizing daily cadence of political life in the age of Trump. But for a novice author, determined to prove that an elected official could write a serious policy book, the process was also filled with trepidation and many moments when I was convinced I was in way, way over my head. To the extent I kept my nostrils above water, it is undoubtedly due to the indispensable cast of family, friends, and colleagues who supported me throughout this herculean endeavor.

I originally envisioned writing a much less personal, much more policy-focused book, and it was my friend Charlie Melcher who first challenged me to view authorship as an extension of my advocacy. I didn't end up writing the book we envisioned, but his early confidence in me was inflating. My agent, Jennifer Joel, believed in this project from the beginning, and was resolute in making sure I got to write the book that my heart pointed me toward. Mark Warren, my editor at Random House, was also an early believer in this project, and it was so comforting to go through this process with an editor who was equally passionate about addressing this crisis head-on. And as a novice author, he treated me kindly and patiently, and for that I am deeply grateful. Victoria Bassetti, my brilliant research partner, helped form and mold this book from the moment I began it. She was my copilot for every step of this journey, reviewed and edited every word, and made the product so much better in every way. Max Lehman-Ludwig gave a nice assist to Victoria down the home stretch, and for that we are both thankful.

Thank you to all those who read all or portions of this book: Cory Booker, John King, Jim Johnson, Pamela Cantor, David Bonine, Kenny Curran, Jamie Geller, and Allison Herwitt. David, Kenny, Jamie, and Allison all help lead my Senate office, and without their patience as I balanced Senate responsibilities with the process of writing, I could not have done this. Additional heartfelt thanks to my friend and right hand in the Washington office, Maya Ashwal, who helped guard writing time, especially as deadlines approached. Many smart people assisted Victoria in her research, but a special shout-out goes to Kristin Goss at Duke University, Eric Ruben of Southern Methodist University, John Kowal and Lauren-Brooke Eisen at the Brennan Center for Justice, and Daniel Webster of Johns Hopkins (who makes a few appearances in the book) for being on call to lend a hand.

The book opens with the story of Sam Saylor and Janet Rice and their slain son, Shane, and I am so grateful that they chose to share their story with me. I am, at all times, in awe of the parents and relatives of the slain who muster the courage to tell their stories publicly and speak truth to power so that fewer parents ever have to go through what they have endured. So many stories are included in this book, but I am especially grateful to my great friends Mark and Jackie Barden and Nicole and Ian Hockley for, as usual, baring their souls to help move our common cause forward. And thanks to Nelba Márquez-Greene, Merry Jackson, Michael Scholtes, Kelly Murphy, Walker Gladden III, Joni Holifield, Marcus Cole, G. Travis Miller, and all the other individuals who agreed to talk with me about their (often heartbreaking) experiences inside America's gun violence epidemic. I hope I have done all your stories justice.

Of course, most specifically, a thank-you to the community of Newtown, and the families of the children we lost that day, who have let me become part of your lives during the last seven years. I hope you see this book as simply another mechanism by which to tell the story of your grace, and our collective commitment to honor your children's memories. I will not list your names here, but you are with me every day, and our fight is only beginning.

And finally, at the end of that day in December 2012 that my life changed, I came home to Cathy, my moral compass over the past two decades, and knew that she would be there with me for whatever journey which I was about to undertake. I couldn't have done any of this work, nor written this book, without her. Our inquisitive, kind, and precocious boys, Owen and Rider, occasionally appear as characters in this book, but, more important, are my daily joy, and constant reminders of why I have taken on this work to keep children safe from violence. And finally, I cannot imagine being in the place I am today without four and a half decades of unconditional support from my parents, Scott and Cathy, who have believed in and supported every crazy idea I have ever concocted.

I am truly a lucky guy, to be surrounded by so many who inspire and support me, and without my family, my friends, and my fellow activists, none of the pages that precede this one would be possible.

A NOTE ON SOURCES USED IN THIS BOOK

This book is the product of years of thought and research. As I wrote, I was deeply influenced by two books, Norbert Elias's *The Civilizing Process* and Steven Pinker's *The Better Angels of Our Nature*. The two books' clear-eyed depiction of the human capacity for violence coupled with their profound optimism about our ability to do good make them required reading for anyone exploring the issue of American violence.

The references that follow catalog many, but not all, of the works used in writing this book. The research ranged from deep dives into the scientific literature and crime databases to late-night reading of books and articles intended for a general readership. Many of them are collected here and organized by chapter and theme. So if a reader wants to delve into the scientific studies or popular articles about the so-called warrior gene or about violence and hope in Baltimore, they will be able to find the citations to much of the material used on those topics in one place.

A number of sources defied classification. They were used throughout the book and thread their way through many themes. For example, Adam Winkler's masterful *Gunfight: The Battle Over the Right to Bear Arms in America* and Michael Waldman's excellent *The Second Amendment: A Biography* informed passages on American violence, the NRA, and the history of gun control laws. But this catalog does not duplicate citations to them, or other similar works, when they were used, as Winkler and Waldman were, in multiple chapters. Readers should be aware that the sources detailed in this note were relied upon cumulatively.

CHAPTER ONE: SOS

October 20, 2012

Lewis, Charles J. "Murphy's Record: A Loyal Democrat, a Low-Key Profile." *Connecticut Post*, October 20, 2012. https://www.ctpost.com/local/article/Murphy-s-record-A-loyal-Democrat-a-low-key-3967800.php.

Mascia, Jennifer. "'When I'm the Trauma Surgeon on Call and I Hear About a Gunshot Wound, I Have to Cross My Fingers and Say a Little Prayer': Accounts from the Front Lines of Urban Gun Violence. This Week: Hartford, Connecticut." *The Trace*, August 21, 2015. https://www.thetrace.org/2015/08/city-limits-hartford-connecticut-gun-violence/.

NBC Universal. "Arrest in Hartford Homicide." NBC Connecticut, October 25, 2012. https://www.nbcconnecticut.com/news/local/Arrest-in-Hartford-Homicide--175823931.html.

Owens, David. "Man Gets 40 Years for Hartford Shooting That Destroyed Two Lives." *Hartford Courant*, May 7, 2015. https://www.courant.com/breaking-news/hc-hartford-shane-oliver-murder-0508-20150507-story.html.

Ross, Janell. "In the Shadow of Newtown, a Father Grieves and Fights." *The Root*, December 13, 2013. https://www.theroot.com/in-the-shadow-of-newtown-a-father-grieves-and-fights-1790899324.

Stuart, Christine. "Anti-Gun Protestors Say 'We Are All Newtown.'" *New Haven Register*, March 31, 2013. https://www.nhregister.com/connecticut/article/Anti-gun-protestors-say-We-are-all-Newtown-11387262.php.

S.O.S.

"'S.O.S.'—The Ambulance Call of the Seas: How Famous Wireless Distress Signal Originated—Science in Role of Life Saver at Sea." *New York Times*, February 13, 1910. https://www.nytimes.com/1910/02/13/archives/-sos-the-ambulance-call-of-the-seas-how-famous-wireless-distress.html.

United Wireless to *The New York Times*. "Save 47 After Wireless Call: The Alamo Reaches the Sinking Steamer Kentucky Just in Time to Take Off Crew." *New York Times*, February 5, 1910. https://www.nytimes.com/1910/02/05/archives/save-47-after-wireless-call-the-alamo-reaches-the-sinking-steamer.html.

United Wireless to *The New York Times*. "How Wireless Saved the Kentucky Crew; Operator McGinnis Tells of Fight to Keep Rising Water from the Dynamo." *New York Times*, February 6, 1910. https://www.nytimes.com/1910/02/06/archives/how-wireless-saved-the-kentucky-crew-operator-mcginnis-tells-of.html.

CHAPTER TWO: THE VIOLENCE INSIDE US

Greg Gianforte

Cochrane, Emily. "'That's My Kind of Guy,' Trump Says of Republican Lawmaker Who Body-Slammed a Reporter." *New York Times*, October 19, 2018. https://www.nytimes.com/2018/10/19/us/politics/trump-greg-gianforte-montana.html.

Mele, Christopher. "Montana Republican Greg Gianforte Is Sentenced in Assault on Reporter." *New York Times*, June 13, 2017. https://www.nytimes.com/2017/06/13/us/politics/greg-gianforte-sentenced.html.

Ripley, Brie. "Gianforte 'Body Slams' Reporter, Charged with Assault by Gallatin County Sheriff's Office." *Montana Public Radio*, May 25, 2017. https://www.mtpr.org/post/gianforte-body-slams-reporter-charged-assault-gallatin-county-sheriffs-office.

The Biology of Violence

Archer, John. "The Nature of Human Aggression." *International Journal of Law and Psychiatry* 32, no. 4 (2009): 202–208. https://doi.org/10.1016/j.ijlp.2009.04.001.

Bowles, Samuel. "Did Warfare Among Ancestral Hunter-Gatherers Affect the Evolution of Human Social Behaviors?" *Science* 324, no. 5932 (2009): 1293–1298. https://doi.org/10.1126/science.1168112.

Brower, M. C., and B. H. Price. "Neuropsychiatry of Frontal Lobe Dysfunction in Violent and Criminal Behaviour: A Critical Review." *Journal of Neurology, Neurosurgery, and Psychiatry* 71, no. 6 (2001): 720–726. https://doi.org/10.1136/jnnp.71.6.720.

Burns, Taylor. "Testosterone and Human Aggression (or Why It's Time to Give Your Gonads Some Credit)." *Scitable*, January 22, 2011. https://www.nature.com/scitable/blog/cognoculture/testosterone_and_human_aggression_or_180520.

Carrier, David R., and Christopher Cunningham. "The Effect of Foot Posture on Capacity to Apply Free Moments to the Ground: Implications for Fighting Performance in Great Apes." *Journal of Experimental Biology* 6, no. 2 (2017): 269–277. https://doi.org/10.1242/bio.022640.

Carrier, David R., and Michael H. Morgan. "Protective Buttressing of the Hominin Face." *Biological Reviews of the Cambridge Philosophical Society* 90, no. 1 (2014). https://doi.org/10.1111/brv.12112.

Cohen, Adam. *Imbeciles: The Supreme Court, American Eugenics, and the Sterilization of Carrie Buck*. New York: Penguin Books, 2017.

Côté, Sylvana M., Tracy Vaillancourt, John C. LeBlanc, et al. "The Development of Physical Aggression from Toddlerhood to Pre-Adolescence: A Nation Wide Longitudinal Study of Canadian Children." *Journal of Abnormal Child Psychology* 34, no. 1 (2006): 71–85. https://doi.org/10.1007/s10802-005-9001-z.

Denno, Deborah. "Courts' Increasing Consideration of Behavioral Genetics Evidence in Criminal Cases: Results of a Longitudinal Study." *Michigan State Law Review*, vol. 2011 (2011): 967–1047. https://www.researchgate.net/publication/256020090_Courts'_Increasing_Consideration_of_Behavioral_Genetics_Evidence_in_Criminal_Cases_Results_of_a_Longitudinal_Study.

Ermer, Elsa, Lora M. Cope, Prashanth K. Nyalakanti, et al. "Aberrant Paralimbic Gray Matter in Criminal Psychopathy." *Journal of the American Academy of Child and Adolescent Psychiatry* 121, no. 3 (2012): 649–658. http://doi.org/10.1037/a0026371.

Ermer, Elsa, Lora M. Cope, Prashanth K. Nyalakanti, et al. "Aberrant Paralimbic Gray Matter in Incarcerated Male Adolescents with Psychopathic Traits." *Journal of the American Academy of Child and Adolescent Psychiatry* 52, no. 1 (2013): 94–103. http://doi.org/10.1016/j.jaac.2012.10.013.

Farahany, Nita. "Neuroscience and Behavioral Genetics in U.S. Criminal Law: An Empirical Analysis." *Journal of Law and the Biosciences* 2, no. 3 (2016): 485–509. https://doi.org/10.1093/jlb/lsv059.

Farahany, Nita, William Bernet, Cindy L. Vnencak-Jones, et al. "Bad Nature, Bad Nurture, and Testimony Regarding MAOA and SLC6A4 Genotyping at Murder Trials." *Journal of Forensic Sciences* 52, no. 6 (2007): 1362–1371. http://doi.org/10.1111/j.1556-4029.2007.00562.x.

Fields, Douglas. *Why We Snap: Understanding the Rage Circuit in Your Brain*. New York: Dutton, 2016.

Forget-Dubois, Nadine, Michel Boivin, Ginette Dionne, et al. "A Longitudinal Twin Study of the Genetic and Environmental Etiology of Maternal Hostile-Reactive Behavior During Infancy and Toddlerhood." *Infant Behavior and Development* 30, no. 3 (2007): 453–465. https://doi.org/10.1016/j.infbeh.2006.12.005.

Fuss, Johannes. "Legal Responses to Neuroscience." *Journal of Psychiatry and Neuroscience* 41, no. 6 (2016): 363–365. https://www.ncbi.nlm.nih.gov/pmc/articles/PMC5082506/.

Gabbatiss, John. "Nasty, Brutish, and Short: Are Humans DNA-Wired to Kill?" *Scientific American,* July 19, 2017. https://www.scientificamerican.com/article/nasty-brutish -and-short-are-humans-dna-wired-to-kill/.

Gómez, José María, Miguel Verdú, and Adela González-Megías. "The Phylogenetic Roots of Human Lethal Violence." *Nature* 538: 233–237. https://doi.org/10.1038/nature19758.

Hagerty, Barbara Bradley. "Can Your Genes Make You Murder?" Morning Edition, National Public Radio, July 1, 2010. https://www.npr.org/templates/story/story.php?storyId =128043329.

Hebb, D. O. *A Textbook of Psychology.* Philadelphia: Saunders, 1972.

Henderson, Leslie. "Why Our Brains See the World as 'Us' Versus 'Them.'" *Scientific American,* June 22, 2018. https://www.scientificamerican.com/article/why-our-brains-see -the-world-as-us-versus-them/.

Hermans, Erno J., Nick F. Ramsey, and Jack van Honk. "Exogenous Testosterone Enhances Responsiveness to Social Threat in the Neural Circuitry of Social Aggression in Humans." *Biological Psychiatry* 63, no. 3 (2007): 263–270. https://doi.org/10.1016/j.biopsych.2007.05.013.

Jarrett, Christian. "Neuroscientists Conduct the Most Frustrating Brain Scanning Study Ever." *Wired,* April 16, 2014. https://www.wired.com/2014/04/neuroscientists -conduct-the-most-frustrating-brain-scanning-study-ever/.

Johnston, Ian. "Humans Evolved to Have an Instinct for Deadly Violence, Researchers Find." *The Independent,* September 28, 2016. https://www.independent.co.uk/news/ science/human-evolution-violence-instinct-to-kill-murder-each-other-a7335491.html.

Kiehl, Kent A. "A Cognitive Neuroscience Perspective on Psychopathy: Evidence for Paralimbic System Dysfunction." *Psychiatry Research* 142, no. 2–3 (2006): 107–128. https://doi .org/10.1016/j.psychres.2005.09.013.

Kiehl, Kent A., and Morris B. Hoffman. "The Criminal Psychopath: History, Neuroscience, and Economics." *Jurimetrics: The Journal of Law, Science, and Technology* 51 (2011): 355–397. https://www.ncbi.nlm.nih.gov/pmc/articles/PMC4059069/.

Kubota, Jennifer T., Mahzarin R. Banaji, and Elizabeth A. Phelps. "The Neuroscience of Race." *Nature Neuroscience* 15 (2012): 940–948. https://www.nature.com/articles/nn.3136.

Lacourse, Eric, Michel Boivin, Mara Brendgen, et al. "A Longitudinal Twin Study of Physical Aggression during Early Childhood: Evidence for a Developmentally Dynamic Genome." *Psychological Medicine* 44, no. 12 (2014): 2617–2627. https://doi.org/10.1017/ S0033291713003218.

Mattsson, Åke, Daisy Schalling, Dan Olweus, et al. "Plasma Testosterone, Aggressive Behavior, and Personality Dimensions in Young Male Delinquents." *Journal of the American Association of Child Psychiatry* 19, no. 3 (1980): 476–490. https://www.jaacap.org/ article/S0002-7138(09)61065-7/pdf.

McDermott, Rose, Dustin Tingley, Jonathan Cowden, et al. "Monoamine Oxidase A Gene (MAOA) Predicts Behavioral Aggression Following Provocation." *Proceedings of the National Academy of Sciences of the United States of America* 106, no. 7 (2009): 2118–2123. http://doi.org/10.1073/pnas.0808376106.

McSwiggan, Sally, Bernice Elger, and Paul S. Appelbaum. "The Forensic Use of Behavioral Genetics in Criminal Proceedings: Case of the MAOA-L Genotype." *International Journal of Law and Psychiatry* 50 (2016): 17–23. https://doi.org/10.1016/j.ijlp.2016.09.005.

Mead, Hilary K., Theodore P. Beauchaine, and Katherine E. Shannon. "Neurobiological Adaptations to Violence Across Development." *Development and Psychopathology* 22, no. 1 (2010): 1–22. http://doi.org/10.1017/S0954579409990228.

Meyer-Lindenberg, Andreas, Joshua W. Buckholtz, Bhaskar Kolachana, et al. "Neural Mechanisms of Genetic Risk for Impulsivity and Violence in Humans." *Proceedings of the National Academy of Sciences of the United States of America* 103, no. 16 (2006): 6269–6274. https://doi.org/10.1073/pnas.0511311103.

Mims, Christopher. "Strange but True: Testosterone Alone Does Not Cause Violence." *Scientific American,* July 5, 2007. https://www.scientificamerican.com/article/strange-but-true-testosterone-alone-doesnt-cause-violence/.

Mirazón Lahr, M., F. Rivera, R. K. Power, et al. "Inter-Group Violence among Early Holocene Hunter-Gatherers of West Turkana, Kenya." *Nature* 529: 394–398. https://doi.org/10.1038/nature16477.

Molenberghs, Pascal. "The Neuroscience of In-Group Bias." *Neuroscience & Biobehavioral Reviews* 37 (2013): 1530–1536. https://doi.org/10.1016/j.neubiorev.2013.06.002.

Morgan, Michael H., and David R. Carrier. "Protective Buttressing of the Human Fist and the Evolution of Hominin Hands." *Journal of Experimental Biology* 216, no. 2 (2012): 236–244. http://doi.org/10.1242/jeb.075713.

Panksepp, Jaak. "The Basic Emotional Circuits of Mammalian Brains: Do Animals Have Affective Lives?" *Neuroscience and Biobehavioral Reviews* 35, no. 9 (2011): 1791–1804. http://doi.org/10.1016/j.neubiorev.2011.08.003.

Pinker, Steven. *The Better Angels of Our Nature: Why Violence Has Declined.* London: Penguin Books, 2011.

Rennie, John. "Evolved Fists or the Best Weapons at Hand?" *PLOS,* February 26, 2013. https://web.archive.org/web/20180719044859/https://blogs.plos.org/retort/2013/02/26/evolved-fists-or-the-best-weapons-at-hand/.

Romm, Cari. "A Prehistoric Mass Grave Suggests Hunter-Gatherers Weren't So Peaceful." *The Atlantic,* January 20, 2016. https://www.theatlantic.com/science/archive/2016/01/a-prehistoric-mass-grave-and-the-origins-of-war/424839/.

Sapolsky, Robert M. *Behave: The Biology of Humans at Our Best and Worst.* New York: Penguin Press, 2017.

Sell, Aaron, Liana S. E. Hone, and Nicholas Pound. "The Importance of Physical Strength to Human Males." *Human Nature* 23, no. 1 (2012): 30–44. http://doi.org/10.1007/s12110-012-9131-2.

Siegel, Allan, and Jeff Victoroff. "Understanding Human Aggression: New Insights from Neuroscience." *International Journal of Law and Psychiatry* 32, no. 4 (2009): 209–215. http://doi.org/10.1016/j.ijlp.2009.06.001.

Siever, Larry J. "Neurobiology of Aggression and Violence." *American Journal of Psychiatry* 165, no. 4 (2008): 429–442. http://doi.org/10.1176/appi.ajp.2008.07111774.

Sorrel, Charlie. "The Theory That Human Fists Evolved for Punching Is Put to a Macabre Test." *Fast Company,* October 26, 2015. https://www.fastcompany.com/3052678/the-theory-that-human-fists-evolved-for-punching-is-put-to-a-macabre-test.

Tremblay, Richard. "Development of Physical Aggression from Early Childhood to Adulthood." *Encyclopedia on Early Childhood Development,* December 19, 2002. http://citeseerx.ist.psu.edu/viewdoc/download?doi=10.1.1.569.3682&rep=rep1&type=pdf.

Wade, Lizzie. "Why Do We Kill?" Controversial Study Blames Our Distant Ancestors." *Science,* September 28, 2016. https://www.sciencemag.org/news/2016/09/why-do-we-kill-controversial-study-blames-our-distant-ancestors.

Yu, Rongjun, Dean Mobbs, Ben Seymour, et al. "The Neural Signature of Escalating Frustration in Humans." *Cortex* 54, no. 1 (2014): 165–178. http://doi.org/10.1016/j.cortex.2014.02.013.

A History of Human Violence

Altimari, Dave. "Chief State Medical Examiner Retires." *Hartford Courant*, May 23, 2013. https://www.courant.com/news/connecticut/hc-xpm-2013-05-23-hc-medicalexaminer-carver-retire-20130523-story.html.

Baumeister, Roy F. *Evil: Inside Human Violence and Cruelty*. New York: Henry Holt and Company, 2015.

Beard, Mary. *SPQR: A History of Ancient Rome*. New York: Liveright Publishing Company, 2015.

Carmody, Tim. "10 Reading Revolutions Before E-Books." *The Atlantic*, August 25, 2010. https://www.theatlantic.com/technology/archive/2010/08/10-reading-revolutions-before-e-books/62004/.

Eisner, Manuel. "Long-Term Historical Trends in Violent Crime." *Crime and Justice* 30 (2003): 83–142. https://www.jstor.org/stable/1147697?seq=1/subjects.

Eisner, Manuel. "Modernization, Self-Control, and Lethal Violence: The Long-Term Dynamics of European Homicide Rates in Theoretical Perspective." *British Journal of Criminology* 41, no. 4 (2001): 618–638. https://www.jstor.org/stable/23654286?seq=1#page_scan_tab_contents.

Elias, Norbert. *The Civilizing Process: Sociogenetic and Psychogenetic Investigations*. Oxford: Blackwell Publishers, 2000.

Fry, Douglas P. *War, Peace, and Human Nature: The Convergence of Evolutionary and Cultural Views*. New York: Oxford University Press, 2015.

White, Matthew. *The Great Big Book of Horrible Things: The Definitive Chronicle of History's 100 Worst Atrocities*. New York: W. W. Norton and Company, 2012.

Whitman, Charles. Charles Whitman to unaddressed, July 31, 1966. https://web.archive.org/web/20110708154227/http:/alt.cimedia.com/statesman/specialreports/whitman/letter.pdf.

CHAPTER THREE: AMERICAN VIOLENCE

American Violence

Bailyn, Bernard. *The Barbarous Years: The Peopling of North America—The Conflict of Civilizations, 1600–1675*. New York: Vintage Books, 2013.

Bradford, William. *Of Plimoth Plantation*. 1651. Portcullis Books, 2016.

Brown, Richard Maxwell. *Strain of Violence: Historical Studies of American Violence and Vigilantism*. New York: Oxford University Press, 1975.

Butterfield, Fox. "Historical Study of Homicide and Cities Surprises the Experts." *New York Times*, October 23, 1994. https://www.nytimes.com/1994/10/23/us/historical-study-of-homicide-and-cities-surprises-the-experts.html.

Courtwright, David T. *Violent Land: Single Men and Social Disorder from the Frontier to the Inner City*. Cambridge: Harvard University Press, 2001.

Criminal Justice Research Center at the Ohio State University. "Historical Violence Database." https://cjrc.osu.edu/research/interdisciplinary/hvd.

Friedman, Lawrence. *Crime and Punishment in American History*. New York: Basic Books, 1994.

Frum, David. "The Cultural Roots of Crime: A Conversation About the Rise and Fall of Violence in America with Criminal-Justice Scholar Barry Latzer." *The Atlantic*, June 19, 2016. https://www.theatlantic.com/politics/archive/2016/06/the-cultural-roots-of-crime/487583/.

Gurr, Ted Robert. "Historical Trends in Violent Crime: A Critical Review of the Evidence." *Crime and Justice* 3 (1981): 295–353. https://www.journals.uchicago.edu/doi/abs/10.1086/449082?mobileUi=0.

Hofstadter, Richard, and Michael Wallace. *American Violence: A Documentary History.* New York: Knopf, 1970.

King, Ritchie. "217 Years of Homicide in New York." *Quartz,* December 31, 2013. https://qz .com/162289/217-years-of-homicide-in-new-york/.

Lane, Roger. "Murder in America: A Historian's Perspective." *Crime and Justice* 25 (1999): 191–224. https://www.jstor.org/stable/i248081.

Lane, Roger. *Murder in America: A History.* Columbus: Ohio State University Press, 1997.

Lane, Roger. "Taking the Mystery Out of Murder Rates: Can It Be Done?" *Ohio State Journal of Criminal Law* 8, no. 2 (2011): 553–565. https://kb.osu.edu/handle/1811/73218.

Latzer, Barry. *The Rise and Fall of Violent Crime in America.* New York: Encounter Books, 2016.

Lepore, Jill. "Rap Sheet." *New Yorker,* November 1, 2009. https://www.newyorker.com/ magazine/2009/11/09/rap-sheet.

Lewis, Danny. "The 1873 Colfax Massacre Crippled the Reconstruction Era." *Smithsonian Magazine,* April 13, 2016. https://www.smithsonianmag.com/smart-news/1873-colfax -massacre-crippled-reconstruction-180958746/.

Mann, Charles. *1491: New Revelations of the Americas Before Columbus.* New York: Vintage Books, 2006.

Mitchell, Robert. "'Nattering Nabobs of Negativism': The Improbable Rise of Spiro T. Agnew." *Washington Post,* August 8, 2018. https://www.washingtonpost.com/news/retropolis/ wp/2018/08/08/nattering-nabobs-of-negativism-the-improbable-rise-of-spiro-t-agnew.

Monkkonen, Eric H. "Homicide: Explaining America's Exceptionalism." *American Historical Review* 111, no. 1 (2006): 76–94. https://www.ncbi.nlm.nih.gov/pubmed/21155371.

Monkkonen, Eric H. *Murder in New York City.* Berkeley: University of California Press, 2001.

Roth, Randolph. *American Homicide.* Cambridge: Harvard University Press, 2012.

Roth, Randolph. "Biology and the Deep History of Homicide." *British Journal of Criminology* 51, no. 3 (2011): 535–555. https://www.jstor.org/stable/i23637885.

Roth, Randolph. "How Exceptional Is the History of Violence and Criminal Justice in the United States? Variation Across Time and Space as the Keys to Understanding Homicide and Punitiveness." In *American Exceptionalism in Crime and Punishment,* edited by Kevin R. Reitz, 272–297. New York: Oxford University Press, 2017.

Rothman, Joshua. "New York City Crime in the Nineties." *New Yorker,* December 5, 2012. https://www.newyorker.com/books/double-take/new-york-city-crime-in-the-nineties.

Spierenburg, Pieter. "Democracy Came Too Early: A Tentative Explanation for the Problem of American Homicide." *American Historical Review* 111, no. 1 (2006): 104–114. https:// doi.org/10.1086/ahr.111.1.104.

Strong, George Templeton. *The Diary of George Templeton Strong.* Seattle: University of Washington Press, 1988.

United Nations Office on Drugs and Crime. *Global Study on Homicide 2019.* Vienna, 2019. https://www.unodc.org/documents/data-and-analysis/gsh/Booklet2.pdf.

Zimmerman, Larry. "Mass Grave at Crow Creek in South Dakota Reveals How Indians Massacred Indians in 14th Century Attack." *Smithsonian* 11, no. 6 (1980): 100–109. https:// www.academia.edu/7907221/Mass_Grave_at_Crow_Creek_in_South_Dakota_Reveals _How_Indians_Massacred_Indians_in_14th_Century_Attack.

Firearms History

Barrett, Paul M. *Glock: The Rise of America's Gun.* New York: Broadway Books, 2012.

Cook, Philip J., and Kristin A. Goss. *The Gun Debate: What Everyone Needs to Know.* New York: Oxford University Press, 2014.

Haag, Pamela. "The Commercial Origins of American Gun Culture." *Wall Street Journal,*

April 22, 2016. https://www.wsj.com/articles/american-gun-cultures-commercial-origins-1461335155.

Haag, Pamela. *The Gunning of America: Business and the Making of American Gun Culture.* New York: Basic Books, 2016.

Haag, Pamela. "How Connecticut Made Guns Won the West." *Connecticut Explored* 15, no. 1 (Winter 2016–2017): 26–31. https://www.pamelahaag.com/writing-archive/connecticut-explored.

Henning, Robert A., and Terrence Witkowski. "The Advertising of E. Remington & Sons: The Creation of an Iconic Brand, 1854–1888." *Journal of Historical Research in Marketing* 5, no. 4 (2013): 418–448. http://doi.org/10.1108/JHRM-11-2012-0028.

Lindgren, James. "Forward: The Past and Future of Guns." *Journal of Criminal Law and Criminology* 104, no. 4 (2015): 705–716. https://scholarlycommons.law.northwestern.edu/jclc/vol104/iss4/1.

Lindgren, James, and Justin L. Heather. "Counting Guns in Early America." *William and Mary Law Review* 43, no. 5 (2002): 1777–1842. https://scholarship.law.wm.edu/wmlr/vol43/iss5/2/.

Loo, Dennis, and Ruth-Ellen M. Grimes. "Polls, Politics, and Crime: The 'Law and Order' Issue of the 1960s." *Western Criminology Review* 5, no. 1 (2004): 50–67. https://www.researchgate.net/publication/251312477_Polls_Politics_and_Crime_The_Law_and_Order_Issue_of_the_1960s.

Phelps, M. William. *The Devil's Right Hand: The Tragic Story of the Colt Family Curse.* Lanham: Lyons Press, 2013.

Rattenbury, Richard C. *A Legacy in Arms: American Firearm Manufacture, Design, and Artistry, 1800–1900.* Norman: University of Oklahoma Press, 2014.

Roth, Randolph. "Guns, Gun Culture, and Homicide: The Relationship Between Firearms, the Uses of Firearms, and Interpersonal Violence." *William and Mary Quarterly* 59, no. 1 (2002): 223–240. https://www.jstor.org/stable/i278761.

Roth, Randolph. "Guns, Murder, and Probability: How Can We Decide Which Figures to Trust?" *Reviews in American History* 35, no. 2 (2007): 165–175. https://www.jstor.org/stable/i30031633.

Smith, Solomon K. "Firearms Manufacturing, Gun Use, and the Emergence of Gun Culture in Early North America." *49th Parallel* 34 (2014): 1–48. https://fortyninthparalleljournal.files.wordpress.com/2014/10/solomonsmithautumn2014.pdf.

Smith, Tom W. "The 75% Solution: An Analysis of the Structure of Attitudes on Gun Control, 1959–1977." *Journal of Law and Criminology* 71, no. 3 (1980): 299–316. https://scholarlycommons.law.northwestern.edu/jclc/vol71/iss3/9/.

Witkowski, Terrence H. "Early Brand Development in the U.S. Firearms Industry." *CHARM Association* (2011): 194–209. https://ojs.library.carleton.ca/index.php/pcharm/article/view/1462.

The Second Amendment and Gun Laws

Amar, Akhil Reed. "The Second Amendment as a Case Study in Constitutional Interpretation." *Utah Law Review* 889 (2001): 889–914. https://digitalcommons.law.yale.edu/fss_papers/855.

Brabner-Smith, John. "Firearm Regulation." *Law and Contemporary Problems* 1, no. 4 (1934): 400–414. https://scholarship.law.duke.edu/lcp/vol1/iss4/2/.

Cornell, Saul. "'Half Cocked': The Persistence of Anachronism and Presentism in the Academic Debate over the Second Amendment." *Journal of Criminal Law and Criminology* 106, no. 2 (2016): 203–218. https://scholarlycommons.law.northwestern.edu/jclc/vol106/iss2/2/.

Cornell, Saul. "The Right to Keep and Carry Arms in Anglo-American Law: Preserving Liberty and Keeping the Peace." *Law and Contemporary Problems* 80, no. 2 (2017): 11–54. https://scholarship.law.duke.edu/lcp/vol80/iss2/2/.

Cornell, Saul, and David DeDino. "A Well Regulated Right: The Early American Origins of Gun Control." *Fordham Law Review* 73, no. 2 (2004): 487–528. https://fordhamlawreview.org/wp-content/uploads/assets/pdfs/Vol_73/Cornell_and_DeDino_November.pdf.

DeConde, Alexander. *Gun Violence in America: The Struggle for Control.* Boston: Northeastern University Press, 2001.

Emberton, Carole. "The Limits of Incorporation: Violence, Gun Rights, and Gun Regulation in the Reconstruction South." *Stanford Law and Policy Review* 17, no. 3 (2006): 611–629. https://law.stanford.edu/publications/limits-incorporation-violence-gun-rights-gun-regulation-reconstruction-south/.

Frassetto, Mark. "Firearms and Weapons Legislation up to the Early 20th Century." *SSRN Electronic Journal*, January 15, 2013. http://doi.org/10.2139/ssrn.2200991.

Halbrook, Stephen P. "Encroachments of the Crown on the Liberty of the Subject: Pre-Revolutionary Origins of the Second Amendment." *University of Dayton Law Review* 15 (1989): 91–124. https://www.stephenhalbrook.com/law_review_articles/encroachments_of_the_crown.pdf.

Kopel, David B. "The Second Amendment in the Nineteenth Century." *BYU Law Review* 1998, no. 4 (1998): 1359–1554. https://digitalcommons.law.byu.edu/lawreview/vol1998/iss4/2.

Leff, Sklanik Carol, and Mark Leff. "The Politics of Ineffectiveness: Federal Firearms Legislation, 1919–38." *Annals of the American Academy of Political and Social Science* 455, no. 1 (1981): 48–62. https://doi.org/10.1177/000271628145500106.

Lepore, Jill. "Battleground America." *New Yorker,* April 16, 2012. https://www.newyorker.com/magazine/2012/04/23/battleground-america.

Lepore, Jill. "The Lost Amendment." *New Yorker,* April 19, 2012. https://www.newyorker.com/news/news-desk/the-lost-amendment.

Levinson, Sanford. "The Embarrassing Second Amendment." *Yale Law Journal* 99, no. 3 (1989): 637–659. https://digitalcommons.law.yale.edu/ylj/vol99/iss3/6.

Ruben, Eric M., and Saul Cornell. "Firearm Regionalism and Public Carry: Placing Southern Antebellum Case Law in Context." *Yale Law Journal Forum* 125 (2015): 121–136. https://www.yalelawjournal.org/forum/firearm-regionalism-and-public-carry.

Spitzer, Robert J. "Gun Law History in the United States and Second Amendment Rights." *Law and Contemporary Problems* 80, no. 2 (2017): 55–83. https://scholarship.law.duke.edu/lcp/vol80/iss2/3/.

Spitzer, Robert J. *Guns Across America: Reconciling Gun Rules and Rights.* New York: Oxford University Press, 2015.

Waldman, Michael. *The Second Amendment: A Biography.* New York: Simon & Schuster, 2014.

Winkler, Adam. *Gunfight: The Battle over the Right to Bear Arms in America.* New York: W. W. Norton & Company, 2011.

Zimring, Franklin E. "Firearms and Federal Law: The Gun Control Act of 1968." *Journal of Legal Studies* 4, no. 1 (1975): 133–198. https://www.jstor.org/stable/724104?seq=1#page_scan_tab_contents.

CHAPTER FOUR: THE VIOLENCE WE SEE

Mass Shootings

Cohen, Amy P., Deborah Azrael, and Matthew Miller. "Rate of Mass Shootings Has Tripled Since 2011, Harvard Research Shows." *Mother Jones*, October 15, 2014. https://www .motherjones.com/politics/2014/10/mass-shootings-increasing-harvard-research/.

Fisher, Max, and Josh Keller. "What Explains U.S. Mass Shootings? International Comparisons Suggest an Answer." *New York Times*, November 7, 2017. https://www.nytimes .com/2017/11/07/world/americas/mass-shootings-us-international.html.

Follman, Mark, Gavin Aronsen, and Deanna Pan. "U.S. Mass Shootings, 1982–2019: Data from Mother Jones' Investigation." *Mother Jones*, July 28, 2019. https://www.motherjones .com/politics/2012/12/mass-shootings-mother-jones-full-data/.

Fox, James A., and Emma E. Fridel. "The Tenuous Connections Involving Mass Shootings, Mental Illness, and Gun Laws." *Violence and Gender* 3, no. 1 (2016): 14–19. https://doi .org/10.1089/vio.2015.0054.

Fox, James A., and Jack Levin. "Multiple Homicide: Patterns of Serial and Mass Murder." *Crime and Justice* 23 (1998): 407–455. http://doi.org/10.1086/449274.

Lawler, Dave. "The Deadliest Mass Shootings in Modern U.S. History." *Axios*, June 1, 2019. https://www.axios.com/deadliest-mass-shootings-in-modern-us-history-3b2dfb67-7278 -4082-a78c-d9fdbef367f1.html.

Lemieux, Frederic. "6 Things to Know About Mass Shootings in America." *Scientific American*, June 13, 2016. https://www.scientificamerican.com/article/6-things-to-know -about-mass-shootings-in-america/.

McDonald, Melissa M., Carlos David Navarrete, and Mark Van Vugt. "Evolution and the Psychology of Intergroup Conflict: The Male Warrior Hypothesis." *Philosophical Transactions of the Royal Society B: Biological Sciences* 367, no. 1589 (2012): 670–679. http://doi .org/10.1098/rstb.2011.0301.

Mosher, Dave, and Skye Gould. "The Odds That a Gun Will Kill the Average American May Surprise You." *Business Insider*, October 29, 2018. https://www.businessinsider.com/us -gun-death-murder-risk-statistics-2018-3.

RAND Corporation. "Mass Shootings: Definitions and Trends." March 2, 2018. https:// www.rand.org/research/gun-policy/analysis/essays/mass-shootings.html.

Smith, M. Dwayne, and Margaret A. Zahn. *Homicide: A Sourcebook of Social Research*. Thousand Oaks: SAGE Publications, 1998.

Towers, Sherry, Andres Gomez-Lievano, Carlos Castillo-Chávez, et al. "Contagion in Mass Killings and School Shootings." *PLOS One* 10, no. 7 (2015). https://doi.org/10.1371/ journal.pone.0117259.

Mental Illness and Mass Shootings

Appelbaum, Paul S. "Public Safety, Mental Disorders, and Guns." *JAMA Psychiatry* 70, no. 6 (2013): 565–566. http://doi.org/10.1001/jamapsychiatry.2013.315.

Declercq, Frédéric, and Kurt Audenaert. "Predatory Violence Aiming at Relief in a Case of Mass Murder: Meloy's Criteria for Applied Forensic Practice." *Behavioral Sciences and the Law* 29, no. 4 (2011): 578–591. http://doi.org/10.1002/bsl.994.

Fazel, Seena, and Martin Grann. "The Population Impact of Severe Mental Illness on Violent Crime." *American Journal of Psychiatry* 163, no. 8 (2006): 1397–1403. http://doi.org/ 10.1176/ajp.2006.163.8.1397.

Kalish, Rachel, and Michael Kimmel. "Suicide by Mass Murder: Masculinity, Aggrieved Entitlement, and Rampage School Shootings." *Health Sociology Review* 19, no. 4 (2010): 451–464. http://doi.org/10.5172/hesr.2010.19.4.451.

Knoll, James. "The 'Pseudocommando' Mass Murderer: Part I, the Psychology of Revenge and Obliteration." *Journal of the American Academy of Psychiatry and Law* 38, no. 1 (2010): 87–94. https://www.ncbi.nlm.nih.gov/pubmed/20305080.

Knoll, James. "The 'Pseudocommando' Mass Murderer: Part II, the Language of Revenge." *Journal of the American Academy of Psychiatry and Law* 38, no. 2 (2010): 263–272. https://www.ncbi.nlm.nih.gov/pubmed/20542949.

Knoll, James, and George Annas. "Mass Shootings and Mental Illness." In *Gun Violence and Mental Illness,* edited by Liza Gold and Robert Simon, 81–104. Arlington: American Psychiatric Association Publishing, 2015.

Knoll, James, and John Reid Meloy. "Mass Murder and the Violent Paranoid Spectrum." *Psychiatric Annals* 44, no. 5 (2014): 236–243. http://drreidmeloy.com/wp-content/uploads/2015/12/2014_MassMurderAndT.pdf.

Metzl, Jonathan M., and Kenneth T. MacLeish. "Mental Illness, Mass Shootings, and the Politics of American Firearms." *American Journal of Public Health* 105, no. 2 (2015): 240–249. https://www.ncbi.nlm.nih.gov/pmc/articles/PMC4318286/.

Stone, Michael H. "Mass Murder, Mental Illness, and Men." *Violence and Gender* 2, no. 1 (2015): 51–86. http://doi.org/10.1089/vio.2015.0006.

Swanson, Jeffrey W. "Mental Illness and New Gun Reforms: The Promise and Peril of Crisis-Driven Policy." *Journal of the American Medical Association* 309, no. 12 (2013): 1233–1234. http://doi.org/10.1001/jama.2013.1113.

Swanson, Jeffrey W., Nancy A. Sampson, Maria V. Petukhova, et al. "Guns, Impulsive Angry Behavior, and Mental Disorders: Results from the National Comorbidity Survey Replication (NCS-R)." *Behavioral Sciences and Law* 33, no. 2–3 (2015): 199–212. http://doi.org/10.1002/bsl.2172.

Twenge, Jean M., and W. Keith Campbell. *The Narcissism Epidemic: Living in the Age of Entitlement.* New York: Atria Books, 2010.

The NRA

Carlson, Jennifer. *Citizen-Protectors: The Everyday Politics of Guns in an Age of Decline.* New York: Oxford University Press, 2015.

Davidson, Osha Gray. *Under Fire: The NRA and the Battle for Gun Control.* Iowa City: University of Iowa Press, 1998.

Finn, Peter. "NRA Money Helped Reshape Gun Law." *Washington Post,* March 13, 2013. https://www.washingtonpost.com/world/national-security/nra-money-helped-reshape-gun-law/2013/03/13/73d71e22-829a-11e2-b99e-6baf4ebe42df_story.html.

Harsanyi, David. *First Freedom: A Ride Through America's Enduring History with the Gun.* New York: Threshold Editions, 2018.

Higham, Scott, Sari Horwitz, David S. Fallis, et al. "History of Gun Control Is Cautionary Tale for Those Who Want More Regulations." *Washington Post,* December 22, 2012. https://www.washingtonpost.com/national/history-of-gun-control-is-cautionary-tale-for-those-who-want-more-regulations/2012/12/22/73a07294-4afc-11e2-a6a6-aabac85e8036_story.html.

Hovey, Craig, and Lisa Fisher. *Understanding America's Gun Culture.* Lanham: Lexington Books, 2017.

Ingraham, Christopher. "Just Three Percent of Adults Own Half of America's Guns." *Washington Post,* September 19, 2016. https://www.washingtonpost.com/news/wonk/wp/2016/09/19/just-three-percent-of-adults-own-half-of-americas-guns/.

Ingraham, Christopher. "Nobody Knows How Many Members the NRA Has, But Its Tax Returns Offer Clues." *Washington Post,* February 26, 2018. https://www.washingtonpost

.com/news/wonk/wp/2018/02/26/nobody-knows-how-many-members-the-nra-has
-but-its-tax-returns-offer-some-clues/.

Johnson, Nicholas. *Negroes and the Gun: The Black Tradition of Arms.* Amherst: Prometheus
Books, 2014.

Kohn, Abigail A. *Shooters: Myths and Realities of America's Gun Cultures.* New York: Oxford
University Press, 2005.

Light, Caroline. *Stand Your Ground: A History of America's Love Affair with Lethal Self-Defense.*
Boston: Beacon Press, 2017.

Melzer, Scott. *Gun Crusaders: The NRA's Culture War.* New York: New York University Press,
2009.

New York Times. "President Tells Rifle Association He's for Repeal of Some Gun Curbs." May
7, 1983. https://www.nytimes.com/1983/05/07/us/president-tells-rifle-association-he
-s-for-repeal-of-some-gun-curbs.html.

Rosenfeld, Steven. "The NRA Once Supported Gun Control." *Salon,* January 14, 2013.
https://www.salon.com/2013/01/14/the_nra_once_supported_gun_control/.

Shapira, Ian. "Before Trump's Wild Shifts on the NRA, Ronald Reagan Took on the Gun
Lobby." *Washington Post,* March 2, 2018. https://www.washingtonpost.com/news/
retropolis/wp/2018/03/02/before-trump-defied-the-nra-ronald-reagan-took-on-the-gun
-lobby/.

Sugarmann, Joshua. *National Rifle Association: Money, Firepower, and Fear.* Scotts Valley: Cre-
ateSpace, 2010.

Violence Prevention Campaign. *Blood Money II: How Gun Industry Dollars Fund the NRA.*
Washington, D.C., 2013. http://vpc.org/studies/bloodmoney2.pdf.

Violence Prevention Campaign. *From the Gun War to the Culture War: How the NRA Has Become the Pillar of the Right.* Washington, D.C., 2002. http://vpc.org/graphics/gunwar.pdf.

Whitney, Craig R. *Living with Guns: A Liberal's Case for the Second Amendment.* New York:
PublicAffairs, 2012.

CHAPTER FIVE: THE VIOLENCE WE IGNORE

Newark and the Riots of the 1960s

Cohen, Nathan E. "The Los Angeles Riot Study." *Social Work* 12, no. 4 (1967): 14–21. https://
www.jstor.org/stable/23710409?seq=1#page_scan_tab_contents.

Driver, Justin. "The Report on Race That Shook America." *The Atlantic,* May 2018.
https://www.theatlantic.com/magazine/archive/2018/05/the-report-on-race-that-shook
-america/556850/.

Geary, Daniel. "The Moynihan Report: An Annotated Edition." *The Atlantic,* September 14,
2015. https://www.theatlantic.com/politics/archive/2015/09/the-moynihan-report-an
-annotated-edition/404632/.

George, Alice. "The 1968 Kerner Commission Got It Right, But Nobody Listened." *Smithsonian Magazine,* March 1, 2018. https://www.smithsonianmag.com/smithsonian
-institution/1968-kerner-commission-got-it-right-nobody-listened-180968318/.

Haas Institute for a Fair and Inclusive Society. *1968 Kerner Report: Executive Summary.* Berkeley, 2018. https://haasinstitute.berkeley.edu/1968-kerner-report.

Jan, Tracy. "Redlining Was Banned 50 Years Ago. It's Still Hurting Minorities Today." *Washington Post,* March 28, 2018. https://www.washingtonpost.com/news/wonk/wp/
2018/03/28/redlining-was-banned-50-years-ago-its-still-hurting-minorities-today/.

Levy, Clifford J. "4 High-Rises Torn Down by Newark." *New York Times,* March 7, 1994. https://
www.nytimes.com/1994/03/07/nyregion/4-high-rises-torn-down-by-newark.html.

McGirt, Ellen. "Understanding the 1967 Newark Riots." *Fortune*, July 12, 2017. https://
fortune.com/2017/07/12/understanding-the-1967-newark-riots/.

Risen, Clay. "The Legacy of the 1968 Riots." *The Guardian*, April 4, 2008. https://www
.theguardian.com/commentisfree/2008/apr/04/thelegacyofthe1968riots.

Rothman, Lily. "50 Years Ago This Week: 'Anatomy of a Race Riot.'" *Time*, July 17, 2017.
https://time.com/4852749/1967-newark-riot/.

Stein, Perry. "D.C.'s Poorer Residents Are Increasingly Concentrated East of the Anacostia."
Washington Post, April 14, 2015. https://www.washingtonpost.com/news/local/wp/
2015/04/14/d-c-s-poorest-neighborhoods-now-more-concentrated-east-of-the-anacostia
-study-shows/.

Walsh, Kenneth T. "50 Years After Race Riots, Issues Remain the Same." *U.S. News & World
Report*, July 12, 2017. https://www.usnews.com/news/national-news/articles/2017
-07-12/50-years-later-causes-of-1967-summer-riots-remain-largely-the-same.

Baltimore

Note: Baltimore figures heavily in both chapter 5 and chapter 8. These are the collected citations for both portions of the book.

Anderson, Jessica. "What You Need to Know About the Baltimore Police Consent Decree."
Baltimore Sun, April 6, 2018. https://www.baltimoresun.com/news/crime/bs-md-ci
-consent-decree-explainer-20180403-story.html.

Badger, Emily. "The Long, Painful, and Repetitive History of How Baltimore Became Baltimore." *Washington Post*, April 29, 2015. https://www.washingtonpost.com/news/wonk/
wp/2015/04/29/the-long-painful-and-repetitive-history-of-how-baltimore-became
-baltimore/.

Baltimore Sun. "Interactive: Where Criminals Get Their Guns." 2017. http://data.baltimoresun
.com/gun-trace/?2017.

Banach, Liz. "A Friendship Forged on the Streets of Baltimore." *Behind the Statistics.* http://
behindthestatistics.org/stories/walker/.

Bliss, Laura. "After Nearly a Century, Redlining Still Divides Baltimore." *CityLab*, April 30,
2015. https://www.citylab.com/equity/2015/04/after-nearly-a-century-redlining-still
-divides-baltimore/391982/.

Brown, Lawrence. "Two Baltimores: The White L vs. the Black Butterfly." *Baltimore Sun*,
June 28, 2019. https://www.baltimoresun.com/citypaper/bcpnews-two-baltimores
-the-white-l-vs-the-black-butterfly-20160628-htmlstory.html.

CBS News. "2017 Sees Highest Murder Rate Ever in Shrinking Baltimore." *CBS News*, January 2, 2018. https://www.cbsnews.com/news/baltimore-homicide-murder-rate
-highest-2017-crime-increase-freddie-gray-killing/.

Gately, Gary. "Baltimore Is More Murderous Than Chicago. Can Anyone Save the City from
Itself?" *The Guardian*, November 2, 2017. https://www.theguardian.com/us-news/
2017/nov/02/baltimore-murder-rate-homicides-ceasefire.

Houppert, Karen. "From Gunshot to Grave: The High Cost of Murder in Baltimore." *Baltimore Sun*, January 12, 2016. https://www.baltimoresun.com/citypaper/bcpnews-from
-gunshot-to-grave-the-high-cost-of-murder-in-baltimore-20160112-story.html.

Isaacs, Abby. "A City in Healing: Community Center Helps Baltimore's Youth Stay Away
from Path of Violence." *WMAR Baltimore*, May 8, 2018. https://www.wmar2news
.com/news/region/baltimore-city/a-city-in-healing-community-center-helps-baltimores
-youth-away-from-path-of-violence.

Khazan, Olga. "Being Black in America Can Be Hazardous to Your Health." *The Atlantic*,

July/August 2018. https://www.theatlantic.com/magazine/archive/2018/07/being-black-in-america-can-be-hazardous-to-your-health/561740/.

Lanahan, Lawrence. *The Lines Between Us: Two Families and a Quest to Cross Baltimore's Racial Divide.* New York: The New Press, 2019.

Mitter, Siddhartha. "Gentrify or Die? Inside a University's Controversial Plan for Baltimore." *The Guardian*, April 18, 2018.

Mock, Brentin. "Are Reparations Baltimore's Fix for Redlining, Investment Deprivation?" *CityLab*, February 14, 2019. https://www.citylab.com/equity/2019/02/reparations-baltimore-redlining-segregation-fix-race/582760/.

Morgan, Stephen L., and Joel A. Pally. *Ferguson, Gray, and Davis: An Analysis of Recorded Crime Incidents and Arrests in Baltimore City, March 2010 through December 2015.* For the 21st Century Cities Initiative at Johns Hopkins University. Baltimore: 2016. https://socweb.soc.jhu.edu/faculty/morgan/papers/MorganPally2016.pdf.

Mullins, Luke. "His Brother's Keeper." *The Atlantic*, July 2, 2018. https://www.theatlantic.com/politics/archive/2018/07/baltimore-murder-rate-hits-home/563600/.

Pietila, Antero. *Not in My Neighborhood: How Bigotry Shaped a Great American City.* Chicago: Ivan R. Dee, 2010.

Rector, Kevin. "2017 Homicide Data Provide Insight into Baltimore's Gun Wars, Police Say." *Baltimore Sun*, January 3, 2018. https://www.baltimoresun.com/news/crime/bs-md-ci-2017-homicide-data-breakdown-20180103-story.html.

Rector, Kevin. "Federal Judge Approves Baltimore Policing Consent Decree, Denying Justice Department Request for Delay." *Baltimore Sun*, April 7, 2017. https://www.baltimoresun.com/maryland/baltimore-city/bs-md-ci-consent-decree-approved-20170407-story.html.

Resnick, Brian, and *National Journal*. "Zooming into Baltimore, a Segregated City." *The Atlantic*, April 28, 2015. https://www.theatlantic.com/politics/archive/2015/04/zooming-into-baltimore-a-segregated-city/453606/.

Rosen, Eva. "The Power of Landlords." *The Atlantic*, June 9, 2015. https://www.theatlantic.com/business/archive/2015/06/baltimore-housing-policy-segregation/395039/.

Rothstein, Richard. "From Ferguson to Baltimore: The Fruits of Government-Sponsored Segregation." *Working Economics Blog (Economic Policy Institute)*, April 29, 2015. https://www.epi.org/blog/from-ferguson-to-baltimore-the-fruits-of-government-sponsored-segregation/.

Semuels, Alana. "Where the White People Live." *The Atlantic*, April 10, 2015. https://www.theatlantic.com/business/archive/2015/04/where-the-white-people-live/390153/.

Spies, Mike. "An ATF Official on How Trafficked Guns Are Like Cockroaches." *The Trace*, August 31, 2015. https://www.thetrace.org/2015/08/atf-gun-trafficking-report/.

Thompson, Derek. "The Curse of Segregation." *The Atlantic*, May 5, 2015. https://www.theatlantic.com/business/archive/2015/05/the-curse-of-segregation/392321/.

Urban Institute. "'The Black Butterfly': Racial Segregation and Investment Patterns in Baltimore." February 5, 2019. https://apps.urban.org/features/baltimore-investment-flows/.

U.S. Department of Justice Civil Rights Division. "Investigation of the Baltimore City Police Department." Washington, D.C., 2016. https://www.justice.gov/crt/file/883371/download.

Webster, Daniel W., Shani A. L. Buggs, and Cassandra K. Crifasi. "Estimating the Effects of Law Enforcement and Public Health Interventions Intended to Reduce Gun Violence in Baltimore." *Johns Hopkins Center for Gun Policy and Research*, January 11, 2018. https://www.issuelab.org/resource/estimating-the-effects-of-law-enforcement-and-public-health-interventions-intended-to-reduce-gun-violence-in-baltimore.html.

Webster, Daniel W., Jennifer Medel Whitehill, Jon S. Verrick, et al. "Effects of Baltimore's

Safe Streets Program on Gun Violence: A Replication of Chicago's *CeaseFire* Program." *Journal of Urban Health* 90, no. 1 (2013): 27–40. http://doi.org/10.1007/s11524-012-9731-5.

The Murder of Corey Dodd

Anderson, Jessica. "Father of Four Among Victims Killed in Recent Spate of Violence in Baltimore City." *Baltimore Sun*, January 22, 2019. https://www.baltimoresun.com/news/crime/bs-md-ci-weekend-shootings-follow-20190122-story.html.

CBS Baltimore. "Father Killed After Dropping Off Kids at School in West Baltimore." CBS Baltimore, January 23, 2019. https://baltimore.cbslocal.com/2019/01/23/father-killed-after-dropping-off-kids-at-school-in-west-baltimore/.

Fox Baltimore. "Father of 4 Killed in West Baltimore After Dropping Kids Off at School." Fox Baltimore, January 23, 2019. https://foxbaltimore.com/news/local/father-of-4-killed-in-west-baltimore-after-dropping-kids-off-at-school.

Reed, Lillian. "Police Identify 25-Year-Old Killed in Sandtown-Winchester Shooting." *Baltimore Sun,* January 19, 2019. https://www.baltimoresun.com/maryland/baltimore-city/bs-md-ci-corey-dodd-20190119-story.html.

Chicagoland

Bump, Philip. "Where the Guns Used in Chicago Actually Came From." *Washington Post*, November 7, 2017. https://www.washingtonpost.com/news/politics/wp/2017/11/07/where-the-guns-used-in-chicago-actually-came-from/.

CBS Chicago. "9,000 Firearms and Counting: Illegal Guns Flood Chicago." CBS Chicago, December 11, 2018. https://chicago.cbslocal.com/2018/12/11/9000-illegal-guns-seized-chicago-auburn-gresham-1000-firearms/.

Gossett, Stephen. "How and Why Chicago Violence Became Conservatives' Favorite Talking Point." *Chicagoist*, August 29, 2016. https://chicagoist.com/2016/08/29/how_and_why_chicago_violence_became.php.

Kurtzleben, Danielle. "FACT CHECK: Is Chicago Proof That Gun Laws Don't Work?" National Public Radio, October 15, 2017. https://www.npr.org/2017/10/05/555580598/fact-check-is-chicago-proof-that-gun-laws-don-t-work.

McKay, Tom. "This Is How Chicago Gets Flooded with Illegal Guns." *Mic*, November 3, 2015. https://www.mic.com/articles/127842/this-is-how-chicago-gets-flooded-with-illegal-guns#.pxn06dJw8.

Moser, Whet. "Chicago Gun Violence: Big Numbers, But a Surprisingly Small Network." *Chicago Magazine*, April 15, 2014. https://www.chicagomag.com/city-life/April-2014/Chicago-Gun-Violence-Big-Numbers-But-a-Surprisingly-Small-Network/.

Papachristos, Andrew V., David M. Hureau, and Anthony A. Braga. "The Corner and the Crew: The Influence of Geography and Social Networks on Gang Violence." *American Sociological Review* 78, no. 3 (2013): 417–447. http://doi.org/10.1177/0003122413486800.

University of Chicago Crime Lab. *Gun Violence in Chicago*. Chicago, 2016. https://urbanlabs.uchicago.edu/attachments/c5b0b0b86b6b6a9309ed88a9f5bbe5bd892d4077/store/82f93d3e7c7cc4c5a29abca0d8bf5892b3a35c0c3253d1d24b3b9d1fa7b8/UChicagoCrimeLab%2BGun%2BViolence%2Bin%2BChicago%2B2016.pdf.

Race, Poverty, Trauma, Guns, and Violence

Ahearn, Thomas. "Report Finds More Than One Out of Four Formerly Incarcerated Ex-Offenders are Unemployed." *Employment Screening Resources*, July 16, 2018. http://www.esrcheck.com/wordpress/2018/07/16/report-finds-one-four-formerly-incarcerated-ex-offenders-unemployed/.

Alexander, Michelle. *The New Jim Crow: Mass Incarceration in the Age of Colorblindness.* New York: The New Press, 2010.

Anderson, Elijah. *Code of the Street: Decency, Violence, and the Moral Life of the Inner City.* New York: W. W. Norton & Company, 2000.

Anderson, Elijah. "The Code of the Streets." *The Atlantic,* May 1994. https://www.theatlantic.com/magazine/archive/1994/05/the-code-of-the-streets/306601/.

Bailey, Annette, Camille Hannays-King, Jennifer Clarke, et al. "Black Mothers' Cognitive Process of Finding Meaning and Building Resilience after Loss of a Child to Gun Violence." *British Journal of Social Work* 43, no. 2 (2013): 335–354. http://doi.org/10.1093/bjsw/bct027.

Beard, Jessica H., Christopher N. Morrison, Sara F. Jacoby, et al. "Quantifying Disparities in Urban Firearm Violence by Race and Place in Philadelphia, Pennsylvania: A Cartographic Study." *American Journal of Public Health* 107, no. 3 (2017): 371–373. http://doi.org/10.2105/AJPH.2016.303620.

Bloom, Lisa. *Suspicion Nation: The Inside Story of the Trayvon Martin Injustice and Why We Continue to Repeat It.* Berkeley: Counterpoint, 2014.

Braga, Anthony A., and Rod K. Brunson. "The Police and Public Discourse on 'Black-on-Black' Violence." National Institute of Justice, 2015. https://permanent.access.gpo.gov/gpo92684/248588.pdf.

Braga, Anthony A., Andrew V. Papachristos, and David M. Hureau. "The Concentration and Stability of Gun Violence at Micro Places in Boston, 1980–2008." *Journal of Quantitative Criminology* 26, no. 1 (2010): 33–53. http://doi.org/10.1007/s10940-009-9082-x.

Brezina, Timothy, Robert Agnew, Francis T. Cullen, et al. "The Code of the Street: A Quantitative Assessment of Elijah Anderson's Subculture of Violence Thesis and Its Contribution to Youth Violence Research." *Youth Violence and Juvenile Justice* 2, no. 4 (2004): 303–328. http://doi.org/10.1177/1541204004267780.

Canada, Geoffrey. *Fist Stick Knife Gun: A Personal History of Violence.* Boston: Beacon Press, 2010.

Centers for Disease Control. "Age-Adjusted Rates for Homicides, by Race/Ethnicity—United States, 1999, 2015." *Morbidity and Mortality Weekly Report* 66, no. 31 (2017): 839. https://www.hsdl.org/?abstract&did=803785.

Cole, David. "Who Pays for the Right to Bear Arms?" *New York Times,* January 1, 2013. https://www.nytimes.com/2013/01/02/opinion/who-pays-for-the-right-to-bear-arms.html.

Felson, Richard B., and Paul-Philippe Pare. "Firearms and Fisticuffs: Region, Race, and Adversary Effects on Homicide and Assault." *Social Science Research* 39, no. 2 (2010): 272–284. http://doi.org/10.1016/j.ssresearch.2009.07.004.

Felson, Richard B., and Paul-Philippe Pare. "Gun Cultures or Honor Cultures? Explaining Regional and Race Differences in Weapon Carrying." *Social Forces* 88, no. 3 (2010): 1357–1378. https://www.jstor.org/stable/40645894?seq=1#page_scan_tab_contents.

Giffords Law Center to Prevent Gun Violence. "Annual Gun Law Scorecard." *Giffords Law Center to Prevent Gun Violence,* 2019. https://lawcenter.giffords.org/scorecard/.

Goode, Steven. "Nearing Retirement, The Rev. Henry Brown Remains Passionate in Quest to Quell Violence." *Hartford Courant,* December 17, 2011. https://www.courant.com/community/hartford/hc-xpm-2011-12-17-hc-hartford-henry-brown-1218-20111217-story.html.

Harvard Injury Control Research Center. "Homicide." Harvard School of Public Health, 2019. https://www.hsph.harvard.edu/hicrc/firearms-research/guns-and-death/.

Howard, Jacqueline. "Gun Deaths in U.S. Reach Highest Level in Nearly 40 Years, CDC Data

Reveal." CNN, December 14, 2018. https://www.cnn.com/2018/12/13/health/gun
-deaths-highest-40-years-cdc/index.html.

Johnson, Timothy. "NRA Falsely Claims That Obama Refuses to Enforce Existing Gun Laws
Even as It Attempts to Weaken the Agency Charged with That Task." Media Matters for
America, October 28, 2015. https://www.mediamatters.org/blog/2015/10/28/nra
-falsely-claims-that-obama-refuses-to-enforc/206481.

Keating, Dan. "Gun Deaths Shaped by Race in America." Washington Post, March 22, 2013.
http://www.washingtonpost.com/sf/feature/wp/2013/03/22/gun-deaths-shaped-by
-race-in-america/.

LaFraniere, Sharon, Daniela Porart, and Agustin Armendariz. "A Drumbeat of Multiple
Shootings, but America Isn't Listening." New York Times, May 22, 2016. https://www
.nytimes.com/2016/05/23/us/americas-overlooked-gun-violence.html.

Leovy, Jill. Ghettoside: A True Story of Murder in America. New York: Spiegel & Grau,
2015.

Levin, Benjamin. "Guns and Drugs." Fordham Law Review 84, no. 5 (2016): 2173–2226.
https://ir.lawnet.fordham.edu/cgi/viewcontent.cgi?article=5194&context=flr.

Lopez, German. "Almost 74% of Guns Used in New York Crimes Come from States with
Weaker Gun Laws." Vox, October 26, 2016. https://www.vox.com/policy-and-politics/
2016/10/26/13418208/guns-new-york-iron-pipeline.

Lopez, German. "Americans Are Supposed to Turn to Police after a Murder. In Black Communities, They Often Can't." Vox, August 26, 2016. https://www.vox.com/2016/8/26/
12631962/ghettoside-jill-leovy-black-crime.

McCullom, Rod. "How Indirect Violence Gets Under a Child's Skin—and into the Brain."
Undark Magazine, August 1, 2018. https://undark.org/article/childhood-violence-brain
-development/.

Moore, Matthew. "Firearm Prevalence and Homicide: An Examination of Urban and Suburban Counties." Criminal Justice Review 42, no. 3 (2017): 315–326. http://doi.org/10
.1177/0734016817724198.

O'Brien, Kerry, Walter Forrest, Dermot Lynott, et al. "Racism, Gun Ownership, and Gun
Control: Biased Attitudes in U.S. Whites May Influence Policy Decisions." PLOS One 8,
no. 10 (2013). http://doi.org/10.1371/journal.pone.0077552.

Office of the Attorney General of New York. Target on Trafficking: New York Crime Gun Analysis. New York, 2016. https://targettrafficking.ag.ny.gov/.

Putnam, Robert D. Our Kids: The American Dream in Crisis. New York: Simon & Schuster,
2015.

Riddell, Corinne A., Sam Harper, Magdalena Cerdá, et al. "Comparison of Rates of Firearm
and Non-firearm Homicide and Suicide in Black and White Non-Hispanic Men, by U.S.
State." Annals of Internal Medicine 168, no. 10 (2018): 712–720. https://www.ncbi.nlm
.nih.gov/pubmed/29710093.

Rood, Lee. "'Everything Has Gotten Worse': Violent Crime Is Surging in Rural Iowa, Fueled by the State's Meth and Mental Health Crises." Des Moines Register, May 11, 2018.
https://www.desmoinesregister.com/story/news/investigations/readers-watchdog/
2018/05/06/meth-mental-health-crises-violent-crime-surge-rural-iowa/508683002.

Smiley, Calvin John, and David Fakunle. "From 'Brute' to 'Thug': The Demonization and
Criminalization of Unarmed Black Male Victims in America." Journal for Human Behavior in the Social Environment 26, no. 3–4 (2016): 350–366. http://doi.org/10.1080/
10911359.2015.1129256.

Stewart, Eric A., and Ronald L. Simons. "Race Code of the Street, and Violent Delinquency:
A Multilevel Investigation of Neighborhood Street Culture and Individual Norms of

Violence." *Criminology* 48, no. 2 (2010): 569–605. http://doi.org/10.1111/j.1745-9125 .2010.00196.x.

USA Today. "25 Most Dangerous Cities in America." February 21, 2019. https://www.usatoday .com/picture-gallery/travel/experience/america/2018/10/17/25-most-dangerous-cities -america/1669467002/.

Van Dam, Andrew. "The Surprising Way Gun Violence is Dividing America." *Washington Post*, May 31, 2018. https://www.washingtonpost.com/news/wonk/wp/2018/05/31/ the-surprising-way-gun-violence-is-dividing-america/.

Violence Policy Center. *The Relationship Between Community Violence and Trauma: How Violence Affects Learning, Health, and Behavior.* Washington, D.C., 2017. http://www.vpc .org/studies/trauma17.pdf.

Welch, Kelly. "Black Criminal Stereotypes and Racial Profiling." *Journal of Contemporary Criminal Justice* 23, no. 7 (2007): 276–288. http://doi.org/10.1177/1043986207306870.

Xu, Jiaquan, Sherry L. Murphy, Kenneth Kochanek, et al. "Deaths: Final Data for 2016." *National Vital Statistics Report* 67, no. 5 (2018). https://www.cdc.gov/nchs/data/nvsr/ nvsr67/nvsr67_05.pdf.

The Violence of Despair and Suicide

American Psychiatric Association. "Mental Health Disparities: Diverse Populations." https:// www.psychiatry.org/File%20Library/Psychiatrists/Cultural-Competency/Mental-Health -Disparities/Mental-Health-Facts-for-Diverse-Populations.pdf.

Anglemyer, Andrew, Tara Horvath, and George Rutherford. "The Accessibility of Firearms and Risk for Suicide and Homicide Victimization Among Household Members: A Systematic Review and Meta-Analysis." *Annals of Internal Medicine* 160, no. 2 (2014): 101– 110. http://doi.org/10.7326/M13-1301.

Barber, Catherine, Elaine Frank, and Ralph Demicco. "Reducing Suicides Through Partnerships Between Health Professionals and Gun Owner Groups—Beyond Docs vs. Glocks." *JAMA Internal Medicine* 177, no. 1 (2016): 5–6. https://doi.org/10.1001/jamainternmed .2016.6712.

Berezow, Alex. "Suicides Outnumber Murders 6 to 1 for Whites; Murders Outnumber Suicides 3.5 to 1 for Blacks." *American Council on Science and Health,* April 19, 2018. https:// www.acsh.org/news/2018/04/19/suicides-outnumber-murders-6-1-whites-murders -outnumber-suicides-35-1-blacks-12861.

Boddy, Jessica. "The Forces Driving Middle-Aged White People's 'Deaths of Despair.'" National Public Radio, March 23, 2017. https://www.npr.org/sections/health-shots/2017/ 03/23/521083335/the-forces-driving-middle-aged-white-peoples-deaths-of-despair.

Case, Anne, and Angus Deaton. "Mortality and Morbidity in the 21st Century." *Brookings Papers on Economic Activity* (2017): 397–476. https://www.princeton.edu/~accase/ downloads/Mortality_and_Morbidity_in_21st_Century_Case-Deaton-BPEA-published .pdf.

Case, Anne, and Angus Deaton. "Rising Morbidity and Mortality in Midlife Among White Non-Hispanic Americans in the 21st Century." *Proceedings of the National Academy of Sciences of the United States of America* 112, no. 49 (2015): 15078–15083. http://doi.org/10 .1073/pnas.1518393112.

Choolijan, Lauren. "In New Hampshire, An Unlikely Team Tries to Reduce Gun Suicides." WBUR, June 14, 2018. https://www.wbur.org/hereandnow/2018/06/14/suicide -prevention-gun-sellers.

Crosby, Alex, and Sherry Davis Molock. "Suicidal Behaviors in the African American Community." *Journal of Black Psychology* 32, no. 3 (2006): 1–9. http://doi.org/10.1177/0095798406290552.

Daly, Mary C., Daniel J. Wilson, and Norman J. Johnson. "Relative Status and Well-Being: Evidence from U.S. Suicide Deaths." *FRB of San Francisco Working Paper No. 2007–12* (2007). http://doi.org/10.2139/ssrn.1026351.

Early, Kevin, and Ronald Akers. " 'It's a White Thing': An Exploration of Beliefs About Suicide in the African-American Community." *Deviant Behavior* 14, no. 4 (1993): 277–296. https://doi.org/10.1080/01639625.1993.9967947.

Graham, Carol, and Sergio Pinto. "Unequal Hopes and Lives in the USA: Optimism, Race, Place, and Premature Mortality." *Journal of Popular Economics* 32, no. 2 (2019): 665–733. https://doi.org/10.1007/s00148-018-0687-y.

Griffin-Fennell, Felicia, and Michelle Williams. "Examining the Complexities of Suicidal Behavior in the African American Community." *Journal of Black Psychology* 32, no. 3 (2006): 303–319. https://doi.org/10.1177/0095798406290469.

Harvard School of Public Health. "Suicide Prevention: A Role for Firearm Dealers and Range Owners." Gun Shop Project.

Kaplan, Mark S., Margaret E. Adamek, and Olga Geling. "Sociodemographic Predictors of Firearm Suicide Among Older White Males." *Gerontologist* 36, no. 4 (1996): 530–533. http://doi.org/10.1093/geront/36.4.530.

Keller, Jared. "The U.S. Suicide Rate Is at Its Highest in a Half-Century." *Pacific Standard*, December 4, 2018. https://psmag.com/news/the-suicide-rate-is-at-its-highest-in-a-half-century.

Klinger, David. "Suicidal Intent in Victim-Precipitated Homicide: Insights from the Study of 'Suicide-by-Cop.'" *Homicide Studies* 5, no. 3 (2001): 206–226. https://doi.org/10.1177/1088767901005003002.

McKenzie, Kwame, Marc Serafty, and Michael Crawford. "Suicide in Ethnic Minority Groups." *British Journal of Psychiatry* 183, no. 2 (2003): 100–101. https://doi.org/10.1192/bjp.183.2.100.

Nutt, Amy Ellis. "Suicide Rates for Black Children Twice That of White Children, New Data Show." *Washington Post*, May 21, 2018. https://www.washingtonpost.com/news/to-your-health/wp/2018/05/21/suicide-rates-for-black-children-twice-that-of-white-children-new-data-show/.

Olney, Lisa. "Providing Outreach and Education to Prevent Suicide." Children's Hospital at Dartmouth-Hitchcock, April 1, 2019. https://www.chadkids.org/stories/article/1536.

RAND Corporation. *The Relationship Between Firearm Availability and Suicide.* March 2, 2018. https://www.rand.org/research/gun-policy/analysis/essays/firearm-availability-suicide.html.

Scholtes, Michael J. "Why I Will Never Own a Gun." Scholtes Blog, March 26, 2018. https://thescholtes.com/2018/03/26/why-i-will-never-own-a-gun/.

Spates, Kamesha, and Brittany C. Slatton. "I've Got My Family and My Faith: Black Women and the Suicide Paradox." *Socius: Sociological Research for a Dynamic World* 3 (2017): 1–9. http://doi.org/10.1177/2378023117743908.

Stack, Steven. "The Relationship between Culture and Suicide: An Analysis of African Americans." *Transcultural Psychiatry* 35, no. 2 (1998): 253–269. https://doi.org/10.1177/136346159803500205.

True, Morgan. "NH suicide prevention project focuses on gun shops." *San Diego Union-Tribune*, April 20, 2013. https://www.sandiegouniontribune.com/sdut-nh-suicide-prevention-project-focuses-on-gun-shops-2013apr20-story.html.

Domestic Violence

Auchter, Bernie. "Men Who Murder Their Families: What the Research Tells Us." *NIJ Journal*, no. 266 (2010): 10–12. https://www.ncjrs.gov/pdffiles1/nij/230412.pdf.

Benson, Michael L., and Greer L. Fox. *Economic Distress, Community Context and Intimate Violence: An Application and Extension of Social Disorganization Theory, Final Report.* United States Department of Justice, Washington, D.C., 2002. https://www.ncjrs.gov/pdffiles1/nij/grants/193434.pdf.

Campbell, Jacquelyn, Jane Koziol-McLain, Daniel Webster, et al. *Research Results From a National Study of Intimate Partner Homicide: The Danger Assessment Instrument.* National Criminal Justice Reference Service, Washington, D.C., 2004. https://www.ncjrs.gov/pdffiles1/nij/199710.pdf.

Campbell, Jacquelyn, Daniel Webster, and Jane Koziol-McLain. "Risk Factors for Femicide in Abusive Relationships: Results from a Multisite Case Control Study." *American Journal of Public Health* 93, no. 7 (2003): 1089–1097. https://www.ncbi.nlm.nih.gov/pmc/articles/PMC1447915/.

Capaldi, Deborah M., Naomi B. Knoble, Joann Wu Shortt, et al. "A Systematic Review of Risk Factors for Intimate Partner Violence." *Partner Abuse* 3, no. 2 (2012): 231–280. https://doi.org/10.1891/1946-6560.3.2.231.

Farmer, Amy, and Jill Tiefenthaler. "Explaining the Recent Decline in Domestic Violence." *Contemporary Economic Policy* 21, no. 2 (2003): 158–172. https://doi.org/10.1093/cep/byg002.

Fox, James Alan, and Emma E. Fridel. "Gender Differences in Patterns and Trends in U.S. Homicide, 1976–2015." *Violence and Gender* 4, no. 2 (2017). https://doi.org/10.1089/vio.2017.0016.

Grinshteyn, Erin, and David Hemenway. "Violent Death Rates: The U.S. Compared with Other High-Income OECD Countries, 2010." *American Journal of Medicine* 129, no. 3 (2016): 266–273. https://doi.org/10.1016/j.amjmed.2015.10.025.

Kivivuori, Janne. "Veli Verkko as an Early Criminologist; A Case Study in Scientific Conflict and Paradigm Shift." *Scandinavian Journal of History* 42, no. 2 (2017): 144–165. https://doi.org/10.1080/03468755.2016.1265854.

Loveland, Jennifer E., and Chitra Raghavan. "Coercive Control, Physical Violence, and Masculinity." *Violence and Gender* 4, no. 1 (2017): 5–10. https://doi.org/10.1089/vio.2016.0019.

Mascia, Jennifer. "The Untold Story of Gun Violence." *The Trace*, September 12, 2018. https://www.cosmopolitan.com/sex-love/a23088401/domestic-violence-coercive-control/.

Modi, Monica N., Sheallah Palmer, and Alicia Armstrong. "The Role of Violence Against Women Act in Addressing Intimate Partner Violence: A Public Health Issue." *Journal of Women's Health* 23, no. 3 (2013): 253–259. https://doi.org/10.1089/jwh.2013.4387.

New York Times Editorial Board. "Women's Lives, Cut Short." *New York Times*, December 19, 2017. https://www.nytimes.com/interactive/2017/12/19/opinion/women-guns-domestic-violence.html.

Petrosky, Emiko, Janet M. Blair, Carter J. Betz, et al. "Racial and Ethnic Differences in Homicides of Adult Women and the Role of Intimate Partner Violence—United States, 2003–2014." *Morbidity and Mortality Weekly* 66, no. 28 (2017): 741–746. https://www.cdc.gov/mmwr/volumes/66/wr/mm6628a1.htm.

Silverman, Robert A., and Leslie W. Kennedy. "Relational Distance and Homicide: The Role of the Stranger." *Journal of Criminal Law and Criminology* 78, no. 2 (1987): 272–308. https://www.jstor.org/stable/1143450?seq=1#page_scan_tab_contents.

Smith, S. G., J. Chen, K. C. Basile, et al. *The National Intimate Partner and Sexual Violence Sur-*

vey (NISVS): 2010–2012 State Report. National Center for Injury Prevention and Control, Centers for Disease Control and Prevention, Atlanta, 2017.

Sorenson, Susan B. "Firearm Use in Intimate Partner Violence: A Brief Overview." *Evaluation Review* 30, no. 3 (2006): 229–236. https://doi.org/10.1177/0193841X06287220.

Sorenson, Susan B., and Rebecca A. Schut. "Non-Fatal Gun Use in Intimate Partner Violence: A Systematic Review of the Literature." *Trauma and Abuse* 19, no. 4 (2018): 431–442. https://doi.org/10.1177/1524838016668589.

Sorenson, Susan B., and Douglas J. Wiebe. "Weapons in the Lives of Battered Women." *American Journal of Public Health* 94, no. 8 (2004): 1412–1417. https://www.ncbi.nlm.nih.gov/pmc/articles/PMC1448464/.

Sullivan, Tami P., and Nicole H. Weiss. "Is Firearm Threat in Intimate Relationships Associated with Posttraumatic Stress Disorder Symptoms Among Women?" *Violence and Gender* 4, no. 2 (2017): 31–36. https://doi.org/10.1089/vio.2016.0024.

Tanha, Marieh, Connie J. A. Beck, Aurelio José Figueredo, et al. "Sex Differences in Intimate Partner Violence and the Use of Coercive Control as a Motivational Factor for Intimate Partner Violence." *Journal of Interpersonal Violence* 25, no. 10 (2010): 1836–1854. https://doi.org/10.1177/0886260509354501.

United Nations Office on Drugs and Crime. *Global Study on Homicide 2013.* Vienna, 2013. https://www.unodc.org/documents/data-and-analysis/statistics/GSH2013/2014_GLOBAL_HOMICIDE_BOOK_web.pdf.

United Nations Office on Drugs and Crime. *Global Study on Homicide 2018.* Vienna, 2018. https://www.unodc.org/documents/data-and-analysis/GSH2018/GSH18_Gender-related_killing_of_women_and_girls.pdf.

Violence Policy Center. *American Roulette: Murder-Suicide in the United States.* 6th ed. Washington, D.C., 2018. http://vpc.org/studies/amroul2018.pdf.

Zeoli, April. "Non-Fatal Firearm Uses in Domestic Violence." Battered Women's Justice Project, Minneapolis, Minnesota, 2017. https://www.preventdvgunviolence.org/nonfatal-gun-dv-zeoli-.pdf.

Zeoli, April, Alexander McCourt, Shani Buggs, et al. "Analysis of the Strength of Legal Firearms Restrictions for Perpetrators of Domestic Violence and Their Associations with Intimate Partner Homicide." *American Journal of Epidemiology* 187, no. 7 (2017): 1449–1455. http://doi.org/10.1093/aje/kwx362.

CHAPTER SIX: THE VIOLENCE WE EXPORT

America's Role in International Violence

Arria, Michael. "The Curious Ascent of General Atomics." *Vice,* May 31, 2012. https://www.vice.com/en_us/article/dp4xvw/how-general-atomics-won-the-west.

Bezhan, Frud. "Aftershocks of Iran's 1953 Coup Still Felt Around the World, 60 Years Later." Radio Free Europe/Radio Liberty, August 15, 2013. https://www.rferl.org/a/iran-coup-mossadegh-cia-60th-anniversary/25076552.html.

Blitzer, Jonathan. "The Link Between America's Lax Gun Laws and the Violence That Fuels Immigration." *New Yorker,* March 22, 2018. https://www.newyorker.com/news/news-desk/the-link-between-americas-lax-gun-laws-and-the-violence-that-fuels-immigration.

Brodzinsky, Sibylla. "Inside San Pedro Sula—The Most Violent City in the World." *The Guardian,* May 15, 2013. https://www.theguardian.com/world/2013/may/15/san-pedro-sula-honduras-most-violent.

Brook, Pete. "The 40,000 People Living on Bagram Air Base Haven't Actually Seen Afghanistan." *Wired,* February 24, 2015. https://www.wired.com/2015/02/edmund-clark-the-mountains-of-majeed/.

de Córdoba, José, and Juan Montes. "'It's a Crisis of Civilization in Mexico.' 250,000 Dead. 37,400 Missing." *Wall Street Journal,* November 14, 2018. https://www.wsj.com/articles/its-a-crisis-of-civilization-in-mexico-250-000-dead-37-400-missing-1542213374.

Geographical Imaginations. "Theory of the Drone 12: 'Killing Well'?" December 8, 2013. https://geographicalimaginations.com/tag/hellfire-missile/.

Keller, John. "Air Force Asks General Atomics to Build Year's Worth of MQ-9 Reaper Unmanned Combat Drones." *Military and Aerospace Electronics,* November 6, 2018. https://www.militaryaerospace.com/unmanned/article/16726592/air-force-asks-general-atomics-to-build-years-worth-of-mq9-reaper-unmanned-combat-drones.

Kristian, Bonnie. "Obama's Drone Warfare Makes More Terrorists Than It Kills." *Real Clear Defense,* August 8, 2016. https://www.realcleardefense.com/articles/2016/08/09/obamas_drone_warfare_makes_more_terrorists_than_it_kills_109683.html.

Lawrence, J. P. "Afghan General: There Are a Lot More Taliban Fighters Than Previously Thought." *Stars and Stripes,* June 12, 2018. https://www.stripes.com/news/afghan-general-there-are-a-lot-more-taliban-fighters-than-previously-thought-1.532312.

Levine, Yasha. "The Billionaire Brothers Behind America's Predator Drones—And Their Very Strange Past." *AlterNet,* April 24, 2013. https://www.alternet.org/2013/04/billionaire-brothers-behind-americas-predator-drones-and-their-very-strange-past/.

Linthicum, Kate. "There Is Only One Gun Store in All of Mexico. So Why Is Gun Violence Soaring?" *Los Angeles Times,* May 24, 2018. https://www.latimes.com/world/la-fg-mexico-guns-20180524-story.html.

Luhnow, David. "Latin America Is the Murder Capital of the World." *Wall Street Journal,* September 20, 2018. https://www.wsj.com/articles/400-murders-a-day-the-crisis-of-latin-america-1537455390.

MacGillis, Alec. "Guess Where the Gangs Get Their Guns?" *The New Republic,* August 12, 2014. https://newrepublic.com/article/119026/guns-fueling-immigration-central-america-come-us.

Mackey, Danielle. "Deported into a Nightmare." *The Atlantic,* June 23, 2018. https://www.theatlantic.com/international/archive/2018/06/honduras-immigration-trump-mexico-gang-violence/563465/.

Manna, Emily. "Exploring a Link Between Drone Strikes and Retaliation." *Georgetown Public Policy Review,* July 8, 2016. http://gppreview.com/2016/07/08/exploring-link-drone-strikes-retaliation/.

Pane, Lisa Marie. "How American Guns in Latin America Spur the Immigration Crisis." *Christian Science Monitor,* October 1, 2018. https://www.csmonitor.com/USA/2018/1001/How-American-guns-in-Latin-America-spur-the-immigration-crisis.

Parsons, Chelsea, and Eugenio Wiegend. *Beyond Our Borders: How Weak U.S. Gun Laws Contribute to Violent Crime Abroad.* Washington, D.C.: Center for American Progress, 2018. https://cdn.americanprogress.org/content/uploads/2018/01/31115010/012918_BeyondOurBorders-report-51.pdf.

Robles, Francis. "Fleeing Gangs, Children Head to U.S. Border." *New York Times,* July 9, 2014. https://www.nytimes.com/2014/07/10/world/americas/fleeing-gangs-children-head-to-us-border.html.

Taylor, Gary. "Palm Bay Man at Center of International Firearms Trafficking Probe." *Orlando Sentinel,* August 23, 2010. https://www.orlandosentinel.com/news/os-xpm-2010-08-23-os-firearms-trafficking-20100823-story.html.

Voice of America. "U.S. Official: U.S. Foreign Military Sales Total $55.6B, Up 33 Percent."

October 9, 2018. https://www.voanews.com/usa/us-official-us-foreign-military-sales-total-556b-33-percent.

Watson, Kathryn. "Graham Says Saudi Crown Prince 'Has Got to Go,' Pushing Harder Line Than Trump." CBS News, October 16, 2018. https://www.cbsnews.com/news/graham-saudi-crown-prince-has-got-to-go-pushing-harder-line-than-trump/.

Yablon, Alex. "ATF Documents Show How Traffickers Exploit Lax Sellers and Weak Laws." *The Trace*, September 18, 2018. https://www.thetrace.org/2018/09/atf-documents-crime-guns-us-mexico-trafficking/.

CHAPTER SEVEN: CURBING THE MEANS OF VIOLENCE

Missouri and Connecticut

Bergner, Brad, and Michael Nowicki. "From Armed Rebellions to Permitless Carry: A Brief History of Guns in Missouri." *The Trace*, May 15, 2017. https://www.thetrace.org/2017/05/armed-rebellions-permitless-carry-brief-history-guns-missouri/.

Crisp, Elizabeth. "Missouri Lawmakers Stick to Pro-Gun Trends." *St. Louis Post-Dispatch*, January 28, 2013. https://www.stltoday.com/news/local/govt-and-politics/missouri-lawmakers-stick-to-pro-gun-trends/article_089487cd-3b82-5a06-a5b4-b1e0f63797aa.html.

Guo, Jeff. "Gun Killings Fell by 40 percent After Connecticut Passed This Law." *Washington Post*, June 12, 2015. https://www.washingtonpost.com/blogs/govbeat/wp/2015/06/12/gun-killings-fell-by-40-percent-after-connecticut-passed-this-law/.

Rudolph, Kara E., Elizabeth A. Stuart, Jon S. Vernick, et al. "Association Between Connecticut's Permit-to-Purchase Handgun Law and Homicides." *American Journal of Public Health* 105, no. 8 (2015): 49–54. https://doi.org/10.2105/AJPH.2015.302703.

Spies, Mark. "Missouri Under the Gun." *The Trace*. https://www.thetrace.org/missouri-under-the-gun/.

Tavernise, Sabrina. "In Missouri, Fewer Gun Restrictions and More Gun Killings." *New York Times*, December 21, 2015. https://www.nytimes.com/2015/12/22/health/in-missouri-fewer-gun-restrictions-and-more-gun-killings.html.

Webster, Daniel, Cassandra Kercher Crifasi, and Jon S. Vernick. "Effects of the Repeal of Missouri's Handgun Purchaser Licensing Law on Homicides." *Journal of Urban Health* 91, no. 2 (2014): 293–302. https://doi.org/10.1007/s11524-014-9865-8.

Fewer Guns, Better Laws, Less Violence

Bailey, James E., Arthur L. Kellerman, and Grant W. Somes. "Risk Factors for Violent Death of Women in the Home." *JAMA Internal Medicine* 157, no. 7 (1997): 777–782. http://doi.org/10.1001/archinte.1997.00440280101009.

Crifasi, Cassandra Kercher, Molly Francis-Merrill, Alex McCourt, et al. "Association Between Firearm Laws and Homicide in Urban Counties." *Journal of Urban Health* 95, no. 3 (2018): 383–390. http://doi.org/10.1007/s11524-018-0273-3.

Defilippis, Evan, and Devin Hughes. "Gun-Rights Advocates Claim Owning a Gun Makes a Woman Safer. The Research Says They're Wrong." *The Trace*, May 2, 2016. https://www.thetrace.org/2016/05/gun-ownership-makes-women-safer-debunked/.

Díez, Carolina, Rachel P. Kurland, Emily F. Rothman, et al. "State Intimate Partner Violence–Related Firearm Laws and Intimate Partner Homicide Rates in the United States, 1991 to 2015." *Annals of Internal Medicine* 167, no. 8 (2017): 536–543. http://doi.org/10.7326/M16-2849.

Donohue, John J., Abhay Aneja, and Kyle D. Weber. "Right-to-Carry Laws and Violent Crime: A Comprehensive Assessment Using Panel Data and a State-Level Synthetic

Controls Analysis." *Stanford Law and Economics Olin Working Paper No. 508,* June 19, 2017. https://dx.doi.org/10.2139/ssrn.2990220.

Everytown for Gun Safety Action Fund. "New Analysis of FBI Data Shows Federal Background Check System Works in Washington State: More Than 40,000 Gun Sales Blocked to Prohibited Purchases, Including 24,000 Sales to Felons and More Than 6,000 Sales to Domestic Abusers." Everytown for Gun Safety, August 21, 2014. https://everytown.org/press/new-analysis-of-fbi-data-shows-federal-background-check-system-works-in-washington-state-more-than-40000-gun-sales-blocked-to-prohibited-purchases-including-24000-sales-to-felons-and-more-than-60/.

Fleeger, Eric, Lois K. Lee, Michael C. Mounteaux, et al. "Firearm Legislation and Firearm-Related Fatalities in the United States." *JAMA Internal Medicine* 173, no. 9 (2013): 732–740. http://doi.org/10.1001/jamainternmed.2013.1286.

Hemenway, David. "Survey Research and Self-Defense Gun Use: An Explanation of Extreme Overestimates." *Journal of Criminal Law and Criminology* 87, no. 4 (1997): 1430–1445. https://scholarlycommons.law.northwestern.edu/cgi/viewcontent.cgi?referer=&httpsredir=1&article=6936&context=jclc.

Hemenway, David, and Sara J. Solnick. "The Epidemiology of Self-Defense Gun Use: Evidence from the National Crime Victimization Surveys 2007–2011." *Preventative Medicine* 79 (2015): 22–27. https://doi.org/10.1016/j.ypmed.2015.03.029.

Ingraham, Christopher. "It's Time to Bring Back the Assault Weapons Ban, Gun Violence Experts Say." *Washington Post,* February 15, 2018. https://www.washingtonpost.com/news/wonk/wp/2018/02/15/its-time-to-bring-back-the-assault-weapons-ban-gun-violence-experts-say/.

Kalesan, Bindu, Matthew E. Mobily, Olivia Keiser, et al. "Firearm Legislation and Firearm Mortality in the USA: A Cross-Sectional, State-Level Study." *Lancet* 387, no. 10030 (2016): 1847–1855. https://doi.org/10.1016/S0140-6736(15)01026-0.

Kaste, Martin. "Gun Studies: Permit Laws Reduce Murders; Red Flag Laws Cut Suicides." National Public Radio, June 4, 2018. https://www.npr.org/2018/06/04/616268027/gun-studies-permit-laws-reduce-murders-red-flag-laws-cut-suicides.

Kaufman, Elinore J., Christopher N. Morrison, Charles C. Branas, et al. "State Firearm Laws and Interstate Firearm Deaths from Homicide and Suicide in the United States: A Cross-Sectional Analysis of Data by County." *JAMA Internal Medicine* 178, no. 5 (2018): 692–700. http://doi.org/10.1001/jamainternmed.2018.0190.

Kivisto, Aaron J., and Peter Lee Phalen. "Effects of Risk-Based Firearm Seizure Laws in Connecticut and Indiana on Suicide Rates, 1981–2015." *Psychiatry Online,* June 1, 2018. https://doi.org/10.1176/appi.ps.201700250.

Klarevas, Louis. *Rampage Nation: Securing America from Mass Shootings.* New York: Prometheus Publishing, 2016.

Koper, Christopher S., William D. Johnson, Jordan L. Nichols, et al. "Criminal Use of Assault Weapons and High-Capacity Semiautomatic Firearms: An Updated Examination of Local and National Sources." *Journal of Urban Health* 95, no. 3 (2018): 313–321. http://doi.org/10.1007/s11524-017-0205-7.

Lemieux, Frederic. "Effect of Gun Culture and Firearm Laws on Gun Violence and Mass Shootings in the United States: A Multi-Level Quantitative Analysis." *International Journal of Criminal Justice Sciences* 9, no. 1 (2014): 74–93. https://www.researchgate.net/publication/268804619_Effect_of_Gun_Culture_and_Firearm_Laws_on_Gun_Violence_and_Mass_Shootings_in_the_United_States_A_Multi-Level_Quantitative_Analysis.

McClenathan, Jane, Molly Pahn, Michael Siegel, et al. *The Changing Landscape of U.S. Gun Pol-*

icy: *State Firearm Laws, 1991–2016.* State Firearm Laws, 2017. https://www.statefirearmlaws
.org/sites/default/files/2017-12/report_0.pdf.

Postel, Thérèse. "The Assault Weapons Ban: Did It Curtail Mass Shootings?" The Century Foundation, January 11, 2013. https://tcf.org/content/commentary/the-assault-weapons
-ban-did-it-curtail-mass-shootings/.

RAND Corporation. *The Effects of Bans on the Sale of Assault Weapons and High-Capacity Magazines.* March 2, 2018. https://www.rand.org/research/gun-policy/analysis/ban-assault
-weapons.html.

RAND Corporation. *The Science of Gun Policy: A Critical Synthesis of Research Evidence on the Effects of Gun Policies in the United States.* Santa Monica, California, 2018. https://www
.rand.org/pubs/research_reports/RR2088.html.

Siegel, Michael, Molly Pahn, Ziming Xuan, et al. "Firearm-Related Laws in All 50 U.S. States, 1991–2016." *American Journal of Public Health* 107, no. 7 (2017): 1122–1129. http://doi
.org/10.2105/AJPH.2017.303701.

Siegel, Michael, Ziming Xuan, Craig S. Ross, et al. "Easiness of Legal Access to Concealed Firearm Permits and Homicide Rates in the United States." *American Journal of Public Health* 107, no. 12 (2017): 1923–1929. http://doi.org/10.2105/AJPH.2017.304057.

Wintemute, Karen J., Anthony A. Braga, and David M. Kennedy. "Private-Party Gun Sales, Regulation, and Public Safety." *New England Journal of Medicine* 363, no. 6 (2010): 508–511. http://doi.org/10.1056/NEJMp1006326.

Zeoli, April M., and Daniel W. Webster. "Effects of Domestic Violence Policies, Alcohol Taxes, and Police Staffing Levels on Intimate Partner Homicide in Large U.S. Cities." *Injury Prevention* 16, no. 2 (2010): 90–95. http://doi.org/10.1136/ip.2009.024620.

Mothers and Children of the Movement

Baker, K. C. "Moms Demand Action for Gun Sense Founder Shannon Watts Fights to Keep the Nation's Children Safe." *People,* December 30, 2016.

Blair, Ian F. "'3½ Minutes, 10 Bullets' Examines the Murder of Jordan Davis." *Rolling Stone,* June 23, 2015. https://www.rollingstone.com/politics/politics-news/3-1-2-minutes-10
-bullets-examines-the-murder-of-jordan-davis-33678/.

Coates, Ta-Nehisi. "To Raise, Love, and Lose a Black Child." *The Atlantic,* October 8, 2014. https://www.theatlantic.com/politics/archive/2014/10/to-raise-love-and-lose-a-black
-child/381189/.

Eller, Claudia. "Emma Gonzalez Opens Up About How Her Life Has Changed Since Parkland Tragedy." *Variety,* October 9, 2018. https://variety.com/2018/politics/features/
emma-gonzalez-parkland-interview-1202972485/.

Fisher, Dana R. "Here's Who Actually Attended the March for Our Lives. (No, It Wasn't Mostly Young People.)" *Washington Post,* March 28, 2018. https://www.washingtonpost
.com/news/monkey-cage/wp/2018/03/28/heres-who-actually-attended-the-march
-for-our-lives-no-it-wasnt-mostly-young-people/.

Follman, Mark. "These Women Are the NRA's Worst Nightmare." *Mother Jones,* September/
October 2014. https://www.motherjones.com/politics/2014/09/moms-demand
-action-guns-madd-shannon-watts-nra/.

Giffords, Gabrielle. "A Senate in the Gun Lobby's Grip." *New York Times,* April 17, 2013. https://www.nytimes.com/2013/04/18/opinion/a-senate-in-the-gun-lobbys-grip.html.

Giffords, Gabrielle, and Mark Kelly. *Gabby: A Story of Courage, Love, and Resilience.* New York: Scribner, 2012.

Girouard, April. "Giffords a Longtime Supporter of Gun Rights." Fox News, January 9, 2011 (updated December 23, 2015). https://www.foxnews.com/politics/giffords-a-longtime-supporter-of-gun-rights.

González, Emma. "A Young Activist's Advice: Vote, Shave Your Head, and Cry Whenever You Need To." *New York Times,* October 5, 2018. https://www.nytimes.com/2018/10/05/opinion/sunday/emma-gonzalez-parkland.html.

Goss, Kristin A. *Disarmed: The Missing Movement for Gun Control in America.* Princeton: Princeton University Press, 2006.

Goss. Kristin A. "Whatever Happened to the 'Missing Movement'? Gun Control Politics over Two Decades of Change." In *Gun Studies: Interdisciplinary Approaches to Politics, Policy, and Practice,* edited by Jennifer Carlson, Kristin A. Goss, and Harel Shapira. New York: Routledge, 2018.

Green, Emma. "Her Big Idea: Gabby Giffords." *The Atlantic,* July 2, 2013. https://www.theatlantic.com/politics/archive/2013/07/her-big-idea-gabby-giffords/277446/.

Mead, Rebecca. "Joan of Arc and the Passion of Emma González." *New Yorker,* March 26, 2018. https://www.newyorker.com/culture/cultural-comment/the-passion-of-emma-gonzalez.

Morales, Ed. "Emma González: La Nueva Cara of Florida Latinx." *Washington Post,* March 1, 2018. https://www.washingtonpost.com/news/post-nation/wp/2018/03/01/emma-gonzalez-la-nueva-cara-of-florida-latinx/.

Murphy, Chris. "South Florida School Shooting." *Congressional Record.* 115th Congress, 2nd Session, 2018, Vol. 164, S949. https://www.congress.gov/115/crec/2018/02/14/CREC-2018-02-14-pt1-PgS930-5.pdf.

Schouten, Fredreka. "Giffords' Super PAC Raises $6.5 Million." *USA Today,* July 25, 2013. https://www.usatoday.com/story/news/politics/2013/07/25/gabby-giffords-americans-for-responsible-solutions-fundraising-gun-control/2586975/.

Staples, Gracie Bonds. "Lucy McBath's Son Was Shot to Death Outside a Jacksonville Convenience Store After a Dispute Over Loud Music." *Atlanta Journal-Constitution,* March 29, 2014. https://www.ajc.com/news/crime--law/god-has-told-will/P9NH4PElM0PRnTzk1KO63J/.

Terris, Ben. "What's Wrong with Politicizing a Tragedy? For Sen. Chris Murphy, Nothing at All." *Washington Post,* September 28, 2016. https://www.washingtonpost.com/lifestyle/style/whats-wrong-with-politicizing-a-tragedy-for-sen-chris-murphy-nothing-at-all/2016/09/27/92db2444-7de6-11e6-9070-5c4905bf40dc_story.html.

Vasilogambros, Matt. "Gabby Giffords' Gun-Control Group Brings in $6.6 Million This Year." *The Atlantic,* July 31, 2013. https://www.theatlantic.com/politics/archive/2013/07/gabby-giffords-gun-control-group-brings-in-66-million-this-year/437985/.

Wallace, Wells. "Chris Murphy and the Accelerating Politics of Mass Shootings." *New Yorker,* February 16, 2018. https://www.newyorker.com/news/news-desk/chris-murphy-and-the-accelerating-politics-of-mass-shootings.

CHAPTER EIGHT: PULLING OUT THE ROOTS OF VIOLENCE

Focused Deterrence and Cure Violence

Abt, Thomas. *Bleeding Out: The Devastating Consequences of Urban Violence—and a Bold New Plan for Peace in the Streets.* New York: Basic Books, 2019.

Braga, Anthony A., David M. Kennedy, Elin J. Waring, et al. "Problem Oriented Policing, Deterrence, and Youth Violence: An Evaluation of Boston's Operation Ceasefire." *Journal of Research in Crime and Delinquency* 38, no. 3 (2001): 195–225. http://doi.org/10.1177/0022427801038003001.

Braga, Anthony A., and David Wiesburd. "The Effects of Focused Deterrence Strategies on Crime: A Systematic Review and Meta-Analysis of the Empirical Evidence." *Journal of Research in Crime and Delinquency* 49, no. 3 (2012): 323–358. https://doi.org/10.1177/0022427811419368.

Braga, Anthony A., David Wiesburd, and Brandon Turchan. "Focused Deterrence Strategies and Crime Control: An Updated Systematic Review and Meta-Analysis of the Empirical Evidence." *Criminology and Public Policy* 17, no. 1 (2018): 205–250. https://doi.org/10.1111/1745-9133.12353.

Brantigham, P. Jeffrey, Nick Sundback, Kristine Chan, et al. *GRYD Intervention Incident Response and Gang Crime 2017 Evaluation Report*. Los Angeles, 2017. https://www.lagryd.org/sites/default/files/reports/GRYD%20IR%20and%20Gang%20Crime%20Report_2017_FINALv2_0.pdf.

Brunson, Rod K. "Focused Deterrence and Improved Police–Community Relations." *Criminology and Public Policy* 14, no. 3 (2015): 507–514. https://doi.org/10.1111/1745-9133.12141.

Butts, Jeffrey A., Caterina Gouvis Roman, Lindsay Bostwick, et al. "Cure Violence: A Public Health Model to Reduce Gun Violence." *Annual Review of Public Health* 36 (2015): 39–53. https://doi.org/10.1146/annurev-publhealth-031914-122509.

Elliott, Philip. "The Koch Brothers Are Pushing for Criminal Justice Changes." *The Atlantic*, January 29, 2018. https://time.com/5123969/koch-brothers-criminal-justice-reform/.

Freskos, Brian. "Inside the Ambitious Campaign to Push Chicago Homicides Below 400." *The Trace*, July 11, 2019. https://www.thetrace.org/2019/07/chicago-gun-violence-399-campaign/.

Givens, Ann. "On Patrol with Chicago's Last Violence Interrupters." *The Trace*, February 6, 2017. https://www.thetrace.org/2017/02/chicago-homicides-cure-violence-interrupters/.

Hagen, Lisa. "A Decades-Old Approach to Prevent Gunshot Wounds Is Catching On in Hospitals Around the U.S." WAMU American University Radio, January 23, 2019. https://wamu.org/story/19/01/23/a-decades-old-approach-to-prevent-gunshot-wounds-is-catching-on-in-hospitals-around-the-u-s/.

Kennedy, David M. *Don't Shoot: One Man, a Street Fellowship, and the End of Violence in Inner-City America*. New York: Bloomsbury, 2011.

Purtle, Jonathan, Rochelle Dicker, Carnell Cooper, et al. "Hospital-Based Violence Intervention Programs Save Lives and Money." *Journal of Trauma and Acute Care Surgery* 75, no. 2 (2014): 331–333. http://doi.org/10.1097/TA.0b013e318294f518.

Roberts, Laura. "Waterbury Police Athletic League Keeps Kids off the Street, Crime Down." Fox61, May 1, 2015. https://fox61.com/2015/05/01/waterbury-police-activity-league-keeps-kids-off-the-street-crime-down/.

Rosenberg, Tina. "Taking Aim at Gun Violence, With Personal Deterrence." *New York Times*, April 3, 2018. https://www.nytimes.com/2018/04/03/opinion/gun-violence-personal-deterrence.html.

United States Agency for International Development. *What Works in Reducing Community Violence: A Meta-Review and Field Study for the Northern Triangle*. Bethesda, Maryland, 2016. https://www.usaid.gov/sites/default/files/USAID-2016-What-Works-in-Reducing-Community-Violence-Final-Report.pdf.

van Brocklin, Elizabeth. "What Gun Violence Prevention Looks Like When It Focuses on the Communities Hurt the Most." *The Trace*, July 10, 2019. https://www.thetrace.org/2019/07/gun-violence-prevention-communities-of-color-funding/.

Wolff, Craig. "As Drug Trade Rises in Hartford, So Does Violent Crime." *New York Times*, December 16, 1988. https://www.nytimes.com/1988/12/16/nyregion/as-drug-trade-rises-in-hartford-so-does-violent-crime.html.

Mass Incarceration and Criminal Justice Reform

American Civil Liberties Union. *Cracks in the System: Twenty Years of the Unjust Federal Crack Cocaine Law.* New York, 2006. https://www.aclu.org/sites/default/files/field _document/cracksinsystem_20061025.pdf.

American Civil Liberties Union. *The War on Marijuana in Black and White.* New York, 2013. https://www.aclu.org/sites/default/files/field_document/1114413-mj-report-rfs-rel1 .pdf.

Austin, James, and Lauren-Brooke Eisen. *How Many Americans Are Unnecessarily Incarcerated?* New York: Brennan Center for Justice, 2016.

Berman, Greg, and Julian Adler. *Start Here: A Road Map to Reducing Mass Incarceration.* New York: The New Press, 2018.

Booker, Cory. "Pass the Next Step Act." In *Ending Mass Incarceration: Ideas from Today's Leaders,* edited by Inimai Chettiar and Priya Raghavan, 1–5. New York: Brennan Center for Justice, 2019.

Caulkins, Jonathan P., Bruce Johnson, Angela Taylor, et al. "What Drug Dealers Tell Us About Their Costs of Doing Business." *Journal of Drug Issues* 29, no. 2 (1999): 323–340. https://doi.org/10.1177/002204269902900211.

Drucker, Ernest. *Decarcerating America: From Mass Punishment to Public Health.* New York: New Press, 2018.

Editorial Board of the *Hartford Courant.* "Editorial: Crime Drop Shows Smart Policies at Work." September 26, 2018. https://www.courant.com/opinion/editorials/hc-ed -drop-in-crime-20180925-story.html.

Eisen, Lauren-Brooke, and Inimai Chettiar. *The Reverse Mass Incarceration Act.* New York: Brennan Center for Justice, 2015.

Gao, George. "Chart of the Week: The Black-White Gap in Incarceration Rates." *Fact Tank: News in the Numbers,* Pew Research Center, July 18, 2014. https://www.pewresearch .org/fact-tank/2014/07/18/chart-of-the-week-the-black-white-gap-in-incarceration -rates/.

Ifill, Sherrilyn, Loretta Lynch, Bryan Stevenson, et al. *A Perilous Path.* New York: New Press, 2018.

Jacobs, Josh. "How Long Can Connecticut's Prison Reform Last?" *The Atlantic,* July 15, 2017. https://www.theatlantic.com/politics/archive/2017/07/connecticut-prison-malloy/ 533565/.

Lawlor, Mark. "The Simple Proof That Juvenile Justice Reforms Work: Juvenile Crime Is Down." *Hartford Courant,* May 31, 2019. https://www.courant.com/opinion/op-ed/hc -op-lawlor-juvenile-crime-data-0602-20190531-fdbrittmtvelhcyomvbrpv7iqi-story.html.

Mahoney, Edmund. "A Corner Where Crack Is King." *Hartford Courant,* November 21, 1993. https://www.courant.com/news/connecticut/hc-xpm-1993-11-21-0000001687-story .html.

Moraff, Christopher. "How Connecticut Became a Model for Prison Reform." *The Crime Report,* December 5, 2016. https://thecrimereport.org/2016/12/05/how-connecticut -became-a-model-for-prison-reform/.

Pettus-Davis, Carrie, and Matthew E. Epperson. "From Mass Incarceration to Smart Decarceration." *Grand Challenges for Social Work Initiatives Working Paper No. 4,* 2015. http:// grandchallengesforsocialwork.org/wp-content/uploads/2015/12/WP4-with-cover.pdf.

Pfaff, John F. *Locked In: The True Causes of Mass Incarceration and How to Achieve Real Reform.* New York: Basic Books, 2017.

Schrantz, Dennis, Stephen DeBor, and Marc Mauer. *Decarceration Strategies: How 5 States Achieved Substantial Prison Population Reductions.* The Sentencing Project, 2018. https://

www.sentencingproject.org/publications/decarceration-strategies-5-states-achieved
-substantial-prison-population-reductions/.

Silber, Clarice. "Malloy Leaves Office as National Leader on Criminal Justice Reform." *Connecticut Mirror,* January 4, 2019. https://ctmirror.org/2019/01/04/malloy-leaves-office
-national-leader-criminal-justice-reform/.

Stevenson, Bryan. *Just Mercy: A Story of Justice and Redemption.* New York: Spiegel & Grau, 2015.

United States Sentencing Commission. *Cocaine and Federal Sentencing Policy.* Washington, D.C.,
May 2002. https://www.ussc.gov/sites/default/files/pdf/news/congressional-testimony
-and-reports/drug-topics/200205-rtc-cocaine-sentencing-policy/200205_Cocaine_and
_Federal_Sentencing_Policy.pdf.

United States Sentencing Commission. *Cocaine and Federal Sentencing Policy (as Directed by
Section 280006 of Public Law 103-322).* Washington, D.C., February 1995. https://www
.ussc.gov/sites/default/files/pdf/news/congressional-testimony-and-reports/drug
-topics/199502-rtc-cocaine-sentencing-policy/EXECSUM.pdf.

United States Sentencing Commission. *Cocaine and Federal Sentencing Policy (as Directed by
Section Two of Public Law 104-38).* Washington, D.C., April 1997. https://www.ussc.gov/
sites/default/files/pdf/news/congressional-testimony-and-reports/drug-topics/19970429
_RtC_Cocaine_Sentencing_Policy.pdf.

U.S. Commission on Civil Rights. *Collateral Consequences: The Crossroads of Punishment, Redemption, and the Effects on Communities.* Washington, D.C., 2019.

Wallis, Jim. *America's Original Sin: Racism, White Privilege, and the Bridge to a New America.*
Grand Rapids: Brazos Press, 2016.

Segregation

Cuda, Amanda. "Report: Percent of Bridgeport Children in Poverty Rising." *Connecticut
Post,* November 27, 2012. https://www.ctpost.com/local/article/Report-Percent-of
-Bridgeport-children-in-poverty-4071289.php.

Jackson, C. Kirabo, Rucker C. Johnson, and Claudia Persico. "The Effects of School Spending on Educational and Economic Outcomes: Evidence from School Finance Reforms."
National Bureau of Economic Research Working Paper, January 2015. https://www
.nber.org/papers/w20847.

Johnson, Rucker. *Children of the Dream: Why School Integration Works.* New York: Basic Books,
2019.

Johnson, Rucker. "Long-Run Impacts of School Desegregation & School Quality on Adult
Attainments." National Bureau of Economic Research Working Paper, September
2015. https://www.nber.org/papers/w16664.

Knopov, Anita, Emily F. Rothman, Shea W. Cronin, et al. "The Role of Racial Residential
Segregation in Black-White Disparities in Firearm Homicide at the State Level in the
United States, 1991–2015." *Journal of the National Medical Association* 111, no. 1 (2019):
62–75. http://doi.org/10.1016/j.jnma.2018.06.002.

Phaneuf, Keith M., and Clarice Silber. "Invisible Walls: Among Connecticut Cities and
Towns, the Wealthiest Are the Big Spenders." *Connecticut Mirror,* May 30, 2018. https://
ctmirror.org/2018/05/30/among-connecticut-cities-towns-wealthiest-big-spenders/.

Silver, Christopher. "The Racial Origins of Zoning in American Cities." In *Urban Planning
and the African American Community: In the Shadows,* edited by June Manning Thomas
and Marsha Ritzdorf. Thousand Oaks: Sage Publications, 1997.

Stebbins, Samuel, and Evan Comen. "16 Most Segregated Cities in America." *24/7 Wall St.,*
July 20, 2018. https://247wallst.com/special-report/2018/07/20/16-most-segregated
-cities-in-america-3/3/.

Economic Justice

Board of Governors of the Federal Reserve System. *Report on the Economic Well-Being of U.S. Households in 2017*. Washington, D.C., 2018. https://www.federalreserve.gov/publications/files/2017-report-economic-well-being-us-households-201805.pdf.

Cline, William R. "The New Tax Law's Impact on Inequality." Policy Brief 18-3, Peterson Institute for International Economics, February 2018. https://www.piie.com/publications/policy-briefs/new-tax-laws-impact-inequality.

Fontenot, Kayla, Jessica Semega, and Melissa Kollar. *Income and Poverty in the United States: 2017*. United States Census Bureau, 2018. https://www.census.gov/content/dam/Census/library/publications/2018/demo/p60-263.pdf.

Huffington Post. "CEO-to-Worker Pay Ratio Ballooned 1,000 Percent Since 1950: Report." April 30, 2013. https://www.huffpost.com/entry/ceo-to-worker-pay-ratio_n_3184623.

Ingraham, Christopher. "The Richest 1 Percent Now Owns More of the Country's Wealth Than at Any Time in the Past 50 Years." *Washington Post*, December 6, 2017. https://www.washingtonpost.com/news/wonk/wp/2017/12/06/the-richest-1-percent-now-owns-more-of-the-countrys-wealth-than-at-any-time-in-the-past-50-years/.

Ingraham, Christopher. "Union Membership Remained Steady in 2017. The Trend May Not Hold." *Washington Post*, January 19, 2018. https://www.washingtonpost.com/news/wonk/wp/2018/01/19/union-membership-remained-steady-in-2017-the-trend-may-not-hold/.

Institute on Taxation and Economic Policy. "Who Pays Taxes in America in 2017?" Washington, D.C., 2017. https://itep.org/wp-content/uploads/taxday2017.pdf.

McGaughey, Ewan. "Do Corporations Increase Inequality?" TLI Think! Paper 32, 2016. https://papers.ssrn.com/sol3/papers.cfm?abstract_id=2697188.

Piketty, Thomas. *Capital in the Twenty-First Century*. Cambridge: Harvard University Press, 2017.

Steverman, Ben. "Why American Workers Pay Twice as Much in Taxes as Wealthy Investors." *Bloomberg*, September 12, 2017. https://www.bloomberg.com/news/features/2017-09-12/why-american-workers-pay-twice-as-much-in-taxes-as-wealthy-investors.

Butter or Guns

Berk-Seligson, Susan, Diana Orcés, Georgina Pizzolitto, et al. *Impact Evaluation of USAID's Community-Based Crime and Violence Prevention Approach in Central America: Regional Report for El Salvador, Guatemala, Honduras, and Panama*. Latin American Public Opinion Project, Vanderbilt University, Nashville, Tennessee, 2014. https://www.vanderbilt.edu/lapop/carsi/Regional_Report_v12d_final_W_120814.pdf.

Conover, Ted. "Trucking Through the AIDS Belt." *New Yorker*, August 8, 1993. https://www.newyorker.com/magazine/1993/08/16/trucking-through-the-aids-belt.

Daschle, Tom, and Bill Frist. *Building Prosperity, Stability, and Security Through Strategic Health Diplomacy: A Study of 15 Years of PEPFAR*. Bipartisan Policy Center, Washington, D.C., 2018. https://bipartisanpolicy.org/wp-content/uploads/2019/03/Building-Prosperity-Stability-and-Security-Through-Strategic-Health-Diplomacy-A-Study-of-15-Years-of-PEPFAR.pdf.

Eguizábal, Cristina, Matthew C. Ingram, Karise M. Curtis, et al. *Crime and Violence in Central America's Northern Triangle: How U.S. Policy Responses Are Helping, Hurting, and Can Be Improved*. Wilson Center, Washington, D.C., 2014. https://www.wilsoncenter.org/publication/crime-and-violence-central-americas-northern-triangle-how-us-policy-responses-are.

Fauci, Anthony, and Robert W. Eisinger. "PEPFAR—15 Years and Counting the Lives Saved."

New England Journal of Medicine 378 (2018): 314–316. https://www.nejm.org/doi/10.1056/NEJMp1714773.

Fisher, Max. "The Story of AIDS in Africa." *The Atlantic,* December 1, 2011. https://www.theatlantic.com/international/archive/2011/12/the-story-of-aids-in-africa/249361/.

PEPFAR, *2018 Annual Report to Congress.* Washington, D.C., 2018. https://www.pepfar.gov/documents/organization/279889.pdf.

Rosenberg, Tina. "In Africa, a Glimpse of Hope for Beating H.I.V." *New York Times,* September 19, 2017. https://www.nytimes.com/2017/09/19/opinion/in-africa-a-glimpse-of-hope-for-beating-hiv.html.

World Health Organization. "Prevalence of HIV Among Adults Aged 15 to 49 Estimates by Country." Last Updated July 17, 2018. http://apps.who.int/gho/data/view.main.22500?lang=en.

INDEX

ABOUT THE AUTHOR

Elected in 2012 as the youngest member of the U.S. Senate, CHRIS MURPHY has earned a reputation as a serious legislator who is willing to stand up for his principles and reach across the aisle. Since the Newtown school shooting in December 2012, he has also become the leading voice in Congress confronting the plague of gun violence in America. He is now in his second term representing Connecticut. He and his wife, Cathy, an attorney, have two young sons, Owen and Rider.

Twitter: @ChrisMurphyCT

ABOUT THE TYPE

This book was set in Dante, a typeface designed by Giovanni Mardersteig (1892–1977). Conceived as a private type for the Officina Bodoni in Verona, Italy, Dante was originally cut only for hand composition by Charles Malin, the famous Parisian punch cutter, between 1946 and 1952. Its first use was in an edition of Boccaccio's *Trattatello in laude di Dante* that appeared in 1954. The Monotype Corporation's version of Dante followed in 1957. Though modeled on the Aldine type used for Pietro Cardinal Bembo's treatise *De Aetna* in 1495, Dante is a thoroughly modern interpretation of that venerable face.